SOFTWARE ENGINEERING WITH MODULA-2 AND ADA

Richard Wiener ——————— *Richard Sincovec*

University of Colorado at Colorado Springs

SOFTWARE ENGINEERING WITH MODULA-2 AND ADA

John Wiley & Sons

New York   Chichester   Brisbane   Toronto   Singapore

Library of Congress Cataloging in Publication Data:

Wiener, Richard, 1941–
   Software engineering with Modula-2 and Ada

   Includes index.
   1. Electronic digital computers—Programming.   2. Ada
(Computer program language)   3. Modula-2 (Computer
program language)   I. Sincovec, Richard.   II. Title.
QA76.6.W53   1984   001.64′2   83-21827
ISBN 0-471-89014-6

Printed in the United States of America

10 9 8 7 6 5 4 3 2 1

To Sheila and Deanna

PREFACE

This is a book on modern software engineering. The book is designed to be used by undergraduate students of computer science as well as practicing computer science and software development professionals. We assume that the reader has developed software in at least one high level language, preferably Pascal.

Ada and Modula-2 are presented in the contexts of software design and implementation. It is our belief that neither language will be of much value to practicing software development professionals who do not fully understand the principles of modular and object-oriented software design. One of the main goals of this book is to introduce and illustrate, through several important case studies, the principles and concepts of modular software construction.

The successful development of large software systems is usually a multi-stage process. First a needs and requirements analysis is performed. This stage often results in the development of formal software specifications. The specification stage is followed by several phases of design. After this is the implementation and systematic testing of the software system. The final stage consists of the installation of the software system and further testing. At each stage of the software engineering process, complete documentation is created. This documentation is maintained as changes are made at the various stages of the process.

Unfortunately, experience has shown that software maintenance (postinstallation changes in the software due to errors, new requirements, improvements of design, or a new environment) is difficult and expensive. Indeed, many software organizations spend more than three quarters of their total budgets on this activity. The main reason for the high cost of software maintenance is poor initial software design. One of the principal goals of software engineering is the design of software systems that can be easily maintained. Another principal goal of software engineering is the production of reliable software systems.

Software engineering began as a serious discipline in the late 1960s. The term "software engineering" originated at a conference in 1968 in which the main concern was the emerging "software crisis." The conference addressed the need to deal effectively with the increasing number of software systems that were over budget, delivered late, or not within specifications.

Undergraduate computer science and intensive continuing education courses in software engineering have become increasingly popular. Often these courses present the principles of software engineering independent of any language. Although many of the principles of software development may be stated without concern about the final implementation of the software system, we believe that this approach, although perhaps justified several years ago, is no longer suitable. In recent years, several important languages specifically designed for software engineering have emerged, most notably Ada and Modula-2. These languages may be used at both the software design and the implementation stages of the development process. Indeed, the software engineering methodology employed during design and implementation may be profoundly influenced by the use of these recent software engineering languages. In this book we forge a link between general principles of software engineering and their application in Ada and Modula-2.

Each stage of the software engineering process is examined in this book. Chapter 2 presents an overview of the needs and requirements stage. Chapter 3 focuses on programming languages and their relation to software engineering. In particular, the stage is set for the use of Ada and Modula-2 in the case studies that are presented in later chapters. Chapter 4 presents an overview of the design stage. In the first part of this chapter, the design techniques that are most widely used are presented independent of any language. Modular and object-oriented design are discussed later in the chapter. A new design aid, introduced by the authors, the modular design chart, is presented in Chapter 4. Chapter 5 presents and illustrates modular software development using Ada. Chapter 6 presents and illustrates modular software development using Modula-2. The main focus of Chapter 7 is programming methodology. Chapter 8 presents and illustrates software testing. Chapter 9 presents a comprehensive case study of the software development process from needs analysis to design, to implementation and testing. The subject of the case study is the development of a spelling checker. This example is complex enough to justify the formalism of modern software engineering but simple enough to be contained in one chapter. The design for the spelling checker is given in both Ada and Modula-2, but the detailed implementation is presented in Modula-2 only.

We assume that the reader has access to reference manuals or instructional material giving the detailed syntax of both Ada and Modula-2. It has been our experience that Modula-2 programs are more easily read than Ada programs by anyone with some programming background in Pascal. For this reason, we have presented more detailed case studies in Modula-2 than in Ada. From these case studies, the reader will be able to see the application of the principles of modular software construction and object-oriented design and to appreciate the similarities in designing and implementing software systems using either Ada or Modula-2. Both languages support the same major principles of software design and implementation.

We thank Carol Beasley, Computer Science Editor at Wiley, for her support at every stage of this project. Her suggestions and confidence in us have contributed greatly to making this book a reality.

We thank Gary Ford, Assistant Professor of Computer Science at the University of Colorado at Colorado Springs, for his many helpful suggestions and guidance. In particular, we acknowledge his contribution to the section on rapid prototyping, in Chapter 4.

We are grateful to Bill Bonham, of Sage Computer Technology, for his technical support at a most critical time. Most of the programs in this book were written and tested on a Sage IV. We are also grateful to Roger Sumner, Joel McCormick, and Windsor Brown, all from Volition Systems, Del Mar, California, for their outstanding software support in Modula-2.

We thank James Bankston for his invaluable help in producing a letter-quality version of the manuscript. We acknowledge the support of Marcie Penland and Ruth Wild for their help in the preparation of the manuscript. Thanks also go to our many students who have been involved in the class testing of much of this material and who have given us useful suggestions and ideas.

We are deeply grateful for the continued support of our families during the long hours that we spent writing.

Richard S. Wiener
Richard F. Sincovec

Department of Computer Science
University of Colorado at Colorado Springs

CONTENTS

LIST OF PROGRAMS

MODULAR DESIGN LISTING

SOFTWARE ENGINEERING WITH MODULA-2 AND ADA

Chapter 1

WHAT IS SOFTWARE ENGINEERING? A TOP-DOWN VIEW

The successful development of large software systems represents one of the most difficult challenges in engineering. Experience has shown that large software systems rarely are delivered on time, or within budget or within specifications. The process of later modification or extension of the original software system has proved to be so difficult and expensive that many software organizations spend more than three quarters of their budgets on software maintenance.

Since software complexity increases exponentially with size, it is much easier, in principle, to write and debug 25 programs of 2000 lines each than to write and debug a single program with 50,000 lines of code. Furthermore, significant savings in the cost of software development and maintenance may be achieved by constructing a software system as a set of interrelated modules. To effectively merge a set of separately developed software modules into an integrated entity requires careful attention to sound human management and organization principles as well as to structured software design and implementation methodology. Many of the techniques that have been successful in the development of hardware systems are being used to engineer software systems.

"Software engineering" began as a serious discipline in the late 1960s. The term itself originated at a conference in 1968, when it was recognized that the cost of hardware systems was rapidly falling while the cost of software systems was increasing significantly. The "software crisis," identified in the late 1960s, has intensified. It is estimated that in 1982, software costs in the United States were in excess of $100 billion. Clearly, even modest improvements in software productivity can result in significant reductions in absolute costs.

As the discipline of software engineering has matured, it has become apparent that tools must be created to enhance software reliability, streamline the process of software development, and promote more efficient software maintenance. Programming languages, such as Pascal, Modula-2, and Ada, have been developed since the late 1960s to accomplish these goals. This is a very significant step. Earlier languages were designed with hardware compatibility as the overriding concern. The software practitioner was forced to accept many compromises. The more recent languages have been designed by, and for, software engineers. Pascal, introduced in 1970 as a vehicle for teaching structured programming methodology, has gone beyond its original purpose and is becoming an important commercial language. The fundamental motivation for the development of Ada, in the late 1970s and early 1980s, was the recognition that a powerful software engineering language was necessary.

The principles of software engineering can be presented independent of any programming language. It is our belief that the principles, once presented, should be illustrated and applied to nontrivial problems. We have coupled our presentation of the principles of software engineering to Ada and Modula-2 because these languages include important software engineering features that can be used in both the design and implementation of software systems.

Many software managers have been skeptical about employing software engineering methodology in their projects because of a concern that the benefits will be minimal and the process costly and inefficient. These managers have questioned whether the principles of software engineering can be implemented. Often these people are not aware of the software engineering features available in the newer languages. Never having seen the principles applied in practice, they are naturally wary.

In this book we focus on aspects of software engineering that pertain directly to the specification, design, and implementation process. We forge a link between some of the general principles of software engineering and the implementation of these principles using the language features available in Ada and Modula-2. By so doing, we hope that you will better appreciate the general principles and better understand their actual practice.

1.1 THE SOFTWARE LIFE CYCLE

Many inexperienced software developers view the process of software development as static—write a program and test to see whether it works as desired. "Seat of the pants programming" (a methodology in which the programmer's pants remain glued to his or her seat until the software works) sometimes succeeds for relatively small-scale projects. The bonding between seat and pants may become difficult to endure for large projects.

From a software engineering point of view, of course, a program must "work" according to its specifications. But this is not sufficient. The manner in which the program is designed and written is as important as whether the program works. The ease with which the software can be changed to upgrade performance, meet additional specifications, or rectify errors that are later discovered is directly related to the quality of design and implementation. The "hot-shot" programmer who can quickly throw together cryptic lines of code that only he or she can understand is of questionable value. The programmer who boasts of using clever tricks to reduce the total number of lines of code has probably missed the point. Computer memory is relatively cheap, whereas the modification of software (a process greatly enhanced by program clarity) is generally expensive. Thus, given a choice between a little less economy of code or greater program clarity, the latter is often preferred.

What are the major phases in the software engineering process? We outline briefly the major stages of the software development and usage process, called the software life cycle. In later sections and chapters we discuss each of these stages in detail.

1. **Needs analysis and requirements.** The customer works closely with the software development team to produce a problem definition. A set of requirements is established and approved by both customer and software team.

2. **Specifications.** The analysis team develops a set of formal specifications that includes a detailed description of all functional entities, as well as operational constraints. The formal specifications often serve as a performance contract between the software developers and the customer.

3. **Design.** The major data types that are required to implement the specifications must be identified. Subprogram specifications that include input and output parameters are created. Modules that consist of logically related subprograms and data types are identified and specified. Algorithms for implementing the functional requirements are formulated in pseudo-code.

4. **Implementation.** The modules and subprograms defined during the design phase must be implemented in a high level language that can be executed on the target computer. The various software components must be written and then integrated into an overall program structure.

5. **Installation and testing.** The completed software must be installed and tested on the target computer. Each software requirement must be met by the finished software. Software components must be tested individually and as an integrated entity.

6. **Maintenance.** If errors are discovered, changes must be made to the original software. Additional requirements may be met by modifying the software again later. Improved algorithms may be substituted for their original counterparts to improve the performance of the system. If modular software construction techniques have been employed, these maintenance changes will be highly localized and will produce negligible fall-out effects in the rest of the software system.

Boehm [1] has defined the software life cycle as consisting of:

1. System requirements.
2. Software requirements.
3. Preliminary design.
4. Detailed design.
5. Coding and debugging.
6. Testing.
7. Operation and maintenance.

Freeman [2] has decomposed the software life cycle into the following components.

1. Needs analysis.
2. Specification.
3. Architectural design.
4. Detailed design.
5. Implementation.
6. Maintenance.

All the foregoing descriptions of the software life cycle recognize the stages of specifications, design, implementation, and maintenance. The software development process is iterative. During the design stage it may become necessary to modify the formal specifications (with the customer's approval), perhaps because it is impossible to meet an operational constraint in the design process. Similarly, it may be necessary to rethink part of the design during the implementation stage because of unanticipated problems.

Boehm [1] estimates that analysis, specification, and design account for 40% of development costs, implementation 20%, and testing 40%. However, the cost of maintenance is estimated to be between 4 and 50 times the cost of system development.

1.2 SOFTWARE RELIABILITY

Reliability and maintainability are perhaps the most important attributes of a finished software product. Here we introduce some of the attributes associated with software reliability.

The software must perform according to its specifications, often over a wide range of conditions. Protection against invalid or erroneous inputs must be built into the system. The output that is produced with valid input should fall within an accepted range of values. The software system should have the capability of taking corrective action if an unexpected situation arises. Routines for error handling or exception handling must be designed so that the system will not fail unless further progress would be impossible. If an exceptional situation arises, the software system should notify the user accordingly and specify the appropriate corrective action.

Many of the methods that have been developed for attaining high reliability for hardware systems do not work for software systems. Redundancy, a basic principle of improving the reliability of many hardware systems, has no applicability for software systems. Clearly, the duplication of faulty software does little to ensure reliability! The periodic replacement of components, another frequently used method for sustaining a high level of hardware reliability, also has no applicability for software. Software components do not wear out with age and use. Indeed, it has been observed that whereas hardware systems deteriorate with age, many software systems, like good wines, improve with age. This is because bugs are removed over time.

To achieve high software reliability often requires the writing of significant blocks of extra code. This may slow down program execution because of the numerous error checks being performed. More memory may also be required (certainly for the larger program and maybe for additional data structures required to perform error checking).

Is it reasonable to sacrifice efficiency (program execution speed and memory storage) to attain higher reliability? Although the answer to this question depends on the application, most often it is a decided YES. Often the cost associated with a system failure is considerably greater than the cost of the entire software system. If the software is unreliable—that is, if it fails under special conditions (and often the conditions for failure are not clearly known)—it has almost no value. Data may be lost or destroyed. Incorrect output values may lead to erroneous conclusions in many research applications.

Software reliability is enhanced by a clear and consistent set of software specifications, followed by a clean design, followed by a rigorous program of structured testing. The software should implement all parts of the specifications. Each functional component given in the design should yield to a demonstration of correctness. We discuss software testing in Chapter 8.

1.3 SOFTWARE MAINTENANCE

Software maintenance is a complex process that begins after a software product has been delivered to customers. The provisions for software maintenance are made during the design and implementation stages of software development. If a careful and well-structured design, incorporating a concern about maintenance has been made before the delivery of the "finished" software product, maintenance is straightforward. Unfortunately it often happens that little concern or thought to future software maintenance is built into the software design process. As a result, the process of maintenance is costly, sometimes accounting for more than 80% of the overall life cycle cost for the software product.

We are all accustomed to the concept of maintenance of hardware devices. Automobiles are routinely serviced, say every 15,000 miles. Computers are also serviced by replacing disk drives, electronic circuit boards, and so on. What makes such routine service possible is the modular design and construction of devices. Car engines can be "tuned." It is not necessary to replace the whole component or perform a major overhaul every time engine performance falters. Because automotive subsystems are modular and easily accessible, often a "screwdriver" adjustment can boost engine performance. Such small adjustments are expected and, in fact, a maintenance program is built into the design concept of the device.

It would be wonderful if, say, every 1500 hours of use, a complex software product could be brought into a local software maintenance facility and "tuned up." Let us examine the reasons for software maintenance and then return to the question of how best to prepare for software maintenance.

Sommerville [3] suggests that software maintenance falls into three categories: perfective, adaptive, and corrective. Perfective maintenance encompasses any software changes demanded by the user or suggested by the systems programmer. Adaptive maintenance encompasses any changes that are due to the changing environment in which the software operates. Corrective maintenance involves changes due to system errors that are discovered after the software system has been installed. A survey by Lientz and Swanson [4] revealed that approximately 65% of maintenance was perfective, 18% adaptive, and 17% corrective.

All three types of maintenance are required during the life cycle of many large software systems. New requirements, reflecting changing needs, are often added after the software product has been delivered. The system programmers and designers often produce improved algorithms for components in the system. Often there are changes in the hardware supporting the software system (e.g., new computer, better graphics capability, more RAM, more secondary storage), which suggests either relaxation or tightening of system constraints. In addition, customer feedback often suggests the need to "fine tune" the software product to better serve the end user's needs. Occasionally, obscure bugs are revealed by the same users. Since high software reliability is of supreme importance, corrective maintenance must be given the highest priority. A thorough program of software testing, before the software product is delivered, can minimize the need for corrective maintenance.

The factors that most greatly influence the need for software maintenance and the ultimate cost of that maintenance are: (1) technical factors in the software design and implementation, (2) the dependence of the software on the external environment, (3) the integrity and stability of the hardware that runs the software, (4) the expected lifetime of the software system, and (5) the continuity and stability of the software support staff. The software development team may not be able to exercise much control over items 2, 3, 4, and 5.

But item 1, technical factors, is within the full control of the software development team. Indeed this factor, perhaps more than any of the others, influences the cost of software maintenance. In this book we focus on a central concern of software engineering, namely, the technical factors that affect the cost of software maintenance.

Module independence is perhaps the most significant technical factor in designing software for easy maintenance. Program components should submit to easy tuning and change without affecting other software components (i.e., without producing side effects in other parts of the system). Programming style profoundly affects the cost of software maintenance. The proper use of comments, the wise selection of names for programming entities, and program layout are all factors that determine the ease of later maintenance. Design validation and program testing are two additional technical factors that have an important influence on the cost of software maintenance.

The choice of programming language is related to all the foregoing factors and greatly affects software maintenance. Some languages assist the programmer in developing good programming style. The ability of the software designers to create module independence is very much related to the choice of programming language used in implementing the system. The ability to control and prevent side effects is also dependent on the programming language. The quality and quantity of data structures, and the type of control structures available in a given language, greatly affect the type of design and implementation that is possible. It is well known and often argued that good programs can be written in the poorest of languages and that poor programs can be and often are written in the most powerful and structured languages. This is somewhat analogous to the observation that an excellent mechanic or designer can build a fine device with inadequate tools, whereas a poor designer will mess up a device with the best of tools. These points do not suggest that tools are unimportant. The good designer, supported by high quality tools, will be more productive and generally will produce a higher quality product. The choice of programming language is similar to the choice of a tool.

If the major goal of software engineering is the use of systematic techniques for producing reliable software, then the second most important goal is producing software that is easy to maintain. The procedures and concepts that we discuss in this book are dedicated to achieving both these goals.

1.4   REQUIREMENTS AND SPECIFICATIONS

The most costly errors in the development cycle of a software product usually occur at the requirement and specification stage. All too often, particularly with inexperienced development teams, there is a zeal to get on with the process of design and implementation without a clear definition and agreement between developers and customers concerning the system that will be built.

The first major step in the development of a software product is the establishment of a set of requirements. Most often these requirements result from extensive discussions between the end user (customer) and the development team or its representative. The end user must play an important role in shaping the scope of the software requirements. The language used to express the requirements must be clear, reflecting accurate communication between customer and developer. Both the limitations of the proposed software product and its full range of application must be outlined. The target machine or machines must be identified, and the hardware support environment must be defined. Any and all performance constraints must be stipulated. The nature of the data input process, if any, and the output process (report formats, etc.) must be agreed upon at an early stage.

Quite often, the requirements form the basis for an initial contract between software developer and the customer. The development team translates the informal requirements into a formal specification document, which in turn may form the substance of the contract between customer and developer.

In Chapter 2 we discuss the process of requirements and specifications in greater detail and provide examples of each. Here we briefly introduce the major concepts associated with both processes.

Software requirements and specifications should indicate WHAT THE PROPOSED SYSTEM WILL DO, not how it will be done. The boundaries that define the scope of operations to be performed by the system are defined both in the software requirements and in the specifications documents. Consistency is one of the chief attributes of a well-formulated set of requirements. Because of the well-known tradeoff between execution speed and memory requirements in software systems, the customer and development team must agree, in advance, about the priorities in developing the system. If the target machine has limited memory, then in all likelihood the speed performance of the final product will have to be compromised. If the software requirements demand unreasonably fast execution time as well as extensive memory from the machine, a satisfactory design may prove to be impossible. This type of error at the specification level may be costly later—the requirements and specifications will have to be modified, the design altered, and perhaps many thousands of lines of code changed.

It is not always possible, particularly at the first stage of requirements, to establish precise numerical constraints on either speed or memory performance. General goals should be stated. Priorities should be established. Upper and lower bounds for speed and memory should be established.

The requirements document establishes a general conceptual model of the overall software system. Many software developers have found the use of clear, well-thought-out, and precise English narrative to be the best vehicle for expressing the system model. Graphical techniques, such as data flow diagrams, may play an important role in clarifying the interrelations among the components that make up the system. These graphical tools supplement the narrative. Since the customer may have a limited technical background, the requirements document should be clear and readable. Specialized jargon should be avoided.

There is no generally agreed-upon number of substages in the requirements and specifications phase. Some practitioners develop a single software requirements document. Others prefer a staged approach involving an informal requirements document followed by a formal specification document. The advantage of the two-stage approach is that it supports stepwise refinement: the general scope of the problem is defined, followed by the development of successively more precise and refined functional specifications.

At the latter stage of software specifications, more formal techniques of expressing the software "specs" may be appropriate. Special-purpose specification languages exist and additional languages are being developed. These special languages lead to more precision than can be obtained from ordinary English narrative. Some, in fact, may be automated so that the final specification document is computer generated. In Chapter 2 we present a brief overview of several such specification languages.

The major ingredient of any formal software specification document is a listing of the system's functional and nonfunctional requirements. Numbered paragraphs of narrative are often used to express each functional as well as nonfunctional specification. The document that results may later serve as a checklist for the design team. Both major and minor functional specifications must be stated.

We illustrate many of the concepts of software engineering by examining the process of specifying, designing, and implementing a spelling checker. This important case study is presented in Chapter 9. We chose this problem because of its rich structure and nontrivial solution. Chapter 9 presents the specifications, design, and implementation of a spelling checker as a unified entity. Although in this introductory chapter we mention the spelling checker problem only briefly, we now pick out a few select examples to clarify and illustrate functional and nonfunctional specifications.

Nonfunctional specifications express practical constraints that must be met by the system. For example, suppose it is agreed that the spelling checker software must be able to correctly identify the spelling of 40,000 words. This is a nonfunctional specification. Suppose it is further stipulated that the system must process at least 250 lines of text per minute. This represents another nonfunctional requirement.

Functional specifications define the numerous transformations that are required in the software system. For example, in the spelling checker, a major functional block must parse a text file into individual words. Another major block must allow the user to replace, in the text, a misspelled word with a substitute word. These requirements are both functional requirements. Another example of a minor functional requirement might be a stipulation that the full line of text containing the possibly misspelled word be displayed on the video terminal. Numerous screen layout requirements might also be defined as part of the set of functional requirements. A final example of a major functional requirement, for a spelling checker, would be the stipulation that the user be able to display a subset of dictionary words that contain a particular string of characters that the user inputs. The size of the user's input string (e.g., the first two characters of a word) might be constrained in advance or might be unconstrained. This constraint decision must be made at the specification stage. Obviously, the software design will be affected by the decision.

In Chapter 2 we explore the process of software requirements and specifications in much more depth and begin the formulation of the requirements and specifications of the spelling checker case study.

1.5   DESIGN

The principal purpose of the design stage is to decide HOW TO BUILD THE PROPOSED SYSTEM, not what should be built. Since the overall process of software development is iterative, the design team may recommend that some of the specifications be modified. This is particularly likely to happen when an inconsistency has been detected or an overly constraining nonfunctional requirement has been imposed.

The design team's goal is to formulate the "blueprints" that will easily lead to a software implementation in a given target language. The design team must come up with a solution that meets every formal specification.

Since there are often many ways to design the proposed system, the choices that are made at this stage and the techniques that are employed profoundly affect the cost of later software maintenance. In addition, the ultimate reliability of the software product is dependent on sound design.

Is software design an illusive creative process that defies explanation? Is the process of software design so application dependent that totally different approaches must be used from project to project? We think the answer to both questions is NO.

Clearly, the experience, creative ability, and imagination of the software designers is a factor influencing the success of their work. Most often, the scope and magnitude of the design problem is so great that a systematic approach or methodology must be employed to ensure that the completed design leads to an easily maintainable and reliable product.

Top-down design or stepwise refinement has proved to be a worthy strategy for designing complex systems. Using this approach, the major functional blocks are structured first. Each of the major functional blocks leads to a host of minor functional blocks. These in turn may lead to still other even more refined and "pure" operational blocks. The design team must identify precisely the interrelations that exist between the major and minor blocks that comprise the system. The communication between the functional blocks must be established. The manner in which the work of system design is performed by a team of people is influenced by this top-down approach. Once the tree of major and minor blocks has been defined and the interfaces between the blocks established, the task of block design can be rationally decentralized. The input and output parameters of all subprograms that will comprise the functional blocks of the system must be identified at the early design stage. These formal subprogram parameters are the communication links between the functional components in the system. Most important, the major modules, which consist of abstract data types and functionally related subprograms, must be defined. In Chapters 4, 5, 6, and 9 we focus on modular design methodologies using Ada and Modula-2.

All methods of software design should include a requirements cross-reference in which the designers check off each functional specification against a design component. This process helps ensure that the design will meet all the software specifications.

The modular design method can be implemented efficiently using a software design language. Concepts such as data hiding, side-effect control through the use of proper variable scoping, the use of pseudo-code, the use of automated tools, rapid prototyping, and design validation are discussed later in the book. In Chapter 3 we examine the effect of choice of programming language on the design process. In Chapter 4 we present a survey of some of the major software design methods.

1.6   IMPLEMENTATION

In recent years many large software products have been implemented in a high level language. Although the code generated by a high level language compiler may not be as efficient as that generated directly using a specialized machine language or assembly language, the reliability, the portability, and the maintainability of the final software product are usually improved significantly by the use of a high level language.

A major implementation issue is the choice of programming language. The compilers associated with many recent languages can assist the programmer tremendously in program debugging and reliability improvement. The data structures that are available in a given language may greatly influence the design and implementation of the software product. The manner in which teams of programmers can successfully decentralize and then integrate their work is profoundly affected by the choice of programming language.

Recent languages, such as Modula-2 and Ada, have provided the software developer the mechanisms for dealing with side effects, data hiding, independent modules, and separate compilation units. We explain the relation of these issues to good software engineering practice in Chapter 3, where we also discuss and compare some programming languages.

Programming methodology (somewhat language independent), style, documentation, tools, environments, and portability are other issues related to the implementation of software products. Chapter 7 gives a detailed discussion of these issues.

1.7 TESTING

It is almost a statistical certainty that some errors will be present in a large software system when the work of the implementation team(s) is finished. A software system is typically a huge and complex logical and physical interconnection of subsystems. Although each of the subsystems may have been tested individually, as it was built, the entire system may still have imperfections.

The validation of a completed software system is a continuing process. The entire system and its components should be tested extensively before the product is delivered to any customer. Often, the first set of customers to receive the product are designated an "alpha test site." These customers are told that there will be some additional refinements in the software product before its official release. These alpha-site customers expect bugs and rough edges. Indeed, the major function of the alpha site is to provide immediate feedback to the software developers by reporting bugs and omissions. A second stage often employed before the release of the product is the "beta test site." The beta release should contain fewer bugs and rough edges than the alpha release. Its purpose, like that of the alpha release, is to solicit feedback concerning any remaining bugs. Some minor additional refinements are often made at this stage before the final release of the product.

Testing a software product can no more prove that a program is "correct" than working a numerical example can "prove" a mathematical theorem. Errors may remain in a large software system even after the most comprehensive program of testing has been completed. Only the presence of errors can be detected by program testing, never the absence of errors.

Software testing deliberately attempts to cause a software system to perform in a manner that was not intended by the designers (not according to specifications). The testing process often progresses in stages.

The major stages in the process of software testing are:

1. Function testing.
2. Module testing.
3. Subsystem testing.
4. Integration testing.
5. Acceptance testing.

In Chapter 8 we discuss each of these software testing stages.

Both top-down and bottom-up methodologies are used for testing software systems. Top-down testing begins at the subsystem level. Modules are represented by stubs, surrogate objects that use the interface of the module. After the flow of control among modules at the subsystem level has been tested, each module is tested in the same manner. In module testing, subprograms (procedures and functions) are represented by stubs. When module testing is complete, the subprograms are tested, one by one. Bottom-up testing reverses this process. Testing proceeds from the subprogram level to the module level to the subsystem level. Top-down and bottom-up testing methodologies are described in more detail in Chapter 8. In addition, formal verification, the design of test cases, testing tools, test documentation, and quality assurance are discussed in Chapter 8.

1.8   ADA, MODULA-2, AND SOFTWARE ENGINEERING

The Ada programming language was developed between 1977 and 1983 specifically to lower the cost of software systems, most importantly, embedded systems. In April 1979 a language design team, the Green Team, headed by Jean Ichbiah of CII Honeywell-Bull won a four-way competition for the best language design. The preliminary design for Ada was born. This design was thoroughly tested and revised between April 1979 and July 1980, when the first language specification manual was published. Further development and testing led to a revised language specification in July 1982. At the time of this writing, additional, but small, refinements are being made before the release of the final specifications.

Modula-2 was introduced in 1980 by Niklaus Wirth, the founder of Pascal. The Modula-2 programming language overcomes many of the deficiencies of Pascal, yet it retains much of Pascal's simplicity while achieving much of Ada's power.

The principal applications of Ada and Modula-2 in software engineering are in software design and implementation. Ada and Modula-2 provide facilities for reducing two of the major difficulties associated with large scale software design, namely,

1.   Poor interfaces between separate software components, leading to the production of incompatible components by different programmers.
2.   Interference between the components written by different programmers because of shared data (global data) incorrectly modified by various program units.

Ada and Modula-2 permit the interfaces between the separate components of a software system to be precisely defined so that the components produced by different programmers are compatible. This is achieved by the Ada or Modula-2 compiler's rigorous interface cross-checking mechanisms.

Interference, due to incorrect global data modification, may be eliminated in Ada and Modula-2 by the proper use of data hiding. The Ada "package" and the Modula-2 "module" (described in later chapters) provide the facility for data hiding.

The Ada package, or the Modula-2 module, allows a software developer to clearly distinguish and separate what is to be done (specification) from how it is to be done (implementation).

Ada and Modula-2, perhaps more than any other existing languages, support problem abstraction at both the design and implementation stages. For this reason we have chosen to implement most of the case studies in this book in these two languages. It is possible to emulate some of the techniques illustrated by the case studies in other programming languages.

Let us return now to the beginning of the software engineering process, requirements and specifications.

REFERENCES

1. Boehm, B. W., "The High Cost of Software," in *Practical Strategies for Developing Large Software Systems,* Reading, Mass.: Addison-Wesley, 1975.

2. Freeman, P., "Requirements Analysis and Specification," *Proceedings of the International Computer Technology Conference,* ASME: San Francisco, August 1980.

3. Sommerville, I., *Software Engineering,* International Computer Science Series, Reading, Mass.: Addison-Wesley, 1982.

4. Lientz, B. P., and E. B. Swanson, *Software Maintenance Management,* Reading, Mass.: Addison-Wesley, 1980.

Chapter 2

SOFTWARE REQUIREMENTS AND SPECIFICATIONS

The first major task, which must be performed before even beginning the design or implementation of a software system, is to acquire a full understanding of its requirements. The basic question is, WHAT IS THE SYSTEM TO DO? This may seem obvious, yet many individual programmers and many software companies plunge headstrong into software design and, worse, implementation, before understanding the needs of the customer and before obtaining a general overview of the problem to be solved. The potential costs resulting from poor communication between the customer and the software vendor may be very high. A faulty understanding of the customer's problem may also lead the software organization to misestimate the time and personnel required to do the job.

Too often when the final software product is delivered the customer says something like, "Oh, I thought that the rinks in the system were supposed to do dinks but I see that they are doing kinks." Compare the software system to a house, and imagine how the builder would feel if the customer were to remark at the closing, "We agreed on a four-bedroom house with a family room, and you have built a one-bedroom house with two family rooms." The builder would know that there is trouble.

Needs and requirements are two separate concepts. Needs lead to requirements. The requirements document is a formal and specific statement of what the system is to do based on the customer's needs.

An intensive communication process between the customer and the software vendor should lead to an accurate understanding of what the customer wants. The customer best knows what he or she wants the system to do. The vendor may best know how to do it. The issue of how to do it must be addressed later during the design, not initially during the needs and requirements analysis.

The software requirements document, the SRD, is the launching pad for the software system. It is also a magnetic pole toward which the compass readings of the software design, implementation, and maintenance must always point. It is the frame of reference that will be used to evaluate whether the design is correct and later whether the actual software is correct. It is also the major interface plane between the software vendor and the end user, the customer.

A software requirements document should be complete, consistent, and unambiguous. It often serves as a legal contract between the software developer and the customer. It always serves as the fundamental frame of reference for every later stage of the software development process.

In this chapter we present an overview of the requirements stage of the software life cycle. A short sample SRD for a spelling checker illustrates the flavor of such a document.

There is no standard in-place format or methodology for specifying a software system. Some large software companies have developed automated tools for generating and maintaining SRDs. Other organizations have established formal in-house disciplines involving graphical tools and specialized charts for representing the requirements of a software system. Many organizations use plain, precise, and clear prose for the SRD.

The key to success, regardless of the method used to specify software requirements, is this: the requirements must focus on WHAT THE SYSTEM IS TO DO, **not** HOW THE SYSTEM IS TO DO IT.

2.1 THE SOFTWARE REQUIREMENTS DOCUMENT

The software requirements and specifications should be formalized in a document that will be referenced by the software designers, the system implementors, the system testers, and those responsible for the maintenance of the completed system. Decisions concerning what data structures will be used, what algorithms will be employed, and what control constructs will be used, do not belong in the SRD. These are issues that are addressed in the design stage, which follows the completion of the SRD.

The SRD should be easy to change and maintain because modifications to the original specifications are often suggested at the design or implementation stage. Modifications are facilitated if the sections and specifications are numbered. The Ada *Reference Manual* [1] is an example of an SRD with appropriately numbered specifications.

The SRD may be developed in stages beginning with an informal requirements document followed by a formal document. The staged approach supports stepwise refinement. The formal SRD may be generated using special-purpose specification languages such as those described in Section 2.6.

In the section that follows we present one of many possible structures for a software requirements document.

2.1.1 General Goals

The first section of the SRD describes the system in very general terms and states the overall function and purpose of the system. The presentation tells who will use the system and what needs the system will satisfy. The most important features of the software are outlined. If any special notation or conventions are to be used in the remainder of the document, they are described here.

The physical environment in which the system will be used is described, including any other systems with which the new system will interface. If the system is to be implemented on special hardware, this hardware and its interfaces is described.

The SRD contains constraints on implementation and highlights important performance goals such as execution or memory efficiency, security, or reliability.

2.1.2 Software System Model

The major goal of the second section of the SRD is to develop and describe a conceptual model of the system to illustrate the functions required and the data flow paths in the system. Data flow diagrams with progressive refinement showing more and more detail of the data flow model, information structure charts such as Warnier diagrams, hierarchical block diagrams, and any other graphical or descriptive devices to portray as clearly as possible the flow of information through the software system are presented. As appropriate, pictures of equipment, control flow diagrams, and decision tables may be included to define the system model. Flow charts SHOULD NOT be constructed, since they provide control structure design details that are not appropriate in the requirements specification.

A finite-state machine model of the software system might be appropriate in some instances. In other instances, a Backus-Naur form describing the syntax of the system may be given.

Irrespective of the technique used to describe the software model, all diagrams should be accurately captioned and there should be a key explaining what various boxes, circles, and arrows represent.

2.1.3 Functional Requirements

Functional requirements refer to the operations and transformations that the system must implement. The details concerning possible user interactions with the system are given in the third section of the SRD. There is particular emphasis on describing from the user's point of view the functions that the software will perform.

Each functional requirement of the software system is specified in detail. A description of the input(s) and output(s) is given. No design or implementation features should be presented, just the desired functions of the software.

Included with the functional requirements should be a description of the set of legal values and ranges that the system will accept for inputs, the state changes and actions that the system will take on both legal and illegal inputs, and the outputs that the user will see.

2.1.4 Nonfunctional Requirements

Nonfunctional requirements include a description of all hardware constraints, processing requirements (e.g., the desired speed for certain important operations), and other constraints imposed by the hardware–software environment.

Other nonfunctional requirements to be stated include the required reliability of the system, the level of security for information in the system, the desired level of compatibility with existing software and hardware, and installation constraints.

2.1.5 Project Plan

The project plan indicates the resources committed to the project, the personnel on the project (including their skills and background), the promised delivery date, the computer time and space that will be used to develop the project, and the documents that will be produced, as well as the target audience for these documents.

2.1.6 Maintenance Information

Anticipated changes in the system due to upgrades of hardware, changing user needs, and future enhanced performance should be described. Often it is anticipated that revised versions of a software package will be produced. A clear outline of such possible or planned upgrades in the software should be provided.

The maintenance and information section is written with the system maintenance personnel in mind, since they will reference this document to determine what the system is supposed to do. The functions and constraints that are particularly subject to change should be explicitly identified.

2.1.7 Initial User's Guide

"How can one write a user's guide before the software is developed?" you may ask. If the needs of the customer are fully understood, and if the formal requirements of the system have been identified and specified in the SRD, the initial user's guide should be easy to write.

This user's guide is often reviewed by the people who commissioned the software project. Often it is discovered that the software requirements that were written do not meet all the needs of the user. The user's guide forms an important basis from which the customer can evaluate the SRD for completeness and consistency.

2.1.8 Glossary of All Technical Terms

No assumptions should be made concerning the experience or background of the customer. Since it is common for the customer to lack technical training, it is imperative that the SRD contain a glossary of all specialized terms and jargon. The SRD should contain a detailed table of contents and possibly indexes of several different kinds.

In the next section we illustrate some of the steps just outlined by considering an example.

2.2 THE SOFTWARE REQUIREMENTS FOR A SPELLING CHECKER

As an example, we present a needs statement and SRD for a spelling checker program. This problem forms the basis for an extensive case study in software engineering in Chapter 9 but is used here to illustrate the development of an SRD.

SPELLING CHECKER NEEDS STATEMENT

The customer requests a spelling checker to be used with editor-created files on the customer's microcomputers. The customer requests that the system identify potentially misspelled words and permit the user to correct the misspelled words in-line. The users in the customer's shop are involved in various disjoint and highly specialized activities that require special jargon (e.g., woof, grrr, ghrwoof); hence the spelling checker should contain provisions for adding additional words to the dictionary.

The customer has a number of microcomputers with 128,000 bytes of random access memory (RAM) and two floppy disk drives or one floppy disk drive and one hard disk. In addition, some of the microcomputers have additional memory that is used as a RAM disk. The spelling checker is to operate on these microcomputers.

The customer's needs are analyzed for cost and benefit. User interfaces, functions, and performance are considered and described. A feasibility study is undertaken. In this case, considerable attention is devoted to technical feasibility, since the scope and performance requested may not be possible on a microcomputer. The software development group decides to name the software SPELLCHECK.

SOFTWARE SPECIFICATIONS

1.0 General Goals

SPELLCHECK is a general-purpose spelling checker that operates on an existing editor-created file to produce an output file that has been checked for spelling errors. SPELLCHECK parses out the words from the input file and compares them with the entries it has in its dictionary. Whenever a word is not found in the dictionary, the checker will indicate the word and the line of text that contains the word and seek the user's directions regarding the word.

SPELLCHECK features a large main dictionary and permits words not in the existing dictionary to be added to the dictionary. The user may display the words in the dictionary.

SPELLCHECK is required to run on a microcomputer in an interactive manner. The microcomputer must have at least a video terminal, two floppy disk drives, and at least 128,000 bytes of random access memory.

SPELLCHECK should be able to process at least 250 words per minute.

2.0 Software System Model

The data flow diagram in Figure 2.1 and the accompanying narrative in Section 2.3 serve as the conceptual model for SPELLCHECK. The reader may wish to jump ahead to this material before continuing.

3.0 Functional Requirements

1. When an unidentified word is encountered, the user should have the options of replacing the word with a substitute word, inserting the word in the dictionary, accepting this and all future occurrences of the word as correct, looking up similar words in the dictionary to determine the correct spelling, or exiting the program.

2. The full line of text containing the possibly misspelled word is to be displayed on the video terminal.

3. The user must be able to display a subset of the dictionary words that begin with a particular string of characters that the user inputs.

4. The user must be able to add, delete, and display the words in the dictionary.

5. Unusual or seldom-used words that are not in the dictionary and the user does not wish to add to the dictionary should be "remembered" so that they can be identified as correctly spelled if they should appear later in the text.

6. The program should not fail if the dictionary is full and there is no more space to add words.

7. Statistics should be available to indicate the line that is being processed, the number of words that can be added to the dictionary, and the amount of words that can be "remembered."

8. When SPELLCHECK is exited, the number of words and lines processed should be displayed.

9. Hyphens and all other punctuation marks except the apostrophe should be treated as delimiters of words. Apostrophes should be considered to be legal word characters, except if they occur as the first or last character of a word [e.g., writeln ('Hello')].

10. Wherever possible, all user inputs should be checked for validity and an appropriate message generated if invalid input is detected.

4.0 Nonfunctional Requirements

1. The software must be able to correctly identify the spelling of at least 40,000 words. Dictionary compression techniques are acceptable.

2. The system should be able to process at least 250 words per minute.

3. A word is a string of one or more word characters delimited by nonword characters. Word characters are upper- and lowercase letters (with no distinction between them) and apostrophes.

4. The internal sorting and searching methods are not critical in defining the overall system. The methods should be computationally efficient and should use a minimum amount of memory.

5. Common abbreviations should be considered to be legal words.

6. The dictionary should fit on a 5¼ in. double-sided floppy disk with a capacity of 400,000 bytes.

7. Words up to at least 13 characters long should be analyzed for correct spelling. Provisions should be made to display longer words, thereby permitting the user to identify these long misspelled words.

8. The dictionary should consist of words in uppercase letters and apostrophes.

9. All American Standard Code for Information Interchange (ASCII) characters may appear in the text file.

10. SPELLCHECK should be menu driven with clear, concise menus prompting the user for a response.

5.0 Maintenance Information

1. The software may eventually be incorporated into a word-processing system, and system integration should be easy to perform.

2. The software may be enhanced to do grammatical checking.

3. The user may purchase one large central computer, and it should not be difficult to move the software to the new multiuser system.

4. The dictionary may be expanded with the use of additional dictionary compression techniques.

5. The dictionary may need to be modified by correcting misspelled words, adding new words, or deleting existing words.

6. The system may be modified to allow alternate dictionaries to be used.

6.0 Initial User's Guide

Introduction

SPELLCHECK is a general-purpose spelling checker that will identify more than 40,000 correctly spelled words. SPELLCHECK operates on any system-created text file, allows interactive replacement for incorrectly spelled words, permits the user to display words in the dictionary, allows the user to add and delete words from the dictionary, and permits words that are correctly spelled to be "remembered" if they are not in the dictionary, or added to the dictionary. SPELLCHECK provides the user with statistical information concerning the number of lines of text and the number of words processed.

Details of Operation

The main menu has the following form.

SPELLCHECK: A Spelling Checker

1 → Check a text file for spelling errors.
2 → Display part of the dictionary.
3 → Delete words in the dictionary.
4 → Exit the spelling checker
    program.

We now describe each of these menu items separately.

If menu item 1 is selected from the main menu, the following prompt will be displayed:

Name of disk text file to be examined for spelling errors →

The user inputs the file name. If the file does not exist, SPELLCHECK will notify the user with the message:

FILE_NAME does not exist.

where FILE_NAME is the name input by the user. SPELLCHECK then prompts the user for an appropriate alternative with the following.

Do you wish to try another name (y/n)?

A response of "n" will result in a return to the main menu.

After the file to be checked for spelling errors has been entered, SPELL-CHECK prompts the user for the name of the output file.

What is the name of the text file to be written to →

SPELLCHECK now examines each word in the input file and determines whether it is contained in the dictionary. As the spelling verification proceeds, the user is kept informed of progress with a screen display having the following form.

Line number ###
Word number ###
words may be added to the dictionary

where ### represents an integer. This display is updated after every five lines of text processed.

If a word in the input text file is not found in the dictionary, the line containing the unidentified word is displayed on the screen with a prompt of "T", "A", "R", "D", or "Q" requested by SPELLCHECK. These responses have the following meanings:

T: Accept the word (and all future occurrences of the word in any text files processed during the same session).

A: Add the word to the dictionary. This will enable all future occurrences of the word to be passed by SPELLCHECK. There is a limit to the number of words that can be added to the dictionary. If you attempt to exceed that number, an appropriate message will be displayed.

R: Replace the unidentified word with a word of the user's choice. Presumably, the user will exercise this option whenever an incorrectly spelled word has been discovered. The new word will be placed in the correct location in the output text file.

D: Display similarly spelled words. This permits you to check the spelling of a word in the dictionary. For example, if the unidentified and incorrectly spelled word is "incorect", you may enter the first few characters of the word you wish to search for. If you enter "incor", all words in the dictionary that start with "incor" will be displayed on the screen. You may enter any number of characters for your dictionary search. If no words are found, "None." is displayed. If all the words found will not fit on one screen display, the user prompt "Continue listing (y/n)?" will be displayed. As "n" will return to this menu.

Q: Quit text processing and return to the main menu. The output file that is generated will reflect the amount of processing performed when execution was terminated.

If main menu item 2 is selected, the user can display part of the dictionary. This item is identical to "D" described above.

Main menu item 3 permits the user to delete words that had been added to the dictionary. A prompt will request the user to enter the word to be deleted. If the word entered is not in the dictionary, an appropriate message will be displayed. The user will be prompted for additional words for deletion or, if no further words are to be deleted, control is returned to the main menu.

Menu item 4 exits SPELLCHECK. Statistics indicating the number of words and the number of lines of text that were processed are presented to the user.

2.3 DATA FLOW DIAGRAMS

A data flow diagram is a graphical technique for depicting information flow and transformations that are applied as data moves from input to output. Yourdon and Constantine [2], DeMarco [3], and Myers [4] incorporate data flow diagrams into their proposed analysis and design techniques.

Data flow diagrams can be a valuable tool during software requirements analysis. They depict information flow that describes how an input is transformed to an output. They do not and should not include flow of control.

The basic components of a data flow diagram are labeled arrows and labeled bubbles or circles. The labeled bubbles represent transformations or processes, with the label indicating the transformation. Each bubble may be thought of as a transducer that transforms data inputs into outputs. The arrows represent flow in and out of the transformation, with the label specifying the data. Additional components of a data flow diagram might include data sources and sinks, represented by labeled boxes, and stored information such as data files, represented by a double horizontal line. An information source is the location of data origination, such as from human input, a sensor reading, or machine input. An information sink is the final destination of data as it moves through the system.

Data flow diagrams should be constructed in a top-down manner. The first data flow diagram should represent data flow in the basic system model. Then one bubble at a time should be refined. Significant refinement may be required to obtain a complete conceptual model of the system.

A first-level data flow diagram for the spelling checker problem described in Section 2.2 is shown in Figure 2.1. In the example, a file to be checked for spelling errors (the information source) provides data to the spelling checker in the form of words. Words are processed to determine whether they are in a dictionary (stored information). Words that are in the dictionary flow to an output file of correctly spelled words (the information sink). Words that are not in the dictionary either are correctly spelled and not in the dictionary or are replaced with correctly spelled words. In either case, these words flow to the output file. The user is also an information source, since the user provides data in the form of requests to the spelling checker. These requests are refined in the second-level data flow diagram.

To illustrate information flow refinement, we continue with the spelling checker problem. The requirements analysis for the system indicates that we can refine the information flow. As shown in Figure 2.2, the basic system model illustrated in Figure 2.1 can be refined to show four major functions: the processing of the user request, the splitting of the file to be checked for spelling errors into words, the dictionary lookup and the viewing of selected words from the dictionary, and finally the user processing to handle words that are not

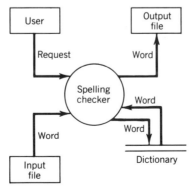

Figure 2.1 First-level data flow diagram for spelling checker.

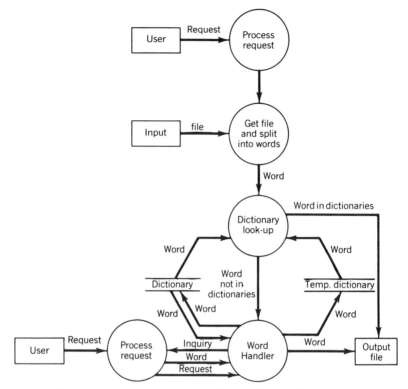

Figure 2.2 Refined data flow diagram for spelling checker.

in the dictionary. Information sources and sinks remain unchanged. In refining a data flow diagram it is important that information continuity be maintained. That is, the input and output to each subgraph in the refinement must remain the same.

The refined data flow diagram (Figure 2.2) defines a temporary dictionary for "remembering" words that the user does not wish to add to the dictionary, although they are flagged as correctly spelled. We now describe each data flow path in the diagram. The user request flows to the "process request" bubble. If the user has requested that a file be checked for spelling errors, the file name flows to the "get file and split into words" transformation. The user may also request that a word be added to the dictionary or that a sublist of words from the dictionary be displayed. Each word flows to the "dictionary lookup and viewer" processor to determine whether the word is in the dictionary or in the temporary dictionary. If the word is in the dictionary, the word is correctly spelled and flows directly to the output file. If the word is not in either dictionary, it may be misspelled, and it is displayed on the user's terminal, where the "user response" transformation performs a requested action. The user may accept the word as correctly spelled by adding it to the temporary or regular dictionary, or the user may replace the word with a correctly spelled word.

Note that continuity of information remains unchanged, since all incoming and outgoing arrows in the original central bubble of Figure 2.1 appear in the refined data flow diagram. There are a number of ways to conceptualize the system. Figure 2.2 is one such way.

Each bubble in Figure 2.2 can be refined further if desired. Since the purpose of the initial data flow diagrams is to present a conceptual model of the system, too much refinement is not desirable. The boundary separating a conceptual model of WHAT the system does from a design description of HOW the system is constructed is thin. If the data flow diagrams are refined too far, this boundary may be crossed.

A principal advantage of a data flow diagram is that transformations can be shown without making any assumptions about the implementation of the transformation. Note that in Figure 2.2 the user is represented as an information source and as a transformation.

There are no "cookbook" rules for creating data flow diagrams. Constructing them is one of the creative processes in requirement analysis. Generally one starts with system inputs and works toward system outputs, with each bubble representing a transformation of the data. Well-developed data flow diagrams permit a reader to determine the overall operation of the system with little or no supporting narrative. Hence, primary input and output files should be explicitly noted; all arrows, bubbles, and boxes should be labeled with meaningful names; and information continuity should be maintained during refinement. The development of data flow diagrams is an iterative process. Early diagrams are refined in stages to produce the final diagram.

2.4 STRUCTURE CHARTS

Structure charts are useful in representing the logical relationships among elements of data. The structure of data can have a significant impact on the design of the software. Hence, complete software requirements analysis implies a careful consideration of information structure. The information structure must be represented in a readable, clear manner. Two methods for representing hierarchical data structures, the block diagram and the Warnier diagram, are presented in this section.

This section does not present actual data structures such as vectors, scalars, stacks, queues, linked lists, trees, or graphs. The definition of the data structures is part of the design process. This section gives notation for presenting information hierarchies in a clear, concise manner.

2.4.1 Block Diagrams

A block diagram displays information hierarchy as a series of multilevel boxes organized as a tree structure. A single block at the top level of the tree repre-

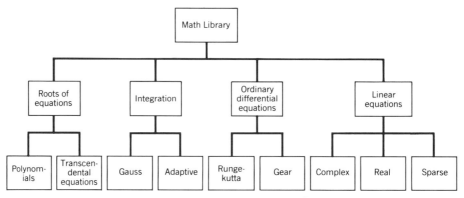

Figure 2.3 Example of a block diagram.

sents the entire information hierarchy. Succeeding levels contain boxes that represent data or information that can be considered to be a subset of boxes further up the tree. At the lowest level, each box contains individual data entries.

An example of a hierarchical block diagram is the organization chart for a company. Another example of a block diagram is given in Figure 2.3. This diagram might appear in the software requirements for a mathematical software library.

The block diagram presents more detail as we move down through the boxes. This mode of representation is useful in requirements analysis because the analyst usually begins with top level information and refines continuously along each branch of the tree until all information detail has been determined.

Block diagrams do not provide much information about the physical characteristics of the data structure. Physical characteristics such as record layout and data format are decided at the design stage. Associativity among information categories in the block diagram is implied but not explicitly shown.

2.4.2 Warnier Diagrams

Warnier diagrams [5] offer an alternative to the block diagram for representing information hierarchy. The Warnier diagram like the block diagram uses a tree structure, but in this case the tree is chopped down (it is lying on its side).

The Warnier diagram contains additional descriptive features that are not available in the block diagrams. These include the ability to specify that certain information is repetitive or that the occurrence of information within a category is conditional. Repetition is indicated by numbers or identifiers in parentheses under the category name. Conditional occurrences of information is indicated by the exclusive-or symbol (Θ). Figure 2.4 illustrates the use of a Warnier diagram to describe an employee data base.

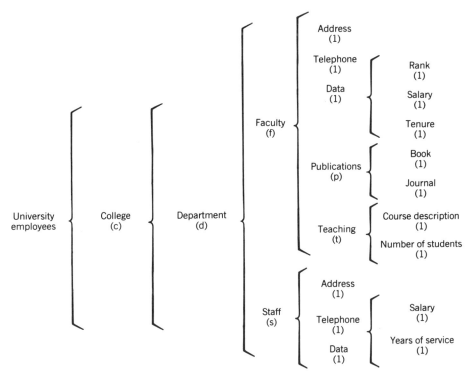

Figure 2.4 Example of a Warnier diagram.

2.5 SOFTWARE COSTS

Software costs are often a surprise to the user. If they are grossly underestimated, however, they are an even bigger surprise to the software development organization. In this section we briefly describe factors that influence software costs and several software cost estimation techniques. An understanding of software productivity coupled with sound software estimation techniques is necessary to meet the increasing demand for new software that is on time and within budget.

Today, software is the most expensive component of many computer-based systems, whereas only several years ago hardware was the most expensive component. Estimating the cost of software is not an exact science, since there are too many variables. These variables relate to human, technical, environmental, and political factors. A reliable approach to software cost estimation is important for the continued success of a software development organization.

One approach to software cost estimation is to do it late in the project. The later it is done, the better the estimated cost will match the actual cost. If it is done at the completion of the project, of course the estimate will match the actual cost exactly. What could be better? Of course, this is totally unrealistic, since a company needs a reliable cost estimate at the beginning of a project. Most software estimating approaches are based on historical data obtained from previous projects. The historical data are used to develop parametric cost estimation models and to support automated costing systems. Historical data are valuable in top-down costing, which involves refining the problem into smaller components for which a cost can be estimated based on prior experience.

Before one can estimate cost it is essential to have an understanding of the factors that affect software productivity. Let us first briefly examine hardware productivity.

Hardware productivity is usually measured with respect to the number of units produced in a predefined time interval. Hardware costs associated with planning, analysis, and design are not included in hardware productivity but are amortized over the total manufacturing time interval. This scheme does not work for measuring software productivity, since the development of a software system is a one-time event. How do we measure software planning, analysis, or design productivity?

Software productivity data are gathered by measuring quantities that can be measured in a practical way. The simplest and most controversial measure is to combine all steps in the software engineering process and determine the average number of validated lines of code per person month. This cannot be measured until a project has been completed. However, new project costs can be estimated based on historical costs for similar projects. The difficult part is estimating the number of lines of validated code that will be delivered.

As an example, suppose that we have just completed a project in which 4600 lines of code were developed. We delivered only 3700 lines of validated code to the customer, with the remaining 900 lines of code used internally for simulation and testing. A breakdown of the project indicated the following:

Requirements	2.0 person-months
Design	4.5 person-months
Coding	2.0 person-months
Testing	4.0 person-months
Total	12.5 person-months

The productivity of the software development team that worked on this project is 3700/12.5 = 296 lines of code per person-month (LOC/PM). If this team or a similar team decides to work on a project of similar scope and difficulty in which the deliverable number of lines can be estimated as 6200 lines of validated code, we can estimate that it will take 6200/296 = 21 person-months for the project.

What are the factors that affect software productivity? The personnel assigned to the project constitute a major factor. The size of the team and their experience affect productivity. As discussed in Chapter 6, the personality of the team members greatly affects productivity, as well. Another factor is the complexity of the problem. If there are changes in requirements or design during the development cycle, productivity may be adversely affected. The software design techniques that are applied and the review process that is used may affect productivity. The implementation language, the software development tools, the computer hardware, and other software resources that are available will also affect productivity. If the software under development has stringent reliability or performance requirements, productivity may be affected.

In an attempt to understand the impact of a wide variety of conditions on software productivity, Walston and Felix [6] identified 29 factors that affect productivity and attempted to show how productivity varied with each factor. Their results provide a qualitative feel for the relative impact of a factor on the LOC/PM productivity measure. However, their study did not take into account the interrelations that clearly exist among the various factors, and thus their work is not sufficient for cost estimation.

Estimation models are empirically derived mathematical equations. They are usually derived from a relatively small number of observation or samples. The models are designed to be used on projects similar to those on which the model was derived. The basic idea for an estimation model is to develop equations that give the personnel required for the project as a function of time, the project cost as a function of various software characteristics, the project duration as a function of the size of the team and the programming environment, and the software quality as a function of software characteristics.

As an example, Basili and Zelkowitz [7] describe four classes of resource models, the simplest being a static single-variable model of the form:

$$\text{Resource} = c * (\text{characteristic}) ** e$$

where c and e are empirically derived constants based on past projects and the "characteristic" is lines of code, person-months, and so on. "Resource" may be "person-months," "project duration," "team size," and so on. The reader is urged to consult Reference 7 for details.

Several other software cost models include the Putman [8] estimation model, the Esterling [9] estimation model, and the constructive cost model (COCOMO) [10]. The Putman model is a dynamic multivariable model that assumes a specific distribution of effect over the development cycle. It is based on large projects involving 30 or more person-years. This model is very sensitive to the estimate of the LOC. A change of only 10% in LOC results in a change of 33% in development effort. The Esterling model looks at the microscopic characteristics of the work environment—for example, "number of interruptions per day" and "fraction of time spent per day on administrative work." This model requires parameters that are hard to collect and does not explicitly consider software characteristics.

COCOMO is the most comprehensive software cost model available. CO-COMO predicts effort in person-months, schedule, the distribution of effort by project phase and activity, staffing levels, productivity, and maintenance costs. The model enables the effects of product characteristics, computer facilities, personnel, and project requirements to be individually considered and is a useful tool for sensitivity analysis. In addition, the model provides insight into major controllable factors that can increase software productivity. The model has been validated against a data base of 63 completed software projects of various sizes. Effort was predicted within 20% of actuals 25% of the time for Basic COCOMO and 70% of the time for Intermediate and Detailed COCOMO.

All the preceding cost estimation techniques require an estimate of the lines of code to be delivered. How do we obtain an accurate estimate of the LOC? An estimate is often based on historical data for implementing similar functions. If both optimistic and pessimistic estimates are made, some measure of risk can be obtained for the project.

Another technique is to break the project into individual functions and then estimate the requirements, design, coding, and testing efforts required for each function. Specific pay rates can be associated with each software engineering task depending on the personnel assigned. The total cost and effort can be estimated by simply adding the appropriate figures.

To gain some degree of confidence in an estimated cost for a software project, at least two methods of estimation should be used. When there is a gross difference between the two estimates, a third estimate should be obtained and/or the factors that went into the original estimates should be carefully reanalyzed.

Automated costing techniques require a data base of the software company's resources and experience. Project characteristics such as the magnitude of the project, the type or category of software, and the difficulty of the project are input into the cost model. The cost model takes the developer profile and the project profile and produces cost estimates for design, implementation, and testing, determines the consistency of the input and the sensitivity of the estimates, and establishes a schedule for the project.

The cost estimation techniques mentioned above reflect an older and traditional methodology for developing software. The next chapters introduce very modern software development methodologies based on object-oriented design and modular software construction. These newer methodologies are supported by the recent languages Ada and Modula-2. We believe that there is a need for new techniques for software cost estimation that reflect the new approaches to software development. We believe this to be an important area for future research.

2.6 SURVEY OF IMPORTANT REQUIREMENTS METHODOLOGIES

Several important methodologies have been developed to assist in requirements specification. In this section we briefly describe one manual methodology and two automated methods. The reader is urged to consult the references to obtain the details associated with these methods.

2.6.1 Structured Analysis and Design Technique (SADT)

SADT (a trademark of Softech, Inc.) is a methodology developed by Ross [11] that has been widely used for system planning, requirements analysis, and system design. SADT was developed to support the definition of system requirements. The underlying principle of SADT is top-down decomposition. SADT is applicable to general system problems including software development. It is generally not used for software design because it contains no constructs for sequence, selection, and iteration, which are necessary in the design stage.

SADT consists of a set of methods that assist the analyst in understanding a complex problem, a graphical language for communicating that understanding, and a set of management and human factors considerations for guiding and controlling the use of the methods and the language.

The SADT graphic language consists of diagrams composed predominantly of boxes, arrows, and natural language names. Each diagram consists of three to six boxes and arrows drawn on a standardized single-page form. There are two diagram types: actigrams and datagrams.

For actigrams, the boxes correspond to activities and the arrows correspond to data. For datagrams, the boxes correspond to data and the arrows correspond to activities. An SADT model consists of a hierarchical set of diagrams. The diagrams are precisely related so that they fit together to form a coherent model.

There are two SADT model types: activity models are oriented toward the decomposition of activities, whereas data models are oriented toward the decomposition of data. Each type of model contains both activities and data; the difference lies in the primary focus of the decomposition. The top-level diagram shows the complete system. Each box in the top-level diagram is then detailed on separate diagrams. This process is continued until the model contains breadth and depth sufficient for understanding the particular problem.

The successful use of SADT requires disciplined teamwork and management. SADT requires systematic review, modification, and approval processes for all diagrams. The process is designed to ensure that the SADT models reflect the best thinking of the team. The documentation produced as the SADT

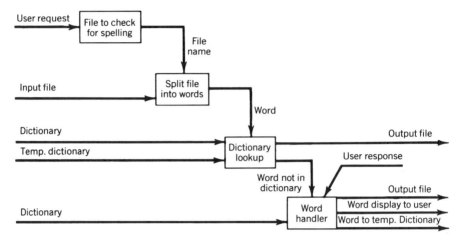

Figure 2.5   SADT diagram for the spelling checker.

model evolves provides information on the various stages of the model and visibility for the project.

Figure 2.5 illustrates an SADT diagram for the spelling checker problem.

2.6.2   Problem Statement Language/Analyzer (PSL/PSA)

PSL/PSA is a computer-aided structured documentation and analysis tool for analysis and documentation of requirements and for the preparation of require-ments for software systems. PSL/PSA was developed by Teichroew and Hershey [12].

PSL is a language for describing systems. The use of PSL involves defining and naming objects and specifying the relationships among them. The objective of PSL is to express in syntactically analyzable form as much as possible of the information that normally appears in an SRD.

The language contains features that permit the description of system input-output flow, the hierarchical structure of objects in the system, the relation-ships among data and the manipulation of data by the system, the identification of which data objects are involved in particular processes in the system, the size of the system and the volume of processing required, the behavior of the system as time passes, and details of project management including schedules, personnel, and responsibilities.

The problem statement analyzer (PSA) accepts PSL descriptions of the system and records the description in a data base. PSA also permits incremen-tal addition, deletion, or modification of the data base, performs a number of different types of analysis, and generates a variety of reports.

The reports generated by PSA include data base modification reports, reports listing all objects in the data base with their respective types and dates of last change, reports showing all properties and relationships for a particular object, summary reports including project management information, structure reports, reports that show data flow in graphical form, and analysis reports that present similarities of inputs and outputs, gaps in information flow, unused data objects, or the dynamic behavior of the system. These reports improve the ability of the analyst to detect discrepancies and inconsistencies.

After the requirements have been completed, the SRD document may be produced semiautomatically.

Several hoped-for benefits of using the automated approach provided by PSL/PSA include improved documentation in terms of preciseness, consistency, and completeness due to the standardization that is required; improved coordination because the data base is available to all; improved ability of the analyst to detect omissions, discrepancies, and inconsistencies by using the reports; and improvements in tracing modifications in the system.

2.6.3 Software Requirements Engineering Methodology (SREM)

SREM [13] is a methodology for generating consistent and correct requirements. It includes techniques and procedures for requirements decomposition and for managing the requirements development process. The principal components of SREM are the requirements statement language (RSL) and the requirements engineering and validation system (REVS). RSL is a machine-processable language for stating requirements. REVS consists of a translator for the RSL, a centralized data base referred to as the abstract system semantic model [ASSM (we appreciate the "M")], and a set of automated tools for processing the information in the ASSM.

RSL is a simple language consisting of only four distinct primitives: elements, relationships, attributes, and structures. Elements correspond to nouns in English. Examples of elements are functional processing steps, conceptual pieces of data necessary in the system, and processing flow information. Relationships are comparable to English verbs and define an association of some type between two elements. Attributes are modifiers of elements, like adjectives in English, which formalize important properties of elements. Structures are used to describe information flow.

The RSL statements that an engineer inputs to REVS are analyzed and an abstract representation of the information is put into the relational data base, ASSM. ASSM also maintains the concepts used to express the requirements. Since the ASSM provides a central repository for all information about the system, it enables a team to work with the same current information and to access the impact of their work on other requirements input by other engineers.

RSL is an easily extensible language, and REVS contains features to permit the user to add tools specialized to a particular application and to create special reports.

SREM was initially developed for embedded computer systems involving the specification of a real-time environment.

2.7 SUMMARY

- A needs analysis should be performed to fully understand the problem and to develop a definition of the software system.
- A good requirements definition is the most cost-effective task that can be performed during the software life cycle.
- The requirements analysis defines the software interface details, the functional attributes of the software, the performance characteristics of the software, the design constraints, and the validation criteria.
- The software requirements document specifies what the software will do but not how it will do it.
- A data flow diagram is a graphical technique for depicting information flow and transformations that are applied as data moves from input to output. Data flow diagrams may be a valuable tool during software requirements analysis and may aid in program modification during the maintenance stage of the software life cycle.
- Structure charts such as block diagrams and Warnier diagrams are useful in representing the logical relationships among elements of data.
- Software costs are affected by human, technical, environmental, and political factors. Software cost estimation techniques are usually based on historical data obtained from previous projects.
- Newer cost estimation techniques need to be developed to reflect recent software development methodologies such as object-oriented design and modular software construction.
- Several manual and automated methodologies have been developed to assist in requirements specifications.

REFERENCES

1. *Reference Manual for the Ada Programming Language,* Draft Revised MIL-STD 1815 ACM Ada Tec Special Publication, Washington, D.C.: U.S. Department of Defense, July 1982.
2. Yourdon, E., and L. Constantine, *Structured Design,* Englewood Cliffs, N.J.: Prentice-Hall, 1979.
3. DeMarco, T., *Structured Analysis and System Specification,* Englewood Cliffs, N.J.: Prentice-Hall, 1979.
4. Myers, G., *Composite Structured Design,* New York: Van Nostrand, 1978.

5. Warnier, J. D., *Logical Construction of Programs,* New York: Van Nostrand, 1974.

6. Walston, C., and C. Felix, "A Method of Programming Measurement and Estimation," *IBM Syst. J.,* Vol. 16, No. 1, 1977, pp. 54–73.

7. Basili, V., and M. Zelkowitz, "Analyzing Medium Scale Software Development," *Proceedings of the Third International Conference on Software Engineering,* Munich, IEEE, 1978, pp. 116–123.

8. Putman, L., *Software Cost Estimating and Life Cycle Control,* New York: IEEE Computer Society Press, 1980, pp. 324–328.

9. Esterling, R., "Software Manpower Costs: A Model," *Datamation,* March 1980, pp. 164–170.

10. Boehm, B. W., *Software Engineering Economics,* Englewood Cliffs, N.J.: Prentice-Hall, 1981.

11. Ross, D. T., "Structured Analysis (SA): A Language for Communicating Ideas," *IEEE Trans. Software Eng.,* Vol. SE-3, No. 1, January 1977, pp. 16–34.

12. Teichroew, D., and E. Hershey, "PSL/PSA: A Computer Aided Technique for Structured Documentation and Analysis of Information Processing Systems," *IEEE Trans. Software Eng.,* Vol. SE-3, No. 1, January 1977, pp. 41–48.

13. Davis, C., and C. Vick, "The Software Development System," *IEEE Trans. Software Eng.,* Vol. SE-3, No. 1, January 1977, pp. 69–84.

EXERCISES

1. Write the requirements for a text formatter for Pascal programs.

2. Write the requirements for a screen-oriented text editor.

3. Write the requirements for a registration program that manages scheduling and includes printing student status, class lists for instructors, and other features that you believe are appropriate.

4. Write the requirements for a business inventory system.

5. Develop the requirements for a grammar checker.

6. Write the requirements for an airline reservation system. Use block diagrams and Warnier diagrams to represent the data elements present in the system.

7. Write the requirements and develop an SADT model for a teacher rollbook program.

8. Estimate the cost of each of the preceding projects in person-days.

9. For each of the preceding exercises, draw data flow diagrams that provide conceptual models for the respective systems.

10. Develop a data flow diagram that represents the computer resources and the flow of information for a computer system that you are familiar with.

Chapter 3

PROGRAMMING LANGUAGES AND SOFTWARE ENGINEERING

The principal end product of the software development process is a software system written in a programming language. Many programming languages are available to support the implementation of a software system. Indeed, many large and successful software systems have been implemented in a variety of programming languages. How important is the choice of a programming language in implementing a large software system? To what extent are the features of a programming language related to software engineering?

We believe that the choice of a programming language for implementing a large-scale software system is critical because the features of a programming language are strongly related to the software engineering process. Languages differ in the degree to which they support:

1. Readability.
2. Modules for modular software construction.
3. Separate compilation with strong cross-reference checking.
4. The control of side effects.
5. Data hiding.
6. Data abstraction.
7. Structured control of flow.
8. Dynamic memory management.
9. Type consistency checking between various subprograms.
10. Run-time checking.

Languages that offer strong support in the above-listed areas provide the basis for constructing reliable and maintainable software. As we indicated in Chapter 1, a superior programming language does not guarantee a superior program. A language merely offers the programmer a set of tools. Only when these tools are properly used, incorporating the principles of sound software engineering, will the finished software product be reliable and easily maintainable.

It is important for software practitioners to understand the relationship of the attributes above to improving software reliability and maintainability. In this chapter we explore such relationships and examine some important older and some more recent programming languages using, as a frame of reference, the foregoing list of language attributes.

3.1 CLASSIFICATION AND TYPES OF PROGRAMMING LANGUAGES

When the first digital computers were developed shortly before and during World War II, all programming was done in machine language. In 1946 von Neumann, Burks, and Goldstein in a paper entitled "Preliminary Discussion of the Logical Design of an Electronic Computing Instrument," suggested the concept of a stored computer program. In 1955 the IBM 650 computer using the Symbolic Optimizer and Assembly Program (SOAP) became a commercial success. A few years later, in 1959, the first major high level language, FORmula TRANslation language, FORTRAN, was born. It was initially used to support the IBM 704 computer. Shortly after the release of FORTRAN, the Association for Computing Machinery (ACM) and the European professional association of computer specialists (GAMM) developed ALGOL (ALGorithmically Oriented Language). Perhaps because of the strong influence of the IBM Corporation, FORTRAN became the dominant high level language used for scientific computing in the United States during the 1960s and the 1970s. ALGOL was used quite extensively in Europe during this period.

A multitude of additional high level languages have been developed and used since the advent of FORTRAN and ALGOL. Indeed, thousands of high level language compilers have been written. But only a relatively small number of these languages have enjoyed extensive use and commercial success. Just a few of the most widely used and successful high level languages are COBOL (COmmon Business-Oriented Language, 1959–1960), PL/1 (Programming Language 1, 1963–1964), BASIC (Beginners All-purpose Symbolic Instruction Code, 1963), APL (A Programming Language, 1966), and Pascal (1971–1973). More recently, two significant high level languages have been developed, Modula-2 (1978–1980) and Ada (1977–1983). We examine the reasons for the development of these two languages later in this chapter.

What about machine and assembly languages? Although some complete software systems are still written in assembly language, and quite often parts of a software system are written in assembly language, most software systems are implemented using a high level language. Why has there been a shift from the use of assembly language to high level language for implementing software systems?

3.1.1 Assembly Language versus High Level Language

Assembly code has been used quite extensively at the systems level. That is, compilers, operating systems, and interpreters have been written using assembly code. In recent years many system-level programs including compilers and operating systems have been written in high level languages.

An assembly language employs a one-to-one relation between language statements and machine operations. Each assembly language is specific to a given computer. A high level language must be compiled (translated) into machine language. The one-to-one relation between language statements and machine operations does not exist. This often results in less efficient code being produced by a high level language compiled to machine code.

Is it not more efficient for a programmer to implement a software design in terms that may be immediately implemented by the machine, that is, using an assembly language? The answer is most often NO! Many programming errors have been found to frequently exist in assembly language programs. Shooman [1] has compiled a listing of the most common errors that occur in assembly language programming but do not occur or are less likely to occur in a high level language. Among these errors are array overwrite, stack overflow, off-by-1 indexing or shifting, complement arithmetic problems, floating point arithmetic problems, pointer problems, and indirect address problems.

In addition to the common assembly language errors named above, an assembly language code is generally less readable than the code written in almost any high level language. This suggests that assembly language code is much more difficult to maintain. Significant reliability problems have been reported in connection with large assembly language programs. An efficient means of expression for a computer assembly language has proved to be a most inefficient means of expression for a programmer.

Some "superassembly" languages have been developed to overcome the difficulties associated with regular assembly languages without significantly degrading their performance. For example, the IF THEN ELSE and DO WHILE control constructs are included on the General Instruments 16-bit CP1600 microprocessor assembly language.

The main motivation for the use of assembly languages has been the increased execution speed that often results because of their use. Some modern optimizing compilers have produced code as efficient as that produced by all but the best assembly language programmers.

There appears to be general agreement that assembly language code should be relegated to short segments of a software system implemented in a high level language. These segments should implement severely time-constrained operations. Frequency counting tools and program analyzers are being used to determine the portions of a software system at which faster execution speed might best improve the overall performance of the entire system. In these locations, the use of assembly code might be justified.

3.1.2 System Implementation Languages

System implementation languages allow the programmer direct access to machine operations. They therefore permit the programmer to implement a design at the machine level. Typical system implementation languages also provide many of the features commonly found in high level languages such as control of flow constructs (e.g., IF THEN ELSE) and variable type checking. The major application areas for system implementation languages are compilers and operating systems. A major system implementation language is C. Only a relatively small number of specialists are responsible for the development of systems software. Surveys have indicated that more than 90% of business and data processing software systems are written in high level languages that do not require direct machine addressing. In scientific software development this fraction is estimated to exceed 98%. Outside of system-level programming, the greatest need for machine language has been associated with embedded real-time systems. This need is expected to diminish with the advent of Ada.

3.1.3 Static High Level Languages

In static high level languages the programmer has no direct control over machine-level operations. Usually such languages offer a range of control structures and data types. The key element in static high level languages is static storage allocation. The memory space required for program variables is computed by the compiler and reserved before program execution. This provides advantages to the compiler writer but imposes constraints on the programmer. For example, the programmer must dimension all data structures in advance by estimating the maximum size that each structure will attain during the course of program execution. The two most popular and widely used static languages are COBOL and FORTRAN.

3.1.4 Block-Structured and Limited Dynamic High Level Languages

Block-structured languages are an evolution of static languages. They generally support additional control constructs and data types. These languages use a limited form of dynamic storage allocation (memory allocated while a program is running), and a memory management system is required to support them. In these languages a block structure is introduced, with appropriate syntax, so that during program execution, entry to a program block requires the allocation of memory and exit from a program block requires the deallocation of memory. In addition to blocks, some languages in this class permit the dynamic allocation and deallocation of memory through the use of "pointer" variables— variables that reference memory locations for data storage. In addition to limited dynamic allocation, block-structured languages support the partitioning of variables into global and local variables, thus providing the programmer with scoping and visibility rules not found in static languages. Some of the important block-structured languages are ALGOL, PL/1, Pascal, Modula-2, and Ada.

3.1.5 Dynamic High Level Languages

In dynamic high level languages, all memory management is carried out during program execution. The execution of individual language statements may cause memory to be allocated or deallocated. Dynamic languages are most often designed for a particular application and do not serve as general-purpose programming languages. Although they have not found extensive commercial application, they have been widely used in artificial intelligence investigations and other types of research. Two major dynamic high level languages are APL and LISP.

3.2 LANGUAGE FEATURES RELATED TO SOFTWARE ENGINEERING

In the introduction to this chapter we listed 10 software engineering attributes associated with a language. For convenience, we repeat this list in Table 3.1.

Table 3.1 Language Attributes Associated with Software Engineering

1. Readability.
2. Modules for modular software construction.
3. Separate compilation with strong cross-reference checking.
4. The control of side effects.
5. Data hiding.
6. Data abstraction.
7. Structured control of flow.
8. Dynamic memory management.
9. Type consistency checking between various subprograms.
10. Run-time checking.

In this section we discuss these attributes in the context of software maintainability and reliability. We examine how these attributes relate to several important older languages such as FORTRAN and BASIC and how they relate to several newer languages such as Pascal, Modula-2, and Ada.

We do not wish to condemn some languages and promote others. Most of the principles of software engineering may be applied in any high level language. However some languages support the attributes listed in Table 3.1 more than others. Our goal in this section is to make the practitioner aware of language features that support software engineering and the problems that may arise when some language features are absent.

3.2.1 Naming Objects

The flexibility that a language offers to the programmer in choosing the names for the various identifiers that are used in a program may greatly affect program readability and thus maintainability. For example, if the name of a data object is constrained to a maximum of two characters, variable names such as X3, Q7, and V5 may be typical. Under these circumstances, it is incumbent on the programmer to create an identifier glossary or data dictionary in which a description of every program variable is listed. When a program is large, the cross-referencing that must be done to check such an identifier glossary is inconvenient. If a language allows larger identifiers to be used, descriptive names should be employed for programs, modules, subprograms, data types, constants, and variables. The importance of this practice cannot be overemphasized. Significant improvements in program readability will result from the use of descriptive names. Most recent versions of high level languages allow the programmer tremendous flexibility in the length and the choice of symbols, such as the use of underscores for identifier names.

A general principle of good software engineering is that to promote program readability, the names of entities (e.g., constants, types, variables, subprograms) should be introduced close to where they are used.

3.2.2 Declaring Objects

In BASIC the first use of a variable name serves as its declaration. This implicit technique for variable declaration has been considered by some programmers to be an advantage in the sense that lower programming overhead is required when compared to the requirements imposed by strongly typed languages such as Pascal, Modula-2, and Ada. In these latter languages, each variable or object that is used in a program must be declared in a location separate from its use. In FORTRAN, separate declarations are optional. If a name is introduced without prior declaration, the first letter of the name determines its type (e.g., if the name starts with any letter in the range I to N, it is taken as an integer variable; otherwise it is taken as a real variable).

A potential danger is lurking in FORTRAN because type declarations are not required. Suppose the statement

$$MPOINT = MP0INT + 5$$

were to appear in a FORTRAN program. This is a legal statement that would be processed by the FORTRAN compiler without error. Unfortunately, it would lead to program error (although this error would never be indicated by the system). In typing in the variable "MP0INT" on the right-hand side of the assignment statement, the character "0" was inadvertently substituted for the symbol "O". This is a common error. The FORTRAN compiler may assign the integer 0 to MP0INT (since by default, the first character "M" of MP0INT makes this variable an integer) and thus assign the value 5 to MPOINT. Of course, the programmer intended to add the current value of MPOINT to 5 to produce the new value of MPOINT. We indeed have a TYPING error?

If FORTRAN were a strongly typed language and the variable POINT were declared to be of TYPE integer, the compiler would flag this error before program execution could ever begin. Programming errors that are revealed during compilation are much less costly than errors detected during or after running a program.

Formal object declarations, required in languages such as Pascal, Modula-2, and Ada, serve as an identifier glossary. If the programmer provides comments next to the important identifier declarations, program readability and maintainability may be enhanced. The example that follows is from a segment of a Pascal program.

```
const ARRAY_SIZE = 5000;
type REAL_ARRAY = array[1..ARRAY_SIZE] of REAL;
var
    X                      : REAL_ARRAY; {X is an array of 5000 real numbers.}
    SUM_OF_NUMBERS : REAL;
. . .

function SUM_NUMBERS_IN_ARRAY (NUMBER: REAL_ARRAY): REAL;
var
    INDEX        : INTEGER;{Used as summing index in array}
    SUM          : REAL;    {Used to form running sum of numbers in array}
begin
    SUM:=0.0;                              {Set the running sum to zero initially.}
    for INDEX:=1 to ARRAY_SIZE do
        SUM :=SUM + X[INDEX];
    SUM_NUMBERS_IN_ARRAY:= SUM {Value returned by function}
end{SUM_NUMBERS_IN_ARRAY};
```

```
. . .
SUM_OF_NUMBERS:=SUM_NUMBERS_IN_ARRAY(X);
writeln(SUM_OF_NUMBERS);
. . .
```

In this program segment a TYPE called REAL_ARRAY is declared. The formal parameter NUMBER in the function subprogram is declared to be a REAL_ARRAY. The descriptive name given to the function subprogram, SUM_NUMBERS_IN_ARRAY, serves to explain the purpose of this software component. The purposes of the variables declared internal to this subprogram (declared locally) are explained by accompanying comments. The operation of assigning a real value of SUM_OF_NUMBERS in the next to the last line is self-explanatory because of the identifier names used in this expression.

We provide a small segment of a BASIC program below that performs the same function as the Pascal segment. Compare the readability of the BASIC program segment to that of the Pascal segment.

```
5        SIZE = 5000
10       DIM X(SIZE)
. . .
100      SUM = 0
105      GOSUB 1000
110      PRINT SUM
. . .
1000     FOR I = 1 TO SIZE
1005     SUM = SUM + X(I)
1010     NEXT I
1015     RETURN
```

The BASIC program segment does not explicity reveal its purpose. Because of the simplicity of the operations performed, however, one might glean from the context the purpose of the operations performed in this BASIC segment.

3.2.3. Type Declarations

Many high level programming languages provide predefined scalar types, INTEGER, CHARACTER, and REAL (the syntax for these scalar types varies from language to language), as well as the structured type ARRAY. Data objects must be expressed in terms of these predefined types. For example, in a traffic control simulation, the signal light colors RED, YELLOW, and GREEN might be represented by the integers, 1, 2, and 3, since the colors are not predefined data types in the language. Integers are an unnatural form of representation for colors. Corruption of data might occur if during program maintenance, the "value" of a signal light's color were inadvertently added to some other integer variable in the program. What is the color 4?

The reliability of the software system would be improved if the compiler prevented the addition of a traffic signal's color with some other integer variable. This is possible if strong type checking is enforced. Suppose the data object COLOR were defined as:

```
type COLOR is (RED, YELLOW, GREEN);
```

This is a programmer-defined enumeration type declaration in Ada. Not only is this declaration readable, but the possibility of performing invalid operations on variables declared to be of type COLOR has virtually been eliminated. The small segment of an Ada program that follows uses type COLOR.

```
C: COLOR; -- Variable C is of type COLOR.
. . .
    if C = RED then
        STOP_SEQUENCE;      -- Subprogram for stopping the traffic
    elsif C = YELLOW then
        PREPARE_SEQUENCE;-- Subprogram for slowing the traffic
    else
        GO_SEQUENCE;        -- Subprogram for counting the traffic
    end if;
```

The operations that are predefined on objects of type COLOR or any enumeration type in Ada include assignment, equality (inequality) testing, and relational operations. If an attempt were made to perform the operation

```
W := C + V
```

where variable V had been declared to be of type INTEGER, the compiler would flag this error. The operation of " + " is not defined for the data object C. The programmer may wish to define his or her own special operations on a programmer-defined data object. For example, color "addition" might be defined as in the following Ada subprogram. The use of the " + " symbol in the function definition is called overloading the symbol " + ". The symbol " + " is overloaded because it is also used for other operand types. Ada is unique in its ability to overload operators.

```
function "+"(A,B: COLOR) return COLOR;
--This function returns a color
SUM: COLOR;
begin
    if (A = RED) and (B = YELLOW) then
        SUM:= GREEN;
    end if;
    if (A = YELLOW) and (B = RED) then
        SUM:= YELLOW;
    end if;
    if (A = GREEN) or (B = RED) then
        SUM:= RED;
    end if;
    if (A = RED) and (B = GREEN) then
        SUM:= RED
    else
        SUM:= YELLOW;
    end if;
    return SUM;
end "+";
```

To further illustrate how programmer-defined enumeration types may promote program readability, we reproduce in Program 3.1 a short Ada program from Reference 2.

PROGRAM 3.1   Ada Program Illustrating Enumeration Types

```
with TEXT_IO; use TEXT_IO;
procedure USER_DEFINED_ENUMERATION_TYPES is
    type MONTHS is (JAN,FEB,MAR,APR,MAY,JUN,JUL,AUG,SEP,OCT,NOV,
                    DEC);
    subtype DAYNUMBER is INTEGER range 1..31;
    type WEATHER_RECORD is array(MONTHS,DAYNUMBER) of INTEGER;
    LOTEMP,HITEMP : WEATHER_RECORD;
    DAY,DAYS    : DAYNUMBER;
        ANSWER : CHARACTER;
        MONTH  : MONTHS;
    --This program creates a table containing the lowest and highest
    --temperature recorded for each day of the month for one year.
    --After the table is completed, the user can query the table
    --by specifying a month and a day.
```

```
begin
    for M in MONTHS loop
        case M is
            when SEP|APR|JUN|JUN|NOV
                                        => DAYS:=30;
            when FEB                    => DAYS:=28; --Ignore leap year.
            when others                 => DAYS:=31;
        end case;
        for D in 1..DAYS loop
            put("Enter lowest temperature for ");
            put(M); put(" "): put(D); --Assume TEXT_IO package
            get(LOTEMP(M,D));       --has been instantiated to
            put_line;               --print months.
            put("Enter highest temperature for ");
            put(M); put(" "); put(D);
            get(HITEMP(M,D));
        end loop;
    end loop;
    put_line;
    put("Do you wish to fetch information from table(y/n)? ");
    get(ANSWER);
    while (ANSWER = 'Y') or (ANSWER = 'y') loop
        put("Enter month: ");
        get(MONTH);
        put_line;
        put("Enter day of month: ");
        get(DAY);
        put_line;
        put("Low temperature = "); put(LOTEMP(MONTH,DAY)); put_line;
        put("High temperature = "); put(HITEMP(MONTH,DAY)); put_line;
        put("Do you wish to fetch more information from table(y/n)? ");
        get(ANSWER);
    end loop;
end USER_DEFINED_ENUMERATION_TYPES;
```

Let us examine the consequences of strong typing in Program 3.1.

Strong typing provides consistency checking within the software. For example, if on the fourth line down from the "begin" statement, the programmer had written

```
            when FEB     => DAYS:=38;
```

by mistake, the compiler would raise the CONSTRAINT_ERROR exception because an attempt had been made to assign to DAYS a value outside its permissible range (1. .31).

Strong typing also protects the program during program execution. The Ada compiler generates code to check, at run time, that assignments to various data objects do not violate type or range constraints. For example, if the user in response to the command "Enter month" enters "JIBBERISH", an exception will be raised by the system because "JIBBERISH" is not of type MONTHS. Similarly, if in response to the command "Enter day of month" the user enters 40, an exception will be raised by the system because 40 is out of the range associated with type DAYNUMBER.

The feature of strong typing helps to ensure internal program consistency as well as error checking against erroneous data inputs.

Type declarations serve as more than just a mechanism for error checking. They allow a programmer to define data objects in a software system (via type declarations) in a natural and readable way in terms of the entities that occur in the problem. This is a form of problem abstraction. The programmer can manipulate data objects defined by type declarations (using supporting subprograms) without regard to how these data objects are represented internally within the computer.

A language's support for problem abstraction through data abstraction (which has other ramifications, discussed in the section on data hiding) is an important indicator of its ability to support software engineering.

3.2.4 Control Structures

In this section we examine how the control structures available in programming languages are related to the software engineering process. But first we look at Program 3.2.

PROGRAM 3.2 A BASIC Program

```
10      DIM A(100)
20      DIM B(10)
30      GOTO 100
40      GOTO 150
50      GOTO 200
60      B(1) = B(1) + 1
61      RETURN
62      B(2) = B(2) + 1
63      RETURN
64      B(3) = B(3) + 1
65      RETURN
```

```
66      B(4) = B(4) + 1
67      RETURN
68      B(5) = B(5) + 1
69      RETURN
70      B(6) = B(6) + 1
71      RETURN
72      B(7) = B(7) + 1
73      RETURN
74      B(8) = B(8) + 1
75      RETURN
76      B(9) = B(9) + 1
77      RETURN
78      B(10) = B(10) + 1
79      RETURN
80      PRINT ''   The Number Of Objects Stored In Each Bin''
90      GOTO 320
92      SUM = 0
94      GOTO 360
95      PRINT ''The sum of numbers in the array = ''; SUM
96      GOTO 400
100     FOR I = 1 TO 100
110     A(I) = 0.1*I
120     NEXT I
130     GOTO 40
150     FOR J = 1 TO 10
160     B(J) = 0
165     NEXT J
170     GOTO 50
200     FOR I = 1 TO 100
210     IF A(I) <= 1 THEN GOSUB 60 : GOTO 305
220     IF A(I) <= 2 THEN GOSUB 62 : GOTO 305
230     IF A(I) <= 3 THEN GOSUB 64 : GOTO 305
240     IF A(I) <= 4 THEN GOSUB 66 : GOTO 305
250     IF A(I) <= 5 THEN GOSUB 68 : GOTO 305
260     IF A(I) <= 6 THEN GOSUB 70 : GOTO 305
270     IF A(I) <= 7 THEN GOSUB 72 : GOTO 305
280     IF A(I) <= 8 THEN GOSUB 74 : GOTO 305
290     IF A(I) <= 9 THEN GOSUB 76 : GOTO 305
300     IF A(I) <= 10 THEN GOSUB 78 : GOTO 305
305     NEXT I
310     GOTO 80
320     FOR I = 1 TO 10
330     PRINT B(I)
340     NEXT I
350     GOTO 92
```

```
360    FOR I = 1 TO 100
370    SUM = A(I) + SUM
380    NEXT I
390    GOTO 95
400    END
```

Is the purpose of Program 3.2 clear? Would this program be easy to maintain? We rework this program in Pascal. The main difference between Programs 3.2 and 3.3 concerns the use of control structures.

PROGRAM 3.3   Pascal Rework of Program 3.2

```
program ILLUSTRATION_OF_CONTROL_STRUCTURES_IN_PASCAL;
const ARRAY_SIZE        = 100;
      SIZE_BIN_ARRAY    = 10
type REAL_ARRAY         = array[1..ARRAY_SIZE] of REAL;
     BIN_ARRAY          = array[0..SIZE_BIN_ARRAY] of INTEGER;
     ARRAY_RANGE        = 1..ARRAY_SIZE;
     BIN_RANGE          = 0..SIZE_BIN_ARRAY;
var WORK_ARRAY          : REAL_ARRAY;
    BIN                 : BIN_ARRAY;
    INDEX               : ARRAY_RANGE;

procedure FILL_ARRAY(var A: REAL_ARRAY);
var I: ARRAY_RANGE;
begin
    for I:=1 to ARRAY_SIZE do
    A[I]:=0.1*I;
end{FILL_ARRAY};

function SUM_ARRAY_ELEMENTS(B: REAL_ARRAY): REAL;
var I     : ARRAY_RANGE;
    SUM : REAL;     {Represents cumulative sum of numbers in array}
begin
    SUM:=0;
    for I:=1 to ARRAY_SIZE do
        SUM:=SUM + B[I];
    SUM_ARRAY_ELEMENTS:=SUM
end{SUM_ARRAY_ELEMENTS};

procedure INITIALIZE_BIN_ARRAY(var C: BIN_ARRAY);
var I: BIN_RANGE;
```

```
begin
    for I:=0 to SIZE_BIN_ARRAY do
        C[I]:=0
end{INITIALIZE_BIN_ARRAY};


procedure ALLOCATE_NUMBERS_TO_BINS(R: REAL; var B: BIN_ARRAY);
var CHOICE: BIN_RANGE;
begin
    CHOICE:=TRUNC(R); {CHOICE will range from 0 to 10.}
    B[CHOICE]:=B[CHOICE] + 1
end{ALLOCATE_NUMBERS_TO_BINS};


procedure OUTPUT(H: BIN_ARRAY);
var I: BIN_RANGE;
begin
    for I:=0 to SIZE_BIN_ARRAY do
        writeln(H[I],' numbers stored in bin ',I)
end{OUTPUT};


begin {Main Program}
    INITIALIZE_BIN_ARRAY(BIN);
    FILL_ARRAY(WORK_ARRAY);
    for INDEX:=1 to ARRAY_SIZE do
        ALLOCATE_NUMBERS_TO_BINS(WORK_ARRAY[INDEX],BIN)
    OUTPUT(BIN);
    writeln('The sum of numbers in the array = ',
            SUM_ARRAY_ELEMENTS(WORK_ARRAY))
end.
```

Have you carefully compared Programs 3.2 and 3.3? The control structures that are employed are significantly different.

We distinguish macroscopic control structures from microscopic control structures. In the Pascal version, the main body of the program directs control to five subprograms, and therefore the main program is very short. This kind of macroscopic control (at the very highest level of the program) reveals the functional components of the software system. Furthermore, it permits maintenance to be performed on separate functional components. We later show how subprogram components may be designed so that the maintenance on one subprogram does not produce fall-out effects on the rest of a program.

At the microscopic level (within a small block of code), the BASIC program employs a cumbersome set of IF THEN statements with accompanying GOTO statements. In fact, the entire BASIC program is riddled with GOTO statements. Do these add to program clarity and readability? We believe the answer is no. Program maintenance becomes very difficult when using a structure similar to the one displayed in the BASIC version, Program 3.2. Since it may be possible to reach a given line of code from many different paths, any change in such a line of code may destroy the integrity of some other transfer statement (e.g., GOTO) elsewhere in the program. Furthermore, since the functional components of the BASIC version of the software system are difficult to identify, the problem of determining where corrections need to be made, in the event of some error, may be next to impossible when such a program becomes large.

The use of CONST (ARRAY_SIZE, and SIZE_BIN_ARRAY) in the Pascal version permits the program to be scaled up or down in size by changing just two numbers. This significantly reduces the amount of later program maintenance if changes of scale are required. How many lines of code must be changed in the BASIC version to change the scale of the solution?

Some software engineering practitioners (e.g., Dijkstra) suggest that the GOTO command should never be used. It was demonstrated by Bohm and Jacopini [3] in 1966 that any software system may be constructed without the use of GOTO statements, provided the implementation language supports a WHILE loop, an IF-THEN-ELSE conditional transfer construct, and sequence. These authors showed that any program constructed using GOTO commands can be transformed into a program without GOTOs. This transformation may require increasing the size of a program.

We believe that the occasional use of a GOTO statement, or the use of an exit statement within a loop (a special type of GOTO), or the use of an exit statement from a subprogram, will not lead to the "spaghetti" syndrome of tangled logic so often associated with the overuse of GOTOs. Program readability may in fact be increased if a loop exit statement tied to some Boolean test is employed. Boolean variables and a conditional transfer test may be required to circumvent the need for an exit statement from a loop. This technique often distracts from program clarity.

We illustrate this point by considering two short Ada segments, each performing the same function.

Ada Segment One

```
loop
    I:=I+1;
    exit when I*I−14*Y > 16; ––Y is an integer variable.
    . . .
end loop;
```

Ada Segment Two

```
B:=TRUE;
while B loop
    I:=I+1;
    if I*I−14*Y <= 16 then   ––Y is an integer variable.
```

```
...
    else B:=FALSE;
end loop;
```

In our view, the first segment, which uses an exit from loop (a form of GOTO), is cleaner and easier to read than the second segment, which does not use any GOTO statement.

The major constructs for conditional transfer of control available in recent structured languages include (at the microscopic level): IF THEN ELSIF ELSE and CASE. The CASE construct is employed when control may transfer to one of several alternatives. The case control structure is illustrated by the following Ada segment.

Ada Segment Illustrating CASE Control

```
type PERFORMANCE =
    (FAILING,VERY_POOR,POOR,AVERAGE,GOOD,EXCELLENT);
QUALITY: PERFORMANCE;
GRADE  : CHARACTER;
...
case QUALITY of
    when FAILING|VERY_POOR => GRADE:='F';
    when POOR               => GRADE:='D';
    when AVERAGE            => GRADE:='C';
    when GOOD              => GRADE:='B';
    when EXCELLENT         => GRADE:='A';
    when others            => null;
end case;
```

Instead of assigning a character to the variable GRADE, the transfer of control to an appropriate subprogram might have been suitable. The option "when others" allows the Ada programmer a default in the event that the discrete variable QUALITY has a value not present in the list of alternatives presented in the case statement. Pascal's CASE statement does not support such a default alternative. Some Pascal implementations fail when presented with a CASE variable not present in the alternative list.

3.2.5 Data Structures

In the most fundamental sense, a software system is composed of data objects and a set of algorithms that manipulate these data objects. In the early days of "programming" it was felt that the problem of software design and implementation was finding the "correct" control of flow. The construction of a detailed set of flow charts was sometimes equated with the design of a software system.

In a large software system, data structures are defined and distributed throughout the system. Some "global" data structures have a scope that covers the entire software system. These global data structures may be modified anywhere in the software system. Other data structures are defined to have a "local" scope and are thus available only in select segments of the software system. The issue of data hiding, which is covered later in this chapter, has become important in the design and implementation of software systems. The manner in which data are transferred from one functional component (subprogram) to another is another significant design issue, which we discuss in this and other chapters.

For scientific programming, the major data structures that have been required are single and multidimensional arrays. For this as well as other reasons, FORTRAN has enjoyed great popularity as the language for implementing many scientific and engineering software systems.

A major data structure problem inherent in FORTRAN is the inability to naturally represent a collection of dissimilar data objects. The array is the only structured data type available in FORTRAN. An array constrains the programmer to use homogeneous data types. Since the only data types other than the array that are available in FORTRAN are scalar types (e.g., floating point, integer, and character), FORTRAN programmers have been forced to resort to parallel arrays for representing sets of dissimilar objects. For example, to represent a group of names and associated annual incomes, one array must be dedicated to representing the list of names, and a parallel array (with an index set correlated to the first array) must be used to store the appropriate incomes. Access to the data base requires fetching information from two separate arrays.

PL/1, Pascal, Module-2, and Ada, to name a few languages, offer the programmer a richer set of predefined data types. The RECORD structure, in particular, allows a programmer to represent objects of different types under the umbrella of the same data structure. The following Pascal segment illustrates the RECORD structure that might be used to represent a group of names and associated incomes.

```
type
    DATA_RECORD = record
        NAME    : array[1..25] of CHAR;
        INCOME : REAL
    end;
    DATA_BASE = array[1..1000] of DATA_RECORD;
var
    COMPANY_DATA : DATA_BASE;
```

The appropriate mechanism to access the income of the 230th individual in the data base would be:

```
R:= COMPANY_DATA[ 230 ].INCOME;  {R declared to be type REAL.}
```

In the Pascal segment above, a programmer-created data structure called DATA_BASE is constructed in terms of the basic predefined building blocks available in the language. Here the ARRAY structure, which requires homogeneous elements, is combined with the RECORD structure, to form an ARRAY of RECORDS. In fact, the RECORD structure contains an ARRAY of characters. This ability to nest one data structure inside another gives the programmer and the designer tremendous flexibility in modeling the entities and information present in the problem in a natural way.

In recent years it has become increasingly evident that a central challenge in the design of software systems is the determination of the abstract data types to be used to represent the entities and information in the system. Associated with the data abstractions are operations that are designed to manipulate the underlying data structures.

3.2.6 Subprograms

A subprogram is a block of code, separate from the main body of a program, that is often used to implement a functional requirement given in the software specifications document. Subprograms provide the functional ''nuts and bolts'' of a software system. They allow a complex system to be partitioned into a set of functional software components.

It would seem, from the foregoing description, that the main purpose of subprograms is to aid in program readability and maintainability. After all, the blocks of code, grouped as subprograms, could easily be integrated into the main body of a program without compromising program correctness. Clearly, the readability and maintainability of a large system is enhanced if the system is decomposed into many smaller blocks, each block performing a well-defined function. Blocks should be of a size that allow the programmer total comprehension of the entire subprogram entity, which assists tremendously in program debugging.

Although program readability and maintainability are important motivations for defining subprograms, the primary motivation for using subprograms is that their proper use may significantly enhance program reliability. In recent languages such as Pascal, Modula-2, and Ada, subprograms allow the programmer to control the scope and visibility of data objects. They allow a programmer to decentralize object declarations across a large software system. They provide programmers working on separate parts of the software system tremendous freedom to create identifiers without concern for name duplication.

In FORTRAN, subprograms are constructed using SUBROUTINES and FUNCTIONS. BASIC offers a weak version of the SUBROUTINE in the form of code groupings that may be referenced by a GOSUB call. In Pascal, Modula-2, and Ada, PROCEDURES and FUNCTIONS serve as subprograms. Subprograms typically have parameters. These parameters may be of three possible types: input, input-output, and output. These allow information to be passed from the outside into the subprogram (input), passed from the outside into the subprogram and from the subprogram to the outside (input-output), and finally from the subprogram to the outside (output).

3.2.6.1 Scope and Visibility

The scope of an identifier is defined as the region of the program in which the identifier may be potentially accessed or modified. The visible region for an identifier is defined as the portion of the program in which the identifier may actually be accessed or modified. Therefore, the scope and the visible region for an identifier may not be the same.

Older languages such as FORTRAN and most system implementation languages offer the programmer exactly one level of identifier locality (i.e., no procedures nested within procedures). More recent block-structured languages such as Pascal, Modula-2, and Ada offer the programmer multiple levels of identifier locality.

One-level locality suggests that the scope of entities declared in a subprogram is confined to that subprogram and that the local entities are not accessible outside that subprogram. Subprograms cannot be nested within subprograms. All subprograms are at the same hierarchical level. In a FORTRAN main program, unless there is a COMMON declaration, variables declared in the main program (either by formal declaration or by default) are not accessible to all subroutines. Communication between main program and subroutines takes place through the subroutine parameters.

In block-structured languages that support multiple-level locality, identifier scope rules are more complex. Identifiers are declared within a block (usually a subprogram) and have a scope that covers the block. Identifiers declared at the outermost level of a program (global identifiers) have a scope that covers the entire program. Blocks may be nested within blocks (i.e., subprograms nested within subprograms). This nesting may affect the visibility of objects defined in outer blocks.

We illustrate scoping and visibility with the following Pascal program segment.

Pascal Program Segment Illustrating Scoping and Visibility

```
var A,B,C,D,E : REAL;

procedure OUTER;
var A,B,C : INTEGER;

    procedure INNER;
    var A,E: CHAR;
    begin {INNER}
        {Character variables A and E are visible.
        Variables A and E are masked out. Integer
```

```
        variables B and C are visible. Global real
        variables B and C are masked out. Global
        variable D is visible.                                    }
        . . .
    end {INNER};

begin {OUTER}
    {Integer variables A,B,C are visible. Global
    variables A,B,C are masked out. Global variables
    D,E are visible.                                              }
    . . .
end {OUTER};

begin {Main Program}
    {Global real variables A,B,C,D,E visible.}
    . . .
end.
```

We note that the name "A" takes on three identities. At the global level (main program level) it is defined as a floating point number, at the level of subprogram "OUTER" it is defined as an integer, and finally, at the nested subprogram level "INNER", it is defined as a character. How can we manage this multiple personality "A"?

When the main program begins to execute, the variable "A" may be used as an ordinary real variable. For example, the assignment statement

$$A := 3.67;$$

may be invoked anywhere in the main program. If the subprogram "OUTER" is called, memory is dynamically set aside (during program execution) for the new entity "A" defined to be an integer. Within the subprogram "OUTER", the global real variable "A" is not visible. Thus an assignment such as

$$A := 3.67;$$

would be illegal and would be flagged by the compiler. An assignment of the form

$$A := 3;$$

would be perfectly legal. If such an assignment were made within subprogram "OUTER", the current value of the real variable "A" in the main program would not be changed. Indeed, two "A"'s would coexist in different memory locations in the same software system. If subprogram "OUTER" were to call subprogram "INNER", the third entity "A" would be dynamically created. Within subprogram "INNER", the assignment

$$A := \text{'H'};$$

would be perfectly legal. In fact, within the scope of subprogram "INNER", the other two entities "A" would be invisible. Three "A"'s (every student's dream) would coexist in different memory locations within the same software system.

Subprogram "INNER" cannot be called or invoked from the main program. All locally declared identifiers within "OUTER" such as "A", "B", "C", and, yes, "INNER", are invisible at the level of the main program. In fact, memory locations to support these entities are allocated only when "OUTER" is called. When subprogram "OUTER" is finished executing (the "end" statement is encountered), the memory that was allocated for these local entities is deallocated. Thus, in some sense, subprogram "INNER" and the local integer variables "A", "B", and "C" do not even exist until subprogram "OUTER" is called. In a similar manner, the local character variables "A" and "E" come into existence only after subprogram "INNER" has been called from within subprogram "OUTER". Confusing? Think of the work the Pascal compiler must do, during program execution, to dynamically manage computer memory and keep track of the various personalities of these global and local variables.

To clarify these points, let us closely examine the scope and visible regions of global variable E. The scope of E covers the entire program. Within subprogram "INNER", E is invisible because of the presence of a local variable name "E". Thus the visible region of global variable "E" starts with its declaration and extends down to the declaration of "E" in procedure "INNER". Then it temporarily stops. It picks up again just below the "end" statement for procedure "INNER" and continues down to the end of the program (Figure 3.1).

Modula-2 and Ada support similar types of scoping and visibility rules. Of what real value, from a software engineering viewpoint, are these scope and visibility capabilities?

3.2.6.2 Scope, Visibility, and Software Engineering

An obvious consequence of multiple levels of locality for identifiers is the tremendous flexibility afforded the programmer(s) in reusing identifier names many times in the same program at different levels of locality. This flexibility promotes software reliability in a team programming environment by permitting smoother interfaces when meshing the work of more than one programmer. Indeed, even in large single-programmer software development projects,

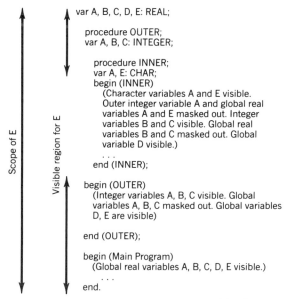

```
var A, B, C, D, E: REAL;

    procedure OUTER;
    var A, B, C: INTEGER;

        procedure INNER;
        var A, E: CHAR;
        begin (INNER)
            (Character variables A and E visible.
            Outer integer variable A and global real
            variables A and E masked out. Integer
            variables B and C visible. Global real
            variables B and C masked out. Global
            variable D visible.)
            . . .
        end (INNER);

    begin (OUTER)
        (Integer variables A, B, C visible. Global
        variables A, B, C masked out. Global variables
        D, E are visible)

    end (OUTER);

    begin (Main Program)
        (Global real variables A, B, C, D, E visible.)
        . . .
    end.
```

Figure 3.1 Scope and visibility of variable E.

program reliability is improved when it is possible for a programmer to reuse some variable names whenever this results in a more natural and readable expression. It must be cautioned that the overuse of the same identifiers might lead to confusion.

We illustrate the vulnerability present in languages that do not support levels of locality. In these languages the management of the name space used for identifiers is difficult to control. We present a toy problem for illustrative purposes only. Suppose that we wish to input 5000 integers into an array, and after each integer has been entered, print out the cumulative sum of all the integers previously entered (including the one just entered). We first show an implementation of this in BASIC, admittedly contrived to make our point (Program 3.4)!

PROGRAM 3.4 BASIC Program for Cumulative Sum

```
10      DIM A(5000)
20      FOR I = 1 TO 5000
30      PRINT "Enter integer "; I
40      INPUT A(I)
45      K = I
50      GOSUB 100
60      NEXT I
70      GOTO 160
100     SUM = 0
```

```
110    FOR I = 1 TO K
120    SUM = SUM + A(I)
130    NEXT I
140    PRINT "Cumulative sum of first "; K;" terms is "; SUM
150    RETURN
160    END
```

Next, we show an implementation of this in Pascal (Program 3.5).

PROGRAM 3.5   Pascal Program for Cumulative Sum

```
program CUMULATIVE_SUM;
type INTEGER_ARRAY = array[1..5000] of INTEGER;
var A        : INTEGER_ARRAY;
    I        : INTEGER;
    K        : INTEGER;
    RESULT : INTEGER;

procedure SUM(W: INTEGER_ARRAY; L: INTEGER; var ANSWER: INTEGER);
var TOTAL : INTEGER;
        I : INTEGER;
begin
    TOTAL:=0;
    for I:=1 to L do
        TOTAL:=TOTAL + W[I];
    ANSWER:=TOTAL
end{SUM};

begin {Main Program}
    K:=0;
    for I:=1 to 5000 do
    begin
        K:=K+1;
        write('Enter integer ',K,': ');
        readln(A[K]);
        SUM(A,K,RESULT);
        writeln('The cumulative sum after ',K,' terms is ',RESULT)
    end{do loop}
end.
```

In the BASIC version, Program 3.4, the variable I is declared, in line 20, as an INTEGER variable. It is used as a loop index variable. In line 110, within the ''subroutine'' starting at line 100, the variable I is reassigned a new set of values. When control returns to the original loop, line 60, the value of I, controlling this original loop, has been corrupted and lost. After a FOR NEXT loop in BASIC, the value of the loop control variable (I in this case) is lost. Of course this short and simple program has been contrived to make this point. But in a larger BASIC program, it is quite easy to inadvertently reuse a variable name for some other purpose, thus corrupting the original value. This type of error is the worst kind of programming error. It is difficult to detect.

In the Pascal version, Program 3.5, two variables named ''I'' exist. The first, at the global main program level, is used to control the main loop. The second, defined as a local variable in subprogram ''SUM'' is used to control the cumulative sum loop. This local variable ''I'' (also an INTEGER variable) is stored in a separate memory location from the global variable I. In fact, it comes into existence only when procedure ''SUM'' is called. The value of the main loop index variable ''I'' is not changed when the local ''I'' takes on its appropriate sequence of values. This decoupling of the two ''I'''s resulting from the visible region of the global variable ''I'' (which does not include subprogram ''SUM'') clearly improves program reliability.

We remark here that the ''var'' preceding the formal parameter ''AN-SWER'' in subprogram ''SUM'', indicates an input-output or purely output mode for the transfer of information. The ANSWER is generated each time the subprogram ''SUM'' is executed.

3.2.6.3 Subprograms and Top-Down Design

The feature of nested subprograms in a language supports top-down design. Top-down design proceeds from the general to the specific—from an identification of major system components to subcomponents and sub-subcomponents, and so forth. Many software designers construct the software system architecture as a hierarchy of software components, each to be later implemented as a subprogram. The hierarchical levels of the system architecture are realized in the implementation by mapping the functional components onto the set of nested subprograms that are used to implement the functional components.

3.2.6.4 Subprograms and Data Abstraction

Earlier we discussed the desirability of data abstraction. To better appreciate the meaning, significance, and utility of data abstraction, we must reexamine the concept of a data type and relate this concept to subprograms.

A data type introduces an abstract entity and a set of allowable operations on the entity. For example, among the operations predefined for entities of type REAL, in Pascal, are multiplication, division, addition, subtraction, comparison, assignment, and unary negation.

Quite often, data types are created by the programmer as a vehicle for providing a natural representation of problem variables. See, for example,

Program 3.1. The designer may wish to introduce special operations on the new data types, to permit manipulation of these data types to meet the needs of the given problem. The ability to create new data types as well as to define special operations on these new data types allows the designer to employ a much higher level of abstraction in solving the problem. Instead of having to map the entities of the problem onto a limited set of predefined data types and operations, the designer may instead invent new types and new operations that naturally mirror the objects and their transformations found in the problem.

As we examine software systems ranging from machine language programs to recent high level language implementations, we observe a dramatic increase in the level of data abstraction evident in the design and implementation of these systems.

The final and perhaps most important component associated with data abstraction is data hiding. Language support for data hiding is very recent. To discuss data hiding and its relation to data abstraction and software engineering, we must introduce the concept of the module.

3.2.7 Modules

3.2.7.1 Data Hiding; True Data Abstraction

Modula-2 and Ada permit a programmer to manipulate abstract data types without regard to their representational details. Furthermore, it is possible in these language to make the representational details of the abstract data types inaccessible outside of the module in which they are defined. This important feature of Modula-2 and Ada distinguishes these languages from most other languages.

The inability to hide data represents an area of vulnerability for large software systems. The global data structures that subprograms transform and manipulate may be unwittingly corrupted. We illustrate this phenomenon by considering a set of subprograms, in Pascal, for stack manipulations.

Suppose we wish to enter a name and then print out the reverse sequence of characters in the name. We may easily accomplish this using a stack structure, as in Program 3.6.

PROGRAM 3.6 Pascal Stack Manipulations

```
program NAME_REVERSAL;

const
    STACKSIZE = 40;

type
    STACKITEM = CHAR;
```

```pascal
STACK       = record
                    ITEM:  array[1..STACKSIZE] of STACKITEM;
                    TOP : 0..STACKSIZE
              end;

var
    NAME,REVERSE : packed array[1..STACKSIZE] of CHAR;
    A                : STACK;
    CHAR_NUM, J   : INTEGER;

function EMPTY(S: STACK) : BOOLEAN;
begin
    if S.TOP = 0 then
        EMPTY:=TRUE
    else EMPTY:=FALSE
end{EMPTY};

function POP(var S: STACK) : STACKITEM;
begin
    if EMPTY(S) then
        writeln('Stack underflow.')
    else begin
        POP:=S.ITEM[S.TOP];
        S.TOP:=S.TOP−1
    end
end{POP};

procedure PUSH(var S: STACK; X: STACKITEM);
begin
    if S.TOP = STACKSIZE
        then writeln('Stack overflow.')
    else begin
        S.TOP:=S.TOP + 1;
        S.ITEM[S.TOP]:=X
    end
end{PUSH};

begin {Main Program}
    for J:=1 to STACKSIZE do NAME[J] :=' ';
    REVERSE:=NAME;
    write('Enter first name, middle initial, last name  : ');
    CHAR_NUM:=0;
    while (CHAR_NUM <= 40) and (not EOLN) do
    begin
        CHAR_NUM:=CHAR_NUM+1;
        read(NAME[CHAR_NUM])
```

```
    end{while loop};
    A.TOP:=0;
{This is an example of an all too typical Pascal
statement that although correct, accesses the
internal structure of the abstract type STACK,
and therefore represents poor software engineering
practice. A procedure INITIALIZE should be available
as part of the supporting operations for the abstract
data type STACK.                                          }
    for J:=1 to CHAR_NUM do
        PUSH(A,NAME[J]);
    for J:=1 to CHAR_NUM do
        REVERSE[J]:= POP(A);
    writeln;
    writeln(REVERSE)
end.
```

Program 3.6 works as it should to reverse the sequence of characters in NAME. The stack, with its first-in/last-out structure, easily accomplishes the desired goal.

Now suppose, as a later maintenance task, we wish to print out the middle initial of the name before printing the reversed name. In Program 3.7 we exhibit a modified version of Program 3.6, which purports to implement the minor modification required for the program.

PROGRAM 3.7   Maintenance Modification of Program 3.6

```
program NAME_REVERSAL_WITH_MIDDLE_INITIAL;

const
    STACKSIZE = 40;

type
    STACKITEM = CHAR;

    STACK      = record
                    ITEM: array[1..STACKSIZE] of STACKITEM;
                    TOP : 0..STACKSIZE
                 end;

var
    NAME,REVERSE    : packed array[1..40] of CHAR;
    A               : STACK;
    CHAR_NUM, J     : INTEGER;
```

```
function EMPTY(S: STACK) : BOOLEAN;
begin
    if S.TOP = 0 then
        EMPTY:=TRUE
    else EMPTY:=FALSE
end{EMPTY};

function POP(var S: STACK) : STACKITEM;
begin
    if EMPTY(S) then
        writeln('Stack underflow.')
    else begin
        POP:=S.ITEM[S.TOP];
        S.TOP:=S.TOP−1
    end
end{POP};

procedure PUSH(var S: STACK; X: STACKITEM);
begin
    if S.TOP = STACKSIZE then
        writeln('Stack overflow.')
    else begin
        S.TOP:=S.TOP + 1;
        S.ITEM[S.TOP]:=X
    end
end{PUSH};

function FIND_MIDDLE(var S: STACK): CHAR;
begin
    S.TOP:=0;
    repeat
        S.TOP:=S.TOP+1;
    until S.ITEM[S.TOP] = ' ';
    FIND_MIDDLE:=S.ITEM[S.TOP+1]
end{FIND_MIDDLE};

begin {Main Program}
    for J:=1 to 40 do NAME[J]:=' ';
    REVERSE:=NAME;
    write('Enter first name, middle initial, last name  : ');
    CHAR_NUM:=0;
    while (CHAR_NUM <= 40) and (not EOLN) do
    begin
        CHAR_NUM:=CHAR_NUM+1;
        read(NAME[CHAR_NUM])
    end{while loop};
```

```
    A.TOP:=0;          {Initialize stack A to empty.}
    for J:=1 to CHAR_NUM do
        PUSH(A,NAME[J]);
    writeln;
    writeln('The middle initial is ',FIND_MIDDLE(A));
    writeln;
    for J:=1 to CHAR_NUM do
        REVERSE[J]:=POP(A);
    writeln;
    writeln(REVERSE)
end.
```

Do you see the serious maintenance error in Program 3.7?

Subprogram FIND_MIDDLE, by accessing the global STACK data structure directly, corrupts the TOP index pointer. This causes a series of stack underflow errors when an attempt is made to print the reversed name.

The underlying cause of the maintenance error is Pascal's inability to hide the data representation of STACK to which procedure FIND_MIDDLE is bound. Of course poor programming is directly responsible for the error. If parameter S, in subprogram FIND_MIDDLE, were a value parameter rather than a reference parameter (i.e., if the "var" in front of S were removed), the new program would work as intended. The point, though, is that Pascal's inability to hide the data structure STACK from subprograms that need to perform stack manipulations represents a potentially serious liability from a software engineering viewpoint.

True data abstraction requires that generalized operations be allowed on data objects not bound to particular data representations. This implies data hiding—the control over the accessibility of data objects. The programmer who wishes to use a stack does not need to know how the stack is represented, just as, most often, the programmer who uses an integer does not need to know the internal representation of that data object.

The ability to support data hiding and true data abstraction is the most significant feature that sets Modula-2 and Ada apart from earlier languages. Both recent languages introduce a level of program abstraction higher than the subprogram, namely, the module (called a package in Ada).

In concept, a module is a collection of related subprograms operating on a set of data types. The representational details of these data types may be suppressed. Typically, the modules in a software system are installed in a library, and the software resources (i.e., subprograms and associated data structures) provided by the modules may be accessed by any program. The modules are reusable major software components that may be interfaced to many host programs.

3.2.7.2   The Module and Separate Compilation in Modula-2

Modules are split into specification and implementation parts. Each of these module components is compiled separately. Data types may be specified in the specification (interface) portion of a module without revealing representation details; these must be provided in the implementation part of the module. The specification part of a module contains data types and objects and subprogram stubs (the subprogram name and associated formal parameters). Any host programs that use a library module can "see" only the specification portion of the module that has been explicitly designated as an exportable component. Therefore, these host programs can declare and manipulate data objects given in the module specification without knowledge of the representation details of these data types. Thus, true data abstraction is achieved in the host program. Corruption of a data type, as evidenced in Program 3.7, cannot occur, since the host program can perform only a restricted set of operations (manipulations) on the data type, namely, those given in the module specification.

We illustrate this concept in Program 3.8 by reworking Program 3.7 in Modula-2. The reader is urged to consult Niklaus Wirth's book *Programming in Modula-2* [4] for language details.

PROGRAM 3.8   Modula-2 Version of Program 3.7

```
(* This definition module is a separate compiland and is
   compiled before the program ReverseName is compiled. *)

DEFINITION MODULE Stacks;
(* $SEG:=8; *)
(* This is a compiler directive required by the particular operating system being
   used. It assigns a segment number of a definition module. In general, this is
   not required. *)

    EXPORT QUALIFIED
        (* type *) Stack,
        (* proc *) Empty,
        (* proc *) Pop,
        (* proc *) Push,
        (* proc *) Initialize,
        (* proc *) Remove;

    TYPE Stack;   (* Representational details hidden   *)

    PROCEDURE Empty(S: Stack) : BOOLEAN;
    (* Returns true if stack is empty. *)
```

```
    PROCEDURE Pop(VAR S: Stack) : CHAR;
    (* Strips top element off stack. *)

    PROCEDURE Push(VAR S: Stack; X: CHAR);
    (* Adds element to top of stack. *)

    PROCEDURE Initialize(VAR S: Stack);
    (* Sets stack to empty. *)

    PROCEDURE Remove(VAR S: Stack);
    (* Removes stack from memory. *)

END Stacks.
```

```
MODULE ReverseName;  (* This is the program. *)

(* In Modula-2, all reserved words must be given in uppercase. *)

    FROM Stacks IMPORT Empty, Pop, Initialize, Remove, Stack;

    FROM InOut IMPORT WriteString, WriteLn, Write, Read, EOL;

    PROCEDURE Find Middle (VAR S : Stack) : CHAR;
    (* We use an algorithm different from that in Program 3.7. *)

    VAR LocalStack: Stack;
        ch         : CHAR;

    BEGIN
        Initialize(LocalStack);
        REPEAT
            ch:=Pop(S);
            Push(LocalStack,ch);
        UNTIL ch= '.';
        ch:=Pop(S);
        Push(LocalStack,ch);
        (* Now we restore the stack S to its original form. *)
        WHILE NOT Empty(LocalStack) DO
            Push(S,Pop(LocalStack));
        END;
        RETURN ch
    END FindMiddle;

    VAR Name        : ARRAY[1. .40] OF CHAR;
        A           : Stack;
```

```
        CharNum, j    : CARDINAL;
        ch            : CHAR;

BEGIN (* ReverseName *)
    FOR j:=1 TO 40 DO
        Name[j]:=' ';
    END;
    WriteString("Enter first name, middle initial, last name : ");
    CharNum:=0;
    WHILE (CharNum <= 40) AND (ch # EOL) DO
        INC(CharNum); (* Increment CharNum by 1 *)
        Read(ch);
        Name[CharNum]:=ch;
    END;
    WriteLn;
    Initialize(A);
    FOR j:= TO CharNum DO
        Push(A,Name[j]);
    END;
    WriteLn;
    WriteString("The middle initial is ");
    Write(FindMiddle(A));
    WriteLn;
    WriteString("The reversed name is → ");
    WHILE NOT Empty(A) DO
        ch:=Pop(A);
        IF ch # EOL THEN Write(ch); END;
    END;
    Remove(A);
END  ReverseName.
```

The Modula-2 program ReverseName "imports" the subprograms Empty, Pop, Push, Initialize, and Remove from the library module Stacks. The abstract data type Stack is also imported from the module Stacks. The data type Stack is an example of true data abstraction. The programmer, in program ReverseName, does not know the representation details of type Stack (for that matter neither does the reader of this book, at this point). Therefore the programmer can neither purposely nor inadvertently alter this data structure except by using the procedures provided by the same module Stacks.

To actually execute ReverseName, the implementation module for Stacks must be compiled and available. If these implementation details are later modified—for example, because an algorithm has been improved—the program ReverseName does not have to be recompiled as long as the specification part (definition module) has not been changed. This feature of module construction supports software maintenance.

What are the implementation details of module Stacks? How was the Stack data structure represented? How do the subprograms Empty, Pop, Push, Initialize, and Remove manipulate this unknown data structure? Before we display the second part of module Stacks, the implementation part, we ask you to consider two important questions. Did your understanding of ReverseName depend on a knowledge of the representation details of Stack? Would you be able to use this abstract Stack type in your own programs?

We trust that your understanding of ReverseName was not dependent on knowing the representation details of Stack. We also trust that you would be able to use the abstract type Stack, coupled with the subprograms Empty, Pop, Push, Initialize, and Remove. Since the abstract data type Stack is exported from the module Stacks, you, the programmer, may create many objects of this data type. You will note that the abstract type Stack is a parameter to each of the procedures in module Stacks. This permits Pop, Push, and the other stack operations to be performed on the entire set of stack objects that the programmer has created.

Your facility for using the subprograms associated with type Stack would be enhanced if a user's guide were included in the form of comments under each subprogram stub. We believe that rather than supply a separate user's guide with each software module, the specification part of the module (definition module in Modula-2) should include this user's guide.

Well, now that you are convinced that you do not need to know the representation details of module Stacks to use it, we now present these details anyway.

Implementation Details of Module Stacks

```
IMPLEMENTATION MODULE Stacks;

    FROM Terminal IMPORT WriteString, WriteLn;

    FROM Storage  IMPORT ALLOCATE, DEALLOCATE;

    CONST STACKSIZE = 80;

    TYPE Objects = ARRAY [1..STACKSIZE] OF CHAR;

            Stack = POINTER TO RECORD
                            ITEM: Objects;
                            TOP : CARDINAL
                        END;
```

```
    PROCEDURE Empty(S: Stack) : BOOLEAN;
    BEGIN
        IF S↑.TOP = 0 THEN
            RETURN TRUE
        ELSE
            RETURN FALSE
        END
    END Empty;

PROCEDURE Pop(VAR S: Stack) : CHAR;
(* Strips top element off stack. *)
BEGIN
    IF Empty(S) THEN
        WriteString("Stack underflow.");
        WriteLn;
        HALT;
    ELSE
        DEC(S↑.TOP);
        RETURN S↑.ITEM[S↑.TOP+1];
    END
END Pop;

PROCEDURE Push(VAR S: Stack; X: CHAR);
(* Adds element to top of stack. *)
BEGIN
    IF S↑.TOP = STACKSIZE THEN
        WriteString("Stack overflow.");
        WriteLn
    ELSE
        INC(S↑.TOP);
        S↑.ITEM[S↑.TOP]:=X
    END
END Push;

PROCEDURE Initialize(VAR S: Stack);   (* Sets stack to empty. *)
BEGIN
    NEW(S);
    S↑.TOP:=0
END Initialize;

PROCEDURE Remove(VAR S: Stack);
BEGIN
    DISPOSE(S)
END Remove;

END Stacks.
```

Modula-2, with virtually no loss of generality, requires hidden types to be pointer variables.

We indicated above that an implementation module may be modified without affecting a client program that imports the module. Recall, from Chapter 1, our discussion of modular system design and the example of car maintenance (not having to overhaul an entire engine every time there is a fault in the performance—because of the modularity of the engine design). If module implementations are decoupled from client programs, faults in these modules may be repaired without concern about "fall-out" effects to the rest of the system (the client programs that import the module).

The implementation details of module Stacks may be changed without requiring any change in the program(s) that import this module. We present another version of IMPLEMENTATION MODULE Stacks. In this version, the abstract data type Stack is represented dynamically. Thus, the amount of memory consumed by the stack structure changes as the size of the stack changes. This version is superior to the preceding version because the system designer does not have to impose a predetermined upper limit on the size of the stack.

A New Implementation of MODULE Stacks

```
IMPLEMENTATION MODULE GenStacks;

    FROM InOut IMPORT WriteString, WriteLn;

    FROM Storage  IMPORT ALLOCATE, DEALLOCATE;

    FROM SYSTEM IMPORT WORD;

    TYPE
        Stack  = POINTER TO NODE;

        NODE = RECORD
                    ITEM: CHAR;
                    NEXT: Stack
                END;

    PROCEDURE Empty(S: Stack) : BOOLEAN;
    BEGIN
        IF S = NIL
            THEN RETURN TRUE
            ELSE RETURN FALSE
        END(* if then *)
    END Empty;
```

```
PROCEDURE Pop(VAR S: Stack) : CHAR;

VAR
    P: Stack;
    W: CHAR;
BEGIN
    IF Empty(S) THEN
        WriteString("Stack underflow");
        WriteLn;
        HALT
    ELSE
        P:=S;
        W:=P↑.ITEM;
        S:=S↑.NEXT;
        DISPOSE(P);
        RETURN W
    END
END Pop;

PROCEDURE Push(VAR S: Stack; X: CHAR);

VAR
    P: STACK;

BEGIN
    NEW(P);
    P↑.ITEM:=X;
    P↑.NEXT:=S;
    S:=P
END Push;

PROCEDURE Initialize(VAR S: Stack);   (* Sets stack to empty. *)
BEGIN
    NEW(S);
    S↑.NEXT:=NIL
END Initialize;

END GenStacks.
```

Have you carefully compared the new version of IMPLEMENTATION MODULE Stacks with the preceding version? Why do we not have to have a procedure Remove in this second version?

We illustrate the importance of separating the specification of a module from its implementation with another example. Suppose we create a module that sorts an array of integers (there may be a fault in the algorithm that we use in this module). We create a short client program that imports this Sorting module. Then we modify the implementation details of module Sorting (we repair the algorithm for sorting), without doing any damage to the original client program (Program 3.9).

PROGRAM 3.9 Sorting Module and Associated Client Program

```
DEFINITION MODULE Sorting;
(* $SEG:=9; *)

    EXPORT  QUALIFIED
                (* proc *) Sort;

    PROCEDURE Sort(VAR A: ARRAY OF INTEGER);

END Sorting.
```

```
MODULE WeSort;

    FROM Sorting IMPORT Sort;

    FROM InOut IMPORT WriteString, WriteInt, WriteLn, ReadInt;

    VAR
        i           : CARDINAL;
        NUMBERS : ARRAY[11..20] OF INTEGER;

BEGIN
    FOR i:= 11 TO 20 DO
        WriteString("Enter number ");
        WriteInt(i,1);
        WriteString(" : ");
        ReadInt(NUMBERS[i]);
        WriteLn;
    END;
    WriteLn;
    Sort(NUMBERS);
    WriteLn;
    WriteString("     The Sorted Numbers");
    WriteLn;
    WriteString("     ---------------");
    WriteLn;
```

```
    FOR i:=11 TO 20 DO
        WriteInt(NUMBERS[i],15);
        WriteLn
    END
END WeSort.
```

```
IMPLEMENTATION MODULE Sorting;

    PROCEDURE Sort(VAR A: ARRAY OF INTEGER);

    (* In Modula-2, the open array type A has a lower index
       bound of 0 and an upper index bound given by the predefined
       function HIGH.                                                    *)

        PROCEDURE Maximum(A: ARRAY OF INTEGER; VAR  pos : CARDINAL);

        Var i    : CARDINAL;  (* Natural numbers from 0 to MAXCARD *)
        max      : INTEGER;

        BEGIN
            max:=A[0];
            pos:=0;
            FOR i:=1 TO HIGH(A) DO
                IF A[i] > max THEN
                    max:=A[i];
                    pos:=i;
                END
            END(* do loop *)
        END Maximum;

        PROCEDURE Interchange(VAR A: ARRAY OF INTEGER; x,y: CARDINAL);

        VAR Z: INTEGER;

        BEGIN
            IF x # y THEN
                Z:=A[x];
                A[x]:=A[y];
                A[y]:=Z
            END
        END Interchange;

    VAR
        pos    : CARDINAL;
        Index, j : CARDINAL;
```

```
BEGIN (* Sort *)
    Index:=HIGH(A) + 1;
    REPEAT
        DEC(Index);  (* DEC means decrement Index by 1. *)
        Maximum(A,pos);
        Interchange(A,pos,Index);
    UNTIL Index = 0;
END Sort;

END Sorting.
```

We note that the subprogram Sort in module Sorting uses an open, undimensioned array. This allows it to interface with an array of any size. The subprograms Maximum and Interchange, used in the implementation part of module Sorting, are invisible to program Sort or to any program importing module Sorting. Unfortunately, there is an error in the implementation of module Sorting. The error involves the algorithm used. Can you find it?

Once the error has been detected, a repaired implementation part is compiled. The program WeSort does not have to be recompiled.

The repaired implementation of module Sorting is as follows.

Correct Implementation Module Sorting

```
IMPLEMENTATION MODULE Sorting;

    PROCEDURE Sort(VAR A: ARRAY OF INTEGER);

        PROCEDURE Maximum(A: ARRAY OF INTEGER; UPPER: INTEGER;
                          VAR  pos : CARDINAL);

        VAR i       : CARDINAL;
            max  : INTEGER;

        BEGIN
            max:=A[0];
            pos:=0;
            FOR i:=1 TO UPPER DO
                IF A[i] > max THEN
                    max:=A[i];
                    pos:=i;
                END
            END(* do loop *)
        END Maximum;
```

```
PROCEDURE Interchange(VAR A: ARRAY OF INTEGER; x,y:
                                CARDINAL);

    VAR Z: INTEGER;

    BEGIN
        IF x # y THEN
            Z:=A[x];
            A[x]:=A[y];
            A[y]:=Z
        END
    END Interchange;

VAR pos     : CARDINAL;
    Index, j : CARDINAL;

BEGIN (* Sort *)
    Index:=HIGH(A) + 1;
    REPEAT
        DEC(Index);
        Maximum(A,Index,pos);
        Interchange(A,pos,Index);
    UNTIL Index = 0;
END Sort;


END Sorting.
```

The correction was in subprogram Maximum, which got another parameter in the revised version. This third parameter is used in the main body of module Sorting.

To illustrate the power of reusable library modules in Modula-2, we present a powerful module for controlling screen input-output. This module was developed by Joel McCormick of Volition Systems (P.O. Box 1236, Del Mar, California 92014). With the permission of Volition Systems we present the screen input-output module Windows as Program 3.10. This example will also give you an additional flavor of the Modula-2 programming language.

Program 3.10, library module Windows, is an excellent example of a major software component that offers the software system developer a host of functional components. Module Windows treats the screen like an abstract data object, permitting the programmer six generalized manipulations to facilitate screen input-output. Any programmer who wishes to access the functional components Write, WriteLn, Open, Close, Borders, and Title, in doing screen windowing, may "plug in" to the module Windows. All that the potential Windows user must know are the precise interface details given in the definition portion of this module.

You may wish to skip over the fine details of this long library module for your first reading, focusing on the basic structure of this software system until you have gained additional familiarity with Modula-2.

PROGRAM 3.10 **Library Module Windows for Screen Input-Output**

```
DEFINITION MODULE Windows;      (* May 82 J. McCormack *)
(* Copyright 1982, Volition Systems. All rights reserved. *)
(*$SEG := 17; *)

EXPORT QUALIFIED WINDOW, WriteString,
    Write, WriteLn, Open, Close, Borders, Title;

CONST rows       = 24;
      columns    = 80;

TYPE WINDOW:

    RowRange    = [0 .. rows-1];
    ColRange    = [0 .. columns-1];  (* Range for text *)

    RowLength   = [1 .. rows];
    ColLength   = [1 .. columns];    (* Range for virtual cursor *)

PROCEDURE Open (VAR w      : WINDOW;
                    row    : RowRange;
                    column: ColRange;
                    height : RowLength;
                    width  : ColLength);
(* Open window for writing. No checks for overlap of windows. *)

PROCEDURE Close (VAR w     : WINDOW);
(* Close window. *)

PROCEDURE Title (w       : WINDOW;
                 name : ARRAY OF CHAR;
                 under : CHAR);
(* Put name at the top of the window. If under <> 0C or ' ',
   underline the title. *)

PROCEDURE Borders (w    : WINDOW;
                   corner, down, across: CHAR);
(* Draw border around current writable area in window with characters.
   Good to call this BEFORE Title. *)
```

```
PROCEDURE GotoRowColumn (w     : WINDOW;
                         row   : RowRange;
                         column : ColRange);
(* Relative to writable window boundaries, of course. *)

PROCEDURE Write (w: WINDOW; ch: CHAR);
(* Write one character to window.
   If end of column, go to next row.
   If end of window, go to top of window. *)

PROCEDURE WriteString (w: WINDOW;
                       s: ARRAY OF CHAR);
(* Write a string to window. *)

PROCEDURE WriteLn (w: WINDOW);
(* Go to beginning of next line. Next line is
   not blanked until next character is written  *)

END Windows.
```

```
IMPLEMENTATION MODULE Windows;  (* 27 May 82 J. McCormack.  *)
(* Copyright 1982, Volition Systems. All rights reserved. *)

FROM Screen IMPORT GotoXY;
FROM Storage IMPORT ALLOCATE, DEALLOCATE;
IMPORT Terminal;

TYPE
    XColRange = [0 .. columns];
    WINDOW = POINTER TO
                RECORD
                    row,                        (* Current cursor row *)
                    firstrow,
                    lastrow      : RowRange;
                    column       : XColRange; (* Current cursor column*)
                    firstcolumn,
                    lastcolumn   : ColRange;
                END

VAR  Row: RowRange;                        (* Current cursor position *)
     Col : XColRange;

PROCEDURE Open (VAR w   : WINDOW;
                    row: RowRange;
```

```
                                column: ColRange;
                                height: RowLength;
                                width: ColLength);
(* Allocate window, and put virtual cursor in upper left corner. *)
BEGIN
    NEW(w);
    w↑.row := row;
    w↑.firstrow := row;
    w↑.lastrow := row + height − 1;
    w↑.column := column;
    w↑.firstcolumn := column;
    w↑.lastcolumn := column + width − 1;
END Open;

PROCEDURE Close (VAR w: WINDOW);
BEGIN
    DISPOSE(w)
END Close;

PROCEDURE Title (w      : WINDOW;
                 name   : ARRAY OF CHAR;
                 under  : CHAR);
(* Put name at the top of the window.
   If under <> 0C or ' ', underline the title. *)
   VAR i: ColRange;
BEGIN
    WITH w↑ DO
        column := firstcolumn;
        row := firstrow;
        WriteString (w, name);
        WriteLn (w);
        IF (under = 0C) OR (under = ' ') THEN
            firstrow := firstrow + 1
        ELSE
            FOR i := firstcolumn TO lastcolumn DO
                Write (w, under)
                END;
            WriteLn(w);
            firstrow := firstrow + 2;
            END;
        END (* WITH *)
END Title;

PROCEDURE GotoRowColumn (w      : WINDOW;
                         row    : RowRange;
                         column : ColRange);
```

```
(* Relative to writable window boundaries, of course. *)
BEGIN
    w↑.row := w↑.firstrow + row;
    w↑.column := w↑.firstcolumn + column
END GotoRowColumn;


PROCEDURE Borders (w      : WINDOW;
                        corner, down, across: CHAR);
(* Draw border around current writable area in window with characters.
   Good to call this BEFORE Title.   *)
   VAR i: RowRange;
       j: ColRange;
BEGIN
    WITH w↑ DO
        GotoXY (firstcolumn, firstrow);
        Terminal.Write (corner);
        FOR j := firstcolumn + 1 TO lastcolumn − 1 DO
            Terminal.Write (across)
            END;
        Terminal.Write (corner);
        FOR i := firstrow + 1 TO lastrow − 1 DO
            GotoXY (firstcolumn, i);
            Terminal.Write (down);
            GotoXY (lastcolumn, i);
            Terminal.Write (down)
            END;
        GotoXY (firstcolumn, lastrow);
        Terminal.Write (corner);
        FOR j := firstcolumn + 1 TO lastcolumn − 1 DO
            Terminal.Write (across)
            END;
        Terminal.Write (corner);
        Row := lastrow;
        Col := lastcolumn + 1;
        firstrow := firstrow + 1;
        row := firstrow;
        lastrow := lastrow − 1;
        firstcolumn := firstcolumn + 1;
        column := firstcolumn;
        lastcolumn := lastcolumn − 1;
        END (* WITH *)
END Borders;


PROCEDURE EraseToEndOfLine (w: WINDOW);
    VAR i: ColRange;
```

```
BEGIN
    WITH w↑ DO
        GotoXY (column, row);
        FOR i := column TO lastcolumn DO
            Terminal.Write (' ')
            END;
        GotoXY (column, row);
        Col := column,
        Row := row
        END (* WITH *)
END EraseToEndOfLine;

PROCEDURE Write (w: WINDOW;
                    ch: CHAR);
(* If after end of line, move to first character of next line
   If about to write first character on line, blank rest of line.
   Write character. *)

BEGIN
    IF ch = 15C THEN
        WriteLn(w);
        RETURN;
        END;

    WITH w↑ DO
        IF column > lastcolumn THEN
            IF row = lastrow THEN
                row := firstrow
            ELSE
                INC (row)
                END;
            column := firstcolumn
            END;
        IF column = firstcolumn THEN
            EraseToEndOfLine (w);
            END;
        IF (Col # column) OR (Row # row) THEN
            GotoXY (column, row);      (* Put physical cursor
                                            at virtual cursor *)
            Row := row;
            END;
        IF ch = 10C THEN
            IF column # firstcolumn THEN
                Terminal.Write(ch);
                DEC(column);
                END;
```

```
        ELSE
            Terminal.Write (ch);
            INC (column);
            END;
        Col := column;
        END (* WITH w↑ *);
END Write;

PROCEDURE WriteLn (w: WINDOW);
    VAR col: ColRange;

(* If not after line, blank rest of line.
   Move to first character of next line. *)

BEGIN
    WITH w↑ DO
        (*
        IF column <= lastcolumn THEN
        *)
        IF column = 0 THEN
            EraseToEndOfLine (w);
            END;
        IF row = lastrow THEN
          row := firstrow
        ELSE INC (row)
            END;
        column := firstcolumn
        END;
END WriteLn;

PROCEDURE WriteString (w: WINDOW;
                            s: ARRAY OF CHAR);
    VAR i: CARDINAL;
BEGIN
    i := 0;
    WHILE (i <= HIGH (s)) & (s[i] # 0C) DO
        Write (w, s[i]);
        INC (i)
        END;
END WriteString;

BEGIN (* Windows *)
    Row := 0;
    Col := 0;
    GotoXY (0, 0)
END Windows.
```

In Chapter 5 using Ada, and in Chapter 6 using Modula-2, we discuss and illustrate modular software design. For now, we are tempted to draw an important analogy to hardware engineering. In the design of hardware systems, the designer typically consults a handbook (e.g., integrated circuit handbook—in the "old" days, transistor or vacuum tube handbook) and selects from a large set of "off-the-shelf" components the particular component or components whose input-output characteristics meet the needs of the hardware design. The software module offers the software engineer that same approach to design. Once a large library of modules has been constructed, and the specification parts of this library published in a "handbook," the software designer can choose the particular module or modules that may be "plugged" into his or her own system. Each of these modules can offer the system designer a powerful set of related functional components. Furthermore, it would be reasonable to expect each of the modules in the "handbook" to have been thoroughly tested and verified.

With the advent of the programming languages Modula-2 and Ada, this type of major software components industry not only is possible, but indeed is developing.

3.2.7.3 The Module in Ada

The "package," in Ada, represents the highest level of program abstraction and serves as a module. Data hiding is accomplished through the use of "private" or "limited private" types. Assignment and equality testing are the only operations that are defined in the language for private types (the programmer must create all other operations). For limited private types no predefined operations are provided by the language. The programmer must supply all supporting operations, including assignment and equality testing.

We display a sample Ada package in Program 3.11.

PROGRAM 3.11   Specification of an Ada Package

```
with MATH_LIB; use MATH_LIB; -- Imported library modules

package VECTORS is -- Specification portion

    type RECTANGULAR is private; -- Abstract and hidden data

    type type POLAR is private;     -- Abstract and hidden data type

    function CREATE_RECT(A,B: in FLOAT) return RECTANGULAR;

    function CREATE_POLAR(A,B: in FLOAT) return POLAR;

    function RECT_POLAR_CONV(A: RECTANGULAR) return POLAR;
```

```
function POLAR_RECT_CONV(A: POLAR) return RECTANGULAR;

function HORZ_VECT(A: RECTANGULAR) return FLOAT;

function VERT_VECT(A:RECTANGULAR) return FLOAT;

function MODULUS_VECT(A: POLAR) return FLOAT;

function ANGLE_VECT(A: POLAR) return FLOAT;

private
    type RECTANGULAR is
            record
                HORZ, VERT: FLOAT;
            end record;

    type POLAR is
            record
                MODULUS, ANGLE: FLOAT;
            end record;

end VECTORS; -- End of specification part
```

Have you noticed that in Ada, the representations of limited and limited private types are listed explicitly in the specification part of the module? Although types RECTANGULAR and POLAR were listed, they are just as inaccessible to the user of this package as if they had been specified in the implementation portion of the package.

Modula-2 and Ada differ in their approaches to module and package exportation into client programs. Modula-2 allows a subset of the identifiers declared in the specification portion of a module to be exported to client programs. In Ada, it is all or nothing. When a client program imports an Ada package, all identifiers in the specification part of the package (except those declared to be of type private or limited private) become accessible to the client program. Ada's lack of selective importation rules can make it difficult, in a large program, to determine which package a particular imported entity comes from.

3.2.7.4 Scope and Visibility of Identifiers in Ada Packages

The specification part of an Ada package opens a window to the rest of an Ada program. Normally, packages are compiled separately and act as library modules. To access the resources (data objects and subprograms) contained within a package, the "with" statement makes the package name visible. Objects may then be accessed using dot notation consisting of the name of the package, followed by a dot, followed by the name of the subprogram or data object required. If within the scope of a "with" command, an additional "use" command is employed, all the resources of the package may be directly accessed as if they were declared at that point. The scope of these package resources is the same as if these resources were declared at the point of the "use" command. Most often, a "with" is immediately followed by a "use" as in Program 3.11.

A tricky problem arises if name duplication occurs between imported package entities and locally declared identifier names. In Ada, an identifier made visible by a "use" statement can never hide another identifier, although it may overload it. The name clash is resolved by according precedence to the innermost scope (the locally declared objects). In the event that two packages with name clashes are imported (using a "with" followed by a "use"), qualified reference (e.g., package_A.name or package_B.name) using dot notation can resolve the clash.

The reader is urged to consult the Ada reference manual [5] or an Ada programming book [2] for a more detailed discussion concerning Ada package scoping rules. Situations such as nesting a package within the specification portion of another package, and other such issues are dealt with.

The reader with extensive FORTRAN programming experience may be wondering at this point, "What else is new? Separate compilation and program libraries have been available in FORTRAN since the late 1950s." Not true. In the next section we distinguish separate compilation (available in Modula-2 and Ada) from independent compilation.

3.2.7.5 Separate versus Independent Compilation

Independent compilation implies that program units may be compiled separately and subsequently integrated to form a complete "program." The integration process is performed by a utility program called a linker or linkage editor. Without the facility of independent compilation, a language would be ill suited for large-scale software engineering.

When independent compilation is supported in a language, if a compiland is modified, it is not necessary to recompile the whole program. Only the modified unit must be recompiled and the system relinked.

FORTRAN has enjoyed widespread use, in part, because it supports independent compilation. Extensive precompiled FORTRAN subroutine libraries exist and form the environment for many software engineering projects. All the identifiers used in a subroutine (the basic library unit in FORTRAN) either are formal parameters, are locally declared, or are explicitly declared in a COMMON block. This COMMON block specifies the variables that are visible outside the subroutine. If reference is made to other subroutines (from within a subroutine), the compiler treats them as if they are externally declared and creates a list of external references to be resolved by the system linker. Because the programmer does not have to explicitly specify external references (through an IMPORT list, as in Modula-2), the compiler assumes that all external references to both COMMON variables as well as subroutines are correct.

Many FORTRAN programmers consider this a blessing. It is clear from the description above that a FORTRAN compiler is very forgiving. A programmer can invent a subroutine call within another subroutine even if that subroutine doesn't exist. Top-down design! But there is a problem. Indeed, there is a very serious problem!

The FORTRAN compiler does not check whether a subroutine call has the correct number of parameters or the correct type of parameters. This can potentially lead to absolute chaos in large system software development. Either because of the absence of subroutines, assumed by the compiler to exist, or because of erroneous subroutine transfers (both go undetected by the compiler), very serious run-time errors may occur. These, unfortunately, are usually the most serious and expensive to repair.

The organization of compilation units in FORTRAN does not support the module. Linkage from one unit (e.g., main program) to another is at the subprogram (subroutine) level. The attribute of true data abstraction, achieved through data hiding, is not available. The basic software engineering principle, MAKE VISIBLE ONLY WHAT IS NEEDED AT EACH POINT IN A SYSTEM, cannot be implemented in FORTRAN because any type of external reference can be invoked anywhere in a FORTRAN program. The subtleties associated with scope and visibility rules do not exist. Earlier in this chapter we discussed some of the vulnerabilities present in FORTRAN due to the lack of strong typing. These factors suggest that FORTRAN lacks many of the language attributes considered to be useful and important for the engineering of large-scale software systems. Nevertheless, an extensive investment has already been made in building FORTRAN systems; therefore FORTRAN remains a viable and important language.

Modern software engineering requires that an implementation language support both independent compilation and strong type checking across compilation boundaries. We have seen that FORTRAN lacks the feature of strong type checking across compilation boundaries. Pascal suffers from the deficiency that it does not support independent compilation. We refer to the combination of independent compilation with strong type checking across compilation boundaries as separate compilation. It must be emphasized that this type checking is performed at the time of compilation. Any external subprogram reference (perhaps to a module procedure) implies:

1. A check to ensure that the referenced subprogram exists on file in precompiled form.

2. A check to ensure that the calling parameters agree with the formal parameters of the subprogram both in number and in type.

3. A version number for the specification part of the module is recorded. This protects the system from a swap being made in the module specification

without recompilation of the client program. Note that a change in the implementation part of the module does not require the client program to be recompiled.

4. Information is stored to allow access to the various compilands at program execution time.

The rigorous cross-checking that is required of a compiler that supports separate compilation allows software construction to be decentralized (as is the case with existing independent compilation languages) while preserving the benefits of strong typing, complex scoping, and data abstraction.

Modula-2 and Ada, as we have seen, do support separate compilation. In Chapters 5 and 6 we discuss modular software design and use the important features of separate compilation as part of the software construction process.

3.3   DEFICIENCIES OF PASCAL; MODULA-2 TO THE RESCUE

Pascal was introduced in 1970, by Niklaus Wirth, as a vehicle for teaching structured programming principles. Because it is a relatively simple and readable language, it has become very popular. Many useful extensions to the original language definition statement have been implemented. Pascal is currently being used for an increasing number of commercial applications.

The important language attributes of strong typing, readability, side-effect control through the use of local and global identifiers, structured control of flow, dynamic memory management, and strong run-time checking are all present in Pascal. Notably missing, however, are features that support modular software construction, separate compilation, and data hiding.

Specific shortcomings of Pascal include:

1. Fixed size arrays. Writing general purpose numerical software is difficult in Pascal.

2. The absence of static variables, other than global variables. The use of global variables often forces a scope larger than desired.

3. Short-circuiting of Boolean expressions is not specified. This requires the writing of cumbersome code.

4. No "else" clause in the case statement.

5. No facilities for separate compilation.

6. No facilities for data hiding. Subprograms are bound to a particular data representation. This limits the level of data abstraction that is possible.

7. The declaration order (i.e., constants, types, variables, subprogram) inhibits declarations from being positioned near their point of application.

8. Type checking can never be suppressed. This facility might be desired in exceptional circumstances.

9. No facilities for concurrent processing.

Modula-2 was introduced in 1980 by Niklaus Wirth to correct these Pascal language problems. The corrective features of Modula-2 are given next, in the same order as the Pascal problems listed above, which they rectify.

Corrective Features Present in Modula-2

1. Modula-2 supports dynamic arrays.

2. Variables declared in a library module stay "alive" for the duration of a program's existence. The scope of these variables can be carefully controlled.

3. Short-circuiting of the Boolean "and" and "or" operators is prescribed in the language.

4. Case statements can use an "else" clause.

5. Separate compilation with rigorous cross-reference checking is provided by the language.

6. Data hiding is achieved through the module and the opaque type.

7. The declaration order for data objects is totally relaxed.

8. Type checking may be suppressed by using the WORD type. This practice is not recommended except in extraordinary circumstances.

9. Modula-2 provides complete support for concurrent processes.

Ada also provides a similar set of corrective features removing every deficiency noted for Pascal.

3.4 EXCEPTION HANDLING

FORTRAN and Pascal offer the programmer relatively little help in detecting and handling errors. With these languages, the programmer must use the control constructs available in the language to detect an exception and transfer control to an exception handler.

Exception tracking may be performed, in FORTRAN and Pascal, by using COMMON (global in Pascal) Boolean variables, which may be set at any layer of nesting. More commonly, Boolean "flag" variables are transmitted among subprograms. Although this technique allows exceptions to be transmitted from subprogram to subprogram, it has proved to be an unreliable scheme in complex and large software systems.

PL/1 and Ada provide the system designer and programmer a set of constructs for declaring and handling exceptions. Exception propagation can be carefully controlled using these languages and a graceful course of action taken when an unexpected event occurs.

In Ada, programmer-defined exceptions may be declared. For example, one might declare

```
DIVIDE_BY_ZERO : exception;
```

This exception could then be "raised" within some unit in the scope of the declaration above as, for example,

```
if B = 0.0 then raise DIVIDE_BY_ZERO;
```

or as another example,

```
MY_SALARY : exception;

if I_DO_WELL then raise MY_SALARY;

-- Ada is a readable language!
```

When an exception is raised, control is transferred to a block of code called an exception handler. In the following illustration of Ada code,

```
exception
    when DIVIDE_BY_ZERO => RESET_PARAMETERS;
    -- Other exceptions would be listed here also.
```

subprogram RESET_PARAMETERS performs the appropriate corrective action. An Ada exception handler may be defined in a program unit that is at an outer nesting level from where the actual exception was raised. The exception is automatically propagated to the outer unit. In fact the exception handler may exist at the outermost level of the program. Then all exceptions, no matter how deeply nested, will propagate to this outer exception handler. In Ada, when an exception is detected, the offending logical unit (e.g., block, subprogram, task) is immediately suspended. Since it is expected that Ada will be used (among other places) for embedded systems, this exception handling strategy makes sense for such systems. By contrast, in PL/1, after an exception has been handled, control returns to the offending unit, directly to the point at which the exception occurred. It is easy to mimic this strategy in Ada by having the Ada exception handler direct control back to the offending unit, hopefully after some corrective action has been taken to prevent the exception from occurring again.

3.5 CHOOSING A PROGRAMMING LANGUAGE

Although some purists might argue that good software design can be pursued independent of the implementation language, we believe that the software design process may be significantly enhanced by using the highest level features of the implementation language in the software design. For example, if the software system is to be implemented in Modula-2 or Ada, the architecture of the system can be structured using the module and package as building blocks. That is, they may be used to express and represent the design.

The manner in which the software development may be decentralized and later centralized depends largely on the implementation language features available that support multiple name use, information transfer, data hiding, and separate compilation. Although structured, well-documented design may be implemented with almost any language, the newer languages Modula-2 and Ada have features specifically created to support modular software construction.

Other factors, such as the availability and cost of compilers, the availability of software development tools, and the need for portability, influence the choice of programming language. If the software system under development must interface with a large in-place system, language compatibility is a key issue. Quite often the language of choice, under these circumstances, is the language that the first system is implemented in.

In Chapters 5 and 6 we discuss modular software construction using Modula-2 and Ada. We demonstrate how the features of these powerful software engineering languages influence the design process.

3.6 SUMMARY

- Language features that support good software engineering are: readability, modules, separate compilation, data hiding, data abstraction, structured control of flow, dynamic memory management, type consistency checking within and between various subprograms, and run-time checking.

- The most common use of assembly language has been connected with system-level programming mainly for compilers and operating systems.

- Descriptive names should be chosen for programs, subprograms, modules, constants, data types, and variables.

- Strong typing in languages provides a programmer with consistency checking on the use of defined data objects.

- A data type introduces an abstract entity and a set of allowable operations on the entity.

- Type declarations allow a programmer to define data objects in a software system in a natural and readable way in terms of the entities that occur in the problem. This supports problem abstraction.

- In programming languages that provide the WHILE loop, IF THEN ELSE, and sequence, GOTO statements are never required. The occasional use of an EXIT statement or a GOTO statement may improve program readability.

- In the most fundamental sense, a software system is composed of data objects and a set of algorithms that manipulate these data objects.

- The ability to nest one data structure within another, in Pascal, Modula-2, and Ada, offers the software engineer tremendous flexibility in representing complex data objects.

- Subprograms provide the functional "nuts and bolts" of a software system. They allow a complex system to be partitioned into a set of functional software components.

- Subprograms allow the programmer to control the scope and visibility of data objects.

- Subprograms provide programmers working on separate parts of a software system freedom to create identifiers without concern for name clashes.

- True data abstraction requires that generalized operations be allowed on data objects not bound to particular data representations. This implies data hiding.

- The ability to support data hiding and true data abstraction is the most significant feature that sets Modula-2 and Ada apart from previous languages.

- A module is a collection of related subprograms and data types.

- Modula-2 modules and Ada packages are split into specification and implementation parts. Each of these module components is compiled separately.

- Data types may be named in the specification (interface) portion of a module without making accessible their representational details.

- Independent compilation implies that program units may be compiled separately and subsequently integrated to form a complete "program." The integration process is performed by a utility program called a linker or linkage editor. Without the facility of independent compilation, a language would be ill suited for large-scale software engineering.

- Separate compilation involves rigorous cross-reference checking at the time of compilation.

- Pascal does not support either independent compilation or separate compilation.

- The manner in which the software development process may be decentralized and later centralized depends largely on the implementation language features available that support multiple name use, data hiding, and separate compilation.

REFERENCES

1. Shooman, M. L., *Software Engineering,* New York: McGraw-Hill, 1983.
2. Wiener, R., and R. Sincovec, *Programming in Ada,* New York: Wiley, 1983.
3. Bohm, C., and G. Jacopini, "Flow Diagrams, Turing Machines and Languages with Only Two Formulation Rules", *Commun. ACM,* Vol. 9, 1966, pp. 366–371.
4. Wirth, N., *Programming in Modula-2,* New York: Springer-Verlag, 2nd Edition, 1983.
5. *Reference Manual for the Ada Programming Language,* Draft Revised MIL–STD 1815 ACM AdaTec Special Publication, Washington, D.C.: U.S. Department of Defense, July 1982.

EXERCISES

1. Make a table cross-referencing as many programming languages as you can against the attributes listed in Table 3.1. Indicate, for each language in your table, the extent to which the specific language attribute is supported.

2. Define an abstract data type, QUEUE. Identify the operations that support this abstract type. Use either Modula-2 or Ada to define the specification for the QUEUE.

3. Repeat Exercise 2 for the abstract type TREE.

4. Repeat Exercise 2 for the abstract type LIST.

5. Repeat Exercise 2 for the abstract type GRAPH.

6. Write a FORTRAN program that reworks Program 3.1. Compare the readability of your program with Program 3.1. Does the use of enumeration types in Program 3.1 allow a more natural expression of the problem solution?

7. Make up a short Pascal program that demonstrates the vulnerability of the program resulting from the use of global data structures during the maintenance process.

8. Write a Modula-2 or Ada program that corrects the deficiency in the program of Exercise 7.

9. Rework Program 3.8 in Ada. Compare the two programs.

10. Rework Program 3.10 in Ada.

11. Write the package body for the package specification given in Program 3.11.

12. Identify a set of data abstractions and associated procedures that relate to the specification of the spelling checker given in Chapter 2.

Chapter 4

GENERAL PRINCIPLES OF SOFTWARE DESIGN

4.1 GENERAL GOALS

In this chapter we present an overview of the design phase in the software engineering life cycle. It has been well documented that difficulties encountered in large software projects usually are due not to poor programming practice or poor management but to inadequate attention to the design process. Simple programs usually can be developed with little design activity. However, a large software program cannot be successfully created without a formal design. In this chapter we describe a number of software design methodologies that are currently being used. We then introduce a modular and object-oriented design methodology. One of the principal goals of this book is to make a case for this software development methodology. In Chapters 5, 6, and 9, we further develop and illustrate this methodology with case studies using Ada and Modula-2, and in Chapter 8 we indicate the impact of this methodology on software testing.

What is a design methodology? A design methodology is a collection of methods that if faithfully carried out and applied to a particular problem should, at least in theory, achieve a software design. Since the design of software is a creative process unique to each situation and problem, a methodology cannot be considered a simple recipe that can be applied blindly to yield a good design. A design methodology provides form and structure to the design process by requiring the use of design aids and associated documentation, which are intended to produce a clear statement of the design and its objectives. Form and structure can never replace creativity! Successful designs are usually the result of several iterations on preliminary designs. A side benefit of many design methodologies is that the resulting documentation makes the status of the project more visible, thus allowing management a better opportunity to track the process of software development.

How does one teach another person to become a good software designer? This may be an impossible question to answer. However, it is clear that becoming a good software designer does require experience. It also requires adherence to sound principles of software engineering.

In this chapter we present some commonly used design aids and methodologies that facilitate the design process. We present an overview of top-down, bottom-up design, HIPO charts, Warnier–Orr diagrams, the Jackson design methodology, data flow design, and structure charts. All these design methodologies and their associated design aids were developed before the existence of Ada and Modula-2.

Later in this chapter we introduce two recent and significant design methodologies, object-oriented design and modular software construction. In addition, we introduce a new design tool, the modular design chart. Ada and Modula-2 may be directly linked to these design methodologies. In this and later chapters we use both Modula-2 and Ada as program design languages to support object-oriented design and modular software construction.

The use of any design aid or methodology is usually an improvement over ad hoc methods and usually leads to better communication between those involved in the design process, management, and the customer.

We do not emphasize any single pre-Ada and pre-Modula-2 methodology or design aid in this chapter. It would require several books to describe in detail some of the design techniques that we briefly outline in this chapter. Our goal is not to present a ''reader's digest'' of design methods but rather to make you aware of some of the more significant methods that have enjoyed some success and to briefly characterize these methods. You are urged to consult some of the references mentioned in this chapter if you wish to become conversant with a particular method of design.

The objective of the design process is to build a coherent, well-planned representation of the required software. The principal goal of design is to determine HOW THE SYSTEM WILL WORK. Badly designed systems are expensive to maintain, difficult to test, and usually unreliable. The overall architecture for the system is established in the design phase. Tradeoffs are made to meet various requirements such as reliability, generality, portability, and user friendliness. To accomplish this usually requires several levels of detail in the design process.

The last sections of this chapter cover the use of prototypes in the design process, the automated tools that are available to assist in the design process, and some strategies for design validation.

In summary, good software design is the principal ingredient for effective software engineering. The design stage is the most critical part of the software engineering cycle. Well-designed software is straightforward to implement and maintain, is easy to understand, is reliable, and can be verified. Poorly designed software may work correctly, but maintenance is likely to be expensive, testing may be difficult or impossible, and the software may be unreliable.

4.2 HARDWARE CONSIDERATIONS

To obtain optimum performance from any computer, it is necessary to tailor the computer software to suit the architecture of the computer. Significant changes have taken place in computer hardware over the past two decades. All indications are that computer hardware changes during the next 10 years will be even greater, particularly with the introduction of novel forms of computer architecture, largely made possible by advances in semiconductor technology, and the convergence of computing and communications. Such topics as super-computers and parallel algorithms, microcomputers, local area networks, graphics, and security and privacy are now of particular importance to the software designer.

The design of software for parallel processors requires parallelism in the design to take advantage of the architecture. This involves the design of algorithms that execute efficiently and computer languages and design strategies to express and develop these algorithms. Hockney and Jesshope [1] describe various parallel computers, parallel languages, and parallel algorithms.

The design of software for microcomputers requires the careful consideration of the constraints imposed by limited memory, limited disk space, and sometimes limited execution speed. An example illustrating the interplay of these constraints and their consideration in the design process is presented in Chapter 9.

4.3 AN OVERVIEW OF THE DESIGN PROCESS BEFORE ADA AND MODULA-2

The typical design process has several distinct phases. In our discussions of pre-Ada and pre-Modula-2 design methodologies, we find it useful to view the design process as consisting of three distinct phases: high level design, intermediate level design, and low level design. Figure 4.1 presents a simple data flow diagram that illustrates the process. High level data flow diagrams and the software specifications are the inputs to high level design. High level design establishes the major subsystems or modules. The output of this level of design is the high level architecture of the system and the global data structure specifications. The output from high level design provides the input for the intermediate level design. The intermediate level of design partitions the subsystems into clusters of interacting subprograms. This level is iterated until the algorithm used in each subprogram unit must be specified in detail. The output of the intermediate design is the modular software structure including all subprograms, interfaces, and data structures. Finally, we reach the low level of the design process. This involves the design of each algorithm in each subprogram.

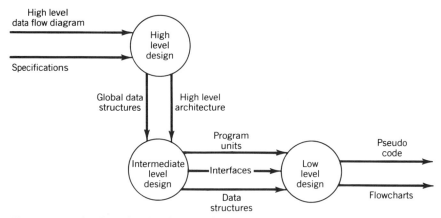

Figure 4.1 The three levels of the design process.

4.3.1 High Level Design

High level design identifies the initial high level architecture of the system by identifying and naming the major parts (modules or subsystems) of the system. In this stage, major decisions of a structural nature are made and choices are made between major design alternatives. The software specifications document must be carefully analyzed to determine that the proposed structure is compatible with the requirements. High level data flow diagrams are useful in specifying the software architecture. The inputs and outputs to the system are identified and the major data flow paths through the system are established. The global data structures are identified.

Techniques and aids for this stage of the design process are given in Section 4.4. Top-down design, HIPO charts, and data flow diagrams are useful for high level design. Structure charts are often used to illustrate the high level architecture of the system.

4.3.2 Intermediate Level Design

Intermediate level design is an iterative process that decomposes the modules or subsystems into separate subprograms. Each module is designed in terms of interacting program units. The logical relationships of control and data between components are established. This involves the specification of the interfaces, control, and linkage between parts of the system and other systems that the software must interact with.

This phase of the design should acknowledge the importance of future maintenance. As indicated in Chapter 1, 65% of maintenance is perfective, so the design should permit easy upgrading and modification. The importance of reliability should also be emphasized at this stage of the design process. Reliability must be designed into a system from the start rather than added at the implementation stage. Program description (or design) languages may be used to define the intermediate level design. Structure charts are often used to illustrate the hierarchical structure of each module. The Jackson and Warnier–Orr methods are used by some designers for intermediate level design.

4.3.3 Low Level Design

Low level design specifies the operation of the individual subprogram units of the system. The level of detail approximates programs but does not involve code. The algorithm for each program unit is designed. This involves the definition of local data structures and identifier names and may involve the specification of housekeeping functions local to the program unit. Design aids associated with low level design include pseudo-code, structured design, and flow charts. A programmer should be able to take the low level design and turn it into a program written in a specific computer language that will execute on a specific machine.

4.4 DESIGN METHODOLOGIES BEFORE ADA AND MODULA-2

In this section we briefly describe several design methodologies in use today that were developed before computer languages such as Ada and Modula-2. The methodologies are top-down—bottom-up design, HIPO charts and their use in the design process, the Warnier–Orr diagram and associated design methodology, the Jackson design methodology, and data flow design. The reader is referred to the references for additional details concerning any of these methodologies.

4.4.1 Top-Down–Bottom-Up Design

The terms "top-down design" and "bottom-up design" are used extensively in the computer science literature. Niklaus Wirth [2] proposed stepwise refinement as an early top-down design strategy. In each step, one of several functions or tasks is decomposed into a number of subfunctions or subtasks. This strategy, sometimes called functional decomposition, develops the architecture of a program by successively refining levels of procedural detail. The refinements can be continued through intermediate level design, whereby more and more detail is developed concerning how the software is to be organized. Finally, if the process is continued to low level design, it will terminate when all instructions are expressed in pseudo-code or a computer language.

As each function or task is refined, the data may also need to be refined, decomposed, or structured to accommodate the means of communication between the subfunctions and subtasks. Program and data refinement should be done in parallel with each level of refinement.

Every refinement implies that some design decision has been made. The designer should analyze the consequences of each decision and explore alternatives. Design criteria such as efficiency, storage, clarity, and modularity of structure should be examined for each design decision. The evolving design can be thought of as a tree, with each node representing a design deliberation and decision. Each successive tree represents a design with successively more detail added.

During the process of stepwise refinement, the notation that is used during high level design should be natural to the problem and, as the refinements progress through intermediate and finally to low level design, the notation should become similar to the language in which the software will be developed.

An important feature of top-down design is that at each level of refinement the details of the design at lower levels of refinement are hidden. Only the data and control information required to interface with the next level need to be defined. If a data structure is local to a lower level function or task, it need not be specified until that level is reached in the design process. However, if a data structure is shared by several functions or tasks at the same level, it must be specified before proceeding to a lower level in the design.

To illustrate top-down design, we consider an example. Suppose that we wish to sort a file of employee records that exist on disk. Each record contains the name of each employee along with other relevant information. The desired output is an alphabetical listing of all employees along with the other information contained in each record. The statement of the problem is

Produce employee list

A refinement of this problem statement is given in Figure 4.2. The next refinement of "Read employee records" requires data structure information on the specific data fields contained in the record.

Note that in the successive refinements, eventually we replace functions and tasks that describe what is to be done by an algorithm, which specifies how to perform the function or task.

The design process is one of trial and error. As we make refinements, we may eventually wish to modify a previous design decision. This modification of design may require us to change other parts of the design and associated data structures. The modification should be done in a systematic way. One technique is to back up to an earlier level in the design that the modification does not affect and redo all the top-down refinements, taking the modification into account.

For example, suppose that a top-down analysis has produced the refinements illustrated in Figure 4.3, where F1 through F18 represent program units

Figure 4.2   Refinement of produce employee list.

or pseudo-code for the operations that need to be performed. Suppose that in attempting to refine F18, we discover an error, or we learn that a change in data structure defined earlier will make F18 more efficient in terms of execution speed and/or storage. To make the change, we must back up to the point where the change has no effect. If this is F13, we must redo F13 and all refinements of F13 (i.e., F17 and F18). If this is F2, we must redo all refinements of F2 (i.e., F4–F7, F11–F14, F17, and F18).

Backing up in this manner is essential if a correct design is to be achieved. The more complicated the software system, the more important it is to back up in a systematic manner.

The goal of bottom-up design is to establish a set of general-purpose resources while maintaining application independence. Bottom-up design proceeds from the specific to the general. It effectively enhances the software development environment by making available more powerful instructions or functions to the software developers. Typical examples of this include building a set of "screen display" utilities and building a mathematical library of subroutines. For other examples, consider the construction of subprograms for performing operations on commonly used data structures such as stacks, queues, linked lists, and trees. In practice, top-down design is usually accompanied by bottom-up design.

4.4.2 HIPO Charts

HIPO (hierarchy plus input-process-output) charts are a design aid useful in the top-down design of systems. HIPO charts were originally developed at IBM [3] to serve primarily as a documentation tool. They consist of two basic compo-

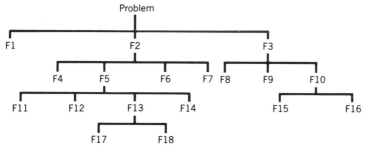

Figure 4.3   Top-down design and backing up.

nents: a hierarchy (H) chart and input-process-output (IPO) diagrams. The H chart displays in block form the relationships among major functions, minor functions, and modules of the system. The IPO diagrams express each function and module in the hierarchy chart in terms of its input and output variables and describes the processes and transformations that take place in the function or module.

We illustrate the two components of HIPO by considering a KWIC (keyword in context) index problem. A KWIC index is a list of titles of books, research articles, and so on, arranged so that each title that contains a "key" word can be easily found. Associated with the title is the location of the title (e.g., a library call number, a book shelf number, an office number, or a filing cabinet drawer). For example, consider the following two titles.

```
SOFTWARE ENGINEERING USING ADA AND PASCAL       Shelf 1
THE EVOLUTION OF THE UNIVERSE                    Room 25
```

The KWIC index for this list with the "key" words in the first column would be:

```
ADA AND PASCAL              SOFTWARE ENGINEERING USING  Shelf 1
ENGINEERING USING ADA AND PASCAL               SOFTWARE  Shelf 1
EVOLUTION OF THE UNIVERSE                            THE  Room 25
PASCAL SOFTWARE ENGINEERING USING ADA AND                Shelf 1
SOFTWARE ENGINEERING USING ADA AND PASCAL                Shelf 1
UNIVERSE                         THE EVOLUTION OF THE  Room 25
```

Often the KWIC index is printed with the "key" words in the center of the page and the title not circularly shifted. For example, the preceding KWIC index might be printed as follows.

```
    SOFTWARE ENGINEERING USING   ADA AND PASCAL
                     SOFTWARE   ENGINEERING USING ADA AND PASCAL
                          THE   EVOLUTION OF THE UNIVERSE
SOFTWARE ENGINEERING USING ADA AND   PASCAL
                                SOFTWARE ENGINEERING USING ADA AND PASCAL
          THE EVOLUTION OF THE   UNIVERSE
```

We omitted the "location" information because of the longer line length.

In each title, words that are articles, prepositions, or trivial are called "nonkeywords." In the KWIC index, each title occurs once in the list for each keyword in the title. The titles are usually aligned so that all the keywords occur in the same column. In the first sample listing of the KWIC index, we have chosen the left-hand column and shifted that portion of the title that appears before the keyword to the end of the line. Note that the location of the title is printed to the right of the title. In the second, we aligned the keywords in the middle of the page. The titles are printed in alphabetical order of the keywords.

Such a KWIC index is useful in finding books and articles. To find titles on a particular subject, one just searches the KWIC index for keywords related to the subject and jots down the corresponding title and its location. A typical KWIC index may contain thousands of titles.

A software system to produce a KWIC index is given the titles, the locations, and the list of nonkeywords as input. The system reads the titles and nonkeywords, identifies possible keywords and creates entries for the KWIC index, alphabetizes the entries according to the keywords, and then prints the KWIC index. The list of nonkeywords may be modified from run to run by adding or deleting words. A file of titles and locations should be permanently saved. It should be possible to edit the titles and locations and to add additional titles or to delete existing titles on future runs.

Figure 4.4 shows the H (hierarchy) diagram and Figure 4.5 shows the IPO (input-processing-output) chart for the highest level of the KWIC index system.

The HIPO design process is an iterative top-down activity in which the hierarchy chart and the input-process-output charts are developed concurrently. This leads to a systematic functional decomposition of the system.

Note that in the H diagram for the KWIC index given in Figure 4.4, we have denoted the top level control unit as 0.0 and that the functions on the second level are numbered successively from 1.0 to 6.0. Figure 4.4 shows only the third level for the editing of existing titles. The functions on the third level related to Edit Title are denoted 3.1, 3.2, 3.3, and 3.4. A fourth level for function 3.1 might be denoted by 3.1.1, 3.1.2, etc. Other second-level functions may also be expanded to the third and lower levels as the design proceeds. Usually a numbering scheme is used so that each function in the overall H diagram may be associated with its corresponding IPO chart. IPO charts are

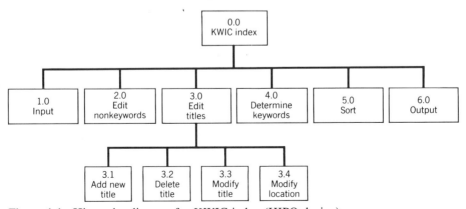

Figure 4.4   Hierarchy diagram for KWIC index (HIPO design).

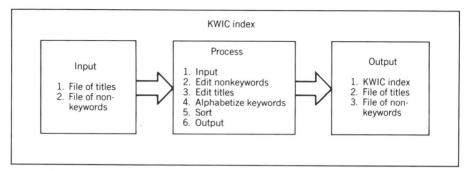

Figure 4.5 Input-process-output chart for KWIC index (HIPO design).

constructed for each box in the H diagram as the design proceeds. For example, the IPO chart for the Edit Titles function is shown in Figure 4.6.

Thus the total use of the HIPO design method consists of one H diagram that presents in block form the relationships among the functions and modules in the program, an overview IPO diagram that provides input variables, process functions, and output variables for the highest level of the H diagram, and a set of detailed, lower level IPO diagrams for each block in the H diagram. The H diagram should be properly labeled so that it can serve as a table of contents for the design. The process part of the IPO chart is mostly verbs, whereas the input and output sections are nouns. Solid arrows are often used to indicate flow of control and open arrows used to represent data flow.

An obvious question concerns the level to which one should continue the decomposition. The lowest level of detail may contain pseudo-code in the process portion of the IPO diagram and the input and output portions may contain the actual parameters to the function or procedure. Clearly some functions will be more complex than others, and so not all branches of the H diagram need to terminate at the same level.

The HIPO design method has been successfully used on a wide variety of projects. The principal difficulty of the method is that on large projects the number of diagrams becomes difficult to manage if the method is used for low

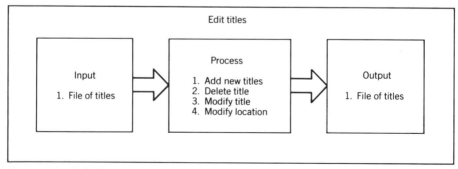

Figure 4.6 IPO diagram for Edit Titles.

level design. The solution is to use HIPO diagrams for high level and intermediate level design only. HIPO diagrams have proved to be useful at a number of different stages of the software life cycle including high level and intermediate level design, design reviews, testing, and maintenance.

4.4.3 Warnier–Orr Diagrams

A design aid initially proposed by Warnier [4] and continued by Orr [5] is the Warnier–Orr diagram (introduced in Chapter 2). This diagram uses nested sets of braces, some pseudo-code, and logic symbols to indicate the structure of a system. The features of the Warnier–Orr diagram are best illustrated by an example.

Suppose that we have a contract to design an inventory control system for a computer store that markets new and used computers. After carefully studying the SRD, we arrive at a data structure that will support the inventory system. In Figure 4.7, a Warnier–Orr diagram that describes the data structure, the numbers in parentheses indicate the number of times the data item may be encountered. The notation (0,1) would indicate that the data may be encountered not at all, or once. The symbol ⊕ indicates exclusive "or".

The Warnier–Orr diagram may be used to define a design methodology. The methodology, known as the logical construction of programs (LCP), is described in detail by Warnier [4,6]. The LCP design approach begins with the specification of the input and output data structures as Warnier–Orr diagrams. Warnier's approach assumes that the program is simply an information struc-

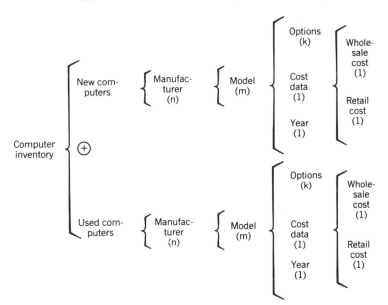

Figure 4.7 Warnier–Orr diagram for computer inventory.

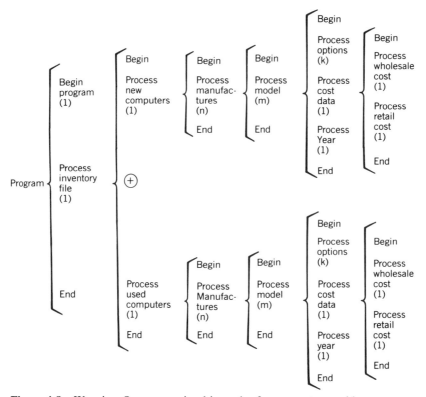

Figure 4.8 Warnier–Orr processing hierarchy for computer problem.

ture that can be represented by a Warnier–Orr diagram that can be derived by systematic methods from the input-output diagrams. That is, the input-output Warnier–Orr diagrams are mapped to processing structure Warnier–Orr diagrams.

To illustrate the general idea, we consider the computer inventory example described above. Suppose that the output that is required is simply a printout of the inventory containing the information described in the data structure for either new or used computers. Then a processing hierarchy for the program can be derived from the structure of the input data. In Figure 4.8, a program that can process the input data file, we introduce notation to indicate the beginning and end of processes. Other notation not used in this figure is available to indicate branching and nesting. To indicate that a process may not be executed, a bar is usually placed above the word "process". The Warnier–Orr representation of the software can be transformed into conventional flow chart representation as indicated in Figure 4.9.

We can see from Figure 4.9 that repetition in the data structure is translated into a "repeat-until" construct. Conditional occurrences would translate into the "if-then-else" construct.

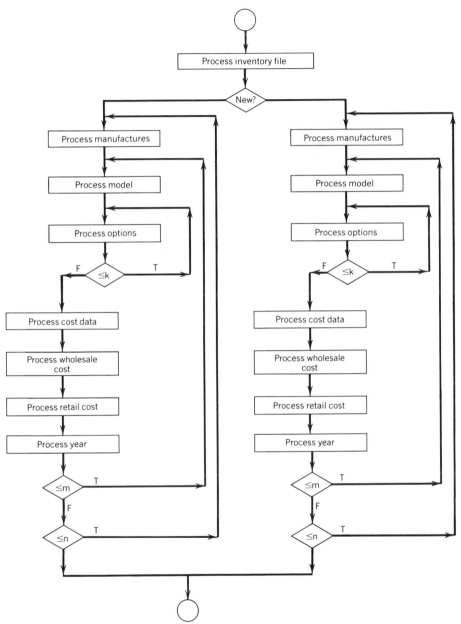

Figure 4.9 Flow chart representation of computer inventory example.

The Warnier–Orr method is most suitable for intermediate level design. However, Warnier does not stop here but continues with a technique called "detailed organization," which systematically produces a set of detailed instructions from the logical organization of the program. At this stage the LCP method is a low level design methodology, which we will not pursue further; the reader is referred to the textbooks by Warnier [4,6] for additional details.

4.4.4 The Jackson Design Methodology

The Jackson design methodology [7,8] attempts to transform data structure to program structure. Jackson's view is that paralleling the structure of the input and output data will result in a good software design. Jackson defines a data structure notation that resembles a hierarchical diagram. The methodology consists of a set of mappings or transformations that may be applied to variations in data structure to obtain program structure.

Figure 4.10, a simple representation of Jackson's data structure notation, can be described as follows: a collection of data A is composed of multiple occurrences (denoted by *) of data substructure B and a single occurrence of data substructure C. Substructure B includes a single occurrence of D and another substructure E that contains data item H or I (alternative data are denoted by an o). Substructure C contains multiple occurrences of F that contain the data item J and a single occurrence of G, which may or may not contain the data item K. Jackson indicates that this representation of information hierarchy can be applied to input, output or data base structures.

The next step in the Jackson design methodology is to map the data structure to a processing hierarchy. This is illustrated in Figure 4.11. Note that the structure of the data presented in Figure 4.10 is identical to the structure of the program of Figure 4.11. The boxes in the processing hierarchy do not necessarily delineate modules.

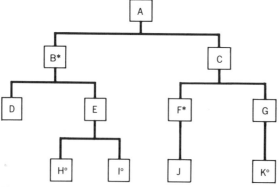

Figure 4.10 Jackson data structure notation.

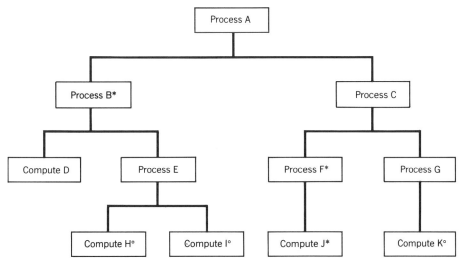

Figure 4.11 Jackson processing hierarchy.

The development of the processing hierarchy is the primary objective of the Jackson design methodology. However, the processing hierarchy can be transformed into a procedural representation of the program in the form of pseudo-code. The Jackson procedural representation is essentially low level design or detailed design. The procedural representation corresponding to the processing hierarchy of Figure 4.11 is:

```
A   sequence
    B   iteration
        do D;
        E   select
            do H;
        E   or
            do I;
        E   end
    B   end
    C   sequence
        F   iteration
            do J;
        F   end
        G   select
            do K;
        G   end
    C   end
A   end.
```

The notation used should be almost self-explanatory. A sequence has two or more parts. In a practical application, the iteration part usually contains a "while" condition or an "until" condition. A selection has two or more parts, of which only one occurs for each occurrence of the selection component. A selection is usually based on whether some condition is true or false.

The preceding example is too simple to illustrate the capabilities of the Jackson design methodology, nor does it contain both an input data structure and an output structure. The books by Jackson [7,8] give many examples that illustrate the methodology on a wide variety of problems. Jackson also introduces a number of supplementary techniques that broaden the applicability and systematize the overall design approach. One of these techniques applies to the treatment of erroneous data, since erroneous data do not exist in a data structure diagram. Another addresses the situation of a program path chosen but later found to be an incorrect path. In this case, a backtracking strategy is proposed along with three new "constructs" for procedural pseudo-code. Jackson recognizes that a structure clash occurs when the input information has little or no structural correspondence to the output information. A series of detailed design maneuvers is proposed to overcome the structure clash. Jackson proposes additional design procedures, which he refers to as program inversion, multithreading, and optimization. These procedures address structure clash, eliminate the use of nonessential intermediate data structure, and attempt to reduce program size. Because of the specialized nature of these techniques, we do not pursue them in this book. The interested reader is urged to consult the references [7,8].

4.4.5 Data Flow Design and Structure Charts

Data flow diagrams lead to software components and structure at the design level. At the specification level, data flow diagrams provide a conceptual framework that relates inputs to outputs. Data flow design attempts to integrate information flow into the design process. Stevens, Myers, and Constantine [9] were among the earliest proponents of data flow design. The book by Yourdan and Constantine [10] refines the process and describes it in detail. Data flow design is usually considered to be a component in what has often been called structured design or composite design. In this section we give a brief overview of the data flow design process. The reader is referred to the references cited for additional details.

Since all software can be represented by a data flow diagram, it follows that data flow design could theoretically be applied to every software development effort. The data flow design method is particularly useful before data structures have been defined or on problems where no formal data structures exist. However, a significant shortcoming of the method is that it does not deal directly with data structure design or its implications. Data flow design can be used on real-time systems but interrupts create some difficulties. Simpson and

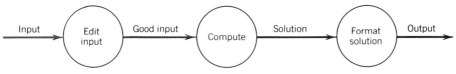

Figure 4.12   Transform flow.

Jackson [11] present an extension of data flow design called MASCOT, which adapts the method to real-time, interrupt-driven systems.

The principal component of data flow design is determining a mapping from the data flow diagram (DFD) to the software structure. The method recognizes two types of data flow: transform and transaction. Transform flow is characterized by flow along incoming paths (called afferent), a transition kernel (called the transform center), and flow along outgoing paths (called efferent). Transform flow is indicated in Figure 4.12.

Transaction flow is characterized by a single data item that triggers other data flow along one of many paths. A reception path converts external input into a transaction that is evaluated; based on the value determined, flow along one of many action paths is initiated. The hub of information flow from which the action paths emanate is called the transaction center. Transaction flow is indicated in Figure 4.13.

Transform flow arises in many scientific and engineering algorithms, in process control applications, and in some commercial (business) applications. Transaction flow arises in compilers and translators, in most interactive systems, and in all menu-driven applications. Large systems usually contain both transform flow and transaction flow. The successful application of data flow design requires the identification of the portions of the data flow diagram that exhibit each type of flow.

The data flow design method begins with a careful review of the software requirements document. Any data flow diagrams in the SRD should be reviewed and refined so that sufficient detail exists to obtain a preliminary design for the software structure. Next the data flow diagrams are analyzed to determine whether transform or transaction flow is present; for transform flow the transform flow boundaries are determined and for transaction flow the transaction centers are identified.

We now describe the process of mapping the DFD to software structure. The identification of the mapping is referred to as transform analysis or transaction analysis, depending on the type of data flow.

Transform analysis consists of a set of steps for transforming a DFD with transform flow characteristics into a predefined template for software structure. To illustrate the steps, consider the DFD given in Figure 4.14. Note that we have identified and named the various transformations. Significant analysis of the problem may be necessary to determine a first description of the information flow.

In evaluating the DFD of Figure 4.14, we see that data objects enter the

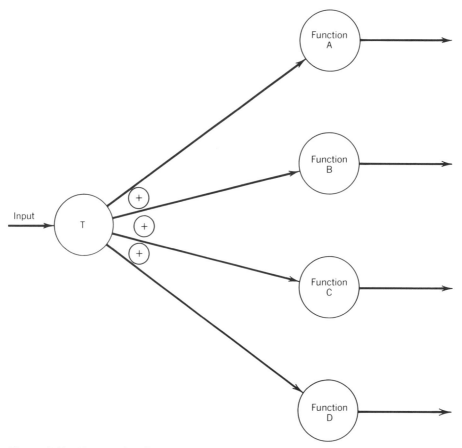

Figure 4.13 Transaction flow.

software system along four incoming paths and exit the software via two paths. There appears to be no distinct transaction center, so transform flow will be assumed. The top level software structure is determined by dividing the data flow diagram into its afferent (input), transform, and efferent (output) elements. Afferent or incoming flow is a path in the DFD in which information is converted from external to internal form. The afferent element of the DFD is the point at which the input data stream is most processed but still considered to be input. All processing before reaching the afferent boundary is the afferent branch of the structure. Efferent or outgoing flow converts information from internal to external form. The efferent element of the DFD is the point at which the output stream is least processed but still considered to be output. All processing after the efferent boundary is the efferent branch of the structure. All processing between the afferent and efferent branches is the transform branch of the DFD.

Suppose that after carefully examining each bubble in Figure 4.14, we

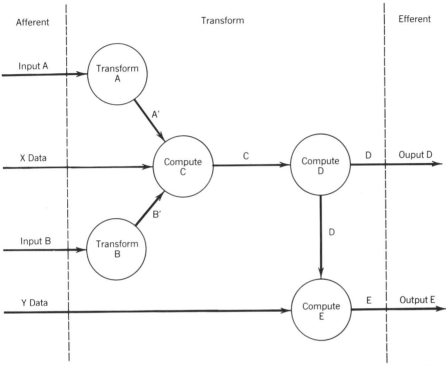

Figure 4.14 Data flow diagram for transform analysis with first specification of afferent and efferent flow boundaries.

decide that bubbles A through E represent the transform center and that the afferent and efferent boundaries are indicated by the dashed lines.

The next step is to perform a first-level factoring of the software structure. Recall that the purpose of transform analysis is to map a DFD into a structure chart. The main difference between a structure chart and a DFD is that a structure chart depicts control. We must provide control for afferent, transform, and efferent information processing. Figure 4.15 illustrates a first-level factoring. The "Afferent control" module coordinates all incoming data, "Transform control" supervises the operations of the central transformations, and "Efferent control" coordinates the output. "System control" coordinates the three subordinate control functions. Complex flows may result in a structure different from the simple structure given in Figure 4.15.

The next step is to perform second-level factoring by mapping individual bubbles of the DFD into appropriate modules of software structure. Transforms are mapped into subordinate levels of the software structure beginning at the transform center boundary and moving outward along afferent and efferent paths. Each module is given a name that implies the function of subordinate modules that it controls (Figure 4.16).

Figure 4.16 illustrates a one-to-one mapping between bubbles in the DFD

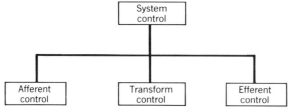

Figure 4.15   First-level factoring.

and software modules. This is seldom the case. Bubbles are often combined and represented as one module, or a single bubble may be expanded to two or more modules. Practical design considerations dictate the outcome of second-level factoring.

The final step is to refine the first-cut structure chart. Modules may be expanded into several new modules or they may be combined. The goal is to produce a structure that has good module independence and good cohesion. Guidelines for performing refinements of first-cut structure charts are given by Page-Jones [12].

The actual placement of afferent and efferent flow boundaries is subject to an interpretation of the functional purpose of each bubble in the DFD. Different designers may specify different flow boundaries, and alternative designs can be examined by varying the placement of the flow boundaries. In Figures 4.17 through 4.22, we show various divisions of the DFD and the resulting software structures. Quite often the preferred structure chart results when the sum of the data streams cut by the afferent and efferent boundaries is a minimum. Figure 4.22 represents such a structure. We urge the reader to carefully review Figures 4.14 through 4.22 and to correlate the data flow diagrams and the associated structure charts. Notice the effect of the choice of afferent and efferent boundaries on the structure chart.

We now direct our attention to transaction analysis. The design steps for transaction analysis are essentially the same as those for transform analysis except for the mapping of the DFD to the software structure. To illustrate

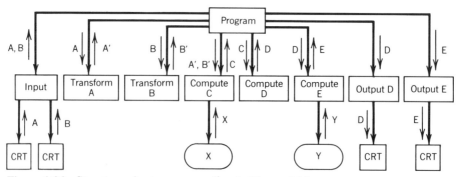

Figure 4.16   Structure chart corresponding to Figure 4.14.

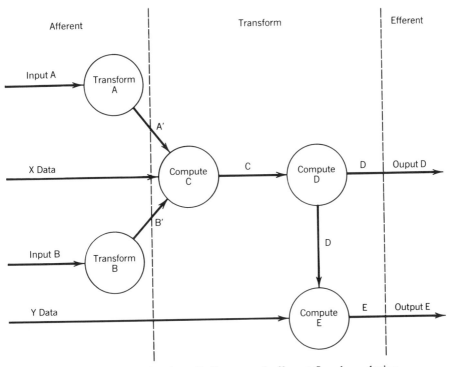

Figure 4.17 Second specification of afferent and efferent flow boundaries.

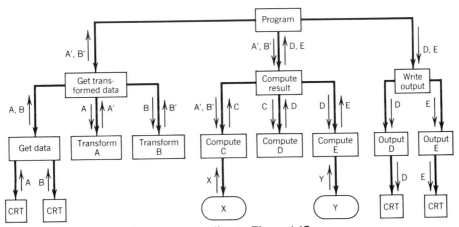

Figure 4.18 Structure chart corresponding to Figure 4.17.

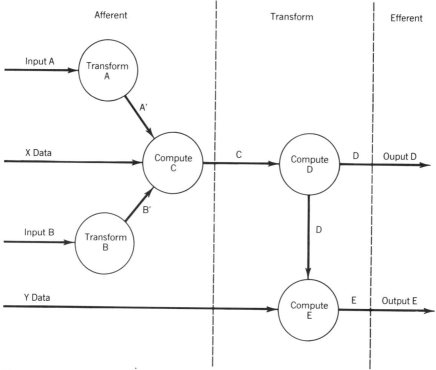

Figure 4.19 Third specification of afferent and efferent flow boundaries.

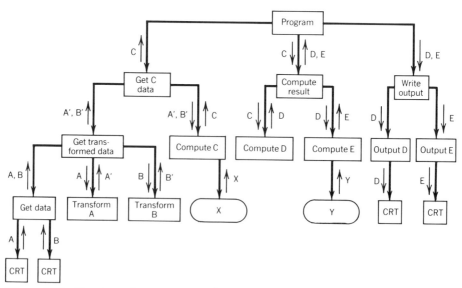

Figure 4.20 Structure chart corresponding to Figure 4.19.

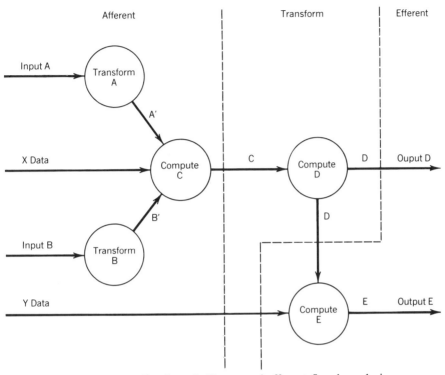

Figure 4.21 Fourth specification of afferent and efferent flow boundaries.

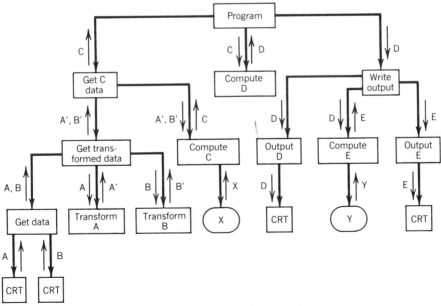

Figure 4.22 Structure chart corresponding to Figure 4.21.

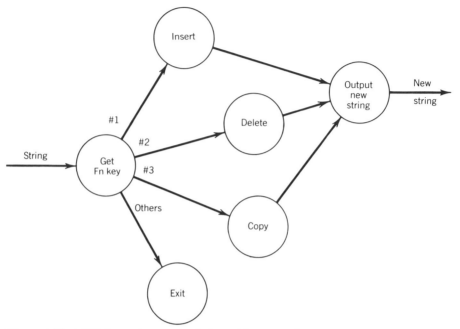

Figure 4.23   DFD for string manipulation with transaction center.

transaction analysis, we consider the DFD given in Figure 4.23, which represents data flow for a simple string manipulation requirement. The string operations are inserting a string in a given string, removing a string from a given string, and copying a portion of a given string to a new string.

The first step is to locate the transaction center; this usually is immediately obvious. The transaction center is the origin of a number of information flow paths that flow radially from it. The reception or input path and all action paths from the transaction center must be identified. Transaction flow can be mapped into a software structure that contains a reception branch and a dispatch branch. Another substructure on the dispatch branch controls all processing actions based on the transaction. The first-level factoring of the DFD in Figure 4.23 is shown in Figure 4.24.

Structure for the "Input" branch is developed using transform analysis. Structure for the "Dispatcher" branch is determined by analyzing the flow characteristics along each action path. That is, we refine the structure of each action path using either transform analysis or transaction analysis, depending on the type of flow. In particular, the "Insert," "Delete," and "Copy" bubbles should now be refined to yield lower level data flow diagrams. For example, in Figure 4.25 we refine the "Insert" operation. We then use transform analysis to obtain the structure chart in Figure 4.26, which represents a refinement of the "Insert" box in Figure 4.24.

Finally, as in transform analysis, we refine the first-cut software structure.

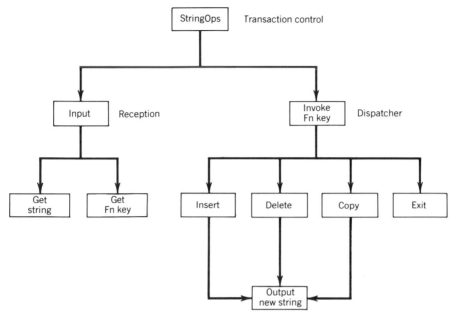

Figure 4.24 First-level factoring for string manipulation.

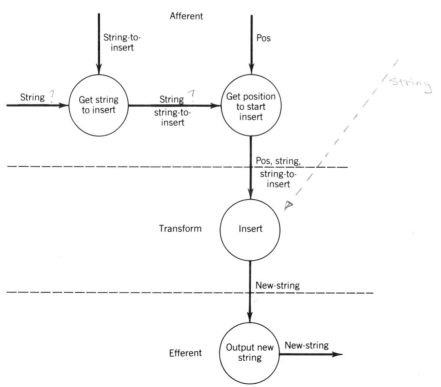

Figure 4.25 Refined DFD for insert operation.

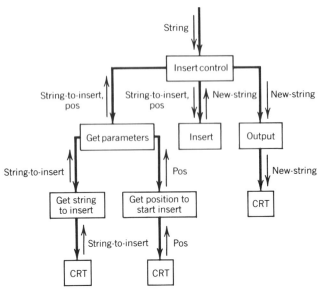

Figure 4.26 Partial second-level factoring of string manipulation.

Page-Jones [13] presents some guidelines for refining software structure for systems that process transactions.

4.4.6 Structured Programming

Structured programming is based on the stepwise refinement process. Dijkstra [14,15] laid the groundwork for structured programming. He strongly advocated the elimination of the "goto" statement from all high level programming languages.

The foundation of structured programming involves the use of only three basic control structures to express program logic. These basic constructs are a sequence mechanism, a selection mechanism, and an iteration mechanism. Sequence refers to the execution of one task followed immediately by the execution of another task. Selection refers to the "if then", "if then else", "if then else elsif", and "case" syntax structures that are found in modern high level programming languages. Some purists might argue that the "case" construct does not belong in a "structured" program. The selection of the task that is to be executed next is based on the result of some decision. Iteration refers to the repeated execution of some task until a predefined condition is satisfied. Bohm and Jacopini [16] established that these three basic constructs are sufficient for expressing any problem logic.

Since structured programming is based on stepwise refinement, one might ask how it differs from top-down design. Top-down design is a technique for decomposing a problem, independent of control structures that might be used.

This means that a top-down design could be implemented in either a nonstructured or a structured fashion.

Some of the advantages of structured programming are the following:

- Structured programs generally have a clear and logical control structure pattern that makes the design easy to understand.

- Programmers who use structured programming are generally more productive than those who do not.

- Maintenance is simplified, since clarity assists in localizing a problem and redesigning a solution.

4.4.7 Low Level Design Aids

Many of the design aids described in the preceding sections can also be used to assist and document low level design. However, several design aids are used almost exclusively in this application. In this section we describe the following low level design representation schemes: flow charts, Nassi-Schneiderman diagrams, and pseudo-code.

Flow charts are the oldest and most controversial program design tool. They are often useful as a low level design and documentation tool.

Shooman [17] presents the symbols used in the flow charts of the American National Standards Institute (ANSI). The most commonly used symbols are boxes, diamonds, and line with arrows. A rectangular box represents a processing step, a diamond indicates a decision point, and arrows show the flow of control. Figure 4.27 uses flow charts to illustrate the three structured constructs described in Section 4.4.6. The structured flow chart that appears in Figure 4.28 shows the nesting of the various constructs.

There are two types of flow chart: high level, macro flow charts and detailed, micro flow charts. Detailed flow charts often can be mapped directly to code. That is, there is a one-to-one correspondence between each symbol in the flow chart and each line of code in the resulting program. Detailed flow charts are cumbersome and usually worthless as an aid to documentation but are a required deliverable in many civilian and military contracts. To satisfy this requirement, almost all large companies have automatic flow charting programs. Clearly, the programmers did not use the flow chart to design their program, since the flow chart was created by using the finished program as data. This is not and never has been the intended use of flow charts. The proper use of flow charts involves a hierarchy of high level flow charts. These are developed as part of the design process, starting with a high level flow chart that identifies the modules or subprograms and then developing high level flow charts for each major module or subprogram. At no time are detailed flow charts drawn.

The Nassi–Schneiderman chart [18] is a graphical design tool that does not allow the violation of the structured programming constructs. The symbols

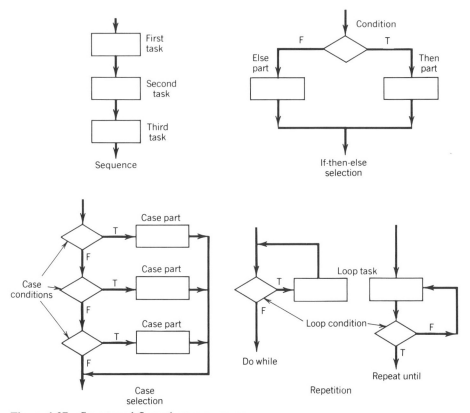

Figure 4.27   Structured flow chart constructs.

used are shown in Figure 4.29. Each box is rectangular and can be nested in any rectangular position in any other box. The boxes are labeled in a manner similar to the labeling of flow charts.

Figure 4.30 illustrates the use of Nassi–Schneiderman charts to represent the flow of control that is identical to the flow chart given in Figure 4.28.

Pseudo-code is an abbreviated notation for the control structures and other features of a programming language. Usually comments are liberally inserted, words often substituted for expressions, and control structures are indented to show the nesting of control. There is no specific syntax associated with pseudo-code; however, designers who are well versed in a particular programming language usually write pseudo-code that looks like an abbreviated form of that language. From pseudo-code it should be possible to implement the design in any language desired. Figure 4.31 is a pseudo-code representation of the example given in Figures 4.28 and 4.30.

Pseudo-code is usually more flexible than flow charts or Nassi–Schneiderman charts because it is easy to create, modify, control, reproduce, and refine using a text editor.

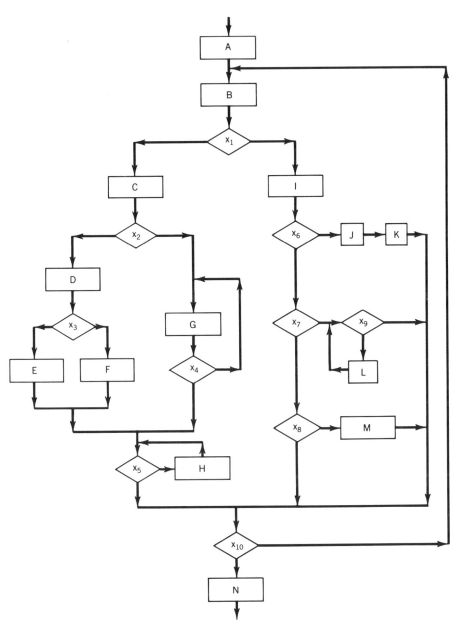

Figure 4.28   An example flow chart.

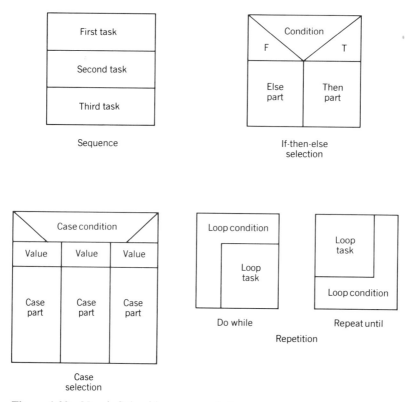

Figure 4.29 Nassi–Schneiderman symbols.

4.4.8 Structured Analysis Design Technique (SADT)

SADT was introduced in Chapter 2 as a specification and analysis technique. SADT can be used for design, but is is quite different from the methods described above. SADT attempts to analyze the problem by breaking it down into smaller and smaller parts, with each part analyzed or broken down further until the problem is completely understood. The actual mapping onto program and modules is not defined by SADT. As such, SADT is useful in analyzing the problem before high level design. Of all the methods described, SADT is the most comprehensive with respect to project control, documentation, and review.

4.5 MODULAR AND OBJECT-ORIENTED DESIGN USING ADA AND MODULA-2

Having presented an overview of the pre-Ada and pre-Modula-2 traditional methods of software design, we now introduce an extremely powerful and very

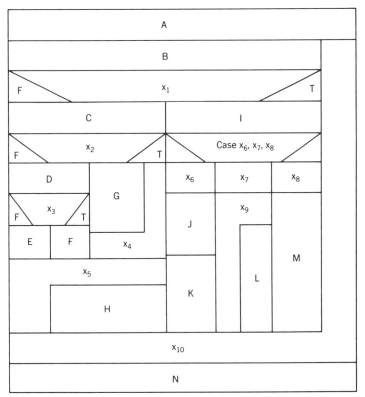

Figure 4.30 Example of Nassi–Schneiderman chart.

modern approach to software design that has gained tremendous currency with the advent of the software engineering languages Ada and Modula-2.

All software design involves a process of abstraction. Objects and operations found in the problem domain or real-world domain must be translated into corresponding objects and operations in the problem-solving domain, namely the software system.

In the early days of software development, circa 1940s and 1950s, when programs were hand wired on a particular machine, the software design process involved a transformation from the problem domain to the 0's and 1's of the particular machine being programmed. Very little abstraction was possible.

In the late 1950s and early 1960s, when the first widely used high level languages like FORTRAN, ALGOL, and COBOL came into existence, the first significant jump in software abstraction took place. Now the objects and operations found in the problem domain could be represented in terms of the predefined data and control structures present in these early high level languages. A list of numbers, a problem-domain entity, could, for example, be represented in FORTRAN as an array of floating point numbers. Two lists of related numbers (e.g., social security number and annual incomes) could, for example, be repre-

```
Start
    A;
    repeat
        B;
        if x₁ then
            I;
            do case xᵢ,  i = 6, 7, 8
                case x₆ :  J;
                            K;
                case x₇ :  do while x₉
                                L;
                            end while;
                case x₈ :  M;
            end case;
        else
            C;
            if x₂ then
                repeat
                    G;
                until x₄;
            else
                D;
                if x₃ then
                    F;
                else
                    E;
                end if;
            end if;
            do while x₅
                H;
            end while;
        end if;
    until x₁₀;
    N;
Stop
```

Figure 4.31 Example of pseudo-code.

sented as two related arrays, with the array index the common factor linking the two arrays.

Several generations of programmers have learned to translate and abstract the entities of the real-world problem they are solving into the basic building blocks (the data and control structures) of the high level language being used. In the 1970s languages like Pascal introduced a richer variety of basic data and control structure building blocks that software developers could use to repre-sent the problem domain. The set structure, the record structure, the pointer type, the repeat and while loops, and the case and if-then-else control structures, are examples of the additional building blocks made available to software developers using Pascal.

Even with the additional Pascal-like constructs introduced in many languages during the 1970s, the fundamental approach to software design remained the same, namely, map the entities of the real-world problem to the structures available in the high level language. Software design continued to be preoccupied with representational details for data and control structures.

In Chapter 3 we illustrate some of the potential problems associated with what we will call data representational design. They include problems associated with tampering with the inner workings of a data structure during software maintenance, leading to lower software reliability. The reliability and maintainability of software may be compromised when its integrity depends on a particular scheme for representing objects. If the representational details must be altered to suit a new environment (e.g., a new computer or operating system), the fall-out effects on the software system are most often profound. Quite often it is cheaper and more reliable to rebuild the entire software system from scratch than to modify the existing system, all because of the strong dependence of the software system on the representational scheme used for the major data types.

Modular and object-oriented design supports the second major jump in abstraction that is possible in the software development process. No longer is it necessary for the system designer to map the problem domain to the predefined data and control structures present in the implementation language. Instead, the designer may create his or her own abstract data types and functional abstractions and map the real-world domain to these programmer-created abstractions. This mapping, incidentally, may be much more natural because of the virtually unlimited range of abstract types that can be invented by the software designer. Furthermore, the software design becomes decoupled from the representational details of the data objects used in the system. These representational details may be changed many times without any fall-out effects being induced in the overall software system.

Is this magic? No! The secret lies in modular software construction and object abstraction—object-oriented design. The term "object-oriented design" is used by Booch [19]. We describe this methodology at greater length in Chapter 5, in connection with Ada, and in Chapter 6 in connection with Modula-2.

The Ada package with its private types, the Modula-2 module with its opaque types, and the complete separation between the specification and implementation of these modules, make modular and object-oriented design a reality. One of the principal goals of this book is to make a case for this approach to software development. In Chapters 5, 6 and 9, we present some case studies that use this process. In Chapter 8 we see how the software testing phase may be affected by modular software construction.

We now present the process of modular and object-oriented design with a short example. We also introduce what we believe to be a powerful design aid, the modular design chart.

4.5.1 The Modular Design Chart; Object-Oriented Design

We illustrate object-oriented design and modular software construction in this section with a short example.

The Problem

We wish to find the youngest common ancestor connecting two arbitrary nodes in a binary tree. The software system must allow the user to do the following.

1. Construct a binary tree with integer values for each node.
2. Input the integer values for the two descendant nodes.
3. Determine and output the node in the tree that is the youngest common ancestor of the two descendant nodes.
4. Provide an error message if the user attempts to input descendant node(s) that do not exist in the tree.

Informal Strategy for Solution

1. Build a binary tree (the type of tree is not important).
2. Locate the positions of the two tree nodes that correspond to the integer values that the user inputs.
3. Compute the levels for each of the two descendant nodes.
4. If the levels are not the same, move up from child to parent, starting at the lower descendant node, to a node whose level is the same as the higher descendant node.
5. With both nodes now at the same level, move up from child to parent along the two branches until convergence to the same node occurs.
6. Output this final node.

For purposes of illustration (see Figure 4.32), let us assume that descendant node 1 is 125 and descendant node 2 is 500. Node 500 is at level 4, if we assume the root node to be at level 0. Node 125 is at level 3.

According to the informal strategy, we move up the tree starting at node 500 until we reach level 3. This takes us to node 400. From nodes 125 and 400, we move up each of the branches to nodes 150 and 300. Then we move up again to node 200, where convergence occurs. We output the resulting youngest common ancestor, namely node 200.

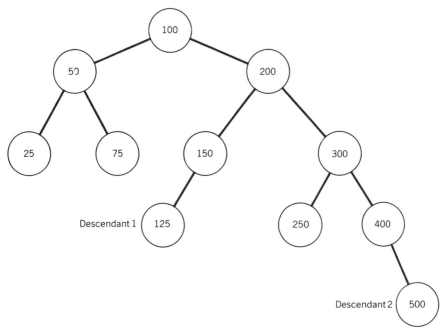

Figure 4.32   Tree to illustrate the youngest-common-ancestor problem.

If two legal nodes are input as the descendant nodes, a solution is guaranteed. In worst case, the root node will be a youngest common ancestor of two descendant nodes.

Object-Oriented Design

We must now find a software solution to the foregoing problem. From the informal problem solution it is evident that we have identified the abstract object, tree, and several important operations on this object. These are given in Table 4.1.

Table 4.1   Data and Functional
Abstractions for Youngest
Common Ancestor Problem

Data abstractions	
Tree	
Functional abstractions	
BuildTree	IsNil
Locate	Equal
Level	Value
MoveUp	

Our design uses an abstract data type called a Tree and will be designed independent of the representational details of this abstract data type. We must pay a price for this. The primitive operations normally available for tree manipulations when the representational details are given are no longer accessible. If we hide the tree structure, then we cannot, for example, access the left child or right child of a given node directly. We cannot assign one node to another or determine whether a tree is empty. In short, we must support the tree data abstraction with functional abstraction—a set of procedures that perform the usual and necessary tree operations.

The overhead of supporting the tree abstraction with general tree manipulation procedures is well worth it. If, in the future, we wish to change the hidden representational details of the tree structure and the procedures that operate on the tree, the software system(s) that use the tree modules will not have to be changed at all. They may not even need to be recompiled. Only the module body that contains the implementation details of the tree and its supporting procedures would have to be changed. This kind of localized maintenance is difficult to achieve using older methods of software design.

We now introduce and illustrate a design tool that we call the modular design chart. This chart provides a graphical overview of the software system architecture. It represents the modular decomposition of the system into its component modules. Each module specification (either definition module or package specification) is represented by a box. The exportable software components including constants, types, objects, and procedures are listed in the box. In addition, the module bodies (either implementation modules or package bodies) are also represented by boxes. A software bus provides the logical interconnection between the modules that make up the software system. The interdependencies that exist among the modules are made evident in the modular design chart. Finally, the main driver program and its connection to the system is shown in the modular design chart.

Complex systems may be partitioned into many different sets of modules. Indeed, the main challenge of modular software design is determining the most sensible decomposition of the software system. This creative process of problem decomposition may be performed using the modular design chart as an aid.

4.5.2 Modular Software Construction

We display the first modular design chart for the youngest-common-ancestor problem, in Figure 4.33. We have partitioned the system into two main modules, GeneralTreeOperations and SpecificTreeOperations. The first module, GeneralTreeOperations, contains a set of basic tree abstractions that are usually implemented directly by a programmer using the predefined building blocks (data structures) given in the language. The operations contained in GeneralTreeOperations might prove useful in other software applications involving trees. The three functional abstractions, namely, IsNil, Equal, and

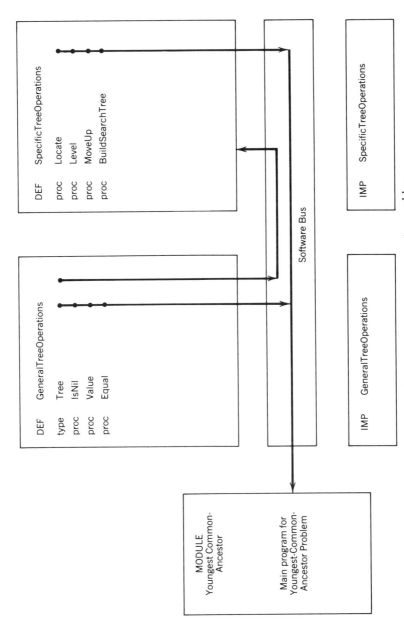

Figure 4.33 First modular design chart for youngest-common-ancestor problem.

Value, are required by the main driver program and are therefore included in GeneralTreeOperations.

The second module, SpecificTreeOperations, contains the more specialized abstractions Locate, Level, MoveUp, and AddNodeToSearchTree not ordinarily used for general tree manipulations. This second module imports the abstract tree type from the first module.

Finally, the modular design chart displays the main program module which must import operations from each of the two system modules. We have chosen not to display standard system library modules such as InOut and Storage even though we import procedures from these modules.

Note that the main program driver reads almost like the informal strategy for the solution to the problem. This is because of the high level of abstraction used in the software design.

Corresponding to the modular design chart given in Figure 4.33, is a modular design listing (Modular Design Listing 4.1). The dashed lines are used to indicate separately compiled units.

MODULAR DESIGN LISTING 4.1   Initial Modula-2 Design

DEFINITION MODULE GeneralTreeOperations;
(* $SEG:=20; *)

EXPORT QUALIFIED
    (* type *) Tree,
    (* proc *) IsNil,
    (* proc *) Equal,
    (* proc *) Value;

TYPE Tree;
(* The representational details of this abstract data type
    are hidden.   *)

PROCEDURE IsNil(T: Tree): BOOLEAN;
(* This procedure returns the value true if the tree node T
    is NIL, and false otherwise.   *)

PROCEDURE Equal(P,Q: Tree): BOOLEAN;
(* This procedure returns true if nodes P and Q are equal,
    false otherwise.   *)

PROCEDURE Value(P: Tree): INTEGER;
(* This procedure returns the value of node P.   *)

END GeneralTreeOperations.

```
DEFINITION MODULE SpecificTreeOperations;
(* $SEG:=21; *)

    FROM GeneralTreeOperations IMPORT Tree;

    EXPORT QUALIFIED
        (* proc *) Locate,
        (* proc *) Level,
        (* proc *) MoveUp,
        (* proc *) BuildSearchTree;

    PROCEDURE Locate(T: Tree; Info: INTEGER: VAR P: Tree);
    (* This procedure returns the memory reference, P,
        of the node in tree T with value Info. Nil is returned
        if a node with value Info doesn't exist in the tree.              *)

    PROCEDURE Level (T: Tree; P: Tree): INTEGER;
    (* This procedure returns the level within tree T of a node
        P. The root node is defined to have level zero.                   *)

    PROCEDURE MoveUp(T: Tree; VAR P: Tree);
    (* Procedure MoveUp replaces node P by its parent.                    *)

    PROCEDURE BuildSearchTree(VAR T : Tree);
    (* A search tree with root T is created.                              *)

END SpecificTreeOperations.
```

```
MODULE YoungestCommonAncestor;

    FROM GeneralTreeOperations IMPORT
            Tree, CreateRoot, IsNil, Equal, Value;

    FROM SpecificTreeOperations IMPORT
            Locate, Level, MoveUp, BuildSearchTree;

    FROM InOut IMPORT
            WriteString, WriteLn, ReadInt, WriteInt;

    VAR
        level1  : INTEGER;
        level2  : INTEGER;
        value1  : INTEGER;
        value2  : INTEGER;
```

```
        T       : Tree;
        n1      : Tree;
        n2      : Tree;

BEGIN (* YoungestCommonAncestor *)
    BuildSearchTree(T);
    WriteString("Enter the value of the first descendant node: ");
    ReadInt(value1);
    WriteLn;
    Locate(T,value1,n1);
    WriteString("Enter the value of the second descendant node: ");
    ReadInt(value2);
    WriteLn;
    Locate(T,value2,n2);
    IF ( IsNil(n1) ) OR ( IsNil(n2) )
    THEN
        WriteLn;
        WriteString("At least one of the values is not in the tree.");
        WriteLn;
        WriteString("Cannot continue processing.");
        HALT
    END(* if then *);
    level1:= Level(T,n1);
    level 2:= Level(T,n2);
    WHILE level1 > level2 DO
        MoveUp(T,n1);
        DEC(level1);
    END(* while loop *);
    WHILE level2 > level1 DO
        MoveUp(T,n2);
        DEC(level2);
    END(* while loop *);
    (* n1 and n2 are now at the same Level *)
    WHILE NOT Equal(n1,n2) DO
        MoveUp(T,n1);
        MoveUp(T,n2);
    END(* while loop *);
    WriteLn;
    WriteString("The youngest common ancestor is ");
    WriteInt( Value(n1),20)
END YoungestCommonAncestor.
```

The modular design listing may be compiled. This assures us of correct high level system integration. We have built the frame of our software system

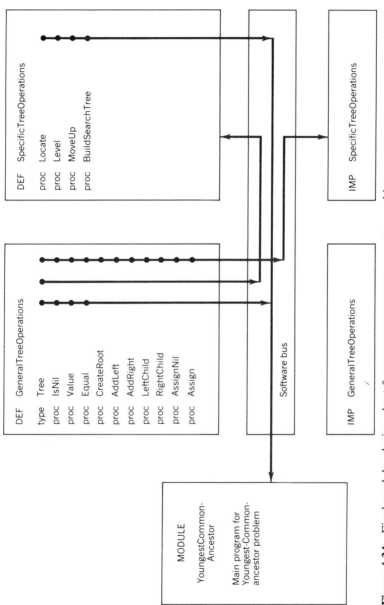

Figure 4.34 Final modular design chart for youngest-common-ancestor problem.

at the design level using the modular design chart and listing as the basis for this design.

As we begin to implement the system (i.e., construct the implementation modules), we expect that additional components will have to be added to some or all of the definition modules because additional tree manipulations such as finding the left and right offspring of a given node may have to be performed at the implementation level. Ordinarily, these low level operations would be performed directly in terms of the global data structure used for the tree. Here, using object-oriented design, additional functional abstractions must be created so that the implementation can proceed smoothly. Thus the design must be iterated as the implementation evolves.

To illustrate this we display the modular design chart for the final software system in Figure 4.34. Note the additional components in GeneralTreeOperations that were added to support the implementation of the system.

We display the complete software system for the youngest common ancestor problem in Program 4.1.

PROGRAM 4.1   Software System For Finding Youngest Common Ancestor

DEFINITION MODULE GeneralTreeOperations;
(* $SEG:=20; *)

    EXPORT QUALIFIED
        (* type *) Tree,
        (* proc *) CreateRoot,
        (* proc *) AddLeft,
        (* proc *) AddRight,
        (* proc *) IsNil,
        (* proc *) LeftChild,
        (* proc *) RightChild,
        (* proc *) Value,
        (* proc *) AssignNil,
        (* proc *) Equal,
        (* proc *) Assign;

    TYPE Tree;
    (* The representational details of this abstract data type
      are hidden.   *)

    PROCEDURE CreateRoot(Info: INTEGER): Tree;
    (* This procedure returns the root node for a new tree
      or subtree.   *)

```
    PROCEDURE AddLeft(P: Tree; Info: INTEGER);
    (* This procedure connects a left offspring with Info
       to node P.                                              *)


    PROCEDURE AddRight(P: Tree; Info: INTEGER);
    (* This procedure connects a right offspring with Info
       to node P.                                              *)


    PROCEDURE IsNil(T: Tree): BOOLEAN;
    (* This procedure returns the value true if the tree node T
       is NIL, and false otherwise.                            *)


    PROCEDURE LeftChild(P: Tree): Tree;
    (* This procedure returns the left child of node P.        *)


    PROCEDURE RightChild(P: Tree): Tree;
    (* This procedure returns the right child of node P.       *)


    PROCEDURE Value(P: Tree): INTEGER;
    (*  This procedure returns the value of node P.            *)


    PROCEDURE AssignNil(VAR P: Tree);
    (*  This procedure assigns the node P to NIL.              *)


    PROCEDURE Equal(P,Q: Tree): BOOLEAN;
    (* This procedure returns true if nodes P and Q are equal,
       false otherwise.                                        *)


    PROCEDURE Assign(P: Tree; VAR Q: Tree);
    (* This procedure assigns node Q to have the same value as P.  *)

END GeneralTreeOperations.
-------------------------------------------------------------------------
DEFINITION MODULE SpecificTreeOperations;
(* $SEG:=21; *)
    FROM GeneralTreeOperations IMPORT Tree;

    EXPORT QUALIFIED
        (* proc *) Locate,
        (* proc *) Level,
        (* proc *) MoveUp,
        (* proc *) BuildSearchTree;
```

```
PROCEDURE Locate(T: Tree; Info: INTEGER; VAR P: Tree);
(* This procedure returns the memory reference P
   of the node in tree T with value Info. NIL is returned
   if a node with value Info doesn't exist in the tree.              *)

PROCEDURE Level(T: Tree; P: Tree): INTEGER;
(*  This procedure returns the level within the tree T of a node
    P. The root node is defined to have level zero.                  *)

PROCEDURE MoveUp(T: Tree; VAR P: Tree);
(*  Procedure MoveUp replaces node P by its parent.                  *)

PROCEDURE BuildSearchTree(VAR T: Tree);
(*  A search tree with root T is created.                           *)

END SpecificTreeOperations.
```

```
IMPLEMENTATION MODULE SpecificTreeOperations;
    FROM GeneralTreeOperations IMPORT
        Tree, IsNil, LeftChild, RightChild, Value, AssignNil,
        Equal, Assign, AddLeft, AddRight, CreateRoot;

    FROM InOut IMPORT WriteLn, WriteString, ReadInt;

    PROCEDURE Locate(T: Tree; Info: INTEGER; VAR P: Tree);

        PROCEDURE L(T: Tree; VAR P: Tree);
        BEGIN
           IF NOT IsNil(T) THEN
               L( LeftChild(T),P );
               IF Value(T) = Info THEN Assign(T,P); END(* if then *);
               L( RightChild(T),P );
           END(* if then *);
        END L;

    BEGIN (* Locate *)
       AssignNil(P);
       L(T,P)
    END Locate;

    PROCEDURE Level(T: Tree; P: Tree): INTEGER;

        VAR found : BOOLEAN;
            count : INTEGER;
```

```
        PROCEDURE L(T,P: Tree; VAR count: INTEGER);
        BEGIN
            IF NOT IsNil(T) THEN
                IF (NOT found) AND
                    NOT ( IsNil(LeftChild(T)) AND IsNil(RightChild(T)) )
                THEN
                    INC(count);
                END(* if then *);
                L(LeftChild(T),P,count);
                L(RightChild(T),P,count);
                IF (NOT found) AND
                    NOT ( IsNil(LeftChild(T)) AND IsNil(RightChild(T)) )
                THEN
                    DEC(count);
                END(* if then *);
                IF Equal(T,P)
                THEN
                    found:=TRUE
                END(* if then *)
            END(* if then *);
        END L;


    BEGIN (* Level *)
        found:=FALSE;
        count:=0;
        IF Equal(P,T)
        THEN
            RETURN 0
        ELSE
            L(T,P,count);
            RETURN count
        END(* if then else *);
    END Level;


    PROCEDURE MoveUp(T: Tree; VAR P: Tree);
    BEGIN
        IF NOT Equal(P,T) THEN
            IF NOT IsNil(T) THEN
                IF ( Equal(LeftChild(T),P)) OR ( Equal(RightChild(T),P) )
                THEN
                    Assign(T,P);
                END(* if then *);
                MoveUp(LeftChild(T),P);
```

```
            MoveUp(RightChild(T),P);
        END(* if then *);
    END(* if then *);
END MoveUp;


PROCEDURE BuildSearchTree(VAR T: Tree);

    PROCEDURE AddNodeToSearchTree(T : Tree; Info: INTEGER);

    VAR P, Q: Tree;

    BEGIN
        Assign(T,Q);
        WHILE NOT ( IsNil(Q) ) DO
            Assign(Q,P);
            IF Info < Value(P)
            THEN
                Assign(LeftChild(P),Q);
            ELSE
                Assign(RightChild(P),Q);
            END(* if then else *);
        END(* while loop *);
        IF Info < Value(P)
        THEN
            AddLeft(P,Info)
        ELSE
            AddRight(P,Info)
        END(* if then else *);
    END AddNodeToSearchTree;

VAR i : INTEGER;

BEGIN (* BuildTree *)
    WriteLn;
    WriteLn;
    WriteString("Enter the first node of the search tree: ");
    ReadInt(i);
    T:=CreateRoot(i);
    WriteLn;
    WriteString("Enter the sequence of values for the search tree");
    WriteLn;
    WriteString("Use  −1 as a terminator to end the sequence");
    WriteLn;
    LOOP
        WriteLn;
```

```
            WriteString("Enter a node in the tree: ");
            ReadInt(i);
            IF i = −1
            THEN
                 EXIT;
            END(* if then *);
            AddNodeToSearchTree(T,i);
        END(* loop *);
    END BuildSearchTree;


END SpecificTreeOperations.
```

```
MODULE YoungestCommonAncestor;

    FROM GeneralTreeOperations IMPORT
             Tree, CreateRoot, IsNil, Equal, Value;

    FROM SpecificTreeOperations IMPORT
             Locate, Level, MoveUp, BuildSearchTree;

    FROM InOut IMPORT
             WriteString, WriteLn, ReadInt, WriteInt;

    VAR
        level1  : INTEGER;
        level2  : INTEGER;
        value1  : INTEGER;
        value2  : INTEGER;
        T       : Tree;
        n1      : Tree;
        n2      : Tree;

BEGIN (* YoungestCommonAncestor *)
    BuildSearchTree(T);
    WriteString("Enter the value of the first descendant node: ");
    ReadInt(value1);
    WriteLn;
    Locate(T,value1,n1);
    WriteString("Enter the value of the second descendant node: ");
    ReadInt(value2);
    WriteLn;
    Locate(T,value2,n2);
    IF ( IsNil(n1) ) OR ( IsNil(n2) )
    THEN
        WriteLn;
```

```
            WriteString("At least one of the values is not in the tree.");
            WriteLn;
            WriteString("Cannot continue processing.");
            HALT
        END(* if then *);
        level1:= Level(T,n1);
        level2:= Level(T,n2);
        WHILE level1 > level2 DO
            MoveUp(T,n1);
            DEC(level1);
        END(* while loop *)
        WHILE level2 > level1 DO
            MoveUp(T,n2);
            DEC(level2);
        END(* while loop *);
        (* n1 and n2 are now at the same Level *)
        WHILE NOT Equal(n1,n2) DO
            MoveUp(T,n1);
            MoveUp(T,n2);
        END(* while loop *);
        WriteLn;
        WriteString("The youngest common ancestor is ");
        WriteInt( Value(n1),20)
END YoungestCommonAncestor.
```

```
IMPLEMENTATION MODULE GeneralTreeOperations;

    FROM Storage IMPORT ALLOCATE, DEALLOCATE;
        (*Procedures NEW and DISPOSE are in ALLOCATE and DEALLOCATE.*)

    FROM InOut IMPORT WriteLn, WriteString;

    TYPE Tree  = POINTER TO node;
         node = RECORD
                    val   : INTEGER;
                    left  : Tree;
                    right : Tree;
                            END(* record *);
                                     Node
    PROCEDURE CreateRoot(Info: INTEGER): Tree;

        VAR T: Tree;

    BEGIN
        NEW(T);
        T↑.val:= Info;
        T↑.left:=NIL;
        T↑.right:=NIL;
```

```
        RETURN T
END CreateRoot;

PROCEDURE IsNil(T: Tree): BOOLEAN;
BEGIN
        RETURN ( T = NIL );
END IsNil;

PROCEDURE LeftChild(P: Tree): Tree;
BEGIN
        RETURN P↑.left
END LeftChild;

PROCEDURE RightChild(P: Tree): Tree;
BEGIN
        RETURN P↑.right
END RightChild;

PROCEDURE AddLeft(P: Tree; Info: INTEGER);

VAR Q: Tree;

BEGIN
        Q:=CreateRoot(Info);
        P↑.left:=Q;
END AddLeft;

PROCEDURE AddRight(P: Tree; Info: INTEGER);

VAR Q: Tree;

BEGIN
        Q:=CreateRoot(Info);
        P↑.right:=Q;
END AddRight;

PROCEDURE Value(P: Tree): INTEGER;
BEGIN
        IF P # NIL
            THEN RETURN P↑.val
        ELSE
            WriteLn;
            WriteString("Cannot return the value of a nil pointer.");
            HALT
        END(* if then *);
END Value;
```

```
PROCEDURE AssignNil(VAR P: Tree);
BEGIN
    P:=NIL
END AssignNil;

PROCEDURE Equal(P,Q: Tree): BOOLEAN;
BEGIN
    RETURN (P = Q);
END Equal;

PROCEDURE Assign(P: Tree; VAR Q: Tree);
BEGIN
    Q:=P
END Assign;

END GeneralTreeOperations.
```

We now display in Program 4.2 a finished Ada software system for the youngest common ancestor problem.

PROGRAM 4.2   Ada Software System for Finding Youngest Common Ancestor

```
package GENERAL_TREE_OPS is

    type TREE is limited private;

    procedure CREATE_TREE (T : in out TREE; INFO : in INTEGER);
        --This procedure returns the root node for a new tree.

    procedure ADD_RIGHT (T : in out TREE;  INFO : in INTEGER);
        --This procedure adds a right child containing INFO to
        --the node T.

    procedure ADD_LEFT (T : in out TREE;  INFO : in INTEGER);
        --This procedure adds a left child containing INFO to
        --the node T.

    function IS_NULL (T : TREE) return BOOLEAN;
        --This function returns the value TRUE if the tree
        --pointer T is NULL and FALSE otherwise.

    function LEFT_CHILD (T : TREE) return TREE;
        --This function returns the left child of node T.
```

```
function RIGHT_CHILD (T : TREE) return TREE;
    --This function returns the right child of node T.

function VALUE (T : TREE) return INTEGER;
    --This function returns the value of node T.

procedure ASSIGN_NULL (T : in out TREE);
    --This procedure assigns the pointer T to NULL.

function EQUAL (T,S : TREE) return BOOLEAN;
    --This function returns TRUE if T and S are equal,
    --FALSE otherwise.

procedure ASSIGN (T : in TREE; S : in out TREE);
    --This procedure assigns S to have the same value as T.

NULL_POINTER : exception;
    --This exception is raised if VALUE is called with
    --a null pointer.

private
    type NODE;
    type TREE is access NODE;
    type NODE is
        record
            VAL   : INTEGER;
            LEFT  : TREE;
            RIGHT : TREE;
        end record;

end GENERAL_TREE_OPS;
--------------------------------------------------------------------------
with GENERAL_TREE_OPS;  use GENERAL_TREE_OPS;

package SPECIALIZED_TREE_OPS  is

        --From GENERAL_TREE_OPS
        --      import type TREE,
        --      import procedures ADD_RIGHT, ADD_LEFT.

procedure LOCATE (T : TREE;  INFO : INTEGER;  S : in out TREE);
    --This procedure returns a pointer S to the node with
    --value INFO.
```

```
function LEVEL (T,S : TREE) return INTEGER;
    --This function returns the level within tree T of a node
    --S. The root node is defined to have level zero.

procedure MOVE_UP (T : in TREE;  S : in out TREE);
    --This procedure replaces node S by its parent in tree T.

procedure BUILD_TREE (T : in out TREE);
    --This procedure takes input from the user and constructs
    --a search tree.

end SPECIALIZED_TREE_OPS;
```

```
with GENERAL_TREE_OPS, SPECIALIZED_TREE_OPS, TEXT_IO;
use  GENERAL_TREE_OPS, SPECIALIZED_TREE_OPS, TEXT_IO;

    --From GENERAL_TREE_OPS
    --      import type TREE,
    --      import functions IS_NULL, EQUAL, VALUE,
    --      import procedures CREATE_TREE, ADD_NODE,
    --      import exception  NULL_POINTER.

    --From SPECIALIZED_TREE_OPS
    --      import function LEVEL,
    --      import procedures LOCATE, MOVE_UP, BUILD_TREE.

    --From TEXT_IO
    --      import put_line, put, get, new_line.

procedure YOUNGEST_COMMON_ANCESTOR is

    T, N1, N2          : TREE;
    LEVEL1, LEVEL2 : INTEGER;
    VALUE1, VALUE2 : INTEGER;

begin  --YOUNGEST_COMMON_ANCESTOR
    BUILD_TREE( T );
    new_line;
    put_line ("We compute the youngest common ancestor of two nodes.");
    put ("Enter the value of the first node: ");
    get ( VALUE1 );
    LOCATE( T, VALUE1, N1 );
    put ("Enter the value of the second node: ");
    get ( VALUE2 );
    LOCATE( T, VALUE2, N2 );
```

```
        if ( IS_NULL( N1 ) or IS_NULL( N2 ) ) then
            new_line;
            put_line ("At least one of the values is not in the tree.");
            put_line ("Cannot continue processing.");
        else
            LEVEL1 := LEVEL( T, N1 );
            LEVEL2 := LEVEL( T, N2 );
            while LEVEL1 > LEVEL2 loop
                MOVE_UP( T, N1 );
                LEVEL1 := LEVEL1 -1;
            end loop;
            while LEVEL2 > LEVEL1 loop
                MOVE_UP( T, N2 );
                LEVEL2 := LEVEL2 - 1;
            end loop;
            --N1 and N1 are now at the same level.
            while not EQUAL( N1, N2 ) loop
                MOVE_UP( T, N1 );
                MOVE_UP( T, N2 );
            end loop;
            new_line;
            put ("The youngest common ancestor is ");
            put ( VALUE( N1 ) );
        end if;
exception
    when NULL_POINTER =>
        put ("Cannot return the value of a null pointer.");
end YOUNGEST_COMMON_ANCESTOR;
-----------------------------------------------------------------------------
package body GENERAL_TREE_OPS is

    procedure CREATE_TREE (T : in out TREE;  INFO : in INTEGER) is
    begin
        T := new NODE;
        T.VAL := INFO;
    end CREATE_TREE;

    procedure ADD_RIGHT (T : in out TREE; INFO : in INTEGER) is
        P : TREE;
    begin
        CREATE_TREE (P, INFO);
        T.RIGHT := P;
    end ADD_RIGHT;

    procedure ADD_LEFT (T : in out TREE; INFO : in INTEGER) is
        P : TREE;
```

```
begin
    CREATE_TREE (P, INFO);
    T.LEFT := P;
end ADD_LEFT;

function IS_NULL (T : TREE) return BOOLEAN is
begin
    if T = null then
        return TRUE;
    else
        return FALSE;
    end if;
end IS_NULL;

function LEFT_CHILD (T : TREE) return TREE is
begin
    return T. LEFT;
end LEFT_CHILD;

function RIGHT_CHILD (T : TREE) return TREE is
begin
    return T.RIGHT;
end RIGHT_CHILD;

function VALUE (T : TREE) return TREE is
begin
    if T /= null then
        return T.VAL;
    else
        raise NULL_POINTER;
    end if;
end VALUE;

procedure ASSIGN_NULL (T : in out TREE) is
begin
    T := null;
end ASSIGN_NULL;

function EQUAL (T,S : TREE) return BOOLEAN is
begin
    if T = S then
        return TRUE;
    else
        return FALSE;
    end if;
end EQUAL;
```

```
    procedure ASSIGN (T : in TREE; S : in out TREE) is
    begin
        S := T;
    end ASSIGN;

end GENERAL_TREE_OPS;
```

```
with GENERAL_TREE_OPS, TEXT_IO;
use  GENERAL_TREE_OPS, TEXT_IO;


package body SPECIALIZED_TREE_OPS is

    --From GENERAL_TREE_OPS
    --      import type TREE,
    --      import functions IS_NULL, LEFT_CHILD, RIGHT_CHILD,
    --              ADD_RIGHT, ADD_LEFT, EQUAL, VALUE,
    --      import procedures CREATE_TREE, ASSIGN_NULL, ASSIGN.


    --From TEXT_IO
    --      import put, get, put_line, new_line.

    procedure LOCATE (T : TREE; INFO : INTEGER; S : in out TREE) is

        procedure L (T : TREE; S : in out TREE) is
        begin
            if not IS_NULL( T ) then
                L( LEFT_CHILD( T ), S );
                if VALUE( T ) = INFO then
                    ASSIGN( T, S );
                end if;
                L( RIGHT_CHILD( T ), S);
            end if;
        end L;

    begin      --LOCATE
        ASSIGN_NULL( S );
        L( T, S );
    end LOCATE;

    function LEVEL (T, S : TREE) return INTEGER is
        FOUND : BOOLEAN;
        COUNT : INTEGER;

        procedure L( T, S : TREE; COUNT : in out INTEGER) is
```

```
        begin
            if not IS_NULL( T ) then
                if ( not FOUND ) and
                    not (IS_NULL( LEFT_CHILD( T ) ) and
                        IS_NULL( RIGHT_CHILD( T ) ) )
                    then
                        COUNT := COUNT + 1;
                end if;
                L( LEFT_CHILD( T ), S, COUNT );
                L( RIGHT_CHILD( T ), S, COUNT );
                if ( not FOUND ) and
                    not (IS_NULL( LEFT_CHILD( T ) ) and
                        IS_NULL( RIGHT_CHILD( T ) ) )
                    then
                        COUNT := COUNT + 1;
                end if;
                if EQUAL( T, S ) then
                    FOUND := TRUE;
                end if;
            end if;
        end L;


    begin --LEVEL
        FOUND := FALSE;
        COUNT := 0;
        if EQUAL( S, T ) then
            return 0
        else
            L( T, S, COUNT );
            return COUNT;
        end if;
    end LEVEL;


    procedure MOVE_UP ( T: in TREE; S : in out TREE) is
    begin
        if not EQUAL( T, S ) then
            if not IS_NULL( T ) then
                if EQUAL( LEFT_CHILD( T ), S ) or
                    EQUAL( RIGHT_CHILD( T ), S )
                then
                    ASSIGN( T, S );
                end if;
                MOVE_UP( LEFT_CHILD( T ), S );
```

```
                    MOVE_UP( RIGHT_CHILD( T ), S );
             end if;
        end if;
    end MOVE_UP;

    procedure BUILD_TREE (T : in out TREE) is

        I : INTEGER;

        procedure ADD_NODE( T : in out TREE; INFOR : in INTEGER) is
            P,Q : TREE;
        begin
            Q := T;
            while Q /= null
                loop
                    P := Q;
                    if INFO < P.VAL then
                        Q := P.LEFT;
                    else
                        Q := P.RIGHT;
                    end if;
                end loop;
            if INFO < P.VAL then
                ADD_LEFT( P, INFO );
            else
                ADD_RIGHT( P, INFO );
            end if;
        end ADD_NODE;

    begin --BUILD_TREE
        put ("Enter the first node of the search tree: ");
        get ( I );
        CREATE_TREE( T, I );
        new_line;
        put_line ("Enter the sequence of values for the search tree");
        put_line ("Use - 1 as a terminator to end the sequence");
        new_line;
        loop
            put ("Enter a node in the tree: ");
            get ( I );
            exit when I = - 1;
            ADD_NODE( T, I );
        end loop;
    end BUILD_TREE;

end SPECIALIZED_TREE_OPS;
```

The reader should observe the close similarity between Programs 4.1 and 4.2. The main differences are in how we access the resources of a package or module from another program unit and the input-output statements. The Ada specification for GENERAL_TREE_OPS contains a private part that indicates to the compiler the data structure for the abstract object TREE. The user of these packages cannot access this data structure directly. In Modula-2 the data structure for type TREE is contained in the implementation details of the module (see Program 4.1). Both languages permit us to do true data abstraction and information hiding.

4.6 RAPID PROTOTYPING

In most branches of engineering, prototyping has long been an important part of the development process of any new product. A prototype is built to assess the system before committing to a final design. Various alternatives are tested using the prototype to determine whether both the functional and nonfunctional specifications for the system can be met. If not, the prototype is modified and reevaluated before hardware construction is permitted to commence. It is not necessary for the prototype to satisfy every requirement for the final system: it must include only the features that need further analysis before a final design can be decided. No engineer would consider beginning production without having thoroughly tested and refined a prototype.

Software engineering, however, has traditionally not considered prototyping as a normal activity, mainly because there is no ''production run'' to produce a large number of copies of the product. Indeed, in software engineering, the prototype IS the production run. For software systems in which multiple copies are needed, the time and cost required are insignificant compared to the development costs. This is certainly not the case in other branches of engineering in which the production costs may greatly exceed the development costs of a product. For such a mass-produced item the cost of a prototype represents a very small fraction of the final unit cost of the product. All too often software developers take the attitude that it is more economical to modify the finished system than to refine the needs before the system is constructed.

In many systems, requirements are incomplete or ill defined, resulting in somewhat arbitrary specification and design decisions. When several competing designs are possible, it is difficult to predict which ones will meet performance specifications. When a user interface is part of the system, it is almost impossible to predict what will be perceived by the users as convenient, consistent, and user friendly.

Software prototyping can address each of these problems. A prototype system can be used to clarify and elaborate requirements and specifications. When the end users of the system and the developers are not the same persons, it is often difficult for the users to define their requirements in sufficient detail that the developers can proceed directly to the design and implementation of the ideal system. Experience shows that much of software maintenance is necessitated by changes or refinements in requirements and specifications. If it were possible to produce quickly a prototype version of a software system, the users could evaluate it and identify where requirements were incorrectly defined or misinterpreted by the developers. Several iterations of this process can lead to virtually complete and correct requirements and specifications.

In designing very complex software systems, there will be many places where a designer must choose among competing methods or algorithms. Each of these choices will have some impact on the overall performance of the system, but it is nearly impossible to predict the ramifications of all these choices together. Again prototyping provides some help. If prototypes of subsystems can be rapidly produced, performance measurements can be made during design. If performance problems are detected, the design can be modified. Iterations of this process can help guarantee that the final design will lead to an implementation that meets all performance specifications.

For example, the nonfunctional requirements for the spelling checker have a significant impact on the design of the software. The primary operation of the spelling checker requires that words in the text be located in the dictionary to verify that they are spelled correctly. The nonfunctional requirements state that the software must correctly identify the spelling of at least 40,000 words, that approximately 250 words be processed per minute, and that it execute on a computer with only 128,000 bytes of memory. Careful consideration of these requirements suggests that rapid prototyping may be useful in determining the search algorithms to use in looking up words in the dictionary, the internal data structure for representing the dictionary, and whether dictionary compression algorithms will be necessary.

The design of user interfaces is one of the most difficult aspects of software system design, partly because the evaluation of interfaces is very subjective, and partly because even the users do not always know in advance what they themselves consider to be desirable interface specifications. Clearly, prototyping provides an important vehicle for iterated refinement of specifications for such interfaces.

For example, in the design of the spelling checker described in Chapter 2, it may be important to prototype the user interface to verify that the menu items and the order in which they are presented to the user are acceptable and that the various screen displays are meaningful. This can be done even though none of the menu items is implemented.

The term "rapid prototyping" is often used in software engineering to reflect the differences between software prototyping and prototyping in other branches of engineering. Clearly, prototyping will be useful in the areas just described only if it can be accomplished substantially faster than producing an entire finished system. To produce software prototypes rapidly, a variety of tools, techniques, and environments are evolving.

There are two major approaches to rapid prototyping: reusable code and executable specifications. There has been some success with each of these, and research in both areas continues. Both these approaches are closely tied to the development of integrated software development environments.

Modern languages such as Ada and Modula-2 make it much easier to reuse existing code than did previous languages. Both languages make it possible to build extensive software libraries and to access individual packages or modules from a library whenever desired. A significant problem that remains to be solved is the development of a library cataloging system. How does a software developer know, given a particular requirement or specification, that there already exists in the library a piece of software that can satisfy that requirement?

A taxonomy of software components is beginning to emerge. Already it is possible to distinguish components such as abstract data types, mathematical routine packages, parsers, scanners, filters, and message channels, to name a few. As use of Ada and Modula-2 increases, general purpose, application specific, and personal libraries will grow and the need for improved classification systems will become increasingly apparent.

The other approach to rapid prototyping, executable specifications, is also the object of intense research efforts. It has long been recognized that the English language is too rich to be an adequate medium for the unambiguous expression of requirements and specifications. More formal languages for requirements and specifications have been developed and investigated for many years. Such languages, with relatively simple syntax and unambiguous semantics, were originally intended to guide human designers. However, it has become apparent that it is also possible to build software systems that can read and use these formal specifications.

In some cases, such software systems use the specifications as a guide to selecting pieces of existing software. This approach seems to be limited, at least at present, to very specific applications areas, with well-defined libraries. More often, executable specifications systems are based on some very general computational model, with a mathematical translation being made between the specifications and the internal model. Many variations of this idea have been developed into working systems.

Software prototyping can be of great value; and as programming environments evolve, prototyping should have considerable impact on the traditional model of the software life cycle. Because it is such a new area of research, there is not yet a consensus on the best approaches. The interested reader is directed to the working papers of the ACM SIGSOFT Rapid Prototyping Workshop [20].

4.7 DESIGN VALIDATION

Validation of the software design is an essential step in the design process. Any undetected errors or omissions that are permitted to progress to the implementation stage of the project probably will not be detected until the testing phase.

This implies that errors that remain in the design are likely to be extremely expensive to correct because they may require a substantial redesign and reimplementation of components of the software system. Consequently, the software may be delivered late, creating additional problems.

The objectives of the design validation process are to show that the software satisfies the requirements in full and to verify that the software design is correct.

A procedure to determine whether all requirements have been addressed by the design is the design review, in which the requirements and the design are studied and compared to determine whether the design satisfies all the requirements. The design review is simplified if the requirements are unambiguous so that uncertainties in the design do not occur.

The process of verifying that the design is correct is potentially a difficult task. One approach is to develop a formal mathematical proof that proves that the software design is correct. This is time-consuming and intellectually demanding, with the consequences that formally proving that a design is correct is expensive. For these reasons, formal proofs of correctness are not generally used for demonstrating design correctness. However, formal verification should be done on the software components or portions thereof that are critical pieces of the system.

Design reviews may be formal or informal. Formal design reviews may be part of the overall management plan consistent with normal procedures within the software development organization, or they may be required by the customer who commissioned the software project. Formal reviews involve the design team, management, and possibly consultants and the customer. A formal design review serves as a major milestone, since a decision to proceed to the implementation phase may be made at this point.

Formal design reviews should be mandatory, since the design team should be able to demonstrate that all software requirements have been met and that the software design is correct. Formal reviews are not intended to detect design errors. All design errors should have been detected and corrected as part of the informal review process.

The purpose of an informal design review is to evaluate all aspects of the software design. Informal design reviews are sometimes referred to as structured walkthroughs. Usually the only participants are members of the design team, but depending on the goals of the review, others may be involved as well. The informal review serves to refine and perfect the design before the formal design review. Any errors in the design should be detected. The informal review should not be used as a mechanism for evaluating the design team or individuals on that team, nor should it be used to review project costs, schedule, or staffing.

After the informal design review, a design review package is made available to the participants. This package contains specific documentation required in the review, supporting material used to arrive at various design decisions, and a history of design tradeoffs. During the review, the reviewers are expected to comment on the completeness, accuracy, and general quality of the design. Major areas of concern should be expressed and identified for potential follow-up. The designers then present a brief overview of the design followed by a "walkthrough," which consists of proceeding through the design step by step, to simulate the function under investigation. The design should be presented in sufficient detail that the concerns expressed are explained away or identified as items to be resolved.

Since formal software verification techniques are rarely used, the informal design review and in particular the walkthrough are intended to detect errors and inconsistencies in the design and point them out to the designer. If errors are detected, they should be noted for subsequent correction by the designer. The review team should not attempt to correct errors during the review. If formal verification has preceded the informal design review, the objective of the review team is to check the verification. This process is more effective than trying to detect design errors by walking through the design with artificial data.

Determining whether the software design meets all the software requirements is often difficult. One approach is to create a requirements cross-reference matrix, listing all the functional requirements down the left-hand column and all the modules (or subprograms) across the top row. A check mark is placed in the appropriate row–column intersection corresponding to the module that implements the requirement.

In the next two chapters we couple Ada and Modula-2 to the exciting and new methodologies of object-oriented and modular design.

4.8 SUMMARY

- Software design is a creative process that is the most critical part of the software engineering cycle. Well-designed software is straightforward to implement and maintain, is easy to understand, is reliable, and can be verified.
- The principal goal of design is to determine HOW THE SYSTEM WILL WORK.
- Hardware considerations play an important role in the design of software systems.
- Top-down design and the HIPO design process arrive at the final design by successive refinements of the problem.
- The Warnier–Orr and Jackson design methodologies are data structure oriented, since they attempt to map data structure into software structure.
- Data flow design maps data flow diagrams into software structure. Depending on the type of flow, transform or transaction analysis is used to define the mapping.
- Structured programming involves three basic constructs: sequence, selection, and iteration.

- Flow charts, Nasi-Schneiderman charts, and pseudo-code are low level design aids.
- Using modular and object-oriented design, the software designer can create abstract data types and functional abstractions that permit a natural mapping from the real-world problem domain to the software system.
- The Ada package and the Modula-2 module make modular and object-oriented design a reality.
- The modular design chart is a useful graphical aid to be used in conjunction with modular and object-oriented design.
- Design validation is an essential part of software design.

REFERENCES

1. Hockney, R. W., and C. R. Jesshope, *Parallel Computers,* Bristol: Adam Hilger Ltd., 1981.
2. Wirth, N. "Program Development by Stepwise Refinement," *Commun. ACM,* Vol. 14, No. 4, April 1971, pp. 221–227.
3. Stay, J. F., "HIPO and Integrated Program Design," *IBM Syst. J.,* Vol. 15, No. 2, 1976, pp. 143–154.
4. Warnier, J. D., *Logical Construction of Programs,* New York: Van Nostrand, 1974.
5. Orr, K. T., *Structured System Design,* New York: Yourdon Press, 1978.
6. Warnier, J. D., *Logical Construction of Systems,* New York: Van Nostrand, 1981.
7. Jackson, M. A., *Principles of Program Design,* New York: Academic Press, 1975.
8. Jackson, M., *System Development,* Englewood Cliffs, N.J.: Prentice-Hall, 1983.
9. Stevens, W., G. Myers, and L. Constantine, "Structured Design," *IBM Syst. J.,* Vol. 13, No. 2, 1974, pp. 115–139.
10. Yourdon, E., and L. Constantine, *Structured Design,* Englewood Cliffs, N.J.: Prentice-Hall, 1979.
11. Simpson, H. R., and K. Jackson, "Process Synchronization in MASCOT," *Comput. J.,* Vol. 22, No. 4, 1979, pp. 332–345.
12. Page-Jones, M., "Transform Analysis," *The Practical Guide to Structured Systems Design,* New York: Yourdon Press, 1980, pp. 181–203.
13. Page-Jones, M., "Transaction Analysis," *The Practical Guide to Structured Systems Design,* New York: Yourdon Press, 1980, pp. 207–219.
14. Dijkstra, E. W., "Programming Considered as a Human Activity," *Proc. IFIPS Congr., 1965,* pp. 213–217.
15. Dijkstra, E. W., "GoTo Statement Considered Harmful," *Commun. ACM,* Vol. 11, No. 3, March 1968, pp. 147–148.
16. Bohm, C., and G. Jacopini, "Flow Diagrams, Turing Machines and Languages with Only Two Formation Rules," *Commun. ACM,* Vol. 9, No. 5, May 1966, pp. 366–371.

17. Shooman, Martin L., *Software Engineering,* New York: McGraw-Hill, 1983.
18. Nassi, I., and B. Schneiderman, "Flowchart Techniques for Structured Programming," *SIGPLAN Notices ACM,* Vol. 8, No. 8, August 1973, pp. 12–26.
19. Booch, Grady, *Software Engineering with Ada,* New York: Benjamin/Cummings, 1983.
20. ACM SIGSOFT Rapid Prototyping Workshop, April 1982, published as *ACM Software Eng. News,* Vol. 7, No. 5, December 1982.

EXERCISES

1. Design a text formatter using the specifications developed in Exercise 1 of Chapter 2. Use data flow design.

2. Design a screen-oriented text editor with the specifications developed in Exercise 2 of Chapter 2. Use HIPO charts and Warnier diagrams to support your design.

3. Design a registration system employing the specifications developed in Exercise 3 of Chapter 2. Use SADT methodology.

4. Design a business inventory system using the specifications developed in Exercise 4 of Chapter 2. Use the Jackson design method.

5. Design a grammar checker. Use the specifications developed in Exercise 5 of Chapter 2. Use object-oriented design coupled with modular design charts.

6. Design an airline reservation system with the specifications developed in Exercise 6 of Chapter 2. Use object-oriented design coupled with modular design charts.

7. Design a rollbook program using the specifications developed in Exercise 7 of Chapter 2. Use data flow design.

8. Develop several design prototypes, using rapid prototyping, for your registration system. Document the performance of each of your prototypes and indicate the reasons for your choice of the final design structure.

9. Display pseudo-code and Nassi–Schneiderman diagrams for the important algorithms used in connection with any of the projects given in Exercises 1 to 7.

10. Compare the design methodologies used in the projects given in Exercises 1 to 7. Are certain design methodologies more suited to particular problem areas? If so, explain in detail.

Chapter 5 ———————————————————————

MODULAR SOFTWARE DEVELOPMENT USING ADA

At the end of Chapter 4 we introduced object-oriented design and modular software construction. We believe that this approach to software design provides the potential for highly reliable and easily maintainable software. Ada and Modula-2 are particularly well suited to support this type of software development.

In this chapter we focus on object-oriented design and modular software construction in Ada. In the next chapter we do the same for Modula-2. To set the stage for our presentation of modular software construction with Ada, we briefly review the rationale for the development of Ada and its relation to software engineering. The reader may wish to consult our previous book [1] for details concerning the syntax of Ada.

5.1 WHY ADA?

For a number of years before 1975, the U.S. Department of Defense (DoD) recognized that the cost of military software systems was increasing at an alarming rate. These software systems tended to be large, consisting of thousands and sometimes millions of lines of code that often had a life cycle of 10 to 15 years. DoD software problems also tended to be subjected to continually changing requirements. Physical constraints such as memory and execution speed and the necessity for high reliability were, and continue to be, typical characteristics of DoD software systems.

Several symptoms of the escalating software cost problem, noted by the DoD, were that software development projects were behind schedule, over budget, unreliable, and often not to the original specifications. The last two symptoms implied that the problem was not only the cost of the software system but also the poor quality of the delivered product. Rapidly escalating life cycle costs, in particular, the high cost of maintenance, constituted another serious symptom. Language proliferation was also identified as a symptom of the problem. Programming languages were being developed and/or used that were not suitable for the application and did not support modern programming and software engineering practices.

The DoD determined that inability to manage complexity was a major factor contributing to the problem. This was attributed to inadequate use of modern software engineering methodologies such as modular programming, top-down and bottom-up development, and software development tools. Often when software development tools were selected they were of marginal usefulness.

Another problem noted by the DoD was the lack of software and programmer portability. Large expenses were associated with moving software from one location to another and with simply moving the software to an upgraded hardware system. Different computing environments also made it necessary to incur the expense of retraining programmers for the new environment.

Many factors have contributed to the "software crisis." The failure of organizations to understand the life cycle implications of software development is certainly one cause of the problem. Related to this is the shortage of personnel properly trained in software engineering. Inertia is another cause. That is, organizations become so entrenched in the use of archaic programming languages and practices that it is very difficult to introduce modern languages and software development practices.

To deal with the escalating costs of military software systems, the DoD formed the High Order Language Working Group (HOLWG) in 1975. The HOLWG identified DoD requirements for high order languages and evaluated many existing languages against these requirements. All existing languages were found to be inadequate for the long term, and no language satisfied the requirements for a common language. The recommendation of the HOLWG was to design a new language and programming environment. The HOLWG determined that a single language to meet all DoD requirements was both feasible and desirable. This language eventually was named Ada and the programming environment is now known as APSE (Ada Programming Support Environment).

Ada was designed and implemented using good standard software engineering practices. That is, there was an analysis phase, a requirements definition phase, a design phase, an implementation phase, and an operational and maintenance phase. Hence, Ada is a product of the software engineering process. The interested reader is referred to Booch [2] for a brief history of the development of Ada from 1975 through 1982.

Ada is a design language that is suitable for the design and implementation phases of the software life cycle. Ada directly embodies, encourages, and enforces modern software engineering principles and methodologies. Ada is not only a programming language but it is also a programming environment and a way of thinking. Ada brings together the best of programming technology in a coherent way designed to meet the needs of practical programmers. It is expected that the many features of Ada will help reduce the cost and improve the quality of software. Specifically, Ada is expected to reduce software life cycle costs, to encourage investment in software support technology, to improve the adaptability of software personnel, to encourage the development of reliable and reusable software, and to encourage disciplined software engineering.

5.2 PRINCIPLES OF SOFTWARE ENGINEERING AND ADA

The most important principles of software engineering are abstraction and modularity.

Abstraction and information hiding are supported in Ada by the typing mechanisms of the language, by the separation between the specification and implementation of program units, by the private part of a package specification, and by the enforcement of defined interfaces.

Ada supports modularity via program units, separate compilation, and generic units. Program units provide a mechanism for the programmer to collect logically related entities in one place. Ada also supports top-down and bottom-up development strategies to assist in modular software design and construction.

5.3 ADA FROM THE TOP DOWN

Ada systems are collections of program units. A program unit is a subprogram (procedure or function), a package, or a task. A subprogram usually defines a single action or operation, a task defines a parallel action, and a package defines a collection of computational resources including data types, data objects, subprograms, tasks, and other packages.

Packages express and enforce the logical abstractions defined by the software developer. They permit the collection of groups of logically related entities and encourage the development of reusable software modules.

A unique and powerful Ada construct is the generic program unit. These program units define high level templates that permit parameterization of subprograms and packages. The generic unit encourages the development of general-purpose software libraries that operate on abstract data objects.

All program units in Ada have two parts: a specification or visible part and a body or hidden part. The body contains the implementation details of the resources indicated in the specification. The body can be logically and textually hidden from the user. Using package specifications, Ada permits a software engineer to develop and specify the software system architecture, thereby creating an enforceable design structure. As development proceeds, the unit bodies or implementation details may be refined.

5.4 ADA TYPES AND DATA STRUCTURES FOR EFFECTIVE DESIGN

A type definition characterizes a set of values and a set of operations applicable to objects of the named type. Carefully defined data types improve and support program readability and maintainability because they allow a problem to be described in terms of the actual objects that arise in the problem definition. Since a problem is more naturally described, it is also more easily understood. The properties of the abstract objects are easily related to the real-world objects. Properly defined types also improve reliability and tend to reduce complexity. Reliability is improved because a strongly typed language guarantees that properties of objects are not violated. Complexity is reduced because implementation details may be hidden.

An Ada attribute is a predefined characteristic of a type, object, or entity. Ada offers a variety of attribute inquiries that provide values that the software engineer may find useful in controlling the course of a computation. Attribute inquiries are also available for determining various characteristics of the underlying computer. The careful use of attributes can lead to more versatile, reliable, maintainable, and readable software.

We now present an example to illustrate how the type features of Ada and the use of attributes and unconstrained types may be used to develop robust software.

Program 5.1 gives a procedure for adding two matrices. Some predefined Ada attributes are used to ensure that the two matrices to be added are dimensionally compatible even though the subscript limits for each matrix are not necessarily the same. The use of the ''+'' for the name of the matrix addition procedure illustrates how the use of operator overloading effectively extends the utility of the language into the domain of matrix processing.

PROGRAM 5.1 **Attributes and Unconstrained Array Types in Ada**

```
type MATRIX is array (INTEGER range <>, INTEGER range <>)
                of FLOAT;

function ''+'' (A, B : MATRIX) return MATRIX is
    C : MATRIX (A'RANGE(1), A'RANGE(2));
        --The resulting matrix will have the subscript
        --range of A.
```

```
  P : constant INTEGER := B'FIRST(1) − A'FIRST(1);
  Q : constant INTEGER := B'FIRST(2) − A'FIRST(2);
    --P and Q are the offsets of the first and second
    --subscripts of B with respect to A.
begin
  if A'LENGTH(1) /= B'LENGTH(1)
    or A'LENGTH(2) /= B'LENGTH(2) then
    raise CONSTRAINT_ERROR;
  else
    for ROW in A'RANGE(1) loop
      for COLUMN in A'RANGE(2) loop
        C(ROW,COLUMN) := A(ROW, COLUMN) + B(ROW+P, COLUMN+Q);
      end loop;
    end loop;
  end if;
  return C;
end "+";
```

For floating point computation, Ada includes at least one predefined type FLOAT. Some implementations of Ada may also include other predefined types such as SHORT_FLOAT and LONG_FLOAT, which have, respectively, substantially less or more precision than FLOAT. One view of software is to consider it an extension to the hardware, and so it might seem reasonable to develop software in terms of these predefined types. However, this would not be desirable for reasons of portability. The Ada language specifications do not state any specific accuracy for FLOAT, and since this is the name assigned, if there is only one floating point type, the actual accuracy is likely to vary considerably.

As an example, consider the following declaration.

```
type REAL is digits 8;
X,Y,Z : REAL;
```

This declaration is guaranteed to be portable because it is a programmer-defined type that is implemented by the compiler to satisfy the accuracy constraint. In this case, we are guaranteed that the objects X, Y, and Z have at least eight significant digits of precision, which, presumably, is required for the problem being solved. If, however, we use the declaration

```
X,Y,Z : FLOAT;
```

we may or may not have eight significant digits of precision, depending on the implementation. If the implementation yields only six significant digits, the software may fail.

Most of the properties of a type or object can be accessed by the use of attributes. This enables a software developer to anticipate the problems of moving the software to another machine. For example, an approximation may be known to be accurate for eight digits but not more, in which case one can write:

```
if REAL'DIGITS <= 8 then
    SIMPLE_APPROXIMATION
else
    MORE_ACCURATE_APPROXIMATION
end if;
```

5.5   USING ADA SUBPROGRAMS FOR EFFECTIVE DESIGN

A program may be conceptualized as a collection of functional components and data objects that interact through a series of sequential or parallel actions. The actions should reflect an abstraction of the processes of the real world. No computer language can be expected to provide operations that mimic every conceivable action that might arise. Instead, computer languages usually provide subprograms as a mechanism for the software developer to specify high level actions that may be synthesized from more primitive instructions that are available in the language. Ada allows us to define subprograms and subprogram stubs. Using program stubs we can defer the implementation of the subprograms while developing additional software that uses the specified facilities of the subprogram stubs.

Subprograms may contain locally declared objects. Global objects may be visible to a subprogram and thus modified by the subprogram. This is not a good practice because this increases the coupling between program units. Instead, it is a better practice to use parameters to pass objects of any type to and from a subprogram. Parameters in Ada may be passed in one of three binding modes.

in	Only the actual value can be used and the subprogram cannot modify the value.
out	The subprogram assigns a value but does not use the value of the parameter.
in out	The subprogram may use the value of the parameter and assign a new value to it.

5.6 USING ADA PACKAGES AND OVERLOADING FOR EFFECTIVE DESIGN

One of the most important features of Ada is the language construct that supports software modules, namely, packages. An Ada package has the same purpose as a Modula-2 module. Generally, the package unit contains functionally related components (data types, objects, and subprograms) that may be used in other programs as a computational resource. The structure of the package dictates its use. Packages whose primary purpose is to collect and name the types and objects that are to be used in the software system may be defined. Packages may be defined as a group of related program units such as a mathematical library of subprograms.

As indicated earlier, Ada permits the software developer to separate the specification of a package from its implementation. This capability is critically important for modular software construction. The specification identifies and describes the accessible parts of a package and indicates how they may be used. Using the terminology of Modula-2, the package exports these entities. It is not important for the other members of a design team to understand how the resources in the package are implemented. Computational resources can be made available without revealing the implementation details.

Since the specification part of a package may be compiled separately from the implementation part, one would create the package specification early in the design process and then develop the body later. The specification would be compiled and placed in the compilation library for the project. Other members of the software development team would then have access to the interface as they develop their respective units.

Good design documentation is part of any software development project. The logical place to locate design documentation related to a package is in the package specification. This might include a user's guide for the package and illustrations that show the actual use of the package resources. The design documentation, user's guide and illustrations may all be presented as comments in the package specification.

To illustrate a package and how a client program gains access to the resources of the package, we consider Program 5.2, a package specification for solving a linear system of equations.

PROGRAM 5.2   Specification for Package Linear Systems

```
package LINEAR_SYSTEMS is
    type MATRIX is array (INTEGER range <>, INTEGER
                      range <>) of FLOAT;
    type VECTOR is array (INTEGER range <>) of FLOAT;
    type PIVOT is array (INTEGER range <>) of INTEGER;
```

```
procedure LU_FACTOR (A : in out MATRIX; P: out PIVOT);
--LU_FACTOR factors the original matrix A into lower
--and upper triangular form via Gaussian elimination
--with partial pivoting. The original matrix A is
--destroyed because the factors LU are saved in A. The
--factored matrix LU and pivot information are
--returned in P for use with SOLVE and MATRIX_INVERSE.

procedure SOLVE (LU : in MATRIX; P: in PIVOT;
                    B : in VECTOR; X: out VECTOR);
--SOLVE solves the system of linear equations
--                     A * X = B.
--LU_FACTOR must be called before calling SOLVE.

procedure MATRIX_INVERSE (LU : in MATRIX; P: in PIVOT;
                    A_INVERSE : out MATRIX);
--MATRIX_INVERSE calculates A_INVERSE such that
                    A * A_INVERSE = I
--where I is the identity matrix. LU_FACTOR must be
--called before calling MATRIX_INVERSE.
end LINEAR_SYSTEMS;
```

The package LINEAR_SYSTEMS is visible to another program unit if it is declared within the program unit and is not hidden by another declaration. However, the usual and preferred method of using packages is to separately compile the package and then to establish accessibility to its features through the ''with'' clause. For example, consider the following program unit, which makes use of the LINEAR_SYSTEMS package to calculate the inverse of a 10×10 matrix.

```
with LINEAR_SYSTEMS;
procedure SIMULTANEOUS_EQUATIONS is
    A,AINVERSE : LINEAR_SYSTEMS.MATRIX(1..10,1..10);
    P          : LINEAR_SYSTEMS.PIVOT(1..10);
    --Other declarations
begin
    --Sequence of statements that create a 10 by 10 matrix
    LINEAR_SYSTEMS.LU_FACTOR(A, P);
    LINEAR_SYSTEMS.MATRIX_INVERSE(A, P, AINVERSE);
    --Sequence of statements that perform other desired
    --operations.
end SIMULTANEOUS_EQUATIONS;
```

In the preceding example, SIMULTANEOUS_EQUATIONS imports the unit LINEAR_SYSTEMS, thereby making the three type declarations and three procedures in LINEAR_SYSTEMS available. This approach supports modularity and localization, hence helps limit the scope of any changes that may occur during software maintenance. Another benefit of this approach is that it encourages reusable software units. The software resources provide by LINEAR_SYSTEMS play an important role in many numerical applications.

Once the package is accessible, parts of the specification may be identified with selected component notation as illustrated in the example above. This is somewhat awkward, so Ada provides the "use" clause to gain direct visibility to the specified package components without requiring the package name as a prefix. We repeat the preceding example using the "use" clause.

```
with LINEAR_SYSTEMS; use LINEAR_SYSTEMS;
procedure SIMULTANEOUS_EQUATIONS is
    A,AINVERSE : MATRIX(1. .10,1. .10);
    P             : PIVOT(1. .10);
    --Other declarations
begin
    --Sequence of statements that create a 10 by 10 matrix
    LU_FACTOR(A, P);
    MATRIX_INVERSE(A, P, AINVERSE);
    --Sequence of statements that perform other desired
    --operations.
end SIMULTANEOUS_EQUATIONS;
```

There is a distinct difference between Ada and Modula-2. In Modula-2 the client program must specifically indicate which module resources are to be imported or made available by using an "import" statement. In Ada, the "use" and "with" clauses make all the resources of the package specification available to the client or host program. Also in Modula-2 the module specification indicates which resources may be exported, whereas in Ada all resources indicated in the package specification are automatically exported. Modula-2's selective import and export statements may contribute to better program readability and scope control than Ada's "with" and "use" features.

From a software maintenance point of view, the implementation details of a package body may be changed without requiring a revision or recompilation of the program units that use the package. Such maintenance may consist of replacing an existing algorithm with an improved algorithm or correcting an error in the implementation.

The next example illustrates how overloading of operators in conjunction with packages may be used to support software modularity in an important problem that arises in many engineering applications. The problem involves solving a system of differential equations of the form

$$\frac{d\mathbf{y}}{dt} = \mathbf{f}(t, \mathbf{y}) \qquad a <= t <= b$$

$$\mathbf{y}(a) = \mathbf{y}_0$$

where $\mathbf{y} = (y_1, y_2, \ldots, y_{NODE})$ and $\mathbf{y}_0$ is the vector of initial conditions. The objective is to approximate the solution to the problem at $N + 1$ equally spaced points in the interval $[a,b]$. The input to the problem is the starting value for t which in this case is a, the final value of t, which is b, the integer N, and the vector of initial conditions. The output is the calculated values for the vector $\mathbf{y}$ at $N + 1$ values of t.

A common algorithm for solving this problem is the Runge–Kutta algorithm, which can be found in many texts on numerical analysis [3]. The steps in the algorithm are usually presented in the following manner.

RUNGE–KUTTA ALGORITHM FOR SYSTEMS OF ORDINARY DIFFERENTIAL EQUATIONS

Step 1: Set $h = (b - a)/N$

$\qquad t = a$

$\qquad y = y_0$

$\qquad$ OUTPUT (t, y)

Step 2: For $i = 1, 2, \ldots, N$ do steps 3–5.

$\qquad$ **Step 3:** Set $k_1 = h\,f(t, y)$

$$k_2 = h f\left(t + \frac{h}{2}, y + \frac{k_1}{2}\right)$$

$$k_3 = h f\left(t + \frac{h}{2}, y + \frac{k_2}{2}\right)$$

$$k_4 = h f(t + h, y + k_3)$$

$\qquad$ **Step 4:** Set $y = y + \dfrac{k_1 + 2k_2 + 2k_3 + k_4}{6}$

$$t = a + i h$$

$\qquad$ **Step 5:** OUTPUT (t, y)

Step 6: Stop.

Note that in step 3 all the k's are vectors of length NODE, that $h\mathbf{f}(\cdot\ \cdot\ \cdot)$ involves multiplying the scalar h times the vector $\mathbf{f}$, that $k_1/2$ and $k_2/2$ involve dividing a vector by a scalar, and that forming $\mathbf{y} + \mathbf{k}_1/2$, $\mathbf{y} + \mathbf{k}_2/2$, and $\mathbf{y} + \mathbf{k}_3$

involves adding two vectors together each of length NODE. Step 4 also involves multiplying a vector by a scalar and adding vectors together.

The usual approach for designing code to perform steps 3 and 4 is the following.

*Call f(t, y), return the vector **ydot**.*

For j = 1, . . . , NODE do
$\quad$*Set **k1**(j) = h * ydot(j)*

$$ytemp(j) = y(j) + \frac{k1(j)}{2}$$

*Call f(t + h/2, **ytemp**), return the vector **ydot**.*

For j = 1, . . . , NODE do
$\quad$*Set **k2**(j) = h * ydot(j)*

$$ytemp(j) = y(j) + \frac{k2(j)}{2}$$

*Call f(t + h/2, **ytemp**), return the vector **ydot**.*

For j = 1, . . . , NODE do
$\quad$*Set **k3**(j) = h * ydot(j)*
$\quad$*ytemp(j) = y(j) + k3(j)*

*Call f(t + h, **ytemp**), return the vector **ydot**.*

For j = 1, . . . , NODE do
$\quad$*Set **k4**(j) = h * ydot(j)*

$$y(j) = y(j) + \frac{k1(j) + 2 * k2(j) + 2 * k3(j) + k4(j)}{6}$$

t = a + i h

We now present a package for performing the vector operations that will support the Runge–Kutta algorithm. Our goal is to produce software that will be as readable as the original algorithm.

The following package, which we have named MATH_LIB, contains the software resources that we need for this problem. We have included the SQRT function to permit easy solution of the problem defined below. The MATH_LIB package is an illustration of an Ada package that contains a group of related program units.

PROGRAM 5.3 Package MATH_LIB

```ada
with TEXT_IO; use TEXT_IO;

package MATH_LIB is

    type VECTOR is array(INTEGER range <>) of FLOAT;

    function "+" (X, Y: VECTOR) return VECTOR;
    function "*" (S: FLOAT; X: VECTOR) return VECTOR;
    function "/" (X: VECTOR; S: FLOAT) return VECTOR;
    function SQRT(N: in FLOAT) return FLOAT;

end MATH_LIB;
```

```ada
package body MATH_LIB is

    function "+" (X, Y: VECTOR) return VECTOR is
        Z: VECTOR(X'RANGE);
    begin
        for I in X'RANGE
            loop
                Z(I):= X(I) + Y(I);
            end loop;
        return Z;
    end "+";

    function "*" (S: FLOAT; X: VECTOR) return VECTOR is
        Z: VECTOR(X'RANGE);
    begin
        for I in X'RANGE
            loop
                Z(I):= S*X(I);
            end loop;
        return Z;
    end "*";

    function "/" (X: VECTOR; S: FLOAT) return VECTOR is
        Z: VECTOR(X'RANGE);
    begin
        for I in X'RANGE
            loop
                Z(I):= X(I)/S;
            end loop;
```

```
            return Z;
      end "/";

      function SQRT(N: in FLOAT) return FLOAT is
            XO,XOLD    : FLOAT;
            CONVERGE : BOOLEAN;
            NMAX       : INTEGER := 8;
            EPS        : FLOAT := 0.000001;
            NEGATIVE,ACCURACY: exception;
      begin
            if N < 0.0 then
                  raise NEGATIVE;
            end if;
            X0 := N/2.0;
            XOLD := X0;
            for I in 1. .NMAX
                  loop
                        CONVERGE := TRUE;
                        exit when abs(X0*X0-N) <= EPS*N;
                        X0 := (X0*X0+N)/(2.0*X0);
                        exit when abs(X0-XOLD) <= EPS*N;
                        XOLD := X0;
                        CONVERGE := FALSE;
                  end loop;
            if not CONVERGE then
                  raise ACCURACY;
            end if;
            return X0;
      exception
            when NEGATIVE =>
                  put("The square root of the negative number ");
                  put(item=>N);
                  put(" is not permitted.");
                  put_line;
                  put("The square root of ");
                  put(item=>-N);
                  put(" will be returned.");
                  return SQRT (-N);
            when ACCURACY =>
                  put("The iteration for square root did not converge.");
                  put_line;
                  put("The square root may not be accurate.");
                  return X0;
      end SQRT;
end MATH_LIB;
```

To illustrate the use of this package, we solve a problem that describes the motion of two bodies under mutual gravitational attraction. The solution is an elliptical orbit. This problem consists of solving four coupled nonlinear differential equations that describe the orbit. The differential equations and the initial conditions are as follows.

$$\frac{dy_1}{dt} = y_2 \qquad\qquad y_1(0) = 2$$

$$\frac{dy_2}{dt} = \frac{-16\, y_1}{(y_1^2 + y_3^2)} \qquad y_2(0) = 0$$

$$\frac{dy_3}{dt} = y_4 \qquad\qquad y_3(0) = 0$$

$$\frac{dy_4}{dt} = \frac{-16\, y_3}{(y_1^2 + y_3^2)} \qquad y_4(0) = 2\sqrt{3}$$

We wish to obtain a calculated solution for the interval $t = 0$ to $t = 13$ at 130 equally spaced points (i.e., $h = 0.1$). At $t = 13$, we have completed one orbit and are beginning the second orbit. Program 5.4 solves this problem. The main program is of particular interest because it is almost identical to the algorithm presented above.

PROGRAM 5.4 Ada ODE Program that Uses MATH_LIB Package

```
with TEXT_IO, MATH_LIB; use TEXT_IO, MATH_LIB;

procedure RUNGE_KUTTA is

    SIZE        : constant INTEGER := 4;
    A,B,H,T     : FLOAT;
    K1,K2,K3,K4 : VECTOR(1..SIZE);
    N           : INTEGER;
    Y           : VECTOR(1..SIZE);

    function F(T: FLOAT; Y: VECTOR) return VECTOR is
        YDOT : VECTOR(1..SIZE);
        TERM : FLOAT;
    begin
        TERM := -16.0/(SQRT(Y(1)**2 + Y(3)**2))**3;
        YDOT(1) := Y(2);
        YDOT(2) := TERM*Y(1);
        YDOT(3) := Y(4);
```

```
        YDOT(4) := TERM*Y(3);
        return YDOT;
    end F;

    function YINITIAL(A: FLOAT) return VECTOR is
        Y: VECTOR(1..SIZE);
    begin
        Y(1) := 2.0;
        Y(2) := 0.0;
        Y(3) := 0.0;
        Y(4) := 2.0*SQRT(3.0);
        return Y;
    end YINITIAL;

    procedure OUTPUT(T: FLOAT; Y: VECTOR) is
    begin
        put_line;
        put(T);
        for I in Y'RANGE
            loop
                    put(Y(I));
            end loop;
    end OUTPUT;

    procedure INPUT(A,B: out FLOAT; N: out INTEGER) is
    begin
        put_line;
        put("Enter initial time: ");
        get(item=>A);
        put_line;
        put("Enter final time: ");
        get(item=>B);
        put_line;
        put("Enter number of time steps: ");
        get(item=>N);
    end INPUT;

begin -- Main program
    INPUT (A,B,N);
    H := (B-A)/FLOAT(N);
    T := A;
    Y := YINITIAL(T);
    OUTPUT (T,Y);
    for I in 1..N
```

```
        loop
            K1 := H*F(T,Y);
            K2 := H*F(T + H/2.0,Y + K1/2.0);
            K3 := H*F(T + H/2.0,Y + K2/2.0);
            K4 := H*F(T + H,Y + K3);
            Y  := Y + (K1 + 2.0*K2 + 2.0*K3 + K4)/6.0;
            T  := T + H;
            OUTPUT (T,Y);
        end loop;
    end RUNGE_KUTTA;
```

Ada packages enforce the principle of abstraction through private types. Private types permit a programmer to create objects whose logical properties are manipulated outside the package but whose structural details are inaccessible. If a package contains a private type definition, the specification for the package must be split into two parts, visible and private (hidden). The private part completes the type definition. It contains information that the compiler needs to allocate storage for the objects declared in the private part. The information in the private part is not invisible to the user, but the user cannot access the information contained in the private part in any way. This is in contrast to Modula-2, where private types are referred to as "opaque" types, which are truly invisible as well as inaccessible to the user.

There are simple private types and limited private types. In either case, the only information available to the client program is that given in the visible part of the package specification. The type name is available to the user program along with those operations declared in the package specification. For simple private types, the operations of assignment and test for equality and inequality are also available. For limited private types, assignment and test for equality and inequality are not available unless explicitly provided for in the package specification.

To illustrate this consider the specification for the package COMPLEX-_ARITHMETIC given in Program 5.5.

PROGRAM 5.5   Package Specification for Complex Arithmetic

```
package COMPLEX_ARITHMETIC is
    type COMPLEX is
        record
            REAL_PART  : FLOAT;
            IMAG_PART  : FLOAT;
        end record;
```

```
    function "+" (A,B : in COMPLEX) return COMPLEX;
    function "−" (A,B : in COMPLEX) return COMPLEX;
    function "*" (A,B : in COMPLEX) return COMPLEX;
end COMPLEX_ARITHMETIC;
```

In the preceding specification the user has access to the real and imaginary parts of complex numbers. So even though COMPLEX is an abstract data type, the abstraction is not enforceable because the type is not private and its structure is therefore accessible. A user could violate this abstraction by manipulating the real and imaginary parts of a complex number and the language would not be able to detect this infraction. To enforce a logical abstraction, we must use private types. The use of private types for the package COMPLEX-_ARITHMETIC is given in Program 5.6.

PROGRAM 5.6 **Package Specification for Complex Arithmetic with Data Hiding**

```
package COMPLEX_ARITHMETIC is
    type COMPLEX is private;
    function MAKE (U,V : in FLOAT)   return COMPLEX;
    function REAL  (A : in COMPLEX) return FLOAT;
    function IMAG  (A : in COMPLEX) return FLOAT;
    function "+" (A,B : in COMPLEX) return COMPLEX;
    function "−" (A,B : in COMPLEX) return COMPLEX;
    function "*" (A,B : in COMPLEX) return COMPLEX;
private
    type COMPLEX is
        record
            REAL_PART  : FLOAT;
            IMAG_PART  : FLOAT;
        end record;
end COMPLEX_ARITHMETIC;
```

Note that we had to add features to the package so that the user can create and obtain the real and imaginary parts of complex numbers. This was necessary because the user of this package no longer has access to the structure of the complex numbers.

Many problems that arise in computing involve the use of stacks, queues, trees, or linked lists as the underlying data type. For a description of each of these data types and the operations usually performed on them you may wish to consult a reference on data structures [4,5]. The operations that need to be performed on each of these data types are independent of the representation details of the data type.

Programs 5.7 and 5.8 illustrate how stacks and queues may be specified as packages so that they can be used as abstract data types by other program units.

PROGRAM 5.7   Package Specification for Stacks

```
package STACKS is
    type STACK (SIZE : POSITIVE) is limited private;
    procedure INITIALIZE ( S : in out STACK);
    function   IS_EMPTY ( S : STACK) return BOOLEAN;
    procedure PUSH ( ITEM : in INTEGER; ON : in out STACK);
    procedure POP   ( FROM : in out STACK; ITEM : out INTEGER);
    function   DEPTH( S : STACK) return INTEGER;
    OVERFLOW, UNDERFLOW : exception;
private
    type LIST is array (INTEGER range <>) of INTEGER;
    type STACK (SIZE : POSITIVE) is
        record
            OBJECTS : LIST(1. .SIZE);
            TOP       : INTEGER range 0. .SIZE;
        end record;
end STACKS;
```

PROGRAM 5.8   Package Specification for Queues

```
package QUEUES is
    type QUEUE (LENGTH : NATURAL) is limited private;
    procedure INITIALIZE (NAME : in out QUEUE);
    procedure INSERT   (ITEM : in INTEGER; ON : in out QUEUE);
    procedure REMOVE (ITEM : out INTEGER; FROM : in out QUEUE);
    function   IS_EMPTY  (NAME : QUEUE) return BOOLEAN;
    function   LENGTH  (NAME : QUEUE) return INTEGER;
    OVERFLOW, UNDERFLOW : exception;
private
    type COLLECTION is array (INTEGER range <> ) of INTEGER;
    type QUEUE (LENGTH : NATURAL) is
        record
            ITEMS  : COLLECTION (0. .LENGTH);
            FRONT : INTEGER;
            BACK   : INTEGER;
        end record;
end QUEUES;
```

The preceding package specifications define a stack and a queue data structure as an abstract type. In the specification for the queue package, note the use of a record discriminant that permits the user to define queues of differing lengths. Since we have defined a stack and a queue to be limited private, the user is prohibited from assigning stack or queue objects to each other and from comparing two stacks or two queues for equality. The principal restriction of these abstractions for stacks and queues is that the items in the respective data structures must be integers. In the next section we show how this restriction may be removed by defining a generic stack and a generic queue that permits the user to define stacks and queues that may operate on objects of any data type.

5.7 GENERICS AND THEIR USE IN EFFECTIVE DESIGN

In the process of designing a software system, we usually encounter subprograms or packages that have a similar purpose but operate on data objects of different types. For example, suppose that we have developed a sorting algorithm for an array of integers. We may be required to sort an array of names, real numbers, or records. Typically, we would have to rewrite the subprogram to take account of the new data type even though the underlying algorithm would remain the same. Generic program units in Ada permit the software developer to create subprograms and packages that provide computational resources for abstract data types. In particular, a generic sorting subprogram would implement a sorting algorithm independent of the type of objects to be sorted. This allows the abstraction of sorting to be taken to its full limit.

Generic units define templates of program units that may be written just once and then tailored to particular needs at translation time. Useful generic units might be subprograms and packages for stacks, queues, linked lists, and trees. Operations on these data types are encountered in many application areas. Other useful generic units might include vector operations, matrix operations, and mathematical libraries. For vector and matrix operations, the size of the vectors and matrices and the elements contained in the vectors and matrices may vary from application to application. A mathematical library may have a floating point precision specification as a generic parameter.

Since sorting is required in many applications, we begin by giving an example of a generic sorting algorithm. The generic prefix to the sorting procedure is:

```
generic
    type OBJECT is private;
    type INDEX is (<>);
    type OBJECT_ARRAY is array (INDEX range <>) of OBJECT;
    with function">"(U,V: OBJECT) return BOOLEAN is <>;
    procedure SORT( A: in out OBJECT_ARRAY);
```

The formal function ''>'' corresponds to the ordering relation on the object type. If the relation''>'' is not currently defined for the objects to be sorted, the package user must provide a function that defines this relation.

To use a generic procedure, the procedure must be instantiated. Instantiation is the process of creating an instance of the generic subprogram or package at compilation time. This requires us to provide an identifier for the program unit and to supply actual parameters for the generic parameters. For example, to instantiate the generic sorting algorithm that will sort an array of integers indexed by the letters of the alphabet, we could do the following.

```
type ALPHABET is  ('a'..'z');
type SPECIAL_ARRAY is array (ALPHABET) of INTEGER;
procedure NEW_SORT is new SORT( OBJECT => INTEGER,
    INDEX => ALPHABET, OBJECT_ARRAY => SPECIAL_ARRAY,
    ">" => ">");
```

To use this sorting procedure, we would call it in the same manner that we would call any other procedure. For example,

```
NEW_SORT( SAMPLE);
```

where SAMPLE is of type SPECIAL_ARRAY.

Ada does not permit function or procedure names as parameters in procedure calls. The generic facility of the language permits us to simulate this capability, which is important in some application areas. For example, suppose that we wish to develop an adaptive integration procedure to integrate a user-defined function over the interval from A to B. We could define the following generic.

```
generic
    with function F(X : REAL) return REAL;
    procedure INTEGRATE (A,B : in REAL; ANSWER : out
                         REAL);
```

To integrate the user-defined function USER_F that has been defined with the declaration

```
function USER_F (X : REAL) return REAL;
```

requires the instantiation

```
procedure INTEGRATE_USER_F is new INTEGRATE (USER_F);
```

followed by a procedure call

```
INTEGRATE_USER_F(A,B,RESULT);
```

As further examples, generic packages that define abstract stacks and queues are given in Programs 5.9 and 5.10. We have modified the internal structure for the abstract types stack and queue so that the user does not have to specify a ''size'' for the stack or queue when objects of these types are declared.

PROGRAM 5.9   Generic Package Specification for Stacks

```
generic
    type OBJECT is private;
package STACKS is
    type STACK is limited private;
    procedure     INITIALIZE ( S : in out STACK);
    function      IS_EMPTY ( S : STACK) return BOOLEAN;
    procedure     PUSH ( ITEM : in OBJECT; ON : in out STACK);
    procedure     POP   ( FROM : in out STACK; ITEM : out OBJECT);
    function      DEPTH( S : STACK) return INTEGER;
    UNDERFLOW : exception;
private
    type NODE;
    type STACK is access NODE;
    type NODE is
        record
            ITEM  : OBJECT;
            NEXT  : STACK;
        end record;
end Stacks;
```

PROGRAM 5.10   Generic Package Specification for Queues

```
generic
    type ELEMENT is private;
package QUEUES is
    type QUEUE is limited private;
    procedure     INITIALIZE  (NAME : in out QUEUE);
    procedure     INSERT   (ITEM : in  ELEMENT; ON     : in out QUEUE):
    procedure     REMOVE (ITEM : out ELEMENT; FROM : in out QUEUE);
    function      IS_EMPTY  (NAME : QUEUE) return BOOLEAN;
```

```
    function      LENGTH ( NAME : QUEUE) return INTEGER;
    UNDERFLOW : exception;
private
    type NODE_PTR is access NODE;
    type NODE is
        record
            ITEM  : ELEMENT;
            NEXT  : NODE_PTR;
        end record;
    type QUEUE is
        record
            FRONT : NODE_PTR:
            REAR  : NODE_PTR;
        end record;
end QUEUES;
```

As a final example of a generic package, we present Program 5.11, a generic unit for performing vector operations in Program 5.10.

PROGRAM 5.11   Generic Package for Vector Operations

```
generic
    type ITEM is private;
        --No operations on ITEM may be assumed.
    type INDEX is (<>);
        --INDEX is a discrete type
    type VECTOR is array (INDEX range <>) of ITEM;
        --with function "+"(X,Y: ITEM) return ITEM is <>;
        --with function "*"(X,Y: ITEM) return ITEM is <>;

package VECTOR_OPERATIONS is

    type VECTOR is private;

    function "+"(X,Y: VECTOR) return VECTOR;
    function "*"(X,Y: VECTOR) return VECTOR;
    function SUM(X: VECTOR) return INTEGER;
    function DOT(X,Y: VECTOR) return INTEGER;

private

    type VECTOR is array (INDEX) of INTEGER;

end VECTOR_OPERATIONS;
```

```
package body VECTOR_OPERATIONS is

    function POS(X: INDEX) return INTEGER is
    begin
        return INDEX'POS(X);
    end POS;

    function VAL(X: INTEGER) return INDEX is
    begin
        return INDEX'VAL(X);
    end VAL;

    function "+"(X,Y: VECTOR) return VECTOR is
        Z: VECTOR;
        B: constant INTEGER := POS(Y'FIRST)-POS(X'FIRST);
    begin
        if X'LENGTH /= Y'LENGTH then
            raise CONSTRAINT_ERROR;
        end if;
        for I in INDEX
            loop
                Z(I) := X(I) + Y(VAL(POS(I)+B));
            end loop;
        return Z;
    end"+";

    function "*"(X,Y: VECTOR) return VECTOR is
        Z: VECTOR;
        B: constant INTEGER := POS(Y'FIRST)-POS(X'FIRST);
    begin
        if X'LENGTH /= Y'LENGTH then
            raise CONSTRAINT_ERROR;
        end if;
        for I in INDEX
            loop
                Z(I) := X(I) * Y(VAL(POS(I)+B));
            end loop;
        return Z;
    end "*";

    function SUM(X: VECTOR) return INTEGER is
        R: INTEGER;
    begin
        if X'LENGTH = 0 then
            raise CONSTRAINT_ERROR;
```

```
    elsif X'LENGTH = 1 then
        return X(X'FIRST);
    else
        R := X(X'FIRST);
        for I in INDEX'SUCC(X'FIRST). .X'LAST
            loop
                R:=R+X(I);
            end loop;
        return R;
    end if;
end SUM;

function DOT(X,Y: VECTOR) return INTEGER is
begin
    return SUM(X*Y);
end DOT;

end VECTOR_OPERATIONS;
```

5.8 MODULAR SOFTWARE CONSTRUCTION IN ADA

In this section we describe modular software construction in Ada, and in Section 5.9 we illustrate portions of this process with a small case study.

The ability to perform the separate compilation of package specifications and package bodies provides the power necessary to do modular software construction in Ada and to use Ada as a program design language (PDL). The architecture of the system and the interfaces may be specified and compiled before the detailed design commences. The compiler enforces these interfaces during the development and implementation of each module.

The modular design chart introduced in Chapter 4 is a useful design aid for system architecture design in Ada. Such a design chart clearly indicates the resources available in each module, the interface connections of the module to the outside world, and the interconnection of the modules that comprise the design. This design chart may be used with packages including generic packages. Collections of related tasks are typically encapsulated in a package so that the modular design chart is also applicable to the design of concurrent real-time processing systems.

Figure 5.1 is a modular design chart containing the various components described above; generic parameters are bounded by dashed lines.

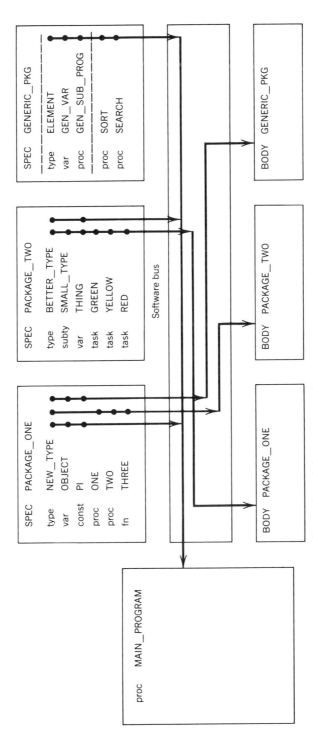

Figure 5.1 Modular design chart for various Ada program units.

5.9 USING ADA FOR MODULAR DESIGN:
A Small Case Study

Booch [2] identifies the following steps in object-oriented design:

1. Define the problem.

2. Develop an informal strategy.

3. Formalize the strategy.
Identify objects and their attributes.
Identify operations on the objects.
Establish the interfaces.
Implement the operations.

Our approach to object-oriented modular design, using as a centerpiece the modular design chart, consists of the steps presented in Table 5.1.

Table 5.1   Our Approach to Object-Oriented and Modular Software Construction

1. Define an informal strategy for the problem solution.
2. Identify objects used in the informal strategy.
3. Identify operations on the objects used in the informal strategy.
4. Define the software system architecture using one or more modular design charts.
5. Create a compilable modular design listing (in either Ada or Modula-2) that includes the initial version of the main driver program.
6. Develop the implementation details for each module.

In step 5 the compiler performs high level integration testing by checking all package and module interfaces for correctness. In step 6 additional software components (data types, procedures, etc.) may need to be created in some of the packages or modules to support the implementation portion of the system. Some of the steps in Table 5.1 may need to be iterated as the software construction progresses.

We now illustrate the process of modular and object-oriented design, modular programming, and program maintenance using Ada on a small case study, the KWIC index system. This case study omits several features mentioned in Section 4.4.2, namely, disk storage of all titles and nonkeywords and editing for these files. Instead, we assume that all titles and nonkeywords are input from the keyboard. We also ignore the location field for each title. This version is still sufficiently complicated to illustrate the use of Ada for modular software design and construction.

The KWIC index problem is described by Parnas [6]. Our design uses the methodology of object-oriented design and modular decomposition.

We begin with the following brief description and informal strategy for the KWIC index system.

Informal Strategy for KWIC Index System

1. Input a set of titles (each title consists of a set of keywords and nonkeywords).
2. Input the set of title words that are nonkeywords.
3. Count the number of words in the title NUM_WORDS.
4. Perform NUM_WORDS circular shifts on each title. Each circular shift involves removing the first word of the title and appending it to the end of the title. If the first word of the circularly shifted title is a keyword, add this title to the set of KWIC index entires.
5. Alphabetize the KWIC index entries.
6. Output the alphabetical listing of all KWIC index entires.

Table 5.2 identifies the basic objects of the KWIC system.

Table 5.2   Objects Identified for KWIC Index Problem

Titles
Keywords
Nonkeywords
KWIC entries

The operations on these objects are listed in Table 5.3.

Table 5.3   Operations for KWIC Index Problem

Input titles.
Input nonkeywords.
Obtains the NUM_WORDS for a title.
Perform all circular shifts for a title forming set of KWIC entires.
Alphabetize KWIC entires.
Output KWIC entires.

The software design for the KWIC index should not depend on the method used to store titles, nor should it depend on the procedure for storing KWIC entries. These implementation details may be modified in the future.

Our main data objects in the KWIC index problem are the titles of books. Data objects, called TITLES, are defined in terms of an abstract data type

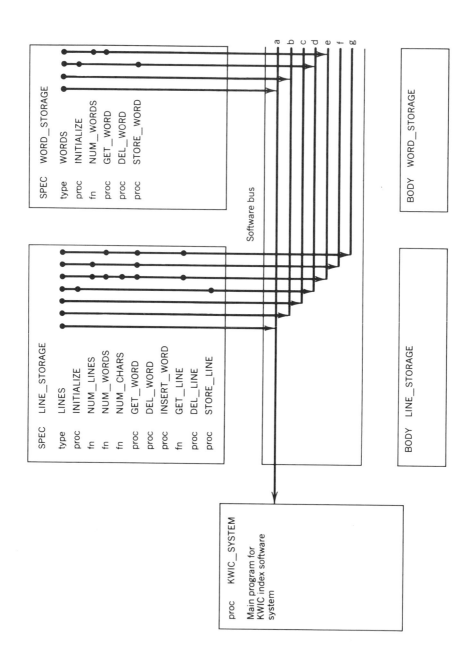

SPEC WORD_STORAGE

type WORDS
proc INITIALIZE
fn   NUM_WORDS
proc GET_WORD
proc DEL_WORD
proc STORE_WORD

SPEC LINE_STORAGE

type LINES
proc INITIALIZE
fn   NUM_LINES
fn   NUM_WORDS
fn   NUM_CHARS
proc GET_WORD
proc DEL_WORD
proc INSERT_WORD
fn   GET_LINE
proc DEL_LINE
proc STORE_LINE

Software bus

a
b
c
d
e
f
g

BODY WORD_STORAGE

BODY LINE_STORAGE

proc KWIC_SYSTEM

Main program for
KWIC index software
system

188

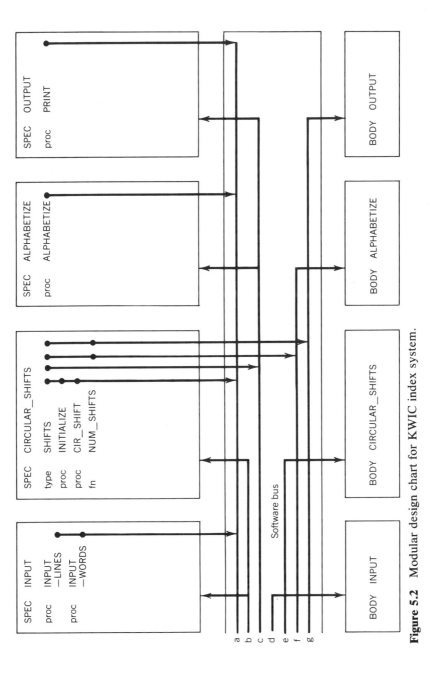

Figure 5.2 Modular design chart for KWIC index system.

LINES. The package LINE_STORAGE defines the abstract data type LINES and provides a variety of subprograms for accessing and storing information for objects of type LINES. The LINES abstraction represents the total set of titles that are input to the system. Almost every action required by the system will require the use of the resources of the LINE_STORAGE package. We have included more features in the LINE_STORAGE package than we need for the KWIC index system; thus this package constitutes a software resource that may be useful in other applications.

A package, named WORD_STORAGE, supports the necessary word handling required for the nonkeywords. This package contains a set of procedures that manipulate an abstract data type called WORDS. For example, procedure GET_WORD returns the *k*th word in a list of words. In this application, the list of words in question is the list of nonkeywords. The procedure STORE_WORD adds a new word to the list of nonkeywords.

A package, named CIRCULAR_SHIFTS, supports the operations of rotating the titles. The abstract data type SHIFTS supports the data object KWIC_ENTRIES. The procedure CIR_SHIFT actually performs circular shifts of all titles in the system, producing as output KWIC entries.

Additional packages called INPUT, ALPHABETIZE, and OUTPUT are defined to handle the other tasks required by the system.

The software system architecture that we have just described is encapsulated in the modular design chart shown in Figure 5.2.

We may use Ada as a program design language to represent the software system architecture depicted in Figure 5.2. Modular Design Listing 5.1 displays the appropriate package specifications for the KWIC index design.

MODULAR DESIGN LISTING 5.1 **System Architecture for KWIC Index System**

```
package LINE_STORAGE is

    type LINES (SIZE : NATURAL) is limited private;

    procedure INITIALIZE( L : in out LINES);
        --Initializes the line storage package. This procedure
        --must be called for each object of type LINES before any
        --other procedures or functions in this package are called
        --for the object.

    function NUM_LINES( L : LINES) return INTEGER;
        --Returns the number of lines.

    function NUM_WORDS( L : LINES; R : INTEGER) return INTEGER;
        --Returns the number of words in line R.
```

function NUM_CHARS (L : LINES; R, W : INTEGER) return INTEGER;
   --Returns the number of characters in the Wth word of
   --the Rth line.

procedure GET_WORD (L : in out LINES; R, W : in INTEGER;
                          WORD : out STRING; POSITION : out INTEGER);
   --Returns the Wth word in the Rth line and its beginning
   --character position in the line.

procedure DEL_WORD (L : in out LINES; R, W : in INTEGER);
   --Deletes the Wth word of the Rth line.

procedure INSERT_WORD (L : in out LINES; R, W : in INTEGER;
                          WORD : in STRING(1..15));
   --Inserts the WORD in the Wth position of the Rth line.

function GET_LINE (L : LINES; R : INTEGER) return STRING;
   --Returns the Rth line.

procedure DEL_LINE (L : in out LINES; R : in INTEGER);
   --Deletes the Rth line.

procedure STORE_LINE (L : in out LINES; LINE : in STRING(1..80));
   --Stores LINE in the line storage.

private

   type COLLECTION is array (INTEGER range <>) of STRING(1..80);
   type LINES (SIZE : NATURAL) is
      record
          DATA : COLLECTION (0..SIZE);
      end record;

end LINE_STORAGE;

----

package WORD_STORAGE is

   type WORDS (SIZE : NATURAL) is limited private;

   procedure INITIALIZE (W : in out WORDS);
      --Initializes the word storage package. This procedure must
      --be called for each object of type WORDS before any other
      --procedures of functions in this package are called for the
      --object.

```
    function NUM_WORDS ( W : WORDS) return INTEGER;
        --Returns the number of words.

    procedure GET_WORD ( W : in out WORDS; K : in INTEGER;
                                    WORD: out STRING);
        --Returns the Kth word.

    procedure DEL_WORD ( W : in out WORDS; K : in INTEGER);
        --Deletes the Kth word.

    procedure STORE_WORD ( W : in out WORDS; WORD : in STRING(1..15));
        --Stores WORD in the word storage.

private

    type LIST is array (INTEGER range <>) of STRING(1..15);
    type WORDS (SIZE : NATURAL) is
        record
            DATA : LIST (0..SIZE);
        end record;

end WORD_STORAGE;
```

```
with LINE_STORAGE, WORD_STORAGE;
use  LINE_STORAGE, WORD_STORAGE;

package INPUT is

        --The procedures in this package are especially tailored
        --for the KWIC index software system.

        --From LINE_STORAGE import type LINES.

        --From WORD_STORAGE import type WORDS.

    procedure INPUT (T : in out LINES);
        --This procedure is used to input a set of titles.

    procedure INPUT (K : in out WORDS);
        --This procedure is used to input the set on nonkeywords.

end INPUT;
```

```
with LINE_STORAGE, WORD_STORAGE;
use  LINE_STORAGE, WORD_STORAGE;
```

```
package CIRCULAR_SHIFTS is

        --From LINE_STORAGE import type LINES.
        --From WORD_STORAGE import type WORDS.

    type SHIFTS is limited private;

    procedure INITIALIZE ( S : in out SHIFTS);
        --Initializes the circular shift package. This procedure must
        --be called for each object of type SHIFTS before any other
        --procedure or function in this package are called for the
        --object.

    procedure CIR_SHIFT ( L : in LINES; W : in WORDS; S : out SHIFTS);
        --Creates circular shifts of all lines in L ignoring those
        --words in WORDS.

    function NUM_SHIFTS ( S : SHIFTS) returns INTEGER;
        --Returns the number of shifts in S.

private

    type WORD_NODE;
    type SHIFTS is access WORD_NODE;
    type WORD_NODE is
        record
            LINE_NO    : INTEGER;
            CHAR_POS  : INTEGER;
            FORWARD   : SHIFTS;
            BACKWARD : SHIFTS;
        end record;

end CIRCULAR_SHIFTS;
-----------------------------------------------------------------------
with LINE_STORAGE, CIRCULAR_SHIFTS;
use  LINE_STORAGE, CIRCULAR_SHIFTS;

package ALPHABETIZE is

        --From LINE_STORAGE import type LINES.

        --From CIRCULAR_SHIFTS import type SHIFTS.

    procedure ALPHABETIZE ( L : in out LINES; S : in out SHIFTS);
        --This procedure alphabetizes a set of circular shifts.

end ALPHABETIZE;
```

```
with LINE_STORAGE, CIRCULAR_SHIFTS;
use  LINE_STORAGE, CIRCULAR_SHIFTS;

package OUTPUT is

        --From LINE_STORAGE import type LINES.
        --From CIRCULAR_SHIFTS import type SHIFTS.

    procedure PRINT ( L : in out LINES; S : in out SHIFTS);
        --This procedure prints a set of circular shifts based on
        --a set of titles. It is especially tailored for the
        --KWIC index software system.

end OUTPUT;
```

```
with LINE_STORAGE, WORD_STORAGE, CIRCULAR_SHIFTS,
     INPUT, OUTPUT, ALPHABETIZE;
use  LINE_STORAGE, WORD_STORAGE, CIRCULAR_SHIFTS,
     INPUT, OUTPUT, ALPHABETIZE;

--This is the main program for the KWIC index software system.

        --From LINE_STORAGE import type LINES.

        --From WORD_STORAGE import type WORDS.

        --From CIRCULAR_SHIFTS import type SHIFTS and procedures
        --INITIALIZE and CIR_SHIFT.

        --From ALPHABETIZE import procedure ALPHABETIZE.

        --From INPUT import procedure INPUT for LINES and
        --procedure INPUT for WORDS.

        --From OUTPUT import procedure PRINT.

procedure KWIC_SYSTEM is

    TITLES        : LINES(SIZE => 10);
    KWIC_ENTRIES : SHIFTS;
    NONKEYWORDS: WORDS(SIZE => 25);

begin  --KWIC_SYSTEM

    INPUT (TITLES);
    INPUT (NONKEYWORDS);
```

```
INITIALIZE (KWIC_ENTRIES);
CIR_SHIFT (TITLES, NONKEYWORDS, KWIC_ENTRIES);
ALPHABETIZE (TITLES, KWIC_ENTRIES);
PRINT (TITLES, KWIC_ENTRIES);

end KWIC_SYSTEM;
```

The main program is simple and easy to read and closely follows the informal strategy given above.

Suppose that later we wish to change the representational details for the data structure LINES used to store the titles. The main program and all other packages in the system are independent of the data structure used to implement LINES. Hence, if the original data structure is changed, no revisions are required outside the package body LINE_STORAGE. In fact, the other program units do not have to be recompiled. Thus, future modification should be less costly and more reliable.

5.10 SUMMARY

- Ada was designed using good software engineering that involved an analysis phase, a requirements definition phase, a design phase, an implementation phase, and an operational and maintenance phase.
- Abstraction and modularity are important principles of software engineering.
- Ada's typing mechanisms, subprograms, packages, generics, and separate compilation, and the Ada programming support environment support effective software design and implementation.
- Ada may be used as a program design language.
- Carefully defined data types improve and support program readability and maintainability. Properly defined types also improve reliability and tend to reduce complexity.
- Ada packages enforce the principle of abstraction through private types. The package specification may be separately compiled from the implementation.
- Generic program units in Ada permit the software developer to create subprograms and packages that provide computational resources for abstract data types.
- The building blocks for modular software construction include abstract data types, subprograms, packages, tasks, and generics.
- The modular design chart is a useful design aid for system architecture design in Ada.
- Data abstraction, information hiding, and modularity can significantly lower software development and maintenance costs.

REFERENCES

1. Wiener, Richard, and Richard Sincovec, *Programming in Ada,* New York: Wiley, 1983.

2. Booch, Grady, *Software Engineering with Ada,* New York: Benjamin/Cummings, 1983.

3. Burden, R. L., J. D. Faires, and A. C. Reynolds, *Numerical Anaylsis,* 2nd ed., Boston Prindle, Weber & Schmidt, 1981.

4. Horowitz, Ellis, and Sartaj Sahni, *Fundamentals of Data Structures,* Woodland Hills, Calif., Computer Science Press, 1976.

5. Tenenbaum, Aaron, M., and Moshe J. Augenstein, *Data Structures Using Pascal,* Englewood Cliffs, N. J.: Prentice-Hall, 1981.

6. Parnas, D. L., ''On the Criteria to be Used in Decomposing Systems into Modules,'' *Commun. ACM,* 15, December 1972, pp. 330–336.

EXERCISES

1. Complete the design and implementation of the KWIC index system described in this chapter. Show your final modular design chart.

2. Design and implement a KWIC index in Pascal. What major differences exist between your Pascal and Ada versions?

3. Write an Ada package specification for screen input-output and implement the procedures specified in a package body.

4. Develop the package bodies for the complex arithmetic package specifications given in Programs 5.5 and 5.6.

5. Write an Ada package specification for string manipulations and implement the procedures specified in a package body.

6. Write an Ada package specification that defines the data type TREE as a limited private type and the operations that are required on this abstract data type. Implement the package body and write a main program that uses the package.

7. Write an Ada package specification that defines the data type LIST as limited private type and the operations that are required for mainipulating linked lists. Implement the package body and write a main program that uses the package.

8. Write the specification for an Ada program text formatter and implement the system. Use the object-oriented and modular software methodology presented in Table 5.1.

9. Using Ada, complete the design and implementation of the screen-oriented editor which was specified in Exercise 2 of Chapter 2. Use the methodology presented in Table 5.1. Use the screen input-output package of Exercise 3 as a module in your design.

10. Use Ada and the methodology given in Table 5.1 to complete the design and implementation of the registration program that was specified in Exercise 3 of Chapter 2.

11. Using the object-oriented and modular software construction methodology, complete the design and implementation, in Ada, of the business inventory system specified in Exercise 4 of Chapter 2.

12. Using Ada, complete the design and implementation of the grammar checker system that was begun in Exercise 5 of Chapter 4. Use the methodology presented in Table 5.1.

13. Using Ada, complete the design and implementation of the airline reservation system of Exercise 6 from Chapter 4. Use the methodology presented in Table 5.1.

14. Write Ada package specifications to develop the system-level architecture via a modular design listing for the rollbook problem of Exercise 7 from Chapter 4.

Chapter 6 ————————————————————————————————

MODULAR SOFTWARE CONSTRUCTION USING MODULA-2

In this chapter we discuss modular software construction using Modula-2.

At the design level, the architecture of a software system is synthesized; the relationships among the functional components are defined, and the major data types are identified. The manner in which the final software product (source and object code) is constructed is driven by the design. In the construction of large and complex software systems, many individual programmers may be involved in the production of the finished software product. Often, software construction is decentralized into a team organization, each team being given the goal of implementing an important subcomponent of the final system. Clearly, if such a human organization is to be employed in constructing the final software product, the design must support this organizational structure.

6.1 THE HUMAN ORGANIZATION AND SYSTEMATIC DEVELOPMENT OF SOFTWARE: TEAM PROGRAMMING

Most computer science students, during the early stages of their professional education, are encouraged to work alone. They are penalized if caught working with a fellow student on a homework assignment. Of course, examinations are administered individually and grades awarded individually. This activity promotes a "lone-wolf" mentality on the part of many computer scientists as they emerge from school into professional practice. The results of a survey by Dan Cougar and Robert Zawacki [1] in 1978 revealed that data processing professional staff believe they have a negligible need to work with other practitioners.

It was discovered, in a survey conducted at IBM in 1978, that 50% of a programmer's time is spent interacting with other team members, 30% working alone, and 20% interacting with others through travel to other organizations. Are universities preparing their students for only 30% of their future activities? Are they failing to encourage the development of group interaction skills that may form the basis for the student's future success as a practitioner?

Some psychologists have speculated that computer and data processing "types" choose this kind of endeavor because they enjoy dealing with (and controlling) a machine rather than interacting with other people. Such people may have limited utility in a large organization solving large-scale problems.

The software development process involves communication at almost every phase in the process. A software engineering group brings individuals together, each with a distinct personality. Bass and Dunteman [2] classify personalities into three types

1. **Task oriented.** An individual who is motivated by the work itself.
2. **Interaction-oriented.** An individual who is motivated by the presence and actions of co-workers.
3. **Self-oriented.** An individual who is motivated by a desire for personal success.

Although most people represent a combination of these three orientations, individuals may have a dominant type of work motivation.

In the experiments conducted by Bass and Dunteman, task-oriented people described themselves as self-sufficient, resourceful, aloof, introverted, aggressive, competitive, and independent. Interaction-oriented individuals considered themselves to be unaggressive, considerate, and helpful. They preferred to work in a group rather than alone. Self-oriented people described themselves as disagreeable, dogmatic, aggressive, competitive, introverted, and jealous. They preferred to work alone. Bass and Dunteman found that males tended to be task oriented whereas females tended to be interaction oriented.

In evaluating the success of group dynamics, it was found that among groups composed entirely of the same personality class, only the groups made up of interaction-oriented persons were successful. Entire groups of either type 1 or type 3 personalities were not successful. Task-oriented and self-oriented group members had a negative feeling about their groups.

The main conclusion emerging from this research is that the most successful group is composed of people from each class, with a group leader who is task oriented.

Gerald Weinberg [3] delineates two basic types in programming groups—task specialists and interaction specialists. The former defines and coordinates the work of the group, whereas the latter deals with conflicts among group members and between group and individual goals.

The fact that many programmers are task oriented (perhaps because of the emphasis on task orientation and individual achievement fostered during early education) suggests concerns about the potential success of a team effort. Will interface specifications be adhered to? Will the implementation teams redesign their separate components (as they are coded) without regard to the overall system architecture?

From the viewpoint of human management in the software development process, serious attention must be paid to the formation of teams. Forming a group with compatible personalities may well be a more important factor in determining the group's success than choosing the best programmers. Managerial control that ensures that group goals are not subverted by some task-oriented individuals is crucial. Formal specifications, design documents, and periodic reviews may help discourage the "lone-wolf" programmer from working at cross-purposes with the team.

An effort should be made to limit the size of each programming team. Individuals may feel a greater sense of personal accomplishment if their effort is shared with only a few other persons. A sense of group loyalty, in which the individual thinks of the group as more important than any one individual, may be more effectively promoted in a small group. One last observation concerning the size of programming teams: as the size of a programming team increases linearly, the number of potential conflicts increases factorially.

The idea of "egoless programming" was introduced by Weinberg [3]. The main feature of egoless programming is that a program is the common property and responsibility of the entire programming team regardless of how and what each individual contributed to the final product. The main argument supporting the philosophy of egoless programming is that it leads to superior program testing and debugging.

In egoless programming, no individual blame is associated with errors. Egoless programming may effectively draw a programming team together, since the emphasis is on the community program (or subsystem) rather than on each individual's contribution.

The problems associated with the human organization of the software development process become amplified when the software design has not properly partitioned the overall system into a sensible set of major component parts. If the interfaces between parts have not been clearly established, confusion among and between teams may result. The authors have observed in their software engineering courses that student teams that have employed modular design using Ada or Modula-2 have generally achieved a higher level of success with their projects than teams that have used more traditional approaches to software construction.

We have indicated that even with good design, the process of human programming organization is not simple. Good software design is a necessary condition that must precede the effective implementation of a final software product using a team structure. In the remainder of this chapter, we address the technical aspects of modular software construction.

6.2 MORE ON MODULAR SOFTWARE CONSTRUCTION

We introduced the notion of modular software construction in Chapters 3, 4, and 5. In this section we continue our general discussion of this approach to software development before launching into a case study.

The payoff for modular software design and implementation occurs when repairs or additions must be made to a software system. In Chapter 1 we used the analogy of car maintenance and pointed out that only because of the modular design of an automobile engine it is easy and inexpensive (at least relatively inexpensive!) to isolate and repair an engine component without having to perform a major overhaul of the entire system. We seek the same benefit with respect to software maintenance by employing a modular design.

As we indicated in earlier chapters, the two key factors contributing to the success of modular design are MODULE INDEPENDENCE and DATA ABSTRACTION. Module independence implies that it should be possible to modify the implementation details of any given module without doing damage to the rest of the system. Data abstraction implies that the client subprograms that import data types or objects from a given module should not have access to the representational details of the data objects. Only the set of specified operations on the given data objects can be used to access or manipulate these data objects.

The main building blocks of modular design are:

1. Abstract data types, representational details hidden.
2. Subprograms, each satisfying a functional specification.
3. Modules, each representing a grouping of functionally related subprograms operating on abstract data types.

The completed software system is an interconnection of modules controlled by the main driver program.

Modular design supports the effective management of complexity. Experience has shown that it is difficult to comprehend large blocks of code (logic) consisting of functionally unrelated components. The reliability of such large code blocks may be poor because the system designer does not have a firm grasp of the complex interrelationships implicit in the code block. It follows that maintenance on such large blocks of code is costly and potentially unreliable.

Although an entire module may be fairly large, each individual component of a module (a subprogram) should be of manageable size. Since a subprogram may be decomposed into a set of nested subprograms, no subprogram component should be unmanageably large.

Since the subprograms within a module are functionally related and all manipulate the same set of module data objects, they are coupled in some sense. Myers [4] has classified seven types of coupling between logical blocks. We list and explain these in Table 6.1.

Table 6.1   Types of Coupling Between Logical Blocks

1. **No direct coupling.** The two blocks do not relate to each other in any way, but relate independently to the main program.
2. **Data coupling.** Data passing between the two blocks is accomplished through the parameters of each block.
3. **Stamp coupling.** Data are shared between the two blocks through a commonly imported module. The shared data are not global.
4. **Control coupling.** One subprogram passes a switch or flag to another. The control path that is executed in the recipient block is dependent on the value of the switch passed.
5. **External coupling.** Data are shared between the two blocks because they each share the same external variables. These external variables may be a subset of the global variables.
6. **Common coupling.** The two blocks share the same global data structures.
7. **Content coupling.** One subprogram directly references the interior of the other (e.g., a that subprogram branches to rather than calls another subprogram).

Myers considers the first type of coupling to be the most desirable, with the desirability of each type of coupling going down from types 1 to 7. Often the actual type of coupling is a combination of several of the types given in Table 6.1.

It is often most desirable for subprogram blocks to be externally coupled. For example, in constructing a module, a set of subprograms all should share the data objects common to the module. Indeed, the very purpose of a module is to provide client blocks a set of abstract data types and a set of corresponding operations on these data types. This may be achieved only by externally coupling each of the module's subprograms to the common data objects of the module.

Control coupling is often desirable for exception handling. Suppose that there are N possible errors to be handled in a software system. We may desire to put all the error messages and corrective control action into the same module and pass the error type into the error-handling module by way of a control parameter. This would promote program readability and the standardization of error message formats.

It is our view that the value of a particular type of coupling is dependent on the type of relationship between the two blocks being coupled. For example, if one subprogram is nested within another, some degree of external coupling (both subprograms have access to some of the local variables of the subprogram of outermost scope) may be desirable. Control coupling may also be desirable in this situation. At the module level, the most desirable situation is clearly no direct coupling. This may not always be feasible. Two modules may both require the facilities of the same input-output module, creating stamp coupling.

At the module level, we should strive to limit the coupling between modules to the most essential resources needed by both modules.

6.3 USING MODULA-2 FOR MODULAR DESIGN: A CASE STUDY

We discussed some of the major concepts associated with modular design in Section 6.2. The reader may wish to refer to Table 5.1 for a summary of the steps involved in the modular construction process. We now illustrate the process of modular design, modular programming, and program maintenance using the new programming language Modula-2. We use Modula-2 at both the design and implementation levels. Our case study is a relatively small but important problem. A larger case study illustrating the entire software development process from specifications to maintenance is presented in Chapter 9. The problem we solve here is important in its own right, however, and to derive value from this case study, you must become involved with many details associated with the problem solution.

What if you couldn't care less about the particular problem area represented in the case study? Why should you waste your time becoming familiar with the multitude of facts related to the problem solution?

We offer two answers to these rhetorical questions. First, the problem area of the case study is central in computer science and therefore extremely important. Second, to bridge the gap between theory and practice, between platitudes about modular software design and reality, you must completely immerse yourself in a case study.

6.3.1 The Problem for the Case Study: An Interactive Mathematical Function Evaluator

We wish to design and implement a software system that allows a user to interactively enter and evaluate a wide range of mathematical functions of one variable, directly from the keyboard. The mathematical function will be entered as a string of characters and converted into a form that may be evaluated.

The first version we develop allows functions only of integer arguments that return only integer values. Later, to demonstrate software maintenance, we convert the system to a second version that allows functions of real (floating point) arguments that return real values. The first version supports combinations of the operations of addition, subtraction, multiplication, and division only. The second version supports sines, cosines, logarithms, absolute value, and exponentials, in addition to the operations of the first version.

A program using the interactive function evaluator should not require recompilation after each new mathematical function is entered. Graceful error handling should be included to prevent crashes in the event of illegal expressions or argument values provided as input to the program.

We note that very few, if any, high level languages provide facilities for the user to directly input a mathematical function that is to be later evaluated. Suppose we wish to tabulate the integer function

$$f(x) = 3*x*x*x + 6*x*x + 2*x + 5$$

for values of the argument x ranging from -10 to 10 in increments of 1, in Pascal. Using the standard facilities of the language, Program 6.1 might be written.

PROGRAM 6.1   Pascal Solution to Function Tabulation Problem

```
program TABULATE_FUNCTION;
var x: INTEGER;

    function F(X: INTEGER): INTEGER;
    begin
        F:=3*X*X*X + 6*X*X + 2*X + 5
    end{F};

begin {Main program}
    writeln('X':8,'F(X)':8);
    writeln;
    for X:=-10 to 10 do
    begin
        X := X + 1;
        writeln(X:8,F(X):8)
    end(* for loop *)
end.
```

If now we wish to tabulate the function

$$f(x) = 2*X*X*X + 12*X*X + 3$$

for values of the argument from -10 to 10, we would have to modify Program 6.1 by changing the assignment statement F, in function F(X). This would entail recompiling the program before reexecuting the program. If the software system is to be truly interactive, the user should not be burdened with the task of modifying and recompiling the whole or part of a program.

Important applications of a function evaluator (for real variables) might occur in building a general-purpose integration program (in which the user might be prompted to enter an integrand interactively), or in constructing a differential equation solver (in which the user might be prompted to enter a forcing function or functions), or finally in building a function graph plotter (in which the user might be prompted to enter the mathematical function or functions to be graphed).

The interactive function evaluator that we wish to design and build is a software tool that will be of value to any programmer writing engineering and mathematical software.

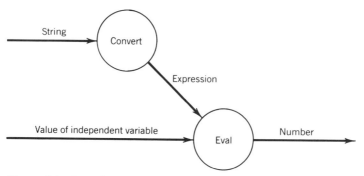

Figure 6.1 Data flow diagram of function evaluator.

6.3.2 Conceptual Model of Proposed System: Version 1

The user enters a string of characters that represents the mathematical expression to be evaluated. This string consists of a sequence of symbols possibly containing: (,), +, −, *, /, 0, 1, 2, 3, 4, 5, 6, 7, 8, 9, X or x. The string must be converted to a form suitable for function evaluation, say the abstract data type Expression. Then a function F, of two arguments, an Expression and an integer argument X (or x), enables the user to interactively enter and evaluate a wide class of mathematical functions. Figure 6.1 is a data flow diagram that depicts the conceptual model just described.

The high level conceptual model of the system depicted in Figure 6.1 may be represented using a definition module in Modula-2. This definition module represents the first cut for the system level architecture of the proposed system. It also represents the system's interface to the "outside world." A software developer importing this module may wish to use the resources Expression, Convert, and Eval connecting the program to the module FunctionEvaluator (using an IMPORT statement).

MODULAR DESIGN LISTING 6.1   **System-Level Architecture for
                                   Function-Evaluator**

```
DEFINITION MODULE FunctionEvaluator;
(* $SEG:=12; *)

    EXPORT QUALIFIED
            (* type *) Expression,
            (* proc *) Convert,
            (* proc *) Eval;
```

TYPE Expression; (∗ An abstract data type derived from the
               original mathematical expression and used
               for function evaluation.   ∗)

PROCEDURE Convert(A: ARRAY OF CHAR): Expression;
(∗ This procedure converts a string representing a
   mathematical function to the abstract type Expression.   ∗)

PROCEDURE Eval(E: Expression; X: INTEGER): INTEGER;
(∗ This procedure combines the abstract data type
   Expression with the argument X to produce the desired
   answer.   ∗)

END FunctionEvaluator.

In Program 6.2 we rewrite Program 6.1 using the module FunctionEvaluator. We can do this even though we do not know the representational details of
the abstract data type Expression, or the implementation details of the subprograms Convert and Eval.

PROGRAM 6.2   Rework of Program 6.1 Using Module FunctionEvaluator

```
MODULE Evaluate;

    FROM FunctionEvaluator IMPORT
            Expression, Convert, Eval;

    FROM InOut IMPORT
            WriteLn, WriteString, WriteInt, ReadInt,Read, EOL;

    VAR   s      : ARRAY[1..80] OF CHAR;
          e      : Expression;
          x      : INTEGER;
          answer : CHAR;
          ch     : CHAR;
          i      : INTEGER;

BEGIN (∗ Main Program ∗)
    WriteLn;
    WriteString("Enter a mathematical function (y/n)? ");
    Read(answer);
    WHILE (answer = 'Y') OR (answer = 'y') DO
        WriteLn;
```

```
WriteString("Enter mathematical function to be evaluated: ");
i:=0;
REPEAT
    INC(i);
    Read(ch);
    s[i]:=ch;
UNTIL ch = EOL;
e:=Convert(s);
WriteString("Evaluate the mathematical expression (y/n)? ");
Read(answer);
WHILE (answer = 'Y') OR (answer = 'y') DO
    WriteLn;
    WriteString("Enter a value for the independent variable: ");
    ReadInt(x);
    WriteLn;
    WriteString("The value of the function F is ––> ");
    WriteInt(Eval(e,x),10);
    WriteLn;
    WriteString("Evaluate the mathematical expression (y/n)? ");
    Read(answer)
END;
    WriteLn;
    WriteString("Enter a mathematical function (y/n)? ");
    Read(answer);
    END;
END Evaluate.
```

A "software bus" connects the program Evaluate to the module FunctionEvaluator. Through this bus flow the software resources available in FunctionEvaluator. For example, the string of characters representing a mathematical expression "s" in Evaluate is converted to "e", a variable declared to be of the abstract data type Expression. The expression "e" is evaluated when an integer argument is supplied to subprogram Eval. The careful reader may see some "sex" in Program 6.2.

The program Evaluate may be successfully compiled even though the software circuitry of FunctionEvaluator has not been designed. Modular software design, from the top down, allows client systems that require some or all of the components of FunctionEvaluator to be designed and implemented before the implementation details have been wired. The definition module, FunctionEvaluator, has a dual role. It serves as a high level system architecture design model of the proposed new subsystem for interactive function evaluation and as an interface to other client systems that are being designed.

6.3.3   Problem Decomposition for Function Evaluator

In Figure 6.1, the highest functional-level components of the proposed software system, namely, Convert and Eval, have been identified. Figures 6.2 and 6.3 are data flow diagrams that depict the major functional components required to implement Convert and Eval, respectively. These data flow diagrams represent a decomposition of the problem into smaller components.

In Figure 6.2, the input string of characters, representing a mathematical expression, is stripped of all internal spaces. This allows the user of the software system flexibility in entering a mathematical expression from the keyboard. The user may include any number of spaces between the symbols of the desired expression.

After spaces have been removed from the input string, the next function that is performed is the replacement of each integer constant in the string of characters with an uppercase letter from the alphabet, using "B" for the first replacement, "C" for the next replacement, and successive letters of the alphabet for additional constants. The letter "X" is excluded because it is used to represent the variable in the mathematical expression. As each integer constant in the input character string is replaced by an uppercase letter, the letter and its associated integer value are stored in a symbol table.

After each integer constant has been replaced by an uppercase letter and an appropriate entry created in the symbol table (the letter and associated

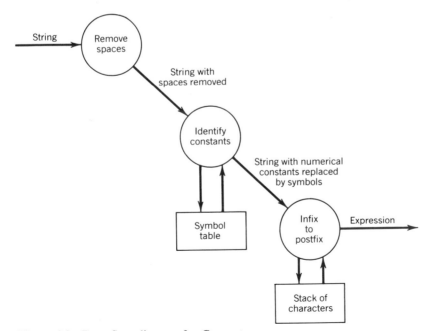

Figure 6.2   Data flow diagram for Convert.

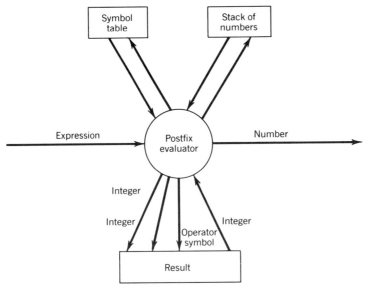

Figure 6.3 Data flow diagram for Eval.

integer), the final function performed by Convert is to put the string of characters in postfix form. The reader is urged to consult a book on data structures, such as Reference 5, for a discussion of infix to postfix conversion. The purpose of the conversion is to produce a string without parentheses that is easier to evaluate. The function Infix to Postfix requires a stack of characters to perform its function.

We illustrate the process described above, for Convert, with the mathematical string,

(5∗x + 6)∗x + 7

The function Remove Spaces converts the input string to the form

(5∗x+6)∗x+7

The function Identify Constants converts the string to the form,

(B∗x+C)∗x+D

The function Infix to Postfix converts the string to the form,

Bx∗C+x∗D+

In Figure 6.3, the expression is processed by a function Postfix Evaluator. The algorithm for evaluating the postfix expression, given in Reference 5, requires the use of a stack of integers. The integer value of each letter is fetched from the symbol table. These integers are put in a stack and combined with the integer value of the variable x to return the numerical answer. The function Result is used to combine two integer values with an operator symbol to return an integer result.

6.3.4 Second Cut of System-Level Architecture for Proposed System

From the data flow diagrams displayed in Figures 6.1 to 6.3, we may identify the functional components Convert, Eval, Remove-Spaces, Identify-Constants, Infix to Postfix, Postfix-Evaluator, and Result. In addition, the data types Symbol Table, Stack, and expression are required. The data type SymbolTable must be shared by the functions Identify-Constants and Postfix-Evaluator. A general stack structure that may be used for both characters and integers must be available for functions Infix to Postfix and Postfix-Evaluator. This suggests a hierarchical decomposition of the functional components in the system.

Figure 6.4, a modular design chart, displays one possible modular design for the software system. Ten proposed separate compilation units that will comprise the software system are shown, namely, definition and implementation modules FunctionEvaluator, SymbolTable, Stacks1, Op1, and Op2. Each box represents a separate compilation unit. The notation DEF indicates a definition module and IMP indicates an implementation module. The functional components exported by each definition module are indicated in the respective boxes. The exact interdependencies among the modules are indicated by the software bus. For example, implementation module Op1 imports type Expression from definition module FunctionEvaluator, as well as the subprograms InitExpr and Assign.

Seven of the ten modules in Figure 6.4 are independent, namely, definition modules FunctionEvaluator, Symboltable, Stacks1, and Op2, as well as implementation modules SymbolTable, Stacks1, and Op2. This module independence promotes more efficient software testing, higher software reliability, and easier maintenance.

In SymbolTable, the operation of creating and initializing a symbol table is performed by InitSymTable, the operation of obtaining a letter to replace an integer constant and storing its associated value in variable Table is performed by Deposit, and the operation of obtaining the integer value for a given letter stored in variable Table is performed by Fetch. The variable Table is exported to subprogram InfixPostfix in implementation module Op1 as well as subprogram Eval in implementation module FunctionEvaluator because both require this variable.

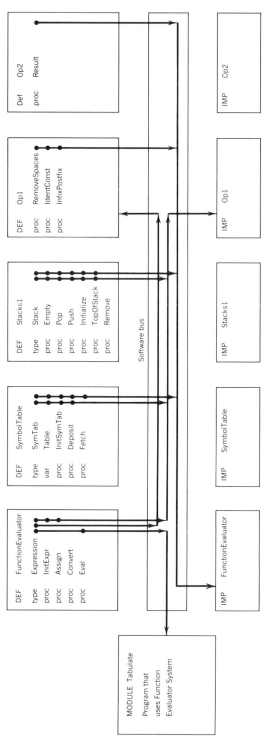

Figure 6.4 Modular design chart for functionevaluator.

In Stacks1, the usual stack operations are defined for a special Modula-2 type called WORD. The type WORD may be used as a surrogate for both characters as well as integers. The stack operators are imported by implementation modules Op1 (in which a stack of characters is used) and Function Evaluator (in which a stack of integers is used).

In Op2, the functional component Result is defined.

In Op1, the functional components RemoveSpaces, IdentConst (for identifying constants and replacing them with letters), and InfixPostfix are defined. These three related functions implement Convert, as indicated in Figure 6.2.

All the functional components that were identified in the data flow diagrams of Figures 6.1, to 6.3 are included in the modular design chart of Figure 6.4. There is a major difference between the information conveyed by a data flow diagram and a modular design chart. In a modular design chart, functional components are grouped according to related function. A hierarchy of components is established. This is not so with a data flow diagram.

We express the system architecture level of design for our proposed system in Modula-2. This is presented in Modular Design Listing 6.2. A Modula-2 library provides a set of utilities that will be used by some of the system modules. A listing of the facilities available in a Modula-2 library is presented in the appendix.

MODULAR DESIGN LISTING 6.2 **System Architecture for FunctionEvaluator**

```
DEFINITION MODULE FunctionEvaluator;
(* $SEG:=12; *)

        EXPORT QUALIFIED
                (* type *) Expression,
                (* proc *) InitExpr,
                (* proc *) Assign,
                (* proc *) Convert,
                (* proc *) Eval;

        TYPE Expression;
        (* An abstract data type derived from the
           original mathematical expression to be used
           for function evaluation.                               *)

        PROCEDURE InitExpr(VAR A: Expression);
        (* Creates and initializes expression.                   *)

        PROCEDURE Assign(VAR A: Expression; B: CHAR; I: INTEGER);
        (* Assigns character B to A in position I.                *)
```

```
    PROCEDURE Convert(A: ARRAY OF CHAR; VAR len: INTEGER): Expression;
    (* This procedure converts a string of length len representing a
       mathematical function to the abstract type Expression.              *)

    PROCEDURE Eval(E: Expression; X: INTEGER): INTEGER;
    (* This procedure combines the abstract data type
       Expression with the argument X to produce the desired
       answer.                                                             *)

END FunctionEvaluator.
```

```
DEFINITION MODULE SymbolTable;
(* $SEG:=14; *)

    EXPORT QUALIFIED
            (* type *) SymTab,
            (* var  *) Table,
            (* proc *) InitSymTab,
            (* proc *) Deposit,
            (* proc *) Fetch;

    TYPE SymTab;
    (* Abstract type for symbol table.                                     *)

    VAR Table: SymTab;
    (* Shared by two modules.                                              *)

    PROCEDURE InitSymTab(VAR A: SymTab);
    (* This procedure creates a symbol table SymTab and initializes
       it to empty.                                                        *)

    PROCEDURE Deposit(A: INTEGER; VAR B: SymTab; VAR C: CHAR);
    (* This procedure deposits an integer A into the symbol table
       B and returns a character C. The character C is associated
       with the integer A in the symbol table B.                          *)

    PROCEDURE Fetch(A: CHAR; B: SymTab): INTEGER;
    (* This procedure returns an integer when a character A
       is input to symbol table B.                                        *)

END SymbolTable.
```

```
DEFINITION MODULE Op1;
(* $SEG:=18; *)
```

(* This module supports the operations necessary for Convert.   *)

    FROM FunctionEvaluator IMPORT Expression;

    EXPORT QUALIFIED
            (* proc *) RemoveSpaces,
            (* proc *) IdentConst,
            (* proc *) InfixPostfix;

    PROCEDURE RemoveSpaces(VAR S: ARRAY OF CHAR; len: INTEGER);
    (* All interior spaces are removed from the input string S,
      producing the output string S.   *)

    PROCEDURE IdentConst(VAR S: ARRAY OF CHAR; VAR len: INTEGER);
    (* All constants in the string S of length len are replaced by
      operand symbols. These symbols are placed in the symbol
      table SymTab with their corresponding numerical values.   *)

    PROCEDURE InfixPostfix(S: ARRAY OF CHAR): Expression;
    (* Converts the string S to Expression. Expression will
      be later used for function evaluation.   *)

END Op1.

DEFINITION MODULE Op2;
(* $SEG:=20; *)

    EXPORT QUALIFIED
            (* proc *) Result;

    PROCEDURE Result(Symb: CHAR; Opnd1,Opnd2: INTEGER): INTEGER;
    (* Returns an integer value when integers Opnd1 and Opnd2 are
      combined with an operator symbol Symb.   *)

END Op2.

DEFINITION MODULE Stacks1;
(* $SEG:=16; *)

    FROM SYSTEM IMPORT WORD;
    (* The word allows the stack structure to support characters
      and integers.   *)

    EXPORT QUALIFIED
            (* type *) Stack,
            (* proc *) Empty,

```
            (* proc *) Pop,
            (* proc *) Push,
            (* proc *) Initialize,
            (* proc *) Remove,
            (* proc *) TopOfStack;

TYPE Stack;

PROCEDURE Empty(S: Stack) : BOOLEAN;
(* Returns true if stack is empty, false otherwise.              *)

PROCEDURE Pop(VAR S: Stack) : WORD;
(* Strips top element off stack.                                 *)

PROCEDURE Push(VAR S: Stack; X: WORD);
(* Adds element to top of stack.                                 *)

PROCEDURE Initialize(VAR S: Stack);
(* Sets stack to empty                                           *)

PROCEDURE Remove(VAR S: Stack);
(* Removes stack from memory.                                    *)

PROCEDURE TopOfStack(S: Stack): WORD;
(* Returns the current top of the stack without changing
   the contents of the stack.                                   *)

END Stacks1.
```

The modules defined above cannot be compiled in random order. A module that imports entities from another module must be compiled after the definition module that exports these entities has been compiled. One of several legal sequences in which to compile these modules is the order in which they are presented above.

We do not require implementation modules to be compiled, or even to exist, before we can successfully compile the design structure given above. The Modula-2 compiler helps check for interface consistency across compiler boundaries. The system architecture Modula-2 design structure provides the ultimate framework within which the final software product will be built.

We must emphasize that the foregoing modules, even though each will compile without error (provided they are compiled in correct sequence), are a design representation of the system that will later be implemented. We are using Modula-2 as a program design language. A hierarchical structure of software components has been identified at this level of design.

6.3.5 **The Detailed Level of Design**

Having identified the major subcomponents of the software system and the hierarchical relationships among these subcomponents at the system architecture level of design, we must focus on each of the subcomponents. High reliability and easy maintainability of the final product are now more probable because of the module independence, data abstraction, and problem decomposition that have been achieved during this phase of the design. Moreover, the modular partitioning of the software system makes the software testing process more efficient.

Pseudo-code is used at the detailed level of design. Documentation for each software component must be created and maintained. If maintenance is performed (ideally at the lowest level of the design), all relevant documents must be modified.

Continuing in a top-down manner, we display the pseudo-code for Convert and Eval. Space does not permit us to show the design of all the subcomponents with pseudo-code. We will, however, show the pseudo-code algorithm for subprogram InfixPostfix. The implementation details of each of the subprograms are revealed in Section 6.3.6, where we display the finished software product.

PSEUDO-CODE FOR SUBPROGRAM CONVERT

Algorithm Convert(A: String): Expression
    RemoveSpaces(A)
    IdentConst(A)
    return InfixPostfix(A)
end Algorithm

PSEUDO-CODE FOR SUBPROGRAM EVAL

Algorithm Eval(A: Expression): integer
    initialize opndstack to empty
    while (more characters to read in A) loop
        symb <–– next input character
        if symb is an operand then push(opndstk,symb)
        else
            opnd2 <–– Pop(opndstk)
            value2 <–– Fetch(opnd2)
            opnd1 <–– Pop(opndstk)
            value1 <–– Fetch(opnd2)
            value <–– Result(symb,value1,value2)
        end else
    end loop
    return <–– Fetch(pop(opndstk))
end Algorithm

PSEUDO-CODE FOR SUBPROGRAM INFIXPOSTFIX

Algorithm InfixPostfix(A: String; B: Expression)
    initialize stack opstk to empty
    initialize B to blank
    while (more characters to read in A) loop
        read(symb) from infix string, A
        if symb is an operand then add symb to B
        else
            if symb = ')' then pop the opstk down to the first left
                            parenthesis and add all the popped
                            operators sequentially to B
                            except the left parenthesis
          else
              while (opstk not empty) and (algebraic precedence of
                  symb on top of stack with symb is true)
              loop
                  topsymb <-- pop(opstk)
                  add topsymb to B if it is not '('
              end loop
              push(opstk,symb) if not ')'
          end else
        end else
    end loop
    while opstk not empty loop
        topsymb <-- pop(opstk)
        add topsymb to Expression
    end loop
end Algorithm

6.3.6 Implementation of Module FunctionEvaluator

As you read this section, carefully observe how the modular structure identified at the system architecture level of design forces the implementation to a modular structure.

The implementation of FunctionEvaluator given in Program 6.3 has been tested and verified. The components may be compiled in the order in which they are presented. We delimit the separately compiled units with a dashed line under the unit. In Section 6.3.7, we walk through this implementation.

PROGRAM 6.3   **Modula-2 Software System for Integer Function Evaluator**

```
DEFINITION MODULE FunctionEvaluator;
(* $SEG:=12; *)
```

```
    EXPORT QUALIFIED
             (* type *) Expression,
             (* proc *) InitExpr,
             (* proc *) Assign,
             (* proc *) Convert,
             (* proc *) Eval;

    TYPE Expression;
    (* An abstract data type derived from the
       original mathematical expression to be used
       for function evaluation.                                        *)

    PROCEDURE InitExpr(VAR A: Expression);
    (* Creates and initializes expression.                             *)

    PROCEDURE Assign(VAR A: Expression; B: CHAR; I: INTEGER);
    (* Assigns character B to A in position I.                         *)

    PROCEDURE Convert(A: ARRAY OF CHAR; VAR len: INTEGER): Expression;
    (* This procedure converts a string of length len representing a
       mathematical function to the abstract type Expression.          *)

    PROCEDURE Eval(E: Expression; X: INTEGER): INTEGER;
    (* This procedure combines the abstract data type
       Expression with the argument X to produce the desired
       answers.                                                        *)

END FunctionEvaluator.
--------------------------------------------------------------------------
DEFINITION MODULE SymbolTable;
(* $SEG:=14; *)

    EXPORT QUALIFIED
             (* type *) SymTab,
             (* var   *) Table,
             (* proc *) InitSymTab,
             (* proc *) Deposit,
             (* proc *) Fetch;

    TYPE SymTab;
    (* Abstract type for symbol table.                                 *)

    VAR Table: SymTab; (* Shared by two modules.                       *)

    PROCEDURE InitSymTab(VAR A: SymTab);
    (* This procedure creates a symbol table SymTab and initializes
       it to empty.                                                    *)
```

```
PROCEDURE Deposit(A: INTEGER; VAR B: SymTab; VAR C: CHAR);
(* This procedure deposits an integer A into the symbol table
   B and returns a character C. The character C is associated
   with the integer A in the symbol table B.                        *)

PROCEDURE Fetch(A: CHAR; B: SymTab): INTEGER;
(* This procedure returns an integer when a character A
   is input to symbol table B.                                      *)
END SymbolTable.
```

```
IMPLEMENTATION MODULE SymbolTable;

FROM Storage IMPORT ALLOCATE, DEALLOCATE;

TYPE SymbolRecord = RECORD
                          Symb: CHAR;
                            Val: INTEGER
                    END;

TYPE SymTab = POINTER TO ARRAY [1..24] OF SymbolRecord;

PROCEDURE InitSymTab(VAR A: SymTab);

VAR I: INTEGER;

BEGIN
    NEW(A);
    FOR I:=1 TO 24 DO
        A↑[I].Symb:=' ';
        A↑[I].Val := 0
    END
END InitSymTab;

PROCEDURE Deposit(A: INTEGER; VAR B: SymTab; VAR C: CHAR);

VAR I: INTEGER;

BEGIN
    C:='A';
    I:=0;
    REPEAT
        I:=I+1;
        INC(C);
        IF C = 'X' THEN INC(C); END;
        (* X is the independent variable *)
```

```
        UNTIL B↑[I].Symb = ' ';
        B↑[I].Symb:=C;
        B↑[I].Val:=A
END Deposit;

PROCEDURE Fetch(A: CHAR; B: SymTab): INTEGER;

VAR C: CHAR;
    I: INTEGER;

BEGIN
    C:='A';
    I:=0;
    REPEAT
        I:=I+1;
        INC(C)
    UNTIL B↑[I].Symb = A;
    RETURN B↑[I].Val
END Fetch;

END SymbolTable.
```

```
DEFINITION MODULE Stacks1;
(* $SEG:=16; *)

    FROM SYSTEM IMPORT WORD;
    (* The word allows the stack structure to support characters
        and integers.                                                    *)

    EXPORT QUALIFIED
                (* type *) Stack,
                (* proc *) Empty,
                (* proc *) Pop,
                (* proc *) Push,
                (* proc *) Initialize,
                (* proc *) Remove,
                (* proc *) TopOfStack;

    TYPE Stack;

    PROCEDURE Empty(S: Stack) : BOOLEAN;
    (* Returns true if stack is empty, false otherwise.                 *)

    PROCEDURE Pop(VAR S: Stack) : WORD;
    (* Strips top element off stack.                                    *)
```

```
PROCEDURE Push(VAR S: Stack; X: WORD);
(* Adds element to top of stack.                                        *)

PROCEDURE Initialize(VAR S: Stack);
(* Sets stack to empty.                                                 *)

PROCEDURE Remove(VAR S: Stack);
(* Removes stack from memory.                                           *)

PROCEDURE TopOfStack(S: Stack): WORD;
(* Returns the current top of the stack without changing
   the contents of the stack.                                          *)

END Stacks1.
```

```
IMPLEMENTATION MODULE Stacks1;

    FROM InOut IMPORT WriteString, WriteLn;

    FROM Storage IMPORT ALLOCATE, DEALLOCATE;

    FROM SYSTEM IMPORT WORD;

    CONST STACKSIZE = 80;

    TYPE Objects = ARRAY [1..STACKSIZE] OF WORD;
         Stack = POINTER TO RECORD
                              ITEM: Objects;
                              TOP : CARDINAL
                          END;

    PROCEDURE Empty(S: Stack) : BOOLEAN;
    BEGIN
        IF S↑.TOP = 0
        THEN
            RETURN TRUE
        ELSE
            RETURN FALSE
        END
    END Empty;

    PROCEDURE Pop(VAR S: Stack) : WORD;
    BEGIN
        IF Empty(S)
```

```
        THEN
            WriteString("Invalid mathematical expression.");
            WriteLn;
            HALT
        ELSE
            DEC(S↑.TOP);
            RETURN S↑.ITEM[S↑.TOP+1];
        END
    END Pop;

    PROCEDURE Push(VAR S: Stack; X: WORD);
    BEGIN
        IF S↑.TOP = STACKSIZE
        THEN
            WriteString("Invalid mathematical expression.");
            WriteLn;
            HALT
        ELSE
            INC(S↑.TOP);
            S↑.ITEM[S↑.TOP]:=X
        END
    END Push;

    PROCEDURE Initialize(VAR S: Stack);
    BEGIN
        NEW(S);
        S↑.TOP:=0
    END Initialize;

    PROCEDURE Remove(VAR S: Stack);
    BEGIN
        DISPOSE(S)
    END Remove;

    PROCEDURE TopOfStack(S: Stack): WORD;
    BEGIN
        RETURN S↑.ITEM[S↑.TOP]
    END TopOfStack;

END Stacks1.
```

```
DEFINITION MODULE Op2;
(* $SEG:=20; *)
```

```
    EXPORT QUALIFIED
         (* proc *) Result;

    PROCEDURE Result(Symb: CHAR; Opnd1,Opnd2: INTEGER): INTEGER;
    (* Returns an integer value when integers Opnd1 and Opnd2 are
        combined with an operator symbol Symb.                           *)

END Op2.
```

```
IMPLEMENTATION MODULE Op2;

    FROM InOut IMPORT      WriteString, WriteLn;

    PROCEDURE Result(Symb: CHAR; Opnd1,Opnd2: INTEGER): INTEGER;
    BEGIN
        CASE Symb OF
            '+': RETURN Opnd1 + Opnd2; |
            '-': RETURN Opnd1 - Opnd2; |
            '*': RETURN Opnd1 * Opnd2; |
            '/': IF Opnd2 = 0
                THEN
                    WriteLn;
                    WriteString("Divide by zero error.");
                    WriteLn;
                    HALT;
                ELSE
                    IF Opnd2 < 0
                    THEN
                        RETURN -(Opnd1 DIV (-Opnd2))
                    ELSE
                        RETURN Opnd1 DIV Opnd2
                    END(* if then else *);
                END(* if then else *);
        END(* case *);
    END Result;

END Op2.
```

```
DEFINITION MODULE Op1;
(* $SEG:=18; *)

(* This module supports the operations necessary for Convert.           *)
```

```
FROM FunctionEvaluator IMPORT Expression;

EXPORT QUALIFIED
        (* proc *) RemoveSpaces,
        (* proc *) IdentConst,
        (* proc *) InfixPostfix;

PROCEDURE RemoveSpaces(VAR S: ARRAY OF CHAR; len: INTEGER);
(* All interior spaces are removed from the input string S
   producing the output string S.                                      *)

PROCEDURE IdentConst(VAR S: ARRAY OF CHAR; VAR len: INTEGER);
(* All constants in the string S of length len are replaced by
   operand symbols. These symbols are placed in the symbol
   table SymTab with their corresponding numerical values.             *)

PROCEDURE InfixPostfix(S: ARRAY OF CHAR): Expression;
(* Converts the string S to Expression. Expression will
   be used later for function evaluation.                              *)

END Op1.
----------------------------------------------------------------------
IMPLEMENTATION MODULE Op1;

    FROM FunctionEvaluator IMPORT Expression, InitExpr, Assign;

    FROM SymbolTable IMPORT SymTab, Table, InitSymTab, Deposit;

    FROM Conversions IMPORT StrToInt;
    (* Provided in Modula Utility Library.                             *)

    FROM Stacks1 IMPORT Stack, Empty, Pop, Push, Initialize,
                        TopOfStack;

    TYPE CharSet = SET OF CHAR;

    PROCEDURE RemoveSpaces(VAR S: ARRAY OF CHAR; len: INTEGER);

        PROCEDURE RemSpace(POS,L: INTEGER);

        VAR I: INTEGER;

        BEGIN
            IF POS < L
```

```
        THEN
            FOR I:=POS TO L DO
                S[I]:=S[I+1];
            END(* for loop *)
        END(* if then *)
    END RemSpace;


VAR I : INTEGER;


BEGIN
    I:=-1;
    REPEAT
        INC(I);
        IF S[I] = ' '
        THEN
            RemSpace(I,len);
            DEC(I);
            DEC(len)
        END (* if then *)
    UNTIL I = len-1;
END RemoveSpaces;


PROCEDURE IdentConst(VAR S: ARRAY OF CHAR; VAR len: INTEGER);


VAR NUMERALS, ALPHABET, ALLOWABLE : CharSet;
    I , J, LenNum, IntVal                : INTEGER;
    Stt                                  : ARRAY[1..20] OF CHAR;
    dummy                                : BOOLEAN;
    ch                                   : CHAR;


    PROCEDURE ADD(POS: INTEGER);
    (* Adds "0" to the position just before the "-" in S              *)


    VAR I: INTEGER;


    BEGIN
        FOR I:=len TO POS + 2 BY -1 DO
            S[I]:=S[I-1];
        END(* for loop *);
        S[POS]:='0';
        S[POS+1]:='-';
        len:=len + 1;
    END ADD;
```

```
PROCEDURE Replace(symb: CHAR; pos, length: INTEGER);
(* This procedure replaces an integer constant by symb.          *)
VAR I: INTEGER;
BEGIN
    S[pos]:=symb;
    IF length > 1
    THEN
        FOR I:=pos+1 TO len−length+1 DO
            S[I]:=S[I+length−1];
        END(* for loop *);
    END (* if then *);
END Replace;


BEGIN (* IdentConst *)
    NUMERALS:=CharSet{'0', '1', '2', '3', '4', '5', '6', '7', '8', '9', '.'};
    ALPHABET:=NUMERALS + CharSet{'A' .. 'Z'} + CharSet{'x'};
    (* We replace any nonoperator minus sign with "0−".            *)
    I:=0;
    WHILE S[I] # ' ' DO
        IF (I = 0) AND (S[I] = '−')
        THEN
            ADD(I);
        ELSE
            IF S[I] = '−'
            THEN
                IF NOT (S[I−1] IN ALPHABET)
                THEN
                (* Minus sign is not an operator.                  *)
                    ADD(I);
                END(* if not then *)
            END(* if then *)
        END(* if then else *);
        INC(I);
    END(* while loop *);
    I:=0;
    InitSymTab(Table);
    WHILE S[I] # ' ' DO
        IF S[I] IN NUMERALS
        THEN
            LenNum:=1;
            WHILE S[I+LenNum] IN NUMERALS DO
                LenNum:=LenNum+1;
            END(* while loop *);
            (* We load the array Stt with the numerals from S
               starting in pos I.                                  *)
```

```
            FOR J:=1 TO 20 DO (* Initialize Stt to a nonnumeric string.   *)
                Stt[J]:='z';
            END;
            FOR J:=1 TO LenNum DO
                Stt[J]:=S[I+J−1];
            END(* for loop *);
            dummy:=StrToInt(Stt,IntVal);
            Deposit(IntVal,Table,ch);
            (* We replace the integer constant by an operand symbol.    *)
            Replace(ch,I,LenNum);
        END(* if then *);
        INC(I);
    END(* while loop *)
END IdentConst;

PROCEDURE InfixPostfix(S: ARRAY OF CHAR): Expression;

VAR
    OPSTK           : Stack;
    index1, index2, I: INTEGER;
    symb, topsymb   : CHAR;
    Allowable       : CharSet;
    Expr            : Expression;

    PROCEDURE Precedence(op1,op2: CHAR): BOOLEAN;
    BEGIN
        IF ((op1 = '+')OR(op1 = '−'))AND (op2 = '*')OR(op2 = '/')
        THEN
            RETURN FALSE
        ELSIF ((op1 = '(' ) AND (op2 # ')' ))OR(op2 = '(')
        THEN
            RETURN FALSE
        ELSE RETURN TRUE
        END(* if then elsif else *);
    END Precedence;

BEGIN (* InfixPostfix *)
    Allowable:=CharSet{'A'..'Z'} + CharSet{'x'};
    Initialize(OPSTK);
    InitExpr(Expr);
    index1:=0; index2:=1;
    WHILE (S[index1] # ' ') DO
        symb:=S[index1];
        IF symb IN Allowable
```

```
            THEN
                Assign(Expr,symb,index2);
                INC(index2);
            ELSE
                LOOP
                    IF (Empty(OPSTK)) OR
                        (NOT Precedence(CHAR(TopOfStack(OPSTK)),symb))
                            THEN EXIT; END;
                    topsymb:=CHAR(Pop(OPSTK));
                    IF (topsymb = '(' ) AND (symb = ')' ) THEN EXIT; END;
                    IF topsymb # '('
                    THEN
                        Assign(Expr,topsymb,index2);
                        INC(index2);
                    END(* if then *);
                END(* loop *);
                IF symb # ')' THEN Push(OPSTK,symb); END;
            END(* if then else *);
            INC(index1);
        END(* while loop *);
        WHILE NOT Empty(OPSTK) DO
            topsymb:=CHAR(Pop(OPSTK));
            IF topsymb # '('
            THEN
                Assign(Expr,topsymb,index2);
                INC(index2);
            END(* if then *);
        END(* while loop *);
        RETURN Expr;
    END InfixPostfix;

END Op1.
------------------------------------------------------------------------
IMPLEMENTATION MODULE FunctionEvaluator;

    FROM Stacks1 IMPORT Stack, Empty, Pop, Push, Initialize,
                        TopOfStack;

    FROM SymbolTable IMPORT SymTab, Table, InitSymTab, Deposit,
                        Fetch;

    FROM Op1 IMPORT RemoveSpaces, IdentConst, InfixPostfix;

    FROM Op2 IMPORT Result;
```

```
FROM Storage IMPORT ALLOCATE, DEALLOCATE;

TYPE Expression = POINTER TO ARRAY [1..80] OF CHAR;
(* Hidden from user.                                          *)

TYPE SetOfChar = SET OF CHAR;

PROCEDURE InitExpr(VAR A: Expression);
VAR I: INTEGER;
BEGIN
    NEW(A);
    FOR I:=1 to 80 DO
        A↑[I]:=' ';
    END(* for loop *);
END InitExpr;

PROCEDURE Assign(VAR A: Expression; B: CHAR; I: INTEGER);
BEGIN
    A↑[I]:=B
END Assign;

PROCEDURE Convert(A: ARRAY OF CHAR; VAR len: INTEGER): Expression;
VAR  I: INTEGER;
     S: ARRAY[1..80] OF CHAR;

BEGIN
    FOR I:=1 TO 80 DO
        S[I]:=' ';
    END(* for loop *);
    (* We copy from A to S. The string S has trailing blanks
       after its useful information.                          *)
    FOR I:=1 TO len DO
        S[I]:=A[I-1];
    END(* for loop *);
    RemoveSpaces(S,len); (* All spaces have been removed from S.     * )
    IdentConst(S,len);       (* All constants have been replaced with
                                operand symbols.                     * )
    RETURN InfixPostfix(S);
END Convert;

PROCEDURE Eval(E: Expression; X: INTEGER): INTEGER;

VAR OPNDSTK          : Stack;
    i, number        : INTEGER;
    symb             : CHAR;
    opnd1, opnd2     : INTEGER;
```

```
        isymb, value          : INTEGER;
        Allowable             : SetOfChar;
    BEGIN (* Eval *)
        Allowable:=SetOfChar{'A'. .'Z'};
        EXCL(Allowable,'X');
        Initialize(OPNDSTK);
        i:=1;
        WHILE E↑[i] # ' ' DO
            symb:=E↑[i];
            IF (symb = 'X') OR (symb = 'x') THEN Push(OPNDSTK,X); END;
            IF symb IN Allowable
            THEN
                isymb:=Fetch(symb,Table);
                Push(OPNDSTK,isymb);
            ELSIF (symb # 'X') AND (symb # 'x')
            THEN
                opnd2:=INTEGER(Pop(OPNDSTK));
                opnd1:=INTEGER(Pop(OPNDSTK));
                value:=Result(symb,opnd1,opnd2);
                Push(OPNDSTK,value);
            END(* if then elsif *);
            INC(i);
        END(* while loop *);
        RETURN INTEGER(Pop(OPNDSTK));
    END Eval;

END FunctionEvaluator.
```

```
MODULE Tabulate;

    FROM FunctionEvaluator IMPORT Expression, Convert, Eval;

    FROM InOut IMPORT WriteLn, WriteString, WriteInt, ReadInt,
                      Read, EOL;

VAR  s       : ARRAY[1. .80] OF CHAR;
     a       : Expression;
     x       : INTEGER;
     answer  : CHAR;
     ch      : CHAR;
     i       : INTEGER;

BEGIN (* Main Program *)
    WriteLn;
    WriteString("Enter a mathematical function (y/n)? ");
```

```
    Read(answer);
    WHILE (answer = 'Y') OR (answer = 'y') DO
        WriteLn;
        WriteString("Enter mathematical function to be evaluated: ");
        i:=0;
        REPEAT
            INC(i);
            Read(ch);
            s[i]:=ch;
        UNTIL ch = EOL;
        s[i]:=' ';
        DEC(i);
        a:=Convert(s,i);
        WriteString("Evaluate the mathematical expression (y/n)? ");
        Read(answer);
        WHILE (answer = 'Y') OR (answer = 'y') DO
            WriteLn;
            WriteString("Enter a value for the independent variable: ");
            ReadInt(x);
            WriteLn;
            WriteString("The value of the function F is → ");
            WriteInt(Eval(a,x),10);
            WriteLn;
            WriteString("Evaluate the mathematical expression (y/n)? ");
            Read(answer)
        END;
        WriteLn;
        WriteString("Enter a mathematical function (y/n)? ");
        Read(answer);
    END;
END Tabulate.
```

6.3.7 Let's Take a Walk: FunctionEvaluator Explained

Suppose the array of characters that we input to FunctionEvaluator is:

$$f(x) = -3 * x * x + 4$$
$$\text{-- -- -- --}$$

where the dashes under the input string indicate the index positions in the array of characters starting with position 1 and ending with position 9. We have purposely inserted a space between the numeral 3 and the "*".

We will walk through the software system FunctionEvaluator, displayed in Section 6.3.6, and by so doing, study the implementation details of each subprogram.

The main control module calls

$$E := Convert(S,9)$$

where S is declared as an ARRAY[1. .80] OF CHAR and E is declared as TYPE E: Expression.

In procedure Convert, in the implementation module FunctionEvaluator, we first copy the nine characters to local array S, which was initialized to blank. Control is then transferred to subprogram RemoveSpaces, in implementation module Op1, with the call

$$RemoveSpaces(S,9)$$

In subprogram RemoveSpaces, since S[3] is blank, control is passed to the nested subprogram RemSpace(3,9). This subprogram shifts the elements of array S down by one with the statement,

$$S[I]:=S[I+1]$$

Upon exiting from subprogram RemoveSpaces, control returns to subprogram Convert. Control is then passed to subprogram IdentConst(S,len), again in module Op1. The array of characters, S, passed to IdentConst, is now

$$-3*x*x+4$$

Since S[0] = '−', control is passed to nested subprogram ADD(0). We add a zero to the expression to avoid the problem of dealing with a unary minus sign operator. This subprogram shifts the characters in S up by one starting in position 0, and then inserts the character "0" in position 0. We note that the lowest array position for a dynamic array, in Modula-2, is 0. When control returns from subprogram ADD back to IdentConst, control is transferred to InitSymTab(Table), in module SymbolTable. This call creates a symbol table data structure dynamically in memory and initializes all the components of the table to blanks and zeros.

The first numeral encountered in the WHILE loop directly below InitSymTab(Table), in subprogram IdentConst, is 0. The length of this numeral, denoted in the program by LenNum, is 1. The standard library routine StrToInt converts the numeral 0 to the integer 0. This integer is deposited in the symbol table by a call to subprogram Deposit, located in module SymbolTable. The character ch returned is 'B'. This happens again for the numeral 3, which gets deposited in the symbol table as the number 3 associated with the character 'C', and then again for the numeral 4, which gets deposited as the number 4 associated with the character 'D'.

When we exit from IdentConst, the array of characters S, is returned to Convert as follows.

$$B-C*x*x+D$$

Convert transfers control to subprogram InfixPostfix, again in module Op1.

In subprogram InfixPostfix, calls to subprogram Initialize, in module Stacks1, and subprogram InitExpr, in module FunctionEvaluator are made. These calls dynamically create and initialize the data structures OPSTK and Expr, respectively. We illustrate the process of infix to postfix conversion in Table 6.2, which was built by traversing the WHILE loop directly under the line

$$index1:=0; index2:=1;$$

The postfix string returned to the main program is, therefore, BCx*x*−D+. The main control module then calls Eval(E,#), where # is some integer value. As an exercise, see whether you can follow the logic of subprogram Eval and confirm that it returns the number $-3*\#*\#+4$ to the control program.

6.3.8 Compilation Order for the Modules of FunctionEvaluator

Because there are some interdependencies among the 10 modules that comprise the software system displayed in Section 6.3.6, the final object code product is produced by compiling the 10 modules in correct sequence. What is the "correct" sequence?

There are several correct sequences. Let us first examine some incorrect sequences. Table 6.3 lists two illegal sequences. We use the suffix "Def" to indicate definition module and the suffix "Imp" to indicate implementation module.

Why are the sequences 1 and 2 illegal?

In sequence 1 module Op1 imports entities from module SymbolTable. Therefore, module SymbolTable must be compiled before module Op1.

The error in sequence 2 is more subtle. Both definition module and the implementation module for Op1 import entities from FunctionEvaluator.

Table 6.2   Infix to Postfix Conversion for
B − C∗x∗x + D

Symbol	OPSTK	Postfix String
B		B
−	−	B
C	−	BC
∗	−∗	BC
x	−∗	BCx
∗	−∗	BCx∗
x	−∗	BCx∗x
+	+	BCx∗x−
D	+	BCx∗x−D
		BCx∗x−D+

Table 6.3   Some Incorrect Sequences for
Compilation

Illegal Sequence 1

FunctionEvaluatorDef
GenStacksDef
GenStacksImp
Op1Def
Op1Imp
SymbolTableDef
SymbolTableImp
Op2Def
Op2Imp
FunctionEvaluatorImp

Illegal Sequence 2

SymbolTableDef
SymbolTableImp
Op1Def
Op1Imp
FunctionEvaluatorDef
GenStacksDef
GenStacksImp
Op1Def
Op2Imp
FunctionEvaluatorImp

**Table 6.4 Some Correct Compilation
Sequences**

Legal Sequence 1

FunctionEvaluatorDef
SymbolTableDef
Op2Def
SymbolTableImp
Op2Def
GenStacksDef
GenStacksImp
Op1Def
Op1Imp
FunctionEvaluatorImp

Legal Sequence 2

FunctionEvaluatorDef
Op2Def
Op2Imp
GenStacksDef
GenStacksImp
SymbolTableDef
SymbolTableImp
Op1Def
Op1Imp
FunctionEvaluatorImp

Therefore, the definition module for FunctionEvaluator must be compiled before either Op1 module is compiled.

Table 6.4 displays two correct sequences for compiling the 10 modules of FunctionEvaluator.

We repeat, once again, the rule for determining legal sequences of compilation.

> *A module that exports resources must be compiled before any module that imports any of these resources.*

6.3.9 Maintenance of FunctionEvaluator

The present version of FunctionEvaluator, given in Section 6.3.6, returns integer values when integer arguments are provided to Eval. We wish to modify the software system to permit real arguments to be input to Eval and to permit Eval to return a real result. Furthermore, we wish to include the important functions sin, cos, exp, ln, and abs as allowable operations. This will make FunctionEvaluator much more useful for general purpose numerical computations.

Normally, maintenance on an unstructured software system as large as FunctionEvaluator would be costly. In addition, the reliability of the resulting product might deteriorate as a consequence of such maintenance. Because of the modular structure of FunctionEvaluator, program maintenance is very simple.

Several subprograms must be modified including subprograms IdentConst and InfixPostfix in implementation module Op1, subprogram Result in implementation module Op2, and subprograms Convert and Eval in implementation module FunctionEvaluator. Module RealStack is developed for importation into implementation module FunctionEvaluator. The type WORD cannot serve as a surrogate for a real value.

In the new subprogram IdentFunct, in implementation module Op1, the key words sin, cos, exp, ln, and abs, in the string S, are replaced by special token symbols. Definition module Op1 is modified to export this new subprogram. In subprogram InfixPostfix, the nested subprogram Precedence must be bolstered with additional code and small changes must be made in the body of InfixPostfix. In subprogram IdentConst, a real value must be transferred to the symbol table rather than an integer value. Additional code must be added to subprogram Result, in module Op2, to permit evaluation of the new functions. Several INTEGER parameters and variables are changed to REAL parameters and variables.

The procedure Convert, in version 2, has no parameters, whereas before it had two parameters. The new version of procedure Convert prompts the user to input a mathematical function, thus removing this responsibility from the user's program.

We display the new version of FunctionEvaluator in Program 6.4.

PROGRAM 6.4   Modula-2 Software System for Real Function Evaluator

```
DEFINITION MODULE FunctionEvaluator;
(* $SEG:=12; *)

    EXPORT QUALIFIED
        (* type *) Expression,
        (* proc *) InitExpr,
        (* proc *) Assign,
        (* proc *) Convert,
        (* proc *) Eval;

    TYPE Expression;
    (* An abstract data type derived from the
       original mathematical expression to be used
       for function evaluation.                              *)
```

```
    PROCEDURE InitExpr(VAR A: Expression);
    (* Creates and initializes expression.                              *)


    PROCEDURE Assign(VAR A: Expression; B: CHAR; I: INTEGER);
    (* Assign character B to A in position I.                           *)


    PROCEDURE Convert(): Expression;
    (* This procedure interactively prompts the user to input a
       mathematical expression as a string of characters and then
       converts this string of characters to an expression.            *)


    PROCEDURE Eval(E: Expression; X: REAL): REAL;
    (* This procedure combines the abstract data type
       Expression with the argument X to produce the desired
       answer.                                                          *)


END FunctionEvaluator.
```

```
DEFINITION MODULE SymbolTable;
(* $SEG:=14; *)


    EXPORT QUALIFIED
            (* type *) SymTab,
            (* var  *) Table,
            (* proc *) InitSymTab,
            (* proc *) Deposit,
            (* proc *) Fetch;


    TYPE SymTab;
    (* Abstract type for symbol table.                                 *)


    VAR Table: SymTab;
    (* Shared by two modules.                                          *)


    PROCEDURE InitSymTab(VAR A: SymTab);
    (* This procedure creates a symbol table SymTab and initializes
       it to empty.                                                    *)


    PROCEDURE Deposit(A: REAL; VAR B: SymTab; VAR C: CHAR);
    (* This procedure deposits a real number A into the symbol table
       B and returns a character C. The character C is associated
       with the number A in the symbol table B.                        *)
```

```
PROCEDURE Fetch(A: CHAR; B: SymTab): REAL;
(* This procedure returns a real number when a character A
   is input to symbol table B.                                    *)

END SymbolTable.
```

```
IMPLEMENTATION MODULE SymbolTable;

    FROM Storage IMPORT ALLOCATE, DEALLOCATE;

    TYPE SymbolRecord = RECORD
                            Symb: CHAR;
                             Val: REAL
                        END;

    TYPE SymTab = POINTER TO ARRAY [1. .24] OF SymbolRecord;

    PROCEDURE InitSymTab(VAR A: SymTab);

    VAR I: INTEGER;

    BEGIN
        NEW(A);
        FOR I:= 1 TO 24 DO
            A↑[I].Symb:=' ';
            A↑[I].Val   :=  0.0
        END
    END InitSymTab;

    PROCEDURE Deposit(A: REAL; VAR B: SymTab; VAR C: CHAR);

    VAR I: INTEGER;

    BEGIN
        C:='A';
        I:=0;
        REPEAT
            I:=I+1;
            INC(C);
            IF C = 'X' THEN INC(C); END;
            (* X is the independent variable. *)
        UNTIL B↑[I].Symb = ' ';
        B↑[I].Symb:=C;
        B↑[I].Val:=A
    END Deposit;
```

```
PROCEDURE Fetch(A: CHAR; B: SymTab): REAL;

VAR C:CHAR;
    I: INTEGER;

BEGIN
    C:='A';
    I:=0;
    REPEAT
        I:=I+1;
        INC(C)
    UNTIL B↑[I].Symb = A;
    RETURN B↑[I].Val
END Fetch;

END SymbolTable.
```

```
DEFINITION MODULE Stacks1;
(* $SEG:=16 *)

    FROM SYSTEM IMPORT WORD;

    EXPORT QUALIFIED
            (* type *) Stack,
            (* proc *) Empty,
            (* proc *) Pop,
            (* proc *) Push,
            (* proc *) Initialize,
            (* proc *) Remove,
            (* proc *) TopOfStack;

    TYPE Stack;

    PROCEDURE Empty(S: Stack) : BOOLEAN;
    (* Returns true if stack is empty, false otherwise.              *)

    PROCEDURE Pop(VAR S: Stack) : WORD;
    (Strips top element off stack.                                   *)

    PROCEDURE Push(VAR S: Stack; X: WORD);
    (* Adds element to top of stack.                                 *)

    PROCEDURE Initialize(VAR S: Stack);
    (* Sets stack to empty.                                          *)

    PROCEDURE Remove(VAR S: Stack);
    (* Removes stack from memory.                                    *)
```

```
    PROCEDURE TopOfStack(S: Stack): WORD;
    (* Returns the current top of the stack without changing
       the contents of the stack.                                    *)

END Stacks1.
```

```
IMPLEMENTATION MODULE Stacks1;

    FROM InOut IMPORT WriteString, WriteLn;

    FROM Storage  IMPORT ALLOCATE, DEALLOCATE;

    FROM SYSTEM IMPORT WORD;

    CONST STACKSIZE = 80;

    TYPE Objects = ARRAY [1..STACKSIZE] OR WORD;
         Stack = POINTER TO RECORD
                                ITEM: Objects;
                                TOP : CARDINAL
                        END;

    PROCEDURE Empty(S: Stack) : BOOLEAN;
    BEGIN
        IF S↑.TOP = 0
        THEN
            RETURN TRUE
        ELSE
            RETURN FALSE
        END
    END Empty;

    PROCEDURE Pop(VAR S: Stack) : WORD;
    BEGIN
        IF Empty(S)
        THEN
            WriteString("Invalid mathematical expression.");
            WriteLn;
            HALT
        ELSE
            DEC(S↑.TOP);
            RETURN S↑.ITEM[S↑.TOP+1];
        END
    END Pop;
```

```
    PROCECURE Push(VAR S: Stack; X: WORD);
    BEGIN
        IF S↑.TOP = STACKSIZE
        THEN
            WriteString("Invalid mathematical expression.");
            WriteLn;
            HALT
        ELSE
            INC(S↑.TOP);
            S↑.ITEM[S↑.TOP]:=X
        END
    END Push;

    PROCEDURE Initialize(VAR S: Stack);
    BEGIN
        NEW(S);
        S↑.TOP:=0
    END Initialize;

    PROCEDURE Remove(VAR S: Stack);
    BEGIN
        DISPOSE(S)
    END Remove;

    PROCEDURE TopOfStack(S: Stack): WORD;
    BEGIN
        RETURN S↑.ITEM[S↑.TOP]
    END TopOfStack;

END Stacks1.
```

```
DEFINITION MODULE RealStack;
(* $SEG:=30; *)

    EXPORT QUALIFIED
            (* type *) Stack,
            (* proc *) Empty,
            (* proc *) Pop,
            (* proc *) Push,
            (* proc *) Initialize,
            (* proc *) Remove,
            (* proc *) TopOfStack;

    TYPE Stack;
```

```
PROCEDURE Empty(S: Stack) : BOOLEAN;
(* Returns true if stack is empty, false otherwise.                    *)

PROCEDURE Pop(VAR S: Stack) : REAL;
(* Strips top element off stack.                                        *)

PROCEDURE Push(VAR S: STACK; X: REAL);
(* Adds element to top of stack                                         *)

PROCEDURE Initialize(VAR S: Stack);
(* Sets stack to empty.                                                 *)

PROCEDURE Remove(VAR S: Stack);
(* Removes stack from memory.                                           *)

PROCEDURE TopOfStack(S: Stack): REAL;
(* Returns the current top of the stack without changing
    the contents of the stack.                                          *)

END RealStack.
```

```
IMPLEMENTATION MODULE RealStack;

    FROM InOut IMPORT WriteString, WriteLn;

    FROM Storage  IMPORT ALLOCATE, DEALLOCATE;

    CONST STACKSIZE = 80;

    TYPE Objects = ARRAY [1..STACKSIZE] OF REAL;
         Stack = POINTER TO RECORD
                                ITEM: Objects;
                                TOP : CARDINAL
                         END;

    PROCEDURE Empty(S: Stack) : BOOLEAN;
    BEGIN
        IF S↑.TOP = 0
        THEN
            RETURN TRUE
        ELSE
            RETURN FALSE
        END
    END Empty;
```

```
    PROCEDURE Pop(VAR S: Stack) : REAL;
    BEGIN
        IF Empty(S)
        THEN
            WriteString("Invalid mathematical expression.");
            WriteLn;
            HALT
        ELSE
            DEC(S↑.TOP);
            RETURN S↑.ITEM[S↑.TOP+1];
        END
    END Pop;

    PROCEDURE Push(VAR S: Stack; X: REAL);
    BEGIN
        IF S↑.TOP = STACKSIZE
        THEN
            WriteString("Invalid mathematical expression.");
            WriteLn;
            HALT
        ELSE
            INC(S↑.TOP);
            S↑.ITEM[S↑.TOP]:=X
        END
    END Push;

    PROCEDURE Initialize(VAR S: Stack);
    BEGIN
        NEW(S);
        S↑.TOP:=0
    END Initialize

    PROCEDURE Remove(VAR S: Stack);
    BEGIN
        DISPOSE(S)
    END Remove;

    PROCEDURE TopOfStack(S: Stack): REAL;
    BEGIN
        RETURN S↑.ITEM[S↑.TOP]
    END TopOfStack;

END RealStack.
```

```
DEFINITION MODULE Op2;
(* $SEG:=20; *)

    EXPORT QUALIFIED
                    (* proc *) Result;

    PROCEDURE Result(Symb: CHAR; Opnd1,Opnd2: REAL) : REAL;
    (* Returns a real value when integers Opnd1 and Opnd2 are
       combined with an operator symbol Symb.                    *)

END Op2.
```

```
IMPLEMENTATION MODULE Op2;

    FROM InOut IMPORT WriteString, WriteLn;

    FROM MathLib0 IMPORT sin,cos,ln,exp;

    PROCEDURE Result(Symb: CHAR; Opnd1,Opnd2: REAL) : REAL;
    BEGIN
        CASE Symb OF
            '+': RETURN Opnd1 + Opnd2; |
            '-': RETURN Opnd1 - Opnd2; |
            '*': RETURN Opnd1 * Opnd2; |
            '/': IF Opnd2 = 0.0
                THEN
                    WriteLn;
                    WriteString("Divide by zero error.");
                    WriteLn;
                    HALT;
                ELSE
                    Opnd2:=Opnd1/Opnd2;
                END(* if then else *);
            '%': RETURN sin(Opnd2); |
            '↑': RETURN cos(Opnd2); |
            '&': RETURN exp(Opnd2); |
            '!': RETURN abs(Opnd2); |
            '#': IF Opnd2 <= 0.0
                THEN
                    WriteLn;
                    WriteString("Cannot take log of nonpositive number.");
                    WriteLn;
                    HALT;
```

```
            ELSE
                RETURN ln(Opnd2);
            END(* if then else *);
        END (* case *);
    END Result;

END Op2.
```

```
DEFINITION MODULE Op1;
(* $SEG:=18; *)

(* This module supports module Convert.                                      *)

    FROM FunctionEvaluator IMPORT Expression;

    EXPORT QUALIFIED
            (* proc *) RemoveSpaces,
            (* proc *) IdentConst,
            (* proc *) InfixPostfix,
            (* proc *) IdentFunct;

    PROCEDURE RemoveSpaces(VAR S: ARRAY OF CHAR; len: INTEGER);
    (* All interior spaces are removed from the input string S,
        producing the output string S.                                       *)

    PROCEDURE IdentConst(VAR S: ARRAY OF CHAR; VAR len: INTEGER);
    (* All constants in the string S of length len are replaced by
        operand symbols. These symbols are placed in the symbol
        table SymTab with their corresponding numerical values.              *)

    PROCEDURES InfixPostfix(S: ARRAY OF CHAR): Expression;
    (* Converts the string S to Expression.  Expression will
        be used later for function evaluation.                               *)

    PROCEDURE IdentFunct(VAR S: ARRAY OF CHAR; VAR len: INTEGER);
    (* We use the following special symbols to replace sin, cos,
        ln, and abs:
            sin--> %
            cos--> ↑
            exp--> &
            abs--> !
            ln--> #                                                          *)

END Op1.
```

```
IMPLEMENTATION MODULE Op1;

    FROM FunctionEvaluator IMPORT Expression, InitExpr, Assign;

    FROM SymbolTable IMPORT SymTab, Table, InitSymTab, Deposit;

    FROM Reals IMPORT StrToReal;

    FROM Stacks1 IMPORT Stack, Empty, Pop, Push, Initialize, TopOfStack;

    TYPE CharSet = SET OF CHAR;

    PROCEDURE RemoveSpaces(VAR S: ARRAY OF CHAR; len: INTEGER);

        PROCEDURE RemSpace(POS,L: INTEGER);

        VAR I: INTEGER;

        BEGIN
            IF POS < L
            THEN
                FOR I:=POS TO L DO
                    S[I]:=S[I+1];
                END(* for loop *)
            END(* if then *)
        END RemSpace;

    VAR I     : INTEGER;

    BEGIN
        I:=-1;
        REPEAT
            INC(I);
            IF S[I] = ' '
            THEN
                RemSpace(I,len);
                DEC(I);
                DEC(len)
            END (* if then *)
        UNTIL I = len-1;
    END RemoveSpaces;

    PROCEDURE IdentConst(VAR S: ARRAY OF CHAR; VAR len: INTEGER);
```

```
VAR NUMERALS, ALPHABET, ALLOWABLE : CharSet;
        I , J, LenNum                    : INTEGER;
        RealVal                          : REAL;
        Stt                              : ARRAY[1..20] OF CHAR;
        dummy                            : BOOLEAN;
        ch                               : CHAR;


    PROCEDURE ADD(POS: INTEGER);
    (* Adds "0" to the position just before the "−" in S.            *)

    VAR I: INTEGER;

    BEGIN
        FOR I:=len TO POS + 2 BY −1 DO
            S[I]:=S[I−1];
        END(* for loop *);
        S[POS]:='0';
        S[POS+1]:='−';
        len:=len + 1;
    END ADD;


    PROCEDURE Replace(symb: CHAR; pos, length: INTEGER);
    (* This procedure replaces an integer constant by symb.          *)

    VAR I: INTEGER;

    BEGIN
        S[pos]:=symb;
        IF length > 1
        THEN
            FOR I:=pos+1 TO len−length+1 DO
                S[I]:=S[I+length−1];
            END(* for loop *);
        END(* if then *);
    END Replace;

BEGIN (* IdentConst *)
    NUMERALS:=CharSet{'0','1','2','3','4','5','6','7','8','9','.'};
    ALPHABET:=NUMERALS + CharSet{'A'..'Z'} + CharSet{'x'};
    (* We replace any nonoperator minus sign with "0−". *)
    I:=0;
    WHILE S[i] # ' ' DO
        IF (I = 0) AND (S[I] = '−')
        THEN
            ADD(I);
```

```
            ELSE
                IF S[I] = '−'
                THEN
                    IF NOT (S[I−1] IN ALPHABET)
                    THEN
                        ADD(I);
                    END(* if not then *)
                END(* if then *)
            END(* if then else *)
            INC(I);
        END(* while loop *);
        I:=0;
        InitSymTab(Table);
        WHILE S[I] # ' ' DO
            IF S[I] IN NUMERALS
            THEN
                LenNum:=1;
                WHILE S[I+LenNum] IN NUMERALS DO
                    LenNum:=LenNum+1;
                END(* while loop *);
                FOR J:=1 TO 20 DO
                    Stt[J]:='z';
                END;
                FOR J:=1 TO LenNum DO
                    Stt[J]:=S[I+J−1];
                END(* for loop*);
                dummy:=StrToReal(Stt,RealVal);
                Deposit(RealVal,Table,ch);
                (* We replace the integer constant by an operand symbol. *)
                Replace(ch,I,LenNum);
            END(* if then *);
            INC(I);
        END(* while loop *)
END IdentConst;


PROCEDURE InfixPostfix(S: ARRAY OF CHAR): Expression;


VAR OPSTK           : Stack;
    index1, index2, I: INTEGER;
    symb, topsymb   : CHAR;
    Allowable       : CharSet;
    Expr            : Expression;
```

```
PROCEDURE Precedence(op1,op2: CHAR): BOOLEAN;
BEGIN
    IF ((op1 = '+')OR(op1 = '−'))AND(op2 = '*')OR(op2 = '/')
    THEN
        RETURN FALSE
    ELSIF ((op1 = '(' ) AND (op2 # ')' ))OR(op2 = '(' )
    THEN
        RETURN FALSE
    ELSIF ((op1='+')OR(op1='−')OR(op1='*')OR(op1='/'))AND
        ((op2='%')OR(op2='↑')OR(op2='&')
            OR(op2='!')OR(op2='#'))
    THEN
        RETURN FALSE
    ELSE RETURN TRUE
    END(* if then elsif else *);
END Precedence;

BEGIN (* InfixPostfix *)
    Allowable:=CharSet{'A'..'Z'} + CharSet{'x'};
    Initialize(OPSTK);
    InitExpr(Expr);
    index1:=0; index2:=1;
    WHILE (S[index1] # ' ') DO
        symb:=S[index1];
        IF symb IN Allowable THEN
            Assign(Expr,symb,index2);
            INC(index2);
        ELSE
            LOOP
                IF (Empty(OPSTK)) OR
                        (NOT Precedence (CHAR(TopOfStack
                        (OPSTK)),symb))
                    THEN EXIT; END;
                topsymb:=CHAR(Pop(OPSTK));
                IF NOT Empty(OPSTK)
                THEN
                    IF ((CHAR(TopOfStack(OPSTK)) = '%') OR
                    (CHAR(TopOfStack(OPSTK)) = '!' ) OR
                    (CHAR(TopOfStack(OPSTK)) = '↑' ) OR
                    (CHAR(TopOfStack(OPSTK)) = '#' ) OR
                    (CHAR(TopOfStack(OPSTK)) = '&')) AND (symb = ')')
                    THEN
                        topsymb:=CHAR(Pop(OPSTK));
                        Assign(Expr,topsymb,index2);
```

```
                        INC(index2);
                        EXIT;
                    END(* if then *);
                END(* if then *);
                IF (topsymb = '(') AND (symb = ')') THEN EXIT; END;
                IF topsymb # '(' THEN
                    Assign(Expr,topsymb,index2);
                    INC(index2);
                END(* if then *);
            END(* loop *);
            IF symb <> ')' THEN Push(OPSTK,symb); END;
        END(* if then else *);
        INC(index1);
    END(* while loop *);
    WHILE NOT Empty(OPSTK) DO
        topsymb:=CHAR(Pop(OPSTK));
        IF topsymb # '(' THEN
            Assign(Expr,topsymb,index2);
            INC(index2);
        END(* if then *);
    END(* while loop *);
    RETURN Expr;
END InfixPostfix;


PROCEDURE IdentFunct(VAR S: ARRAY OF CHAR; VAR len: INTEGER);
(* We use the following special symbols to replace sin, cos
    ln, and abs:
        sin--> %
        cos--> ↑
        exp--> &
        abs--> !
        ln--> #                                          *)


PROCEDURE Replace(symb: CHAR; pos: INTEGER);

VAR i: INTEGER;

BEGIN
    S[pos]:=symb;
    FOR i:=pos+1 TO len-2 DO S[i]:=S[i+2]; END;
END Replace;

VAR k,i: INTEGER;
```

```
    BEGIN (* IdentFunct *)
        k:=0;
        WHILE S[k] # ' ' DO
            IF k >= 1)AND(((S[k]='N')OR(S[k]='n'))AND(S[k-1]='L')OR
                (S[k-1]='1'))
            THEN
                S[k-1]:='#';
                FOR i:=k TO len-1 DO
                    S[i]:=S[i+1];
                END;(* for loop *)
            END(* if then *);
            IF (k >=2)
            THEN
                IF ((S[k]='N')OR(S[k]='n'))AND((S[k-1]='I')OR(S[k-1]='i'))AND
                    ((S[k-2]='S')OR(S[k-2]='s')) THEN Replace('%',k-2); END;
                IF ((S[k]='S')OR(S[k]='s'))AND((S[k-1]='O')OR(S[k-1]='o'))AND
                    ((S[k-2]='C')OR(S[k-2]='c')) THEN Replace('↑',k-2); END;
                IF ((S[k]='P')OR(S[k]='p'))AND((S[k-1]='X')OR(S[k-1]='x'))AND
                    ((S[k-2]='E')OR(S[k-2]='e')) THEN Replace('&',k-2); END;
                IF ((S[k]='S')OR(S[k]='s'))AND((S[k-1]='B')OR(S[k-1]='b'))AND
                    ((S[k-2]='A')OR(S[k-2]='a')) THEN Replace('!',k-2); END;
            END(* if then *);
            INC(k)
        END(* while loop *);
    END IdentFunct;

END Op1.
```

```
IMPLEMENTATION MODULE FunctionEvaluator;

    FROM RealStack IMPORT Stack, Empty, Pop, Push, Initialize,
                            TopOfStack;

    FROM SymbolTable IMPORT SymTab, Table, InitSymTab, Deposit, Fetch;

    FROM Op1 IMPORT RemoveSpaces, IdentConst, InfixPostfix, IdentFunct;

    FROM Op2 IMPORT Result;

    FROM Storage IMPORT ALLOCATE, DEALLOCATE;

    FROM InOut IMPORT WriteLn, WriteString, Read, EOL;

    TYPE Expression = POINTER TO ARRAY [1..80] OF CHAR;
                        (* Hidden from user. *)

    TYPE SetOfChar = SET OF CHAR;
```

```
PROCEDURE InitExpr(VAR A: Expression);

VAR I: INTEGER;

BEGIN
    NEW(A);
    FOR I:=1 TO 80 DO
        A↑[I]:=' ';
    END(* for loop *);
END InitExpr;

PROCEDURE Assign(VAR A: Expression; B: CHAR; I: INTEGER);
BEGIN
    A↑[I]:=B
END Assign;

PROCEDURE Convert(): Expression;

    VAR I, len : INTEGER;
        S     : ARRAY[1..size] OF CHAR;
        ch    : CHAR;

BEGIN
    FOR I:=1 TO size DO
        S[I]:=' ';
    END(* do loop *);
    WriteLn; WriteLn;
    WriteString("Mathematical expression may contain");
    WriteString(" real constants,");
    WriteLn; WriteLn;
    WriteString(" and the operators +, −, /, *, ln, sin,");
    WriteString(" cos, exp, and abs.");
    WriteLn; WriteLn;
    WriteString("Blanks will be ignored in your expression.");
    WriteLn; WriteLn;
    WriteString("Enter your mathematical expression -->");
    WriteLn;
    I:=0;
    REPEAT
        INC(I);
        Read(ch);
        S[I]:=ch;
    UNTIL (ch = EOL) OR (I = size);
```

```
    len:=I−1;
    S[I]:=' ';
    RemoveSpaces(S,len);(* All spaces have been removed from S.          *)
    IdentConst(S,len);    (* All constants have been replaced with
                             operand symbols.                            *)
    IdentFunct(S,len);    (* All mathematical functions have been
                             replaced with special symbols.              *)
    RETURN InfixPostfix(S);
END Convert;


PROCEDURE Eval(E: Expression; X: REAL): REAL;


VAR OPNDSTK          : Stack;
    i                : INTEGER;
    symb             : CHAR;
    opnd1, opnd2     : REAL;
    rsymb, value     : REAL;
    Allowable        : SetOfChar;


BEGIN (* Eval *)
    Allowable:=SetOfChar{'A'..'Z'};
    EXCL(Allowable,'X');
    Initialize(OPNDSTK);
    i:=1;
    WHILE E↑[i] # ' ' DO
        symb:=E↑[i];
        IF (symb = 'X') OR (symb = 'x') THEN Push(OPNDSTK,X); END;
        IF symb IN Allowable THEN
            rsymb:=Fetch(symb,Table);
            Push(OPNDSTK,rsymb);
        ELSIF (symb='%')OR(symb='↑')OR(symb='&')OR(symb='#')OR
            (symb='!')
                THEN
                    opnd2:=Pop(OPNDSTK);
                    value:=Result(symb,opnd1,opnd2);
                    Push(OPNDSTK,value);
        ELSIF (symb # 'X') AND (symb # 'x') THEN
            opnd2:=Pop(OPNDSTK);
            opnd1:=Pop(OPNDSTK);
            value:=Result(symb,opnd1,opnd2);
            Push(OPNDSTK,value);
        END(* if then elsif *);
```

```
            INC(i);
        END(* while loop *);
        RETURN Pop(OPNDSTK);
    END Eval;

END FunctionEvaluator.
```

```
MODULE Tabulate;

    FROM FunctionEvaluator IMPORT Expression, Convert, Eval;

    FROM InOut IMPORT WriteLn, WriteString, Read, EOL;

    FROM RealInOut IMPORT ReadReal, WriteReal;

VAR
    a       : Expression;
    x       : REAL;
    answer : CHAR;
    ch      : CHAR;

BEGIN (* Main Program *)
    WriteLn;
    WriteString("Enter a mathematical function (y/n)? ");
    Read(answer);
    WHILE (answer = 'Y') OR (answer = 'y') DO
        a:=Convert();
        (* Procedure Convert prompts the user for a mathematical
            expression.                                                    *)
        WriteString("Evaluate the mathematical expression (y/n)? ");
        Read(answer);
        WHILE (answer = 'Y') OR (answer = 'y') DO
            WriteLn;
            WriteString("Enter a value for the independent variable: ");
            ReadReal(x);
            WriteLn;
            WriteString("The value of the function F is --> ");
            WriteReal(Eval(a,x),10);
            WriteLn;
            WriteString("Evaluate the mathematical expression (y/n)? ");
            Read(answer)
        END;
```

```
        WriteLn;
        WriteString("Enter a mathematical function (y/n)? ");
        Read(answer);
    END;
END Tabulate.
```

The modifications that were required to convert the software system of Program 6.3 into the software system of Program 6.4 were straightforward because only a few modules in Program 6.4 had to be repaired. This is the real (pun intended) payoff resulting from modular software construction, namely, ease of maintenance!

6.4 MODULAR SOFTWARE CONSTRUCTION IN PASCAL

Standard Pascal provides the software developer no mechanism for separate or independent compilation and no mechanism for data hiding. An important extension to standard Pascal, UCSD Pascal®, developed at the University of California, San Diego, supports separate compilation but does not fully support data hiding.

In UCSD Pascal, compilation units consist of an INTERFACE portion and an IMPLEMENTATION portion. The entire unit must be compiled as a single entity.

Pascal programs may import compilation units by using the key word "uses" at the beginning of the program. All the entities listed in the INTERFACE part of the unit become visible and global to the client Pascal program. Contrast this with Modula-2 in which specific entities are exported and imported. In UCSD Pascal, version checking is not performed automatically as is the case with Modula-2. That is, if an INTERFACE in a Pascal unit is changed and recompiled, the system does not force client programs using the unit to be recompiled. This responsibility rests with the software developer.

Program 6.5 illustrates a UCSD Pascal unit for stacks. Compare this with the Stack units in Program 6.4 written in Modula-2.

PROGRAM 6.5   Stack Unit in UCSD Pascal

```
unit STACK_OPS;

INTERFACE

function POP: CHAR;        {This function is exported.}

procedure PUSH(X: CHAR);   {This procedure is exported.}
```

IMPLEMENTATION   {All data structures defined within
                        this part of the unit are hidden
                        from the user of the unit.   }

const MAX_SIZE = 100;

var STACK: record
                ITEM: array[1..MAX_SIZE] of CHAR;
                TOP : 0..MAX_SIZE
           end;

function POP;
begin
    if STACK.TOP < 1
    then
        writeln('Stack underflow.')
    else
    begin
        POP:=STACK.ITEM[STACK.TOP];
        STACK.TOP:=STACK.TOP-1
    end
end{POP};

procedure PUSH;
begin
    if STACK.TOP > MAX_SIZE
    then
        writeln('Stack overflow.')
    else
    begin
        STACK.TOP:=STACK.TOP+1;
        STACK.ITEM[STACK.TOP]:=X
    end
end{PUSH};

begin   {Initialization code}
    STACK.TOP:=0

end.

The initialization code in Program 6.5 is executed before the code in a client program is executed.

It is important to note that the Pascal stack unit, given in Program 6.5, allows a user only the ability to manipulate a single stack. There is no abstract object, say STACK, exported. Only the operations on this hidden and implicit data type are exported. Since Pascal does not support data hiding, it supports only a limited form of object-oriented design in which the representational details of all data types are accessible.

6.5 SUMMARY

- Programmers tend to be task oriented, self oriented, or interaction oriented.
- Human factors contribute significantly to the success or failure of team programming efforts.
- Roughly 50% of a programmer's time is spent communicating with other programmers.
- Egoless programming requires the individual in a team programming environment to view the software system as community property and not associate ownership with a part of the system.
- In egoless programming, errors are considered to be a norm in the software production process and no individual blame is associated with the errors. Egoless programming may effectively draw a programming team together, since the emphasis is on the community program (or subsystem) rather than on each individual's contribution.
- An egoless approach to programming often results in a more rigorous and effective testing program.
- Two key factors contributing to the success of modular software construction are module independence and data abstraction.
- Module independence implies that it should be possible to modify the implementation details of any given module without doing damage to the rest of the system.
- Data abstraction implies that the client subprograms that import data objects from a given module should not have access to the representational details of the data objects. Only the set of specified operations on the given data objects can be used to access or manipulate these data objects.
- Modula-2 may be effectively used as a program design language.
- The modules that define the system architecture of a software system provide the framework that supports the final software product.
- A strict rule for compilation order must be followed in compiling a software system written in Modula-2. A module that exports entities must be compiled before a module that imports any of these entities.
- Although an entire module may be fairly large, each individual component of a module (a subprogram) should be of manageable size.
- Object-oriented and modular design provides a systematic approach for managing the complexity of large-scale problems.

REFERENCES

1. Cougar, J. D., and R. A. Zawacki, "What Motivates DP Professionals," *Datamation,* Vol. 24, No. 9, 1978.

2. Bass, B. M., and G. Dunteman, "Behaviour in Groups as a Function of Self, Interaction, and Task Orientation," *J. Abnorm. Soc. Psychol.,* Vol. 66, 1963, pp. 419–428.

3. Weinberg, G. M., *The Psychology of Computer Programming,* New York: Van Nostrand, 1971.

4. Myers, G. J., *Reliable Software Through Composite Design,* New York: Van Nostrand, 1975.

5. Tennenbaum, A. M., and M. J. Augenstein, *Data Structures Using Pascal,* Englewood Cliffs, N.J.: Prentice-Hall, 1981.

EXERCISES

1. Determine a strategy for implementing the steps given in Table 5.1 in a team software development environment.

2. Write a pseudo-code description of each of the implementation modules given in Program 6.4.

3. Write a Modula-2 program for graph plotting. Import the procedures Convert and Eval from FunctionEvaluator so that the user may interactively input the function(s) to be graphed. You may wish to identify additional abstract data types associated with the process of drawing a graph, such as axes, lines, and points.

4. Write an integration program that imports Convert and Eval from FunctionEvaluator so that the user may interactively enter the function to be integrated.

5. Write a general "spread-sheet" program that uses the interactive FunctionEvaluator resources given in Program 6.4.

6. List additional legal compilation sequences for the 10 modules that comprise Program 6.4.

7. The module Stacks1 may be reused in other software systems wherever a stack data type is required. Name several applications that might need to import the stack type and its associated operations.

8. Implement each system that you have identified in Exercise 7.

9. Discuss some of the potential problems that might arise if Program 6.4 were implemented in Pascal. In particular, what consequences, if any, might result from Pascal's inability to support data hiding?

10. Redesign the function evaluator so that:
    (a) Variable names may be strings of arbitrary length.

(b) More than one variable may exist in an expression.

(c) The square root operator is added to the list of allowable operations.

11. Using Modula-2, implement the design of the text formatter specified in Exercise 1 of Chapter 2.

12. Using Modula-2, implement the design of the screen-oriented editor specified in Exercise 2 of Chapter 2.

13. Using Modula-2, implement the design of the registration program specified in Exercise 3 of Chapter 2.

14. Using Modula-2, implement the business inventory system program specified in Exercise 4 of Chapter 2.

15. Using Modula-2, implement the teacher rollbook system specified in Exercise 7 of Chapter 2.

16. Write an SRD for the function evaluation described in this chapter.

Chapter 7

PROGRAMMING METHODOLOGY

Is computer programming an art or science? There are many more university departments with the name "computer science" than "computer art"! The practice of software development satisfies some of the attributes of science—"knowledge obtained by study and practice, any department of systematized knowledge, a branch of study concerned with observation and classification of facts, accumulated knowledge systematized and formulated with reference to the discovery of general truths or the operation of general laws" [1]. Software development and programming also satisfy some of the attributes of art—"skill in performance acquired by experience, study or observation, systematic application of knowledge or skill in effecting a desired result, application of skill and taste to production according to aesthetic principles" [1].

Programming involves both form and substance, style as well as structure. Programming indeed encompasses art and science.

In earlier chapters we focused on the stages of the software development cycle that precede the writing of a program: software needs analysis, requirements, and design. Using the principles of modular software construction, described in Chapters 5 and 6, the shell or framework for a program is established. From modular design charts, and accompanying definition modules or package specifications, emerges the structure of the final program. There are many "programs" that comprise the finished software system, if one defines a "program" as a separate compilation unit.

Despite the structure imposed by the modular design process, the programmer may still profoundly influence the quality of the finished software product. The style of the source code (the programs), the internal documentation, the choices for the names of the many objects that are declared, affect the maintainability of the software and therefore the quality of the software.

261

In this chapter we discuss the issues of programming style, tools, environments, portability, and documentation. We examine methods for estimating software complexity—software metrics. In short, in this chapter we worry about how programs are actually written.

7.1 STYLE

The style that a programmer employs in writing source code is the most important factor affecting the clarity and maintainability of the finished software. If the style is poor, the preparatory work performed at the requirements stage and the design stage will be compromised. Although the software requirements and design documents support later maintenance, it is the source code itself that is the main target of later maintenance.

Good programming style suggests good program layout, sensible use of names, meaningful comments, and the use of language constructs that support program security and reliability. If a programmer can feel a pride in workmanship, it is in part connected with his or her programming style.

In Chapter 3 we discussed programming languages and their relation to software engineering. We focused on the software engineering features available in some recent languages such as Modula-2 and Ada. We emphasize again that a well-written program in an older language such as FORTRAN is always superior to a poorly written program in a more powerful language such as Ada even though Ada has many more features that support software engineering.

The power and utility of modern software engineering languages such as Modula-2 and Ada may be realized only if the programmer employs good style and uses the special facilities of these languages when appropriate. To use these recent languages effectively, a programmer must be conversant with the principles of software engineering in addition to being fluent with the language. These recent languages provide the programmer more options at the lowest level. For example, Modula-2 provides the programmer with a choice of four loop constructs: repeat, do, while, and loop. In FORTRAN IV, by contrast, only the do loop is available. This has been changed in FORTRAN 77.

7.1.1 Naming Objects in a Program

The names that are used in a program for labels, constants, data types, variables, subprograms, and modules, that is, the name space, reflect objects or manipulations in the problem space. The names of objects in a program should be related to or identical to the names of the entities that the program is modeling. Inexperienced programmers often choose names that are easy to type rather than names that describe the object or functional entity being modeled. One should be more concerned with the type of name chosen rather than typing names!

As an example, let us compare the Ada statement in an automobile simulation program,

$$A1:=A2 \, / \, A3;$$

with the alternative statement,

$$ANGULAR\_ACCELERATION\_OF\_AXLE:=TORQUE\_APPLIED\_TO\_AXLE \, / $$
$$MASS\_OF\_AXLE;$$

Although both statements "get the job done," the entities used in the first statement have little relation to the problem being solved, whereas the second statement is directly related to the physics of the problem. It is clear that program readability is enhanced by the second Ada statement and diminished by the first Ada statement. This example illustrates that the Ada language does not make programs readable. This is the job of the programmer.

If you are a FORTRAN programmer, you know that the second Ada statement would be impossible in that language. This would be true even if the ":=" were replaced by "=". A curious statement appears in a popular FORTRAN textbook indicating that the language is very considerate because it allows you to name the memory cells in any way you like, as long as you start with a letter, use only letters and numerals, and use no more than six characters.

The last rule, in our opinion makes FORTRAN quite inconsiderate. With a six-character constraint for naming objects and functional entities, abbreviations are often necessary in the FORTRAN name space. Abbreviations, if necessary, should be used consistently. For example, if TOPVEL is used as an abbreviation for top velocity, then TOPACC should be used for top acceleration and not TACCEL, or ACCTOP. A glossary or data dictionary of variable names should be provided as a program comment explaining the meaning of all abbreviations. For example,

```
C    TOPVEL        Top velocity of car
C    TOPACC        Top acceleration of car
```

7.1.2 Program Comments

Most programming languages provide a facility for including nonexecutable program comments. Comments are an essential and integral part of a program. They should not be inserted after a program is finished but rather written, like an ordinary line of code, while the program is being created.

Tight software production schedules should never limit the number or quality of comments inserted in the program code. When a substitute programmer is required to take over the work of the original programmer, this difficult assignment is made much easier if the original programmer exercised care and good judgment in writing comments.

The number and type of comments that are desirable are a function of the complexity and size of the program, the name space that is used, and the programming language. For example, the first Ada statement that we displayed in Section 7.1.1 requires a comment to explain its purpose, whereas the second Ada statement needs no supporting comment because of the clear use of descriptive variable names.

The main purpose of any comment is to relate a portion of a program to the entities being modeled by the program. Every subprogram should include brief comments explaining its functional purpose. Any unusual data objects should be explained with a comment. References, in the form of comments, should be provided to explain any unusual or complex algorithm that is employed in a program. Complex data structures should be explained with comments.

The proper use of names and comments in programs should make the purpose of every part of a program clear to another programmer of equal skill to the original programmer. The relation that parts of a program have to the software design should also be clear. If this relationship is not clear, more or better comments are in order.

In our view, the proper use of object-oriented design coupled with a sensible choice of names for abstract data types, objects, and procedures leads to a program that is as readable as the original problem description. See for example, Section 4.5.

7.1.3 Program Layout

Except for FORTRAN and some assembly language, most modern programming languages allow free format in writing source code. That is, the meaning of the program (from the computer's frame of reference) is not affected by the program layout.

Layout profoundly affects the readability of programs. Indentation and the use of spaces are the two principal degrees of freedom that the programmer may use to control program layout.

Program 7.1 illustrates the importance of program layout by reproducing the Ada Program 3.1, but modifying the layout.

PROGRAM 7.1 Program 3.1 with Different Layout

```
with TEXT_IO; use TEXT_IO; procedure
USER_DEFINED_ENUMERATION_TYPES is type MONTHS is
```

(JAN,FEB,MAR,APR,MAY,JUN,JUL,AUG,SEP,OCT,NOV, DEC); subtype
DAYNUMBER is INTEGER range 1..31; type WEATHER_RECORD is
array(MONTHS,DAYNUMBER) of INTEGER; LOTEMP,HITEMP;
WEATHER_RECORD; DAY,DAYS : DAYNUMBER; ANSWER : CHARACTER;
MONTH : MONTHS; --This program creates a table containing the
--lowest and highest temperature recorded for each day of the
--month for one year. After the table is completed, the user
--can query the table by specifying a month and a day.
begin for M in MONTHS loop case M is when
SEP|APR|JUN|JUN|NOV => DAYS:=30; when FEB => DAYS:=28;
--Ignore leap year.
when others => DAYS:=31; end case; for D in
1..DAYS loop put("Enter lowest temperature for "); put(M);
put(" "): put(D); get(LOTEMP(M,D)); put_line;
put("Enter highest temperature for "); put(M); put(" "); put(D);
get(HITEMP(M,D)); end loop; end loop; put_line;
put("Do you wish to fetch information from table(y/n)? ");
get(ANSWER);while (ANSWER = 'Y') or (ANSWER = 'y') loop
put("Enter month: "); get(MONTH); put_line;
put("Enter day of month: ");
get(DAY); put_line; put("Low temperature = ");
put(LOTEMP(MONTH,DAY)); put_line; put("High temperature= ");
put(HITEMP(MONTH,DAY)); put_line;
put("Do you wish to fetch more information from table(y/n)? ");
get(ANSWER); end loop; end USER_DEFINED_ENUMERATION_TYPES;

PROGRAM 7.2   The Original Program 3.1 Revisited

with TEXT_IO; use TEXT_IO;
procedure USER_DEFINED_ENUMERATION_TYPES is
    type MONTHS is (JAN,FEB,MAR,APR,MAY,JUN,JUL,AUG,SEP,OCT,NOV,
            DEC);
    subtype DAYNUMBER is INTEGER range 1..31;
    type WEATHER_RECORD is array(MONTHS,DAYNUMBER) of INTEGER;
    LOTEMP,HITEMP : WEATHER_RECORD;
        DAY,DAYS : DAYNUMBER;
        ANSWER : CHARACTER;
        MONTH : MONTHS;
    --This program creates a table containing the lowest and highest
    --temperature recorded for each day of the month for one year.
    --After the table is completed, the user can query the table
    --by specifying a month and a day.

```
begin
    for M in MONTHS loop
        case M is
            when SEP|APR|JUN|JUN|NOV => DAYS:=30;
            when FEB                 => DAYS:=28;
                                        --Ignore leap year.
            when others              => DAYS:=31;
        end case;
        for D in 1..DAYS loop
            put("Enter lowest temperature for ");
            put(M); put(" "): put(D);
            get(LOTEMP(M,D));
            put_line;
            put("Enter highest temperature for ");
            put(M); put(" "); put(D);
            get(HITEMP(M,D));
        end loop;
    end loop;
    put_line;
    put("Do you wish to fetch information from table (y/n)? ");
    get(ANSWER);
    while (ANSWER = 'Y') or (ANSWER = 'y') loop
        put("Enter month: ");
        get(MONTH);
        put_line;
        put("Enter day of month: ");
        get(DAY);
        put_line;
        put("Low temperature = "); put(LOTEMP(MONTH,DAY)); put_line;
        put("High temperature= "); put(HITEMP(MONTH,DAY)); put_line;
        put("Do you wish to fetch more information from table (y/n)? ");
        get(ANSWER);
    end loop;
end USER_DEFINED_ENUMERATION_TYPES;
```

Program 7.1 is identical to the one given in Chapter 3, except for layout. The original Program 3.1 is reproduced as Program 7.2 for your convenience. Both versions will run the same way. Which one would you rather maintain?

Hard and fast rules for program layout must occasionally yield to the realities of page size (if the source code is to printed). Very long statements may cause a problem and force a programmer to modify his or her normal program style.

Prettyprinters have been developed to establish a uniform layout format for programs. What kind of program layout conventions are reasonable? We

**TABLE 7.1   A Possible Set of Pascal Program Layout
              Conventions**

---

1. Label, constant, type, and variable declarations made at the outermost block level
    should start in column 1 of a line. Declarations made at subsequent block levels
    should start at column $T*n$ where n is the block level and T is a standard tab indent.
2. In procedure declarations, the procedure header should start at column $T*n$ and the
    procedure body should start at column $T* (n + 1)$.
3. Local declarations should be separated from the procedure header by at least one
    blank line.
4. If the procedure has a header comment, it should appear before the local declara-
    tions and be separated from both the procedure header and the local declaration by
    at least one blank line.
5. The statements within a loop whose initial statement (for, while, repeat) is indented
    by N blanks should be indented by $N + T$ blanks. If this statement is a compound
    statement, the 'begin' and 'end' brackets of that statement should be on a line by
    themselves and should be indented by N spaces. Statements within these brackets
    should be indented by $N + T$ spaces.
6. Where a conditional statement is indented by N spaces, the statement in each arm
    of the conditional should be indented by $N + T$ spaces. If the statement is a
    compound statement, the rule for compound statements given in item 5 should be
    applied. If the conditional statement is a two-armed conditional, the reserved word
    'else' should be indented by N spaces and should be on a line by itself.
7. When records are declared, the reserved words 'record' and 'end' should occur on
    lines by themselves, as should the declaration of each field of the record. The
    indentation of the field name declarations should be consistent and such that the
    field declaration with the greatest number of characters can fit on a single line.
8. Wherever possible, each assignment or input-output statement should appear on a
    line by itself.

---

offer a possible set of conventions, in Table 7.1, as suggested by Sommerville
[2]. Each software organization or programmer must establish a set of conventions.

As is evident by inspecting the programs in this book, we are not following
the conventions listed in Table 7.1.

In the exercises, you are asked to create a table similar to Table 7.1 for a
set of layout conventions for Modula-2 and Ada. What layout conventions do
you use for FORTRAN and Pascal?

7.2   TOOLS

Skilled practitioners in many fields such as law, engineering, and medicine use
tools to increase their productivity. Software engineering practitioners are no
exception. Tools are being developed to assist in every aspect of the software
development process from needs analysis to final testing. In this section we
focus on the tools that assist the programmer.

Brooks, in his classic book *The Mythical Man-Month* [3], suggest that every large software development project retain a tool builder. This individual is responsible for choosing and maintaining any existing tools and building custom tools for particular projects.

What are programming tools? A programming tool is a software utility that expedites the process of software construction. Examples of programming tools are operating systems, compilers, interpreters, editors, assemblers, linkers, prettyprinters, program analyzers, timing analyzers, debuggers, program cross-referencers, and program tracers.

Reifer and Trattner [4] compiled a comprehensive list of program development tools. We reproduce part of this list in Table 7.2. Some of the names for the tools listed in Table 7.2 are not universally applicable; thus they may take on different names in different organizations.

Many of the programming tools listed in Table 7.2 are so essential that programming would be nearly impossible without them. Examples of such essential tools are operating systems, file handlers, editors, and compilers.

Often when one thinks of programming tools, one thinks of special purpose or custom utilities tailored for a particular programming environment. We illustrate this concept by displaying a few such software tools.

7.2.1 Examples of Special Purpose Software Tools in Modula-2

In developing user-interactive software, it is common to query the user during program execution and have the program pause until a response is obtained. Often the user is requested to input a character (in response to a question) from a small set of allowable characters. Frequently the allowable set of characters is: 'Y', 'y', 'N', 'n', if the question is a "yes or no" question [e.g., "Do you wish to continue the program (y/n)? "].

It is important to protect such interactive software from illegal user responses. If, for example, the user is requested to input a character from the set [1, 2, 3, 4] and the user inadvertently enters the character 'T' or '5', what type of error response should the program take? Should the error-handling software be rewritten in every program that requires this type of protection? We think not. Since this type of error handling is so fundamental to any program that employs interactive user queries, some special purpose reusable tools should be developed.

In Program 7.3 we display a definition module, UserResponse, that provides a set of user response tools that may be used by a Modula-2 programmer. In Program 7.4 we display a short Modula-2 program that illustrates the use of these tools. Then in Program 7.5 we display the implementation module UserResponse.

Table 7.2   Program Development Tools

1. Accuracy study processor.
2. Analyzer.
3. Automated test generator.
4. Automated verification system.
5. Bootstrap loader.
6. Comparator.
7. Compiler.
8. Compiler building system.
9. Compiler validation system.
10. Consistency checker.
11. Cross-assembler.
12. Cross-reference program.
13. Data base analyzer.
14. Decompiler.
15. Diagnostics/debugger.
16. Driver.
17. Dynamic simulator.
18. Editor.
19. Environment simulator.
20. Extensible language processor.
21. Instruction simulator.
22. Instruction trace.
23. Interface checker.
24. Interpreter.
25. Interrupt analyzer.
26. Language processor.
27. Linkage editor.
28. Linking loader.
29. Macroprocessor.
30. Map program.
31. Postprocessor.
32. Preprocessor.
33. Production libraries.
34. Program sequencer.
35. Restructuring program.
36. Simulator.
37. Software monitor.
38. Standards enforcer.
39. Test drivers, scripts, data generators.
40. Text editor.
41. Timing analyzer.
42. Trace program.
43. Translator.
44. Utilities.

PROGRAM 7.3   User Response Definition Module

```
DEFINITION MODULE UserResponse;
(* $SEG:=25; *)

    FROM Strings IMPORT STRING;

    EXPORT QUALIFIED
            (* type *) setofchar,
            (* proc *) ReadKey,
            (* proc *) Yes,
            (* proc *) Spacebar,
            (* proc *) CenterMessage;

    TYPE setofchar = SET OF CHAR;

    PROCEDURE ReadKey(okset: setofchar): CHAR;
    (* Used to input a character from the terminal. Returns a
       character in the set okset. Will not accept a character
       outside of okset.
       Example:  ch:=ReadKey(setofchar{'1','2','T'});                    *)

    PROCEDURE Yes(): BOOLEAN;
    (* Use to input 'Y', 'y', 'N', or 'n' from the terminal.
       Returns true if the character is 'Y' or 'y', false if
       the character is 'N' or 'n'.
       Example: IF Yes () THEN HALT;                                     *)

    PROCEDURE Spacebar;
    (* Writes a message "Hit spacebar to continue -->" to the screen.
       Can be used to freeze a screen display until user wishes to
       continue.                                                         *)

    PROCEDURE CenterMessage(s: STRING);
    (* Writes string s to the center of an 80 column screen.            *)

END UserResponse.
```

PROGRAM 7.4   Program That Uses the User Response Tool

```
MODULE TestUserResponse;

    FROM InOut IMPORT WriteString, WriteLn;
```

```
    FROM UserResponse IMPORT setofchar, ReadKey, Yes, CenterMessage,
                            Spacebar;

VAR ch: CHAR;

BEGIN
    WriteLn;
    WriteLn;
    CenterMessage ("This Program Illustrates Some Software Tools");
    CenterMessage ("  ----------------------------------");
    WriteLn;
    WriteLn;
    WriteString("Please enter either a, b, C, or 5 : ");
    ch:=ReadKey(setofchar{'a','b','C','5'});
    WriteLn;
    CASE ch OF
        'a' : WriteString("Take course of action 'a' "); |
        'b' : WriteString("Take course of action 'b' "); |
        'C': WriteString("Take course of action 'C' "); |
        '5' : WriteString("Take course of action '5' ");
    END(* case *);
    WriteLn;
    WriteLn;
    WriteString("Do you wish to continue (y/n)? ");
    WHILE Yes() DO
        WriteLn;
        CenterMessage("It appears that you wish to continue.");
        Spacebar;
        WriteLn;
        WriteString("Do you wish to continue (y/n)? ");
    END(* while loop *);
    WriteLn;
    CenterMessage("We're done.");
END TestUserResponse.
```

PROGRAM 7.5   User Response Implementation Module

```
IMPLEMENTATION MODULE UserResponse;

    FROM Strings IMPORT STRING, Length;

    FROM InOut IMPORT Write, WriteString, WriteLn, Read, EOL;

    FROM Terminal IMPORT BusyRead;

    PROCEDURE CenterMessage(s: STRING);
```

```
CONST Blank = ' ';

VAR len, i  : CARDINAL;

BEGIN
    len:=Length(s);
    FOR i:=1 TO 40 − len DIV 2 DO
        Write(Blank);
    END(* for loop *);
    WriteString(s)
END CenterMessage;

PROCEDURE ReadKey(okset: setofchar): CHAR;

VAR ch          : CHAR;
    good        : BOOLEAN;

BEGIN
    REPEAT
        BusyRead(ch);
        (* Returns the null character 0C if no character is entered.
           Does not echo print character to screen.                    *)
        IF ch = EOL THEN ch:=CHAR(13); END;
        good:=ch IN okset;
        IF NOT good
            THEN
                IF NOT (ch = 0C) THEN Write(CHR(7)); END;
            ELSE
                IF ch IN setofchar{' '..'}'} THEN Write(ch); END;
        END(* if then else *);
    UNTIL good;
    RETURN ch
END ReadKey;

PROCEDURE Yes(): BOOLEAN;
BEGIN
    RETURN ReadKey(setofchar{'Y','y','N','n'}) IN setofchar{'y','Y'};
END Yes;

PROCEDURE Spacebar;

VAR ch: CHAR;

BEGIN
    WriteLn;
```

```
        WriteLn;
        CenterMessage("Hit space bar to continue -->");
        ch:=ReadKey(setofchar{' '})
    END Spacebar;

END UserResponse.
```

The user response tool given in Program 7.3 may be expanded considerably to include other interactive input-output error-handling routines as well as other screen utilities. Whenever a programmer finds that the same sequence of operations is required in many programs, that sequence of operations becomes a prime candidate for inclusion in a tool set.

The definition modules for a tool set entitled "Standard Modula-2 Library" are presented in the appendix. Among the tools included in this standard library are procedures for screen input-output, file input-output, number conversion, exception handling, dynamic allocation and deallocation, and concurrent process control. A Modula-2 Library is one of a set of tools delivered with a Modula-2 software development system. In addition to this standard library are an editor, a compiler, an operating system, other library utilities (some machine dependent), a file handler, a program analyzer, and a debugger [5]. This set of tools provides the Modula-2 programmer considerable leverage in writing programs.

7.2.2 Code Control Tools

The development of large software systems may involve hundreds of programmers writing tens of thousands of lines of code. This code is typically distributed over many distinct files and libraries in the form of both source and object code. Different versions of a system, each tailored to a different environment, may coexist.

The notion of program librarian was put forth by IBM in connection with a management technique known as Chief Programmer Teams [6]. The job of a program librarian is to maintain a comprehensive data base of project information. All project work must pass through the program librarian. The data base keeps track of which files relate to which versions of the system.

A program librarian is particularly useful in a batch programming environment because it ensures a single person interface between the programming team and the computer.

In an interactive environment (the more typical in recent years), there is a need for an automated system to carry out the tasks associated with file information maintenance. This has led to the development of automated program librarian tools.

Some examples of recent automated program librarian tools include

MAKE [7], SCCS [8], and CADES [9]. CADES is a stand-alone system, whereas MAKE and SCCS are available under the UNIX/PWB operating system.

SCCS (Source Code Control System) allows different versions of a system to be maintained without unnecessary code duplication. No part of the system can be updated by more than one programmer at any one time. A record is kept of when updates were made, what source lines were changed, and who was responsible for the change. MAKE ensures the compatibility between source code and its corresponding object code.

The operating systems for both Modula-2 and Ada provide the programmer some automated program librarian tools. Version numbers are automatically created when either a definition module or package specification are compiled. Each program that imports entities from these modules is assigned a version number corresponding to the number associated with the imported module(s). If a specification module is later changed and recompiled, all program units that import this module must be recompiled. If they are not, the incompatibility of version numbers will be detected by the operating system at run time.

7.2.3 Automated Design Tools

There are several levels of automated tool support for software design. The first level is based on hand-written design forms that are interconnected to automated procedures that use the information on the forms. The second level of design tools interacts with the designer. Immediate feedback concerning whether various principles have or have not been followed with the current design are provided to the designer. A third level of design tools displays to the user various forms of the software design (bubble charts, structure charts, etc.) before the next design iteration. Systems that present information on structured designs and generate graphical output fall into this category. Finally, there are systems that attempt to involve the designer in a refinement process by imposing a number of rules that control and/or limit the final design.

Many new automated tools for software design are currently under development. We briefly describe several tools that have been in use for several years.

Campos and Estrin [10] describe a system known as SARA (Systems ARchitects Apprentice), which is a computer-aided system supporting a structured multilevel requirement-driven methodology for the design of concurrent software systems. The software design methodology may be either top-down or bottom-up as appropriate to the problem.

Willis [11] presents an automated system to support design analysis known as DAS. The system is intended to support design verification and also provides a comprehensive set of software testing analyzers including simulation models and metrics. The system addresses software reliability and the control of software life cycle costs. Software design analysis within DAS is based on the use of a central data base for all information describing a software system. Structured design techniques using interactive graphics are also supported by DAS through facilities that allow the construction, modification, and hardcopy documentation of individual software designs. An important feature of DAS is the use of simulation techniques for the evaluation of preliminary designs.

Biggerstaff [12] describes the Unified Design Specification System (UDS2) used by Boeing Computer Services. UDS2 is a set of computerized tools supporting both preliminary and detailed design and also the software construction and maintenance phases. To this end, UDS2 provides tools designers use to produce a precise computer representation, or model, of the desired software system. Because the model can be processed by the computer, a software designer can use UDS2 tools to help ensure that the model design is internally consistent, to obtain feedback and remove design defects early in the design phase, to verify technical aspects of the design throughout the design process, and to determine that the design meets all requirements. A major benefit of UDS2 is that since the document production is automated, the design remains consistent and can be documented at any stage of its evolution.

7.3 ENVIRONMENTS

A programming environment consists of a set of general and specially created tools to aid in program development. Programming environments may typically provide facilities for intercomputer communications, testing and debugging tools, target machine simulators, text processing tools, computer-aided design tools, special-purpose utilities, and program librarian tools.

A popular programming environment is the Unix Programmers Workbench (UNIX/PWB) [13]. This system was originally designed to support software development for IBM, UNIVAC, XDX, and DEC computers. More recently, versions of UNIX/PWB are being made available on smaller machines.

In many existing programming environments, the available set of tools often is weak and incomplete. This deficiency was recognized by the Ada common high order language project. In response, the Ada development team defined a programming environment that would complement the facilities provided by Ada. The outcome of this effort is included in the STONEMAN requirements document. In STONEMAN, an Ada Programming Support Environment (APSE) is defined. Its objective is to "support the development and maintenance of Ada applications software throughout its life cycle, with particular emphasis on software for embedded computer applications" [14].

We represent a brief overview of some of the underlying concepts associated with the APSE. An APSE will be available on a host machine but not necessarily the target machine that will ultimately run the software. For many embedded computer systems, this is quite realistic, since the target machine is often much smaller than the host machine and could not support the program development tools.

The APSE maintains a program data base. An Ada compiler recognizes a program library that contains separately compiled program units. The APSE extends this data base so that it includes source and object code, documentation, and other support files. Facilities for keeping track of revisions are included in the APSE data base. The APSE data base must be extensible, with all new tools being written in Ada.

The APSE is specified as having several levels. At the innermost level is the host operating system, if one exists. This is the level that physically holds the APSE data base. At the next level is the Kernel Ada Programming Support Environment (KAPSE). It provides the logical to physical mapping for the outer layers of the APSE. At a level outside the KAPSE is the Minimal Ada Programming Support Environment (MAPSE). It contains the minimal tool set for program development. At the highest level are the APSE tools themselves. Included are advanced tools to support the various phases of the software life cycle as well as user developed tools. Figure 7.1 gives an overview of an Ada Programming Support Environment.

The KAPSE is the interface at which the APSE relates to the underlying machine. If we want to rehost the environment, we must create a new machine-dependent KAPSE. The KAPSE provides the logical interface to peripheral devices.

The MAPSE contains tools such as text editor, compiler, linker, pretty-printer, static analyzer, control-flow static analyzer, terminal input-output tools, filer, and interpreter. These are the tools that the programmer first encounters and uses for basic program development. STONEMAN only suggests these tools. Each implementation may have a different set of minimal tools.

To facilitate transportability of tools and programs from one machine to another, most implementations use an intermediate language to represent the source code. This intermediate code is called DIANA (Descriptive Intermediate Attributed Notation for Ada).

Ada coupled with APSE is expected to offer a powerful system for the development and maintenance of software.

7.4 PORTABILITY

Often software must be written so that it can be transferred from one operating system to another or from one machine to another. Techniques for achieving program portability are described in Reference 15.

One of the major problems affecting the portability of software is the existence of many dialects for some high level languages. We are all familiar with the multitude of FORTRAN dialects that have been developed over the years. PFORT [16] was developed to ensure that a candidate FORTRAN program is portable over a large class of computers and compilers.

To date, no Ada or Modula-2 dialects have been developed. Indeed, at the time of writing, the DoD will not certify a compiler as an Ada compiler unless it proves itself as satisfying the full language standard. This policy has caused

ADE™
Ada® DEVELOPMENT ENVIRONMENT

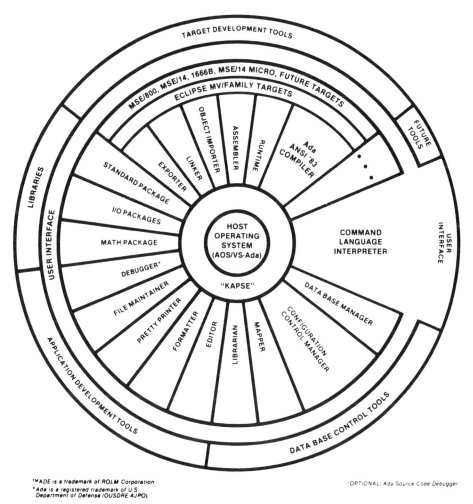

TMADE is a trademark of ROLM Corporation.
*Ada is a registered trademark of U.S.
Department of Defense (OUSDRE·AJPO).

*OPTIONAL: Ada Source Code Debugger

Figure 7.1 An Ada programming support environment. Copyright © ROLM Corporation, San Jose, California 1983.

consternation and debate because some computer scientists argue that useful subsets of Ada should be created for smaller machines.

Total portability of software is difficult to achieve even when using a standard version of a high level language. Machine dependencies often occur in connection with input and output as well as number precision for floating point computation. Number precision is dependent on the word size of the machine.

The character set available on machines may differ, so some program editing may be required to accommodate differing character sets. The two most widely used character sets are ASCII (American Standard Characters for Information Interchange) and EBCDIC (Extended Binary Coded Decimal).

Programs that employ unconventional screen input-output such as inverse video, blinking, and underline may have to be modified to accommodate different terminals.

The architecture of the target machine affects program portability. For example, on a machine with 32-bit words, the largest integer that can be represented is 2,147,483,647, whereas on a machine with 16-bit words the largest integer that can be represented is 32,767. If the software system uses integers larger than 32,767, it will not run on a 16-bit machine.

Quite often, the least portable parts of a program are the sections that involve file manipulations. File access, through a high level language, often depends on operating system primitives. There are no standards that govern how operating systems perform file manipulations. Some typical problems that arise from the lack of file manipulation standards involve file name conventions (the maximum length of a file name), file system directory structure, file system protection (protocols and passwords for protecting files), maximum number of files that may be simultaneously open, and availability of random access to files.

The programmer usually has little control over portability. The best that the programmer can do is to isolate the sections of a software system that may have to be modified because of portability problems. This isolation may be achieved at either the subprogram level or the module level. For example, all terminal-dependent input-output can be put in a special I/O module.

Physical media impose another set of portability problems. Can software developed on a host machine be easily downloaded to a target machine? Unfortunately, at the time of writing, much better solutions to software and media portability problems have yet to be found.

7.5 DOCUMENTATION

We indicated earlier that the major cost in the software life cycle is software maintenance. The cost of maintenance is profoundly affected by the quality of documentation at every phase of the software development process.

For large software systems the documentation effort may rival the programming effort. All too often, the people who are most qualified to write the documentation (the system designers and implementors) are the least inclined to do so. As a result, technical writers are hired to assist in this effort.

The two basic requirements for high quality documentation are:

1. Clarity of expression.
2. Technical accuracy.

In this section we focus on documentation above and beyond program comments (which were discussed in Section 7.1 on programming style).

7.5.1 User Documentation

The first contact an "end user" has with a software system is the user documentation. Ideally, the user documentation should be structured to provide any level of detail appropriate to the user's needs. Most software users are concerned with:

1. A general functional description of the system that explains what the system can do and what its limitations are.

2. An installation guide.

3. A summary manual of the key user commands including how to "fire up" the system.

4. A detailed reference manual that explains each function of the system in detail.

5. A detailed index that allows the user easy access to the reference manual.

6. An operator's guide, if appropriate, that explains how to monitor and correct the operation of the system while it is running.

The use of specialized jargon or "computerese" should be avoided in the user documentation. Terms that are second nature to a software developer may be totally unfamiliar to a software user. For example, terms such as "RAM" or "ROM" or "baud rate" or "prompt" or "page" might be avoided.

Examples that "walk" the user through the solution to a problem are very helpful. Most people learn best by going from the specific to the general, that is, from an example to a generalization. For example, if the software system were a word processor, a sample text file created by the word processor, including all the special codes, would be very helpful to the end user. If the software were a set of mathematical routines, a sample program that uses some or all of the routines would be helpful.

The documentation needs of the end user are different from the needs of the software developer; therefore, the documentation that is supplied with library modules or packages for the software developer must be different from "end-user" documentation.

The documentation supplied with library modules must include precise interface specifications in the form of subprogram stubs with associated data types and data objects. In Ada and Modula-2, these are provided in either a package specification or a module. In addition to the technical specifications, a statement describing the functional purpose of each subprogram or data object should be included in the form of a comment. A small sample program that uses all the features of the library module should be included (commented out) under the formal specification part. In this manner, all the information that the software developer needs to interface the library module to his or her software is available where it counts most—with the specifications.

7.5.2 System Documentation

Documents that describe the requirements, design, implementation, and testing of a software system are essential for software maintenance. Typically this documentation consists of the following components.

1. A needs statement.
2. Formal requirements containing a high level conceptual model of the system.
3. Preliminary design of the system. This may be represented with data flow diagrams and supporting narrative.
4. The software system architecture. This may be represented using modular design chart(s), modular design listing(s), and other graphical aids.
5. The detailed design. This may be represented using pseudo-code.
6. A component test plan that describes how each software component is to be tested.
7. An integrated test plan that describes how the system is to be tested.
8. An acceptance test plan that describes the tests that must be passed before the system will be accepted by the customer.

7.5.3 Data Dictionary

A data dictionary is usually a document that provides information concerning every entity that is relevant to the system being implemented. To be of value, a data dictionary is maintained on line so that any change that is made with respect to an entity in the system is reflected immediately in the data dictionary. The typical entities entered in a data dictionary are subprogram names, record structures, files, module names, block names, data objects, and data types.

Data dictionaries have enjoyed widespread use in data base software systems. The use of extensive data dictionaries predates the development of languages such as Pascal, Modula-2, and Ada. Since these languages require the programmer to declare all entities before they are used, the declarations may serve as a limited form of data dictionary for some applications. The advantage of a centralized on-line data dictionary is that it supports quick reference to the location of an entity in a large software system.

7.5.4 Documentation Maintenance

Every time a software system is modified, the documentation associated with the system must also be modified to reflect the changes in the system. Quite often, the documentation lags the changes that are made in the system. Some changes that are made in a software system are transparent to the end user. In these cases, the only documentation changes that are required are with respect to the system documentation. Some software changes affect the end user, and if so, changes in the user documentation must be made.

The process of documentation maintenance is more efficient if the documentation is available in machine readable form.

In Section 7.2.2, systems for automatic documentation maintenance were described. These systems automate the process of documentation maintenance.

7.6 SOFTWARE METRICS

Since the cost of software maintenance is directly related to the complexity of the software to be maintained, researchers have attempted to estimate the complexity of software systems. The relative complexity of a software system relates to how difficult the software is to understand and maintain compared to other software systems. The complexity of a software system affects its testability and modifiability.

Various types of measures may be used to represent software complexity. Baird and Noma suggest four types of measurement [17].

1. **Nominal measure.** A broad classification is given, for example, "simple," "moderately complex," "complex," "extremely complex."
2. **Ordinal measure.** Classifications are ranked. For example, "program A is more complex than program B, which is more complex than program C."
3. **Interval measure.** Classifications are ranked and the spacing between classifications is measured. For example, "program A is 18 units of difficulty greater than program B."
4. **Ratio measure.** Multiplication and division may be used on the measure. For example, "program A is three times as difficult as program B."

It would of course be most desirable to have a ratio measure for program complexity. But for such a scale to exist, we must define zero complexity. For an interval scale, one must make sense out of a unit of complexity. We adopt the ordinal scale as a frame of reference.

In this section we present an overview of the various factors that have been considered in connection with program complexity. The reader is urged to consult the references cited to obtain the details of how a given method is implemented.

Table 7.3 Halstead's Measures of Program Complexity

1.	Program vocabulary	$-\!\!-\!> n = n1 + n2$
2.	Program length	$-\!\!-\!> N = N1 + N2$
3.	Predicted program length	$-\!\!-\!> N' = n1 * \log2(n1) + n2 * \log2(n2)$
4.	Program volume	$-\!\!-\!> V = N * \log2(n)$
5.	Program potential volume	$-\!\!-\!> V* = n' * \log2(n')$
6.	Program level	$-\!\!-\!> V*/V$
7.	Approximate program level	$-\!\!-\!> L' = 2/n1 * n2/N2$
8.	Program intelligence content	$-\!\!-\!> I = L' * V$
9.	Program development effort	$-\!\!-\!> E = V/L$

7.6.1 Program Size

Many existing measures of program complexity are based on the size of a program. Very large programs have a degree of complexity based simply on their size [18]. Experimental evidence suggests that larger programs have greater maintenance costs than smaller ones [18].

The simplest measure of program size is its number of lines of code. What is a line of code? Is it an executable statement? Does a data declaration qualify as a line of code? Does a comment qualify as a line of code? The number of lines of code (whatever that may mean) is generally an inadequate measure of program size.

Halstead's software science [19] provides a major refinement in estimating the size of a program. The software science measure is widely used in industry and has been supported by empirical studies.

Halstead's Software Science

Halstead's metric is dependent on the number of unique operators $n1$, the number of unique operands $n2$, the total number of operators $N1$, and the total number of operands $N2$. Table 7.3 lists some of Halstead's program measures.

In Table 7.3, n' in line 5 refers to the size of the potential vocabulary. See Reference 19 for details.

Halstead observed empirically that his program intelligence content, $I = L' * V$, correlates well with total programming and debugging time and remains relatively invariant under translation from one programming language to another [19].

7.6.2 Data Structures

Although Halstead's program size metrics appear to work well in ranking programs with widely varying sizes, characteristics such as data structures and flow of control, not accounted for in Halstead's metrics, are important.

An important factor that affects software complexity is the data configuration within a program. The complexity of a program might be related to the way data are organized and allocated.

The SPAN is the number of statements between two references to the same identifier with no intervening references to that identifier. The larger the average SPAN for an identifier, the more complex the program.

The SEGMENT_GLOBAL_USAGE_PAIR is used by Basili as a complexity measure [20]. A segment-global-usage-pair (p,r) is used to signify the instance of a segment p using the global variable r.

The actual usage pair AUP represents the number of times a module actually accesses a global data item. The potential usage pair PUP represents the number of times a module could access a global variable. The relative percentage of actual usage RUP is given by

$$RUP = \frac{AUP}{PUP} \qquad \text{(Have we gone mad?)}$$

This equation yields a rough measure of the likelihood that an arbitrary segment will reference an arbitrary global variable. The greater the likelihood (i.e., the larger the RUP), the greater the possibility that a given global variable may have its value changed in another segment without the knowledge of a maintenance programmer, and the greater the complexity.

7.6.3 Control Structures

Much of the work on complexity theory of the past decade has dealt with the effects of program control of flow. The density and interrelations of control transfers have been related to program complexity. For an excellent discussion and summary of complexity measures see Reference 21.

A program flow graph (Figure 7.2) forms the basis for many control of flow complexity measures. Each node represents a block of code that can be entered only at the beginning of the block and exited only at the end of the block and can contain no transfers of control within the block itself. The edges in the flow graph correspond to the flow of control between various nodes.

The number of edges entering a given node is defined as the indegree of the node, and the number of edges leaving a given node is defined as the outdegree of the node. As an example, node F in Figure 7.2 has an indegree of 2 and an outdegree of 1. If a path exists from some node i to another node j, then node i is said to precede node j.

McCabe's Cyclomatic Complexity Measure

McCabe has originated a widely used complexity measure that is easily calculated [22]. McCabe's measure is based on the cyclomatic number $V(G)$ of a program's flow graph.

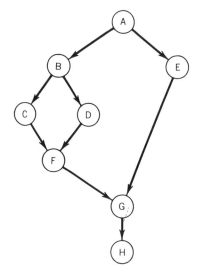

Figure 7.2 A program flow graph.

For a flow graph with e edges, n nodes, and p connected components (usually 1), the cyclomatic complexity is given by

$$V(G) = e - n + 2 \times p$$

For the graph of Figure 7.2, the McCabe cyclomatic complexity is given as follows.

$$V(G) = 9 - 8 + 2 \times 1 = 3$$

The McCabe measure determines the number of linearly independent circuits in a strongly connected graph (for any two nodes, one is reachable from the other). To convert the graph of Figure 7.2 into a strongly connected graph, we must add an edge from node H back to node A. Then the three independent circuits are: (1) nodes A, B, C, F, H, A, (2) nodes A, B, D, F, G, H, A, and (3) nodes A, E, G, H, A.

Myers's Complexity Measure

Myers extends McCabe's measure by taking stock of the fact that predicates with compound conditions are more complex than predicates with a single condition [23]. The Pascal code segments that follows illustrates this.

Code Segment 1

```
if X = Y then P1
        else P2;
```

Code Segment 2

if (X = Y) and (Z = 0) then P1
else P2;

Both code segments produce the same flow graph (see Figure 7.3).

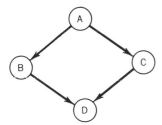

Figure 7.3   Flow graph for one decision.

The McCabe complexity measure for flow graph 2 is

$$V(G) = 4 - 4 + 2 \times 1 = 2$$

Myers suggests that the complexity of the graph be computed as an interval rather than a single number. The interval's lower bound is the number of decision statements plus 1, and the upper bound is the number of individual conditions plus 1. Using the Myers complexity measure, the first code segment produces the interval [2,2] and the second code segment produces the interval [2,3].

7.6.4   Other Complexity Measures

We reference and briefly comment on some additional measures of program complexity that are being used.

A knot measure of complexity, proposed by Woodward, Hennell, and Hedley, is concerned with the physical locations of control transfers not just their numbers [24]. A "knot" occurs in a flow graph whenever the transfer from some point a to another point b is interrupted, and some other transfer outside the a to b scope is required. Please consult Reference 24 for the details.

Chen [25] has originated a program control of flow complexity measure that is sensitive to nested decision structures.

Hansen [26] has developed a complexity measure that combines the cyclomatic complexity of McCabe and an operator count similar to Halstead's $n1$. Hensen's complexity measure is a 2-tuple (a,b) where the first measure is a count of the number of IF, CASE, or other alternate execution constructs and iterative DO, WHILE, REPEAT, or other repetitive constructs. The second measure in Hensen's 2-tuple is a count of operators in the program. Hensen defines these as such primitive operators as $+$, $-$, $*$, AND, and, OR, assignment operators (e.g., $:=$), subroutine or function calls, applications of subscripts to an array, and input and output statements. Consult Reference 26 for the details.

Oviedo [27] has developed a program complexity measure that is a function of both data flow complexity and control flow complexity. Consult the reference for details.

The complexity measures that are a function of both data flow and control flow appear to have the best chance for success, that is, the ability to predict the complexity of future maintenance. With the advent of Modula-2 and Ada and the increased use that these languages will have for engineering software systems, it is our opinion that significant refinements of some existing complexity measures and the introduction of totally new measures that deal with the concept of modules will be necessary.

7.7. SUMMARY

- Programming involves form and substance, style as well as structure. Programming encompasses both art and science.
- The style of source code, its internal documentation, and the choices for the names of the objects that are declared, affect the maintainability of the software and therefore the quality of the software.
- Good programming style suggests good program layout, sensible use of names, meaningful comments, and the use of language constructs that support program security and reliability.
- The names of objects in a program should be related to or identical to the names of the entities that the program is modeling.
- Comments are an essential and integral part of a program that should be inserted while a program is being developed.
- The number and type of comments that are desirable are a function of the complexity and size of a program, the name space that is used and the programming language.
- Every subprogram should include brief comments explaining its functional purpose.
- References, in the form of comments, should be provided to explain any unusual or complex algorithm that is employed in a program.
- Complex data structures and unusual data objects should be explained with comments.
- Layout profoundly affects the readability of programs. Indentation and the use of spaces are the two principal degrees of freedom that the programmer may use to control program layout.

- Software tools have been developed to assist in every aspect of the software development process from needs analysis to final testing.
- Examples of programming tools are operating systems, compilers, interpreters, editors, assemblers, linkers, prettyprinters, program analyzers, timing analyzers, debuggers, program cross-referencers, and program tracers.
- Whenever a programmer finds that the same task must be performed in many programs, the sequence of operations involved in the task becomes a prime candidate for inclusion in a tool set.
- A programming environment consists of a set of general and specially created tools to aid in program development.
- Programming environments may typically provide facilities for intercomputer communications, testing and debugging tools, target machine simulators, text processing tools, computer-aided design tools, special-purpose utilities, and program librarian tools.
- Total portability of software is difficult to achieve even when using a standard version of a high level language.
- The programmer usually has little control over portability. The best that the programmer can do is to isolate the sections of a software system that may have to be modified because of portability problems.
- The cost of maintenance is profoundly affected by the quality of documentation at every phase of the software development process.
- For large software systems the documentation effort may rival or surpass the programming effort.
- The use of specialized jargon or "computerese" should be avoided in the user documentation.
- A data dictionary is usually a document that provides information concerning every entity that is relevant to the system being implemented.
- Every time a software system is modified, the documentation associated with the system must also be modified to reflect the changes in the system.
- The relative complexity of a software system is a function of the difficulty of understanding and maintaining the software compared to other software systems.
- The complexity of a software system affects its testability and modifiability.
- Many existing measures of program complexity are based on estimating the size of a program and the way data are organized and allocated.
- A program flow graph forms the basis for many control of flow complexity measures.
- Complexity measures that are a function of both data flow and control flow appear to have the best chance for success.
- New measures of complexity must be devised to reflect modular and object-oriented design methodologies.

REFERENCES

1. *Webster's New Collegiate Dictionary,* ed., Springfield, Mass.: Merriam, 1951.
2. Sommerville, I., *Software Engineering,* Reading, Mass.: Addison-Wesley, 1982.
3. Brooks, Fredrick P., Jr., *The Mythical Man-Month,* Reading, Mass.: Addison-Wesley, 1975.
4. Reifer, Donald J., and Stephen Trattner, "A Glossary of Software Tools and Techniques," *Computer,* July 1977.
5. Modula-2 System, written by Volition Systems, P.O. Box 1236, Del Mar, Calif., 92014.
6. Baker, F. T., "Chief Programmer Team Management of Production Programming", *IBM Syst. J.,* Vol. 11, No. 1, 1972.
7. Feldman, S. I., "MAKE—A Program for Maintaining Computer Programs," *Software Pract. Exp.,* Vol. 9, pp. 255–265, 1979.
8. Rochkind, M. J., "The Source Code Control System," *IEEE Trans. Software Eng.,* Vol. SE-1, No. 4, pp. 255–260, 1975.
9. McGuffin, R. W., A. E. Elliston, B. R. Tranttner, and P. N. Westmacott, "CADES—Software Engineering in Practice," *Proceeding of the 4th International Conference on Software Engineering,* Munich, 1979.
10. Campos, I. M., and G. Estrin, "Concurrent Software System Design Supported by SARA at the Age of One," *Proceedings of the 3rd International Conference on Software Engineering,* May 1978, pp. 230–242.
11. Willis, R. R., "DAS—An Automated System to Support Design Analysis," *Proceedings of the 3rd International Conference on Software Engineering,* May 1978.
12. Biggerstaff, T., "UDS2—Unified Design Specification System," Boeing Computer Services, Seattle, 1979.
13. Ivie, E. L., "The Programmers Workbench—A Machine For Software Development," *Commun. ACM,* Vol. 20, No. 10, pp. 746–753, October 1977.
14. "Requirements for Ada Programming Support Environments, STONEMAN," Washington, D.C.: U.S. Department of Defense, February 1980.
15. Brown, P. J., Ed. *Software Portability,* Cambridge: Cambridge University Press, 1977.
16. Ryder, B. G., "The PFORT Verifier," *Software Pract. Exp.,* No. 4, pp. 359–377, 1974.
17. Baird, J. C., and E. Noma, *Fundamentals of Scaling and Psychophysics,* New York: Wiley, 1978, pp. 1–6.
18. Elshoff, J., "An Analysis of Some PL/1 Programs," *IEEE Trans. Software Eng.* Vol. SE-2, No. 6, pp. 113–120, June 1976.
19. Halstead, M. *Elements of Software Science,* New York: Elsevier North-Holland, 1977.
20. Basili, V., *"Product Metrics," Tutorial on Models and Metrics for Software Management and Engineering,* New York: IEEE Computer Society Press, 1980, pp. 214–217.

21. Harrison, W. et al., "Applying Software Complexity Metrics to Program Maintenance," *IEEE Comput.* September 1982.

22. McCabe, T., "A Complexity Measure," *IEEE Trans. Software Eng.,* Vol. SE-2, No. 12, pp. 308–320, December 1976.

23. Myers, G., "An Extension to the Cyclomatic Measure Of Program Complexity," *ACM SIGPLAN Notices,* pp. 61–64, October 1977.

24. Woodward, M., et al., "A Measure of Control Flow Complexity in Program Text," *IEEE Trans. Software Eng.,* Vol. SE-5, No.1, pp. 45–50, January 1979.

25. Chen, E., "Program Complexity and Programmer Productivity," *IEEE Trans. Software Eng.,* Vol. SE-4, No. 5, pp. 187–194, May 1978.

26. Hansen, W., "Measurement of Program Complexity by the Pair (Cyclomatic Number, Operator Count)," *ACM SIGPLAN Notices,* pp. 29–33, March 1978.

27. Oviedo, E., "Control Flow, Data Flow and Program Complexity," *Proceedings of COMPSAC 80,* pp. 146–152.

EXERCISES

1. Implement the UserResponse tool presented in Section 7.2, in Ada.

2. Add features to this user response tool and implement your modified version in both Modula-2 and Ada.

3. Test the implementation of the Ada text formatter that you developed in Exercise 8 of Chapter 5, on Program 7.1.

4. Create a software tool that:
   (a) Converts a design input (in some appropriate form) to a modular design chart that may be printed or displayed on some graphical device.
   (b) Converts the modular design chart from part a to a modular design listing.

5. Write modules in Modula-2 that allow the Ada attributes FIRST and LAST to be simulated in Modula-2 for two-dimensional open arrays.

6. Compute the McCabe complexity measure for Program 7.4.

7. Identify the software development tools in the computer environment in which you work.

Chapter 8

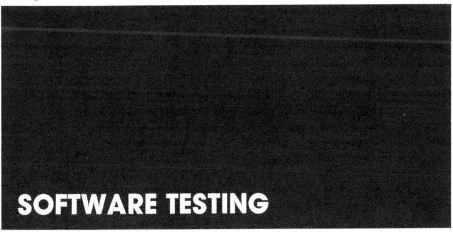

SOFTWARE TESTING

Software testing cannot establish that a program is correct: undetected errors may exist in a software system after even the most comprehensive program of testing. Software testing can demonstrate only the presence of errors in a software system, never the absence of errors.

Planning for testing should start during the design phase. The actual process of software testing begins during the implementation phase of the software life cycle and continues after implementation as a separate phase. The objective of software testing is to detect program errors. Debugging is part of the testing process. The objective of debugging is to locate and correct the errors found during testing. A successful program of testing and debugging establishes the presence of errors and corrects them before they are detected by the customer.

The earlier the errors in a program can be detected, the less costly they generally are to correct. Corrective maintenance involves correcting errors after the system has been delivered and installed. This type of error correction is often very costly. Indeed, the reputation of the software development organization may be damaged if a significant amount of corrective maintenance must be performed. Of course, the reputation of the software development organization will be ruined if such necessary corrective maintenance is not performed!

The testing process should not be viewed as threatening to the people involved in the software development process. Indeed, the reliability of their final product is in large measure assured by the testing process. It is often desirable that an individual or group of people separate from the group that performed the implementation be responsible for software testing.

It has been estimated that software testing takes about the same amount of time as software implementation. Since part of the testing process occurs during implementation, it is difficult to verify this estimate.

In this chapter we present an overview of the seven major stages of software testing.

1. **Code inspection.** A careful walkthrough of the program code conducted by the chief programmer for an inspection team.

2. **Function testing.** Each subprogram (functional component) in a module is tested individually.

3. **Module testing.** The group of subprograms that comprise a module are tested to see whether they cooperate with each other as they are designed to. The module is tested, if possible, as a stand-alone entity, independent of other modules.

4. **Subsystem testing.** A group of related modules are tested as a subsystem. The ability of these modules to communicate properly with each other and cooperate is the central focus of this stage of testing.

5. **System testing (integration testing).** The entire system is tested as an integrated entity, to see that the overall system satisfies the functional specifications given in the requirements document.

6. **Acceptance testing.** In acceptance testing, real data are used to test the system. The customer participates in this stage of testing by suggesting data inputs or by interacting with the software system (if it is a user-interactive system). The software development organization tries to convince the customer that the software system is sound and should be accepted. Based on the results of this stage of testing, additional tests at a lower level may be in order, or the customer may authorize the final stage of testing.

7. **Installation testing.** The delivered and installed system (hardware and software) are tested onsite. The main purpose of the final stage of testing is to ensure that the installation process has been successful.

A successful testing program attempts to detect errors at the lowest possible level. Errors at the subprogram level, if undetected, may induce errors at a higher level in the program. It may be much more costly to detect higher level errors because of the greater number of potential error sources.

The difficulty of software testing for a given system depends on program size as well as program structure. A program that lacks modularity may be much more difficult to test than a modular program.

Since we have emphasized the benefits of modular software construction in Chapters 5 and 6, we illustrate some additional benefits of modular software construction that pertain to software testing in this chapter. We illustrate some stages of the software testing process with the FunctionEvaluator software system presented in Chapter 6, since this software system is sufficiently complex to warrant a systematic test program.

Although all the short testing programs in this chapter are written in Modula-2, the same principles of modular software testing could be illustrated in Ada.

8.1 CODE INSPECTION

It has been suggested by Fagen [1] that four people comprise an inspection team for code inspection. These people are:

1. A competent programmer not involved in the project who acts as moderator.
2. A designer of the software system.
3. A programmer involved in the implementation.
4. An individual responsible for later testing.

The code inspection process requires that the design documents be distributed to the inspection team well in advance of the actual code inspection.

During the code inspection, the programmer explains how the design is implemented by "walking through" the code, line by line. As the presentation is made, the members of the inspection team cross-examine the programmer and attempt to locate logical errors or inefficiencies in the implementation. The task of the inspection team is error detection, not error correction. As errors are detected, they are noted by the moderator and the inspection continues. The advantage of code inspection is that many errors may be detected during a single pass of the software system.

8.2 AN EXAMPLE OF SOFTWARE TESTING AND PERFECTIVE MAINTENANCE

In this section we examine some typical perfective maintenance on a software system and see how central the process of software testing is to the maintenance process. The software subject for our maintenance and testing is the interactive function evaluator system presented and discussed in Chapter 6. Because of the modular construction used in building this software system, the tasks of testing and maintenance are fairly straightforward. The reader may wish to reread and review the sections of Chapter 6 that present and discuss this software system before continuing.

The modules Stacks1 and RealStack, given in Chapter 6, limit the program developer to a maximum stack size of 80. A more reasonable approach to implementing a stack structure might be to dynamically allocate memory each time a new element is pushed onto the stack and to dynamically deallocate memory each time an element is popped from the stack. In this manner, the memory storage required by the stack will exactly equal the memory actually needed. Furthermore, the maximum stack size will no longer be arbitrarily limited to 80, but will be limited by the computer's dynamic memory.

Program 8.1 displays a new implementation for Stacks1. A similar new implementation must be performed for RealStack.

PROGRAM 8.1   New Implementation Module for Stacks1

```
IMPLEMENTATION MODULE Stacks1;

   FROM InOut IMPORT WriteString, WriteLn;

   FROM Storage  IMPORT ALLOCATE, DEALLOCATE;

   FROM SYSTEM IMPORT WORD;

   TYPE
       Stack  = POINTER TO NODE;

       NODE = RECORD
                    ITEM : WORD;
                    NEXT: Stack
                END;

   PROCEDURE Empty(S: Stack) : BOOLEAN;
   BEGIN
       IF S = NIL
           THEN
               RETURN TRUE
           ELSE
               RETURN FALSE
       END(* if then *)
   END Empty;

   PROCEDURE Pop(VAR S: Stack) : WORD;

   VAR
       P: Stack;
       W: WORD;
```

```
BEGIN
    IF Empty(S)
    THEN
        WriteString("Invalid mathematical expression.");
        WriteLn;
        HALT
    ELSE
        P:=S;
        W:=P↑.ITEM;
        S:=S↑.NEXT;
        DISPOSE(P);
        RETURN W
    END
END Pop;


PROCEDURE Push(VAR S: Stack; X: WORD);

VAR
    P: Stack;

BEGIN
    NEW(P);
    P↑.ITEM:=X;
    P↑.NEXT:=S;
    S:=P
END Push;


PROCEDURE Initialize(VAR S: Stack); (∗ Sets stack to empty. ∗)
BEGIN
    NEW(S);
    S↑.NEXT:=NIL
END Initialize;


PROCEDURE TopOfStack(S: Stack): WORD;
BEGIN
    RETURN S↑.ITEM
END TopOfStack;


END Stacks1.
```

The test program Tabulate, shown for your convenience as Program 8.2.

PROGRAM 8.2   Test Program Tabulate

```
MODULE Tabulate;

    FROM FunctionEvaluator IMPORT Expression, Convert, Eval;

    FROM InOut IMPORT WriteLn, WriteString, Read, EOL;

    FROM RealInOut IMPORT ReadReal, WriteReal;

VAR   s        : ARRAY[1..80] OF CHAR;
      a        : Expression;
      x        : REAL;
      answer : CHAR;
      ch       : CHAR;

BEGIN (* Main Program *)
    WriteLn;
    WriteString("Enter a mathematical function (y/n)? ");
    Read(answer);
    WHILE (answer = 'Y') OR (answer = 'y') DO
        a:=Convert();
        WriteString("Evaluate the mathematical expression (y/n)? ");
        Read(answer);
        WHILE (answer = 'Y') OR (answer = 'y') DO
            WriteLn;
            WriteString("Enter a value for the independent variable: ");
            ReadReal(x);
            WriteLn;
            WriteString("The value of the function F is --> ");
            WriteReal(Eval(a,x),10);
            WriteLn;
            WriteString("Evaluate the mathematical expression (y/n)? ");
            Read(answer)
        END;
        WriteLn;
        WriteString("Enter a mathematical function (y/n)? ");
        Read(answer);
    END;
END Tabulate.
```

Sure enough, as is often the case after program maintenance, the test program, Program 8.2, does not run correctly.

Since implementation modules Stacks1 and Realstack were the only program units to be changed and recompiled, the source of the system error is to be
found in these modules. Program 8.3 is a special test program written for
module Stacks1.

PROGRAM 8.3   A Test Program for Module Stacks1

```
MODULE ReverseNumber;

    FROM Stacks1 IMPORT Empty, Pop, Push, Initialize, Stack;

    FROM InOut IMPORT WriteString, WriteLn, ReadInt, WriteInt;

    VAR
        A                : Stack;
        IntNum, j        : CARDINAL;
        i                : INTEGER;

    BEGIN(* ReverseNumber *)
        FOR j:=1 TO 40 DO
            Integers[j]:=0;
        END(* do loop *);
        WriteString("Enter a series of integers (quit with 0) : ");
        IntNum:=0;
        i:=6; (* Any number not equal to 0 will suffice. *)
        Initialize(A);
        WHILE (IntNum <= 40) AND (i # 0) DO
            INC(IntNum);
            ReadInt(i);
            Push(A,i)
        END(* while loop *);
        WriteLn;
        WriteLn;
        WriteString("The reversed numbers --> ");
        WHILE NOT Empty(A) DO
            i:=INTEGER(Pop(A));
            IF i # 0 THEN WriteInt(i,3); END;
        END (* while loop *)
    END ReverseNumber.
```

When the numbers 1, 2, 3, 4, 5, 6 are keyed in as input, the output from
Program 8.3 is:

6 5 4 3 2 117746

This test result suggests an error in subprogram Initialize.

Procedure Initialize, as displayed in Program 8.1, does not assign an initial value to the ITEM field of the dynamic record. To rectify this error, it is necessary to change the definition module (the interface) as well as the implementation module. Therefore, all program units that import Stacks1 (e.g., implementation modules Op1 and FunctionEvaluator) must be recompiled. The revised subprogram Initialize is displayed in Program 8.4.

PROGRAM 8.4   Revised Implementation Module Initialize

```
PROCEDURE Initialize(VAR S: Stack; x: WORD);
(*Sets stack to empty.                                                    *)
BEGIN
    NEW(S);
    S↑.NEXT:=NIL;
    S↑.ITEM:=x
END Initialize;
```

After the subprogram Initialize has been revised in both the definition and implementation modules for Stacks1 and Realstack, an attempt is made to recompile implementation modules Op1 and FunctionEvaluator. This attempt fails. Why?

In both Op1 and FunctionEvaluator any subprogram calls to procedure Initialize must be in error. The old version of Initialize had only one parameter. The new version of this subprogram has two parameters. In addition, the first time a Push operation is to be performed, the operation Initialize must be used as a replacement for Push.

As a consequence of revising Stacks1 and Realstack, changes must be made in Op1 and FunctionEvaluator. This is typical in software testing. A Boolean variable StackInt is introduced into Op1 and FunctionEvaluator. The value of this Boolean variable is set to FALSE initially. When the appropriate stack is initialized (this can happen only when StackInt = FALSE), the Boolean variable StackInt is assigned the value TRUE.

The modified versions of implementation modules Op1 and Function Evaluator are shown in Program 8.5. Each line of code that has been modified is flagged with an arrow.

PROGRAM 8.5   Modified Implementation Modules Op1 and
**   FunctionEvaluator**

```
IMPLEMENTATION MODULE Op1;
```

```
FROM FunctionEvaluator IMPORT Expression, InitExpr, Assign;

FROM SymbolTable IMPORT SymTab, Table, InitSymTab, Deposit;

FROM Reals IMPORT StrToReal;

FROM Stacks1 IMPORT Stack, Empty, Pop, Push, Initialize, TopOfStack;

FROM Strings IMPORT STRING,Copy;

TYPE CharSet = SET OF CHAR;

PROCEDURE RemoveSpaces(VAR S: ARRAY OF CHAR; len: INTEGER);

    PROCEDURE RemSpace(POS,L: INTEGER);

    VAR I: INTEGER;

    BEGIN
        IF POS < L THEN
            FOR I:=POS TO L DO
                S[I]:=S[I+1];
            END(* do loop *)
        END(* if then *)
    END RemSpace;

VAR I   : INTEGER;

BEGIN

    I:=-1;
    REPEAT
        INC(I);
        IF S[I] = ' ' THEN
            RemSpace(I,len);
            DEC(I);
            DEC(len)
        END (* if then *)
    UNTIL I = len-1;
END RemoveSpaces;

PROCEDURE IdentConst(VAR S: ARRAY OF CHAR; VAR len: INTEGER);

VAR NUMERALS, ALPHABET, ALLOWABLE : CharSet;
    I , J, LenNum                 : INTEGER;
```

```
RealVal                              : REAL;
Stt                                  : ARRAY[1..20] OF CHAR;
ST                                   : STRING;
dummy                                : BOOLEAN;
ch                                   : CHAR;

PROCEDURE ADD(POS: INTEGER);
(* Adds "0" to the position just before the "−" in S.              *)

VAR I: INTEGER;

BEGIN
    FOR I:=len TO POS + 2 BY −1 DO
        S[I]:=S[I−1];
    END(* do loop *);
    S[POS]:='0';
    S[POS+1]:='−';
    len:=len + 1;
END ADD;

PROCEDURE Replace(symb: CHAR; pos, length: INTEGER);
(* This procedure replaces an integer constant by symb.             *)

VAR I: INTEGER;

BEGIN
    S[pos]:=symb;
    IF length > 1 THEN
        FOR I:=pos+1 TO len−length+1 DO
            S[I]:=S[I+length−1];
        END(* do loop *);
    END(* if then *);
END Replace;

BEGIN (* IdentConst *)
    NUMERALS:=CharSet{'0','1','2','3','4','5','6','7','8','9','.'};
    ALPHABET:=NUMERALS + CharSet{'A'..'Z'} + CharSet{'x'};
    (* We replace any nonoperator minus sign with "0−". *)
    I:=0;
    WHILE S[I] # ' ' DO
        IF (I = 0) AND (S[I] = '−') THEN
            ADD(I);
        ELSE
            IF S[I] = '−' THEN
                IF NOT (S[I−1] IN ALPHABET) THEN
                    ADD(I);
```

```
                    END(* if not then *)
                 END(* if then *)
             END(* if then else *);
             INC(I);
         END(* while loop *);
         I:=0;
         InitSymTab(Table);
         WHILE S[I] # ' ' DO
             IF S[I] IN NUMERALS THEN
                 LenNum:=1;
                 WHILE S[I+LenNum] IN NUMERALS DO
                     LenNum:=LenNum+1;
                 END(* while loop *);
                 FOR J:=1 TO 20 DO
                     Stt[J]:=' ';
                 END;
                 FOR J:=1 TO LenNum DO
                     Stt[J]:=S[I+J-1];
                 END(* for loop *);
                 Copy(Stt,0,LenNum,ST);
                 dummy:=StrToReal(ST,RealVal);
                 Deposit(RealVal,Table,ch);
                 (* We replace the integer constant by an operand symbol. *)
                 Replace(ch,I,LenNum);
             END(* if then *);
             INC(I);
         END(* while loop *)
END IdentConst;

PROCEDURE InfixPostfix(S: ARRAY OF CHAR): Expression;

VAR   OPSTK          : Stack;
      index1, index2, I: INTEGER;
      symb, topsymb  : CHAR;
      Allowable      : CharSet;
      Expr           : Expression;
───►  StackInt       : BOOLEAN;
                       (* Set to true if stack initialized. *)

PROCEDURE Precedence(op1,op2: CHAR): BOOLEAN;
BEGIN
    IF ((op1 = '+')OR(op1 = '-'))AND(op2 = '*')OR(op2 = '/')
        THEN RETURN FALSE
    ELSIF ((op1 = '(' ) AND (op2 # ')' ))OR(op2 = '(' )
        THEN RETURN FALSE
```

```
          ELSIF ((op1='+')OR(op1='−')OR(op1='*')OR(op1='/'))AND
                ((op2='%')OR(op2='↑')OR(op2='&')OR(op2='!')OR(op2='#'))
             THEN RETURN FALSE
          ELSE RETURN TRUE
          END(* if then elsif else *);
    END Precedence;

    BEGIN (* InfixPostfix *)
 ──► StackInt:=FALSE;
        Allowable:=CharSet{'A'..'Z'} + CharSet{'x'};
        InitExpr(Expr);
        index1:=0; index2:=1;
        WHILE (S[index1] # ' ') DO
            symb:=S[index1];
            IF symb IN Allowable THEN
                Assign(Expr,symb,index2);
                INC(index2);
            ELSE
                LOOP
                    IF (Empty(OPSTK)) OR
                      (NOT Precedence(CHAR(TopOfStack(OPSTK)),symb))
                        THEN EXIT; END;
                    topsymb:=CHAR(Pop(OPSTK));
                    IF (topsymb = '(' ) AND (symb = ')' ) THEN EXIT; END;
                    IF topsymb # '(' THEN
                        Assign(Expr,topsymb,index2);
                        INC(index2);
                        IF ((topsymb='%')OR(topsymb='!')OR(topsymb='↑')OR
                        (topsymb='#')OR
                        (topsymb='&'))AND(symb=')' ) THEN EXIT; END;
                    END(* if then *);
                END(* loop *);
              ►IF symb <> ')'
                THEN
                    IF StackInt
                        THEN Push(OPSTK,symb)
                        ELSE
                            Initialize(OPSTK,symb);
                            StackInt:=TRUE
                        END(* if then else *);
              ► END(* if then *);
            END(* if then else *);
            INC(index1);
        END(* while loop *);
```

```
    WHILE NOT Empty(OPSTK) DO
        topsymb:=CHAR(Pop(OPSTK));
        IF topsymb # '(' THEN
            Assign(Expr,topsymb,index2);
            INC(index2);
        END(* if then *);
    END(* while loop *);
    RETURN Expr;
END InfixPostfix;


PROCEDURE IdentFunct(VAR S: ARRAY OF CHAR; VAR len: INTEGER);
(* We use the following special symbols to replace sin, cos,
    In, and abs:
        sin  --> %
        cos  --> ↑
        exp  --> &
        In   --> #
        abs  --> !                                                      *)


PROCEDURE Replace(symb: CHAR; pos: INTEGER);
VAR i: INTEGER;
BEGIN
    S[pos]:=symb;
    FOR i:=pos+1 TO len-2 DO S[i]:=S[i+2]; END;
END Replace;


VAR k,i: INTEGER;
BEGIN (* IdentFunct *)
    k:=0;
    WHILE S[k] # ' ' DO
            IF (k >= 1)AND(((S[k]='N')OR(S[k]='n'))AND(S[k-1]='L')OR
                (S[k-1]='1'))
        THEN
            S[k-1]:='#';
            FOR i:=k TO len-1 DO
                S[i]:=S[i+1];
            END (* for loop *);
        END(* if then *);
        IF (k >=2) THEN
            IF ((S[k]='N')OR(S[k]='n'))AND((S[k-1]='I')OR(S[k-1]='i'))AND
                ((S[k-2]='S')OR(S[k-2]='s')) THEN Replace('%',k-2); END;
            IF ((S[k]='S')OR(S[k]='s'))AND((S[k-1]='O')OR(S[k-1]='o'))AND
                ((S[k-2]='C')OR(S[k-2]='c')) THEN Replace('↑',k-2); END;
```

```
                IF ((S[k]='P')OR(S[k]='p'))AND((S[k-1]='X')OR(S[k-1]='x'))AND
                    ((S[k-2]='E')OR(S[k-2]='e')) THEN Replace('&',k-2); END;
                IF ((S[k]='S')OR(S[k]='s'))AND((S[k-1]='B')OR(S[k-1]='b'))AND
                    ((S[k-2]='A')OR(S[k-2]='a')) THEN Replace('!',k-2); END;
          END(* if then *);
          INC(k)
      END(* while loop *);
  END IdentFunct;

END Op1.

IMPLEMENTATION MODULE FunctionEvaluator;

    FROM RealStack IMPORT Stack, Empty, Pop, Push, Initialize,
                          TopOfStack;

    FROM SymbolTable IMPORT Table, Fetch;

    FROM Op1 IMPORT RemoveSpaces, IdentConst, InfixPostfix, IdentFunct;

    FROM Op2 IMPORT Result;

    FROM Storage IMPORT ALLOCATE, DEALLOCATE;

    FROM InOut IMPORT WriteLn, WriteString, Read, EOL;

    CONST size = 80;

    TYPE Expression = POINTER TO ARRAY[1..size] OF CHAR;

    TYPE SetOfChar = SET OF CHAR;

    PROCEDURE InitExpr(VAR A: Expression);

    VAR I: INTEGER;

    BEGIN
        NEW(A);
        FOR I:=1 TO size DO
            A↑[I]:=' ';
        END(* do loop *);
    END InitExpr;

    PROCEDURE Assign(VAR A: Expression; B: CHAR; I: INTEGER);
```

```
BEGIN
    A↑[I]:=B
END Assign;

PROCEDURE Convert(): Expression;

VAR I, len : INTEGER;
    S     : ARRAY[1..size] OF CHAR;
    ch    : CHAR;

BEGIN
    FOR I:=1 TO size DO
        S[I]:=' ';
    END(* do loop *);
    WriteLn; WriteLn;
    WriteString("Blanks will be ignored in your expression.");
    WriteLn; WriteLn;
    WriteString("Enter your mathematical expression --> ");
    WriteLn;
    I:=0;
    REPEAT
        INC(I);
        Read(ch);
        S[I]:=ch;
    UNTIL (ch = EOL) OR (I = size);
    len:=I-1;
    S[I]:=' ';
    RemoveSpaces(S,len);
    IdentConst(S,len);
    IdentFunct(S,len);
    RETURN InfixPostfix(S);
END Convert;

PROCEDURE Eval(E: Expression; X: REAL): REAL;

VAR  OPNDSTK         : Stack;
     i               : INTEGER;
     symb            : CHAR;
     opnd1, opnd2    : REAL;
     rsymb, value    : REAL;
     Allowable       : SetOfChar;
 ──► StackInt        : BOOLEAN;

BEGIN (* Eval *)
    Allowable:=SetOfChar{'A'..'Z'};
 ──► StackInt:=FALSE;
```

```
        EXCL(Allowable,'X');
        i:=1;
        WHILE E↑[i] # ' ' DO
            symb:=E↑[i];
            IF (symb = 'X') OR (symb = 'x')
            THEN
              ┌─► IF StackInt THEN Push(OPNDSTK,X)
              │     ELSE
              │         Initialize(OPNDSTK,X);
              │         StackInt:=TRUE
              └──►END(* if then else *);
            END(* if then *);
            IF symb IN Allowable THEN
                rsymb:=Fetch(symb,Table);
              ┌─► IF StackInt THEN Push(OPNDSTK,rysmb)
              │     ELSE
              │         Initialize(OPNDSTK,rysmb);
              │         StackInt:=TRUE
              └──►END(* if then else *);
            ELSIF (symb='%')OR(symb='↑')OR(symb='&')
                                        OR(symb='#')OR(symb='!')
                    THEN
                        opnd2:=Pop(OPNDSTK);
                        value:=Result(symb,opnd1,opnd2);
                    ┌─► IF StackInt THEN Push(OPNDSTK,value)
                    │     ELSE
                    │         Initialize(OPNDSTK,value);
                    │         StackInt:=TRUE
                    └──► END(* if then else *);
            ELSIF (symb # 'X') AND (symb # 'x') THEN
                opnd2:=Pop(OPNDSTK);
                opnd1:=Pop(OPNDSTK);
                value:=Result(symb,opnd1,opnd2);
              ┌─► IF StackInt THEN Push(OPNDSTK,value)
              │     ELSE
              │         Initialize(OPNDSTK,value);
              │         StackInt:=TRUE
              └──► END(* if then else *);
            END(* if then elsif *);
            INC(i);
        END(* while loop *);
        RETURN Pop(OPNDSTK);
    END Eval;


END FunctionEvaluator.
```

When the changes indicated in Program 8.5 are made and the test program Tabulate, Program 8.2, is rerun, it fails again. When the mathematical function *x* is keyed in, the system crashes at run time. On the other hand, when the function (1.0 − *x*) is keyed in, the system runs perfectly. This type of partial failure is also typical in testing large software systems.

More testing must be performed!

Since the most significant changes were made to subprogram InfixPostFix, this subprogram is now thoroughly tested. In Program 8.6 we add code to the procedure InfixPostFix. The lines of code that are added are marked with an arrow.

PROGRAM 8.6   Test Program for Subprogram InfixPostFix

```
PROCEDURE InfixPostfix(S: ARRAY OF CHAR): Expression;

VAR OPSTK            : Stack;
    index1, index2, I: INTEGER;
    symb, topsymb  : CHAR;
    Allowable        : CharSet;
    Expr             : Expression;
    StackInt         : BOOLEAN; (* Set to true if stack initialized. *)

PROCEDURE Precedence(op1,op2: CHAR): BOOLEAN;
BEGIN
    IF ((op1 = '+')OR(op1 = '−'))AND(op2 = '*')OR(op2 = '/')
        THEN RETURN FALSE
    ELSIF ((op1 = '(' ) AND (op2 # ')' ))OR(op2 = '(')
        THEN RETURN FALSE
    ELSIF ((op1 = '+')OR(op1='−')OR(op1 = '*')OR(op1 = '/'))AND
          ((op2='%')OR(op2='↑')OR(op2='&')OR(op2='!')OR(op2='#'))
        THEN RETURN FALSE
    ELSE RETURN TRUE
    END(* if then elsif else *);
END Precedence;

BEGIN (* InfixPostfix *)
    StackInt:=FALSE;
    Allowable:=CharSet{'A'..'Z'} + CharSet{'x'};
    InitExpr(Expr);
    index1:=0; index2:=1;
    WHILE (S[index1] # ' ') DO
        symb:=S[index1];
→       WriteString("Testing Infix ... symb = ");
        Write(symb);
→       WriteLn;
        IF symb IN Allowable THEN
```

```
        ──► WriteString("Testing Infix ... symb in Allowable");
        ──► WriteLn;
            Assign(Expr,symb,index2);
            INC(index2);
        ELSE
            LOOP
            ──► WriteString("Testing Infix ... entered LOOP");
            ──► WriteLn;
                IF (Empty(OPSTK)) OR
                   (NOT Precedence(CHAR(TopOfStack(OPSTK)),symb))
                      THEN EXIT; END;
                topsymb:=CHAR(Pop(OPSTK));
            ──► WriteString("Testing Infix ... topsymb = ");
            ──► Write(topsymb);
            ──► WriteLn;
                IF (topsymb = '(' ) AND (symb = ')' ) THEN EXIT; END;
                IF topsymb # '(' THEN
                    Assign(Expr,topsymb,index2);
                    INC(index2);
                    IF ((topsymb='%')OR(topsymb='!')OR(topsymb='^')OR
                        (topsymb='#')OR
                        (topsymb='&'))AND(symb=')' ) THEN EXIT; END;
                END(* if then *);
            END(* loop *);
            IF symb # ')'
            THEN
                IF StackInt
                    THEN Push(OPSTK,symb)
                    ELSE
                        Initialize(OPSTK,symb);
                        StackInt:=TRUE
                    END(* if then else *);
            END(* if then *);
        END(* if then else *);
        INC(index1);
    END(* while loop *);
    WHILE NOT Empty(OPSTK) DO
    ──► WriteString("Entered WHILE NOT Empty(OPSTK) DO ");
    ──► WriteLn;
        topsymb:=CHAR(Pop(OPSTK));
        IF topsymb # '(' THEN
            Assign(Expr,topsymb,index2);
            INC(index2);
        END(* if then *);
    END(* while loop *);
```

```
    RETURN Expr;
END InfixPostfix;
```

The enhanced version of procedure InfixPostFix, given in Program 8.6, when placed into the system quickly yields the error. It is a subtle logical error!

When the input string is *x,* the WHILE loop pointed to by the last two arrows in Program 8.6 gets entered. This loop should not be entered for this case.

Since OPSTK was never initialized, the value pointed to by OPSTK is indeterminate. For input strings that cause the stack to be initialized [e.g., $(1.0 - x)$], the procedure works just fine. For input strings that do not cause the stack to be initialized, we have problems.

Would you have caught this bug without a test program? What can we do to rectify this problem?

A simple way to correct the error is to again modify procedure Initialize in modules Stacks1 and RealStacks. The final revision for Initialize is shown in Program 8.7. Compare the three versions of procedure Initialize.

PROGRAM 8.7 **Final Revision for Procedure Initialize**

```
PROCEDURE Initialize(VAR S: Stack);
BEGIN
    S:=NIL;
END Initialize;
```

Appropriate modifications must again be made in implementation modules Op1 and FunctionEvaluator. We ask the reader to do this as an exercise.

Our perfective maintenance causes us to go in a circle of module and subprogram modifications. Only through testing is it possible to remove newly introduced bugs and to be assured that the system will work as desired.

8.3 TOP-DOWN AND BOTTOM-UP TESTING

Top-down testing starts at a high level (module level) with subprograms (procedures and functions) represented by stubs. The goal of testing at this level is to confirm that the major architectural blocks of the software system mesh together and that the appropriate interfaces exist between cooperating subprograms. At the next stage of testing, subprogram stubs are replaced by actual code and this code is tested. The process that we are describing is actually top-down software development that incorporates step-by-step testing as an integral part of the process.

Bottom-up testing starts by developing and testing small blocks of code, such as, for example, the implementation of an algorithm. The individual functions and procedures that make up a module are tested thoroughly before an actual module is assembled and tested with other modules.

The main advantage of top-down testing is that serious design errors often are revealed at the highest levels of a software system. Furthermore, testing and software development (i.e., coding) are merged into one operation without the need for a lengthy and separate testing program later. Another major advantage of top-down testing is the early accessibility of a limited but nevertheless working version of the system, which may demonstrate the system's feasibility to customers and management.

A shortcoming of top-down testing and software development is that subtleties of algorithm design may be covered up and not revealed until a lower level of program development is reached. Complex subprograms cannot adequately be simulated by a procedure stub.

Bottom-up testing is usually easier to perform because it is usually easy to construct low level drivers and test cases. Unfortunately, with bottom-up testing, the entire system cannot be integrated and tested as a whole until the very end of the testing process.

The best solution appears to be a mixture of top-down and bottom-up testing. Once the major architectural components of the software system have been identified and blocked out as modules, the more difficult subprograms may be constructed, assembled, and tested, bottom-up. In the meanwhile, integrated system testing, using stubs as surrogates for the yet to be completed subprograms, may commence and yield insights into the overall integrity of the emerging system.

8.4 DESIGNING TEST CASES: A CASE STUDY

The testing of a software system involves the construction of a set of test cases. Each test case requires an input specification, a description of the system functions tested by the input, and a statement of the expected output. Test data consist of the input information that is used in a particular test case.

The goal in designing test cases is to exercise many possible program paths at every level of the software system. For the reasons discussed in section 8.3, it is usually desirable to perform the testing as the software system is developed rather than beginning the testing process after development has terminated.

We illustrate the design of test cases and the integration of test case design with the software development process by considering a relatively simple case study. An illustration of the full test process for a large software system would be prohibitively lengthy. Furthermore, the myriad of details might distract the reader from the essential concepts of test case design.

As our simple illustrative example, we consider a program for sorting that uses a heap data structure for the data to be sorted. We assume that we wish to sort an array of floating point numbers efficiently. We wish to sort in place (without having to use auxiliary data structures such as another array). We assume that the floating point numbers are in an array x, with index values from 1 to n. That is, the numbers to be sorted are contained in $x[1], x[2], \ldots, x[n]$.

The heap sort strategy requires two major steps.

1. Convert the raw data into a heap structure, in place.

A heap may be modeled as an almost complete binary tree such that the value of every node is equal to or less than the value of its parent. An "almost complete binary tree" is a binary tree that satisfies the following conditions.

(a) Every leaf node in the tree is at level k or at level $k + 1$ (the root is at level 1).

(b) If a node in the tree has a right descendant at level $k + 1$, all its left descendants that are leaf nodes must also be at level $k + 1$.

In Figure 8.1a we display a bona fide heap. Figures 8.1b and 8.1c show binary trees that do not qualify as heaps. The tree in Figure 8.1b fails to be a heap because of condition a, and the tree of Figure 8.1c fails because of condition b.

Since every heap node must be equal to or less than its parent, the root node in a binary heap tree must contain the largest key value for the tree. It is this simple fact that we exploit in using the heap tree for sorting numbers.

We use a one-dimensional array to implement the heap structure. If we label the tree nodes so the root node is mapped to the 1 position of the array, the left child of the root to the number 2 position of the array, the right child of the root to the number 3 position of the array, the left off-spring of the left root child to the number 4 position of the array, and so forth, every element position in the one-dimensional array corresponds to a tree node.

For example, we list the key values of the nodes in Figure 8.1a, with their appropriate position numbers as follows.

```
1 <---> 100
2 <--->  75
3 <--->  50
4 <--->  60
5 <--->  70
6 <--->  25
7 <--->  30
8 <--->  20
```

From this mapping, it should be evident that in general, the largest element in the heap is contained in $x[1]$. In the process of building the heap, the largest element in the array will be shifted to the first position.

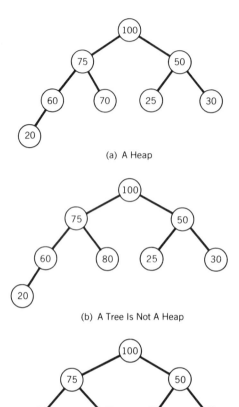

(a) A Heap

(b) A Tree Is Not A Heap

(c) Another Tree That Is Not A Heap

Figure 8.1 Binary trees and heaps. (*a*) A heap. (*b*) A tree that is not a heap. (*c*) Another tree that is not a heap.

2. For $i \longleftarrow n$ down to 2 loop:
    2.1. Interchange $x(1)$ and $x(i)$.
    2.2. Recreate a heap with $i - 1$ elements by readjusting the position of $x(1)$.

The second step of the process resembles a common exchange sort algorithm. In step 2.1, the largest element in the set of remaining elements, namely $x[1]$, is exchanged with the ith element. Then in step 2 the heap structure is rebuilt.

The only feature of the heap structure that proves useful for this sorting technique is the fact that the element in the $x[1]$ position is the largest.

The heap sort method is attractive because the number of comparison operations that must be performed is never greater, for large n, than $n \times \log2(n)$. This is much better than many elementary sorting routines that are of complexity $n \times n$.

We display the algorithms for the in-place creation of a heap (step 1) and the reconstruction of a heap (step 2). Both these algorithms are presented in pseudo-code.

ALGORITHM FOR STEP 1

Algorithm CreateHeap(a: array of real numbers)
    for node ⟵ 2 to k loop
        i ⟵ node
        j ⟵ i div 2 {j is the parent of i}
        while (i is not the root node) and x[j] <= x[i] loop
            interchange x[i] and x[j]
            i ⟵ j   {advance up the tree}
            j ⟵ i div 2
        end loop
    end loop
end CreateHeap

ALGORITHM FOR STEP 2

Algorithm Reconstruction(a: array of real numbers)
    i ⟵ 1
    {Compute the larger of node i's children.}
    j ⟵ 2
    if (k >= 3) and (x[3] > x[2]) then j ⟵ 3
    while (j <= k) and (x[j] > x[i]) loop
        interchange x[i] and x[j]
        i ⟵ j
        *j ⟵ 2*i   {Move down one level in the tree.}*
        if j + 1 <= k then
            if x[j+1] > x[j] then j ⟵ j+1
        end if
    end loop
end ReconstructHeap

Finally Program 8.8, written in Modula-2, displays the full implementation of the heap sort concept.

PROGRAM 8.8 **Modula-2 Program for Heap Sorting**

DEFINITION MODULE HeapSort;
(* $SEG:=16; *)

    EXPORT QUALIFIED Sort;

    PROCEDURE Sort(VAR x: ARRAY OF REAL);

END HeapSort.

IMPLEMENTATION MODULE HeapSort;

    PROCEDURE CreateHeap(VAR a: ARRAY OF REAL);

    VAR
        node, i, j : CARDINAL;
        temp   : REAL;

    BEGIN (* CreateHeap)
        FOR node:= 1 TO HIGH(a) DO
            i:= node;
            j:= i DIV 2;
            WHILE (i # 0) AND (a[j] <= a[i]) DO
                temp:= a[i];
                a[i]:= a[j];
                a[j]:= temp;
                i:= j;
                j:= i DIV 2
            END(* while loop *)
        END(* do loop *)
    END CreateHeap;

    PROCEDURE ReconstructHeap(VAR a: ARRAY OF REAL; k: CARDINAL);
    VAR
        i, j   : CARDINAL;
        temp : REAL;

    BEGIN (* Reconstruct *)
        i:= 1;
        j:= 2;
        IF (k >= 3) AND (a[3] > a[2]) THEN j:= 3; END(* if then*);
        WHILE (j <= k) AND (a [j] > a[i]) DO
            temp:= a[i];
            a[i]:= a[j];

```
            a[j]:= temp;
            i:= j;
            j:= 2*i;
            IF j+1 <= k THEN
                IF a[j+1] > a[j] THEN INC(j); END(* if then *);
            END(* if then *);
        END(* while loop *)
END ReconstructHeap;


PROCEDURE Sort(VAR x: ARRAY OF REAL);

VAR
    i      : CARDINAL;
    temp : REAL;

BEGIN (* Sort *)
    CreateHeap(x);
    FOR i:= HIGH(x) TO 1 BY -1 DO
        temp:= x[0];
        x[0]:= x[i];
        x[i]:= temp;
        ReconstructHeap(x,i-1)
    END(* do loop *)
END Sort;


END HeapSort.
```

The code displayed in Program 8.8 is the first version of HeapSort that we developed. It has not yet been tested.

If you compare procedures CreateHeap and ReconstructHeap in Program 8.8 with the algorithms for CreateHeap and ReconstructHeap, you will notice changes in the index limits on some of the loops. These changes were made to accommodate the open array type in Modula-2. When a procedure parameter is declared to be of open array type, such as, for example, ARRAY OF REAL, the range of the actual array transferred into the procedure is mapped to the range 0 to HIGH. So, for example, if the actual array range is 2 to 10, this range is mapped to 0 to 8.

We will develop a test suite for Program 8.8 that is typical of larger test sets.

We note that there is no input or output in Program 8.8. Any test driver that we write will have to employ its own input and output.

First we informally test the program as an integrated entity. Next we formally test each of the two subprograms, and then the entire program.

In the first informal test program, we allow the user to input any 10 real numbers. We then output the numbers first without sorting (to ensure ourselves that the numbers were properly input) and then after sorting. Before we develop a formal test suite, we display such an informal test program (Program 8.9) and present its output.

PROGRAM 8.9   Informal Test Program for Heap Sort

```
MODULE TestHeapSorting;

    FROM HeapSort  IMPORT Sort;

    FROM InOut      IMPORT WriteLn, WriteString, WriteCard;

    FROM RealInOut IMPORT WriteReal, ReadReal;

    VAR
        x : ARRAY[1..10] OF REAL;
        i : CARDINAL;

    BEGIN (* TestHeapSorting *)
        FOR i:= 1 TO 10 DO
            WriteLn;
            WriteString("Enter x[");
            WriteCard(i,1);
            WriteString("] : ");
            ReadReal(x[i]);
        END(* do loop *);
        FOR i:= 1 TO 10 DO
            WriteLn;
            WriteString("x[");
            WriteCard(i,1);
            WriteString("] = ");
            WriteReal(x[i],1);
        END(* do loop *);
        Sort(x);
        FOR i:= 1 TO 10 DO
            WriteLn;
            WriteString("x[");
            WriteCard(i,1);
            WriteString("] = ");
            WriteReal(x[i],1);
        END(* do loop *)
    END TestHeapSorting.
```

When the input sequence is

1.0, 3.0, 2.0, 4.0, 6.0, 5.0, 7.0, 9.0, 8.0, 10.0

the output sequence is

9.0, 8.0, 6.0, 7.0, 3.0, 2.0, 5.0, 1.0, 4.0, 10.0

The program does not pass the first test! Since component testing was not done as the program was being constructed, it is not surprising that the entire system fails to work the first time.

Before developing our formal test suite, we must find the bug or bugs in the system. We will quickly test each component of the system.

We cannot test the subprograms CreateHeap and ReconstructHeap from outside the module HeapSort. These two procedures are hidden from view. We must perform internal module testing, and to do this, we go inside the implementation module HeapSort.

We first determine whether subprogram CreateHeap is doing its job. To do this we modify procedure Sort by adding code for output. In particular, we print the array *x* after it has been processed by subprogram CreateHeap. We continue to use Program 8.9, TestHeapSorting, as a test driver and use the same input sequence as before. The revised procedure Sort for test purposes is shown in Program 8.10.

PROGRAM 8.10   Revised Procedure Sort for Test Purposes

```
PROCEDURE Sort(VAR x: ARRAY OF REAL);

VAR
    i     : CARDINAL;
    temp : REAL;

BEGIN (* Sort *)
    CreateHeap(x);
    WriteLn;
    WriteString("We are testing CreateHeap");
    WriteLn;
    WriteString("The array after passing through CreateHeap is ");
    WriteLn;
    FOR i:= 0 TO HIGH(x) DO
        WriteLn;
        WriteString("x[");
```

```
        WriteCard(i,1);
        WriteString("] = ");
        WriteReal(x[i],10)
    END(* do loop *);
    FOR i:= HIGH(x) TO 1 BY −1 DO
        temp:= x[0];
        x[0]:= x[i];
        x[i]:= temp;
        ReconstructHeap(x,i−1)
    END(* do loop *)
END Sort;
```

After being processed by CreateHeap, the array is

10.0, 9.0, 8.0, 6.0, 7.0, 3.0, 2.0, 5.0, 1.0, 4.0

If you sketch the corresponding binary tree that corresponds to this array output (10.0 the root, 9.0 the left offspring of the root, 8.0 the right offspring of the root, etc.), the tree is a heap. Thus it appears that the cause of the problem does not lie with CreateHeap. We emphasize that we have not formally tested procedure CreateHeap. But in trying to quickly locate the bug(s) in this program, we bypass CreateHeap for now and focus on Reconstruct.

To test procedure ReconstructHeap, an additional modification is made to procedure Sort. The revision of Sort is shown in Program 8.11.

PROGRAM 8.11   Another Test Revision of Procedure Sort

```
PROCEDURE Sort(VAR x: ARRAY OF REAL);

VAR
    i     : CARDINAL;
    temp : REAL;

BEGIN
    CreateHeap(x);
    WriteLn;
    WriteString("We are testing Createheap");
    WriteLn;
    WriteString("The array after passing through CreateHeap is ");
    WriteLn;
    FOR i:= 0 TO HIGH(x) DO
```

```
        WriteLn;
        WriteString("x[");
        WriteCard(i,1);
        WriteString("] = ");
        WriteReal(x[i],10)
    END(* do loop *);
    FOR i:= HIGH(x) TO 1 BY −1 DO
        temp:= x[0];
        x[0]:= x[i];
        x[i]:= temp;
        ReconstructHeap(x,i−1);
        WriteLn;
        WriteString("We are testing ReconstructHeap");
        WriteLn;
        FOR i:= 0 TO HIGH(x) DO
            WriteLn;
            WriteString("x[");
            WriteCard(i,1);
            WriteString("] = ");
            WriteReal(x[i],10)
        END(* do loop *);
        HALT;
    END(* do loop *)
END Sort;
```

After processing by procedure ReconstructHeap the first time, the array x has the following values.

4.0, 9.0, 8.0, 6.0, 7.0, 3.0, 2.0, 5.0, 1.0, 10.0

This structure is not a heap. The problem becomes clear if you carefully study the output given above.

When the root of the tree (10,9,8,6,7,3,2,5,1,4) produced by CreateHeap, namely 10, is interchanged with 4, the resulting tree is (4,9,8,6,7,3,2,5,1,10). This tree has not changed as a result of being processed by procedure ReconstructHeap. The reason is an off by one error in several indices in procedure ReconstructHeap. In particular, the initial value for index i should be 0 instead of 1. This follows because position 0 corresponds to the tree root rather than position 1 because of the open array mapping.

We display the corrected version of procedure Reconstructheap in Program 8.12.

PROGRAM 8.12 **Corrected Version of Procedure ReconstructHeap**

```
PROCEDURE ReconstructHeap(VAR a: ARRAY OF REAL; k: CARDINAL);

VAR
    i, j    : CARDINAL;
    temp : REAL;

BEGIN
    i:= 0;
    j:= 1;
    IF (k >= 2) AND ( a[2] > a[1] ) THEN j:= 2; END(* if then*);
    WHILE ( j <= k ) AND ( a[j] > a[i] ) DO
        temp:= a[i];
        a[i]:= a[j];
        a[j]:= temp;
        i:= j;
        j:= 2*i;
        IF j+1 <= k THEN
            IF a[j+1] > a[j] THEN INC(j); END(* if then *);
        END(* if then *);
    END(* while loop *)
END ReconstructHeap;
```

Now the array x has the following values after processing by procedure ReconstructHeap the first time.

9.0, 8.0, 7.0, 6.0, 4.0, 3.0, 2.0, 5.0, 1.0, 10.0

This output corresponds to a heap. Please verify this yourself. We now remove all the extra test code from procedure Sort and rerun the test program, Program 8.9.

Happily the output for the same input sequence (1,3,2,4,6,5,7,9,8,10) is

1.0, 2.0, 3.0, 4.0, 5.0, 6.0, 7.0, 8.0, 9.0, 10.0

The program now appears to work as it should, and we are ready to develop a formal test suite.

Module Heapsort must be tested with valid as well as invalid input. It is not necessary to test Heapsort with an array of the wrong type, such as an array of INTEGER or an array of STRING. The Modula-2 compiler would flag

Table 8.1 Test Data Equivalence Partitioning for Heap Sort Program

1. Array x of size 1.
2. Array x of size 2, in order.
3. Array x of size 2, reverse order.
4. Even-numbered array limits, both less than zero, in order.
5. Even-numbered array limits, both less than zero, reverse order.
6. Even-numbered array limits, both less than zero, random order.
7. Repeat steps 4, 5, and 6 with lower limit odd, upper limit even.
8. Repeat steps 4, 5, and 6 with lower limit even, upper limit odd.
9. Lower limit even, less than zero, upper limit even, greater than zero, in order.
10. Lower limit even, less than zero, upper limit even, greater than zero, reverse order.
11. Lower limit even, less than zero, upper limit even, greater than zero, random order.
12. Repeat steps 9, 10, and 11 with lower limit odd, upper limit even.
13. Repeat steps 9, 10, and 11 with lower limit even, upper limit odd.
14. Both limits even, greater than zero, in order.
15. Both limits even, greater than zero, reverse order.
16. Both limits even, greater than zero, random order.
17. Repeat steps 14, 15, and 16 with lower limit odd and upper limit even.
18. Repeat steps 14, 15, and 16 with lower limit even and upper limit odd.

such errors at compilation time because of the strong type checking across compilation boundaries enforced in Modula-2.

We limit our testing to the externally available procedure Sort. The internal, and hidden, procedures CreateHeap and ReconstructHeap will be tested further only if procedure Sort fails to pass one or more tests.

We use equivalence partitioning to design our test data. We choose data equivalence classes so that if the program does not fail for one member of a given class, it should not fail for any member of that class. Table 8.1 illustrates this process for our case study.

There are effectively 30 tests implied in the test suite of Table 8.1. We display a test program, Program 8.13, that supports this test suite. Only two constants must be changed to go from one test case to another, upper limit and lower limit. It is clear that a careful analysis of the program would justify the elimination of some or all of the tests in Table 8.1; they were presented for illustrative purposes only.

PROGRAM 8.13 Program to Generate Test Suite for HeapSort

```
MODULE TestSuiteForHeapSort;

    FROM HeapSort IMPORT Sort;
```

```
FROM InOut      IMPORT WriteLn, WriteString, WriteCard;

FROM RealInOut IMPORT WriteReal, ReadReal;

FROM Utilities    IMPORT Rand, CenterMessage, Spacebar;

CONST
    lowerlimit = −6;
    upperlimit = −2;

(* These limits must be changed to go from one test case
   to another.                                                          *)

VAR
    x              : ARRAY[ lowerlimit. .upper limit ] OF REAL;
    i              : CARDINAL;
    machineseed : BOOLEAN;

PROCEDURE InOrder(VAR a: ARRAY OF REAL);
(* This procedure loads the array with numbers in ascending order.      *)

VAR i: CARDINAL;

BEGIN
    FOR i:= 0 TO HIGH(a) DO
        a[i]:= 5.0 * FLOAT(i);
    END(* do loop *);
END InOrder;

PROCEDURE ReverseOrder(VAR a: ARRAY OF REAL);
(* This procedure loads the array with numbers in descending order.     *)

VAR i: CARDINAL;

BEGIN
    FOR i:= 0 TO HIGH(a) DO
        a[i]:= − 6.8 * FLOAT(i);
    END(* do loop *);
END ReverseOrder;

PROCEDURE RandomOrder(VAR a: ARRAY OF REAL);
(* This procedure loads the array with numbers in random order.         *)

VAR i: CARDINAL;
```

```
    BEGIN
        FOR i:= 0 TO HIGH(a) DO
            a[i]:= −10.0 + 20.0 ∗ Rand(machineseed);
            (∗ The random numbers are uniformly distributed between
                −10.0 and 10.0.                                        ∗)
        END(∗ do loop ∗);
    END RandomOrder;


    PROCEDURE Output(a: ARRAY OF REAL);


    VAR i: CARDINAL;


    BEGIN
        FOR i:= 0 TO HIGH(a) DO
            WriteLn;
            WriteReal(a[i],40);
        END(∗ do loop ∗);
    END Output;

BEGIN(∗ TestSuiteForHeapSort ∗)
    machineseed:= TRUE;
    (∗ Computer seeds random number generator. ∗)
    WriteLn;
    CenterMessage("We perform in order test");
    WriteLn;
    InOrder(x);
    CenterMessage("Before sorting");
    WriteLn;
    Output(x);                          .
    WriteLn;
    Spacebar;
    Sort(x);
    CenterMessage("After sorting");
    WriteLn;
    Output(x);
    WriteLn;
    Spacebar;
    CenterMessage("We perform reverse order test");
    WriteLn;
    ReverseOrder(x);
    CenterMessage("Before sorting");
    WriteLn;
    Output(x);
    WriteLn;
```

```
      Spacebar;
      Sort(x);
      CenterMessage("After sorting");
      WriteLn;
      Output(x);
      WriteLn;
      Spacebar;
      CenterMessage("We perform random order test");
      WriteLn;
      RandomOrder(x);
      CenterMessage("Before sorting");
      WriteLn;
      Output(x);
      WriteLn;
      Spacebar;
      Sort(x);
      CenterMessage("After sorting");
      WriteLn;
      Output(x);
      WriteLn;
      Spacebar
END TestSuiteForHeapSort.
```

Program HeapSort passes the entire battery of tests given in Program 8.13 for each of the cases given in Table 8.1.

8.5 TESTING TOOLS

Software tools have been developed to assist in the often tedious testing process. We discuss a few such testing tools in this section.

8.5.1 Data Generators

Test data generators are programs or modules that automatically generate a large number of test inputs for a given system. As an example, in testing a spelling checker program, a test generator might generate as input to the program a large quantity of words, correctly spelled as well as incorrectly spelled. As another example, in testing a compiler, a test generator might generate as input to the compiler a set of correct as well as incorrect programs. The error messages generated by the compiler under test could be examined for correctness.

8.5.2 Program Analyzers

A typical program analyzer determines how many times each statement in a given program is executed during the run time of the program. To accomplish this mission, most program analyzers must insert additional code into the program to be tested. This "instrumentation" of the program may at times actually alter the measurements being made—a software equivalent of the uncertainty principle!

Quite often, a large fraction of the run time of a given program is spent executing a small portion of the program. A program analyzer can detect this situation. In such cases, it may be warranted to write this small section of code in machine language to better optimize the performance of the system.

Static analyzers examine a program before it is executed. A static analyzer can check that every part of a program is reachable. It can check to make sure that a variable has been initialized with a value before it is used in an assignment statement. The static analyzer DAVE has been developed for use with FORTRAN programs [2].

8.5.3 File Comparators

The software testing process often requires the generation of large quantities of output data. Since the desired output is known before testing commences, this output may be placed on file. Then as the testing begins, the actual test output may be automatically compared to the expected test output. Any errors that are detected must be immediately flagged.

8.5.4 Program Debuggers

The most primitive debugging tool is the core dump. This is a printout of the machine memory at the moment the program error occurs. Since core dumps do not present information directly related to the source program, they are of little value when programming in a high level language.

The software developer needs a debugging tool that relates to the objects used in the program (the variables, procedures, etc.). A symbolic dump debugger does this by providing the programmer a list of all or some of the program variables with their values at the moment of system failure. The programmer does not have the burden of tracing the values of important system variables. A powerful symbolic dump debugger will display the values of both global as well as local variables in all activated procedures. It should associate the name of the appropriate procedure with the variable name, to avoid name confounding where variables of the same name are used in different procedures.

Interactive symbolic dump programs allow the program developer to query the debugger for the values of specific entities in the program at the time of a failure. Unix supports such an interactive debugger with its db program. The program may request the values of variables by name and examine the contents of machine registers.

8.5.5 Program Trace Tools

A trace program provides information about the dynamic properties of a program, that is, the performance of the program as it runs. Subprogram entries and exits, transfers of control within a block, branch selection, and process initiations are the types of event recorded while the program is executing.

Trace programs often generate huge amounts of output data. At times the quantity of output is unmanageable. To avoid unnecessary output, a capability for switching trace logic on and off is desirable.

8.5.6 Interactive Debugging

The most powerful debugging tools are those that allow a programmer to interact with a program while it is running. The instantaneous value of variables may be obtained by freezing program execution. Such debugging tools construct a trace file in which all program state changes are recorded. This trace file may be interrogated later. An example of such a system is EXDAMS [3]. Interactive debugging systems require significant resources.

8.6 PROOF OF PROGRAMS

In this chapter we have described the process of software testing and have indicated that no amount of software testing can establish that a program is correct. Testing can demonstrate only the presence of logical errors, never the absence of such errors. How then can we determine whether a program is correct?

To answer this question, we must be able to specify precisely what a program is intended to do. Then given this specification and a program, we must prove that the program does what the specification says it should do. In this section we introduce this process, which is called program verification. The interested reader is referred to Manna [4] for a more thorough presentation.

Proving that a program is correct is often more difficult than writing the program; however, the consequences of an incorrect program may justify the cost and effort of program verification. By proving that a program conforms to its specification, we can have greater confidence in it. Furthermore, an understanding of program proof techniques is helpful in reading and writing programs and reasoning informally about programs.

In many cases a complete, formal program proof is unnecessary. For large software systems, such a proof is usually infeasible, as is complete testing. However, we can substantially increase our confidence in a program by careful testing, using the style of reasoning developed for program proofs to guide the testing process. In some cases we might mix program proofs of some properties with tests of others.

Program verification is based on assertions about the program variables before, during, and after program execution. Assertions characterize properties of program variables and relationships among them at various stages of program execution. Examples of assertions are:

"y is greater than or equal to zero."

"$a = b$."

"$x + y > z$."

"The components of the vector x are sorted in nondecreasing order."

We use assertions to describe the state of computation before the program begins execution and after each program step has been executed. The variables that appear in an assertion need not be program variables. For example, if x is a vector and i is not a program variable, the assertion

"There exists an i such that $x(i) = a$."

establishes that the value of the variable a is an entry in the vector x. All variables that occur in an assertion must be bound when the assertion applies. Program variables will have an assigned value and so are bound by assignment. Nonprogram variables may be bound by assignment or quantification.

To prove that a program is correct, we must first have a precise specification of what the program is intended to do. This is given by an initial assertion and a final assertion. The initial assertion characterizes what is known or assumed about the program variables before program execution begins. If no assumption is made, the initial assertion is the tautology TRUE. The final assertion specifies what relations are true for the program variables if the program terminates normally. Together, the initial and final assertions specify what the program is intended to do. Determining whether a program is correct may be addressed only if initial and final assertions represent a correct characterization of the task to be performed. That is, program correctness is proved relative to a specified task.

A program or program segment S is said to be correct with respect to an initial assertion P and a final assertion Q if P{S}Q is a tautology. The notation P{S}Q means if P is true before the execution of S, and S is executed and terminates, then Q will be true immediately following the termination of S. We find it convenient to state that

> The program segment
> A1 : P
> S
> A2 : Q
> is correct.

rather than using the notation P{S}Q. We use the notation Ai, where i is an integer, to number our assertions in the program. For example,

> The program segment
> A1: TRUE
> X := 2;
> Y := 5;
> A2: X=2 and Y=5
> is correct.

This is equivalent to

$$\text{TRUE } \{ X:=2; Y:=5 \} X=2 \text{ and } Y = 5.$$

To prove that a program is correct, we need to characterize the effect of each program statement in the programming language on the program variables. Since a program consists of many statements, we also need methods of combining the individual statement characterizations into a description or characterization of executing the entire program. We now present some rules of inference that will permit us to prove that some simple programs are correct.

Rule of Composition

We can break a proof of correctness of a program into a series of proofs of correctness for successive parts of the program. Let S1 and S2 denote program segments and S1;S2 denote the program segment whose execution has the same effect as first executing S1 and then executing S2. The rule of composition states that:

If Q1{S1}Q2 and Q2{S2}Q3, then Q1{S1;S2}Q3.
That is, if the assertion Q1 is initially true and S1;S2 is executed, then after termination of the segment S1;S2, the assertion Q3 will be true.

Using program segments, the rule of composition can be restated as:

```
        A1 : Q1              AI : Q2
If      S1          and      S2
        A2 : Q2              A2 : Q3
are both correct, then
        A1 : Q1
        S1;
        S2
        A2 : Q3
is correct.
```

As an example, if we can establish that

```
A1 :  TRUE          A2 :  X=5
X  := 5;           Y  := X - Z;
A2 :  X=5          A3 :  Y=5-Z
```

are both correct, then using the rule of composition we can conclude that

```
A1   : TRUE
X  := 5;
Y  := X - Z;
A3   : Y=5-Z
```

is correct.

The rule of composition allows us to infer the correctness of a program from the correctness of its program segments. To prove that the program P is correct, given the initial assertion I and the final assertion F, we can break P up into program segments $S1, S2, \ldots, SN$ such that $P = S1; S2; \ldots ; SN$ and then determine "intermediate assertions" $Q1, Q2, \ldots, QNM1$ ($NM1 = N - 1$). If we can prove that $I\{S1\}Q1$, $Q1\{S2\}Q3, \ldots, QNM1\{SN\}F$, it follows from repeated application of the rule of composition that $I\{P\}F$ is correct.

Rules of Consequence

The rules of consequence state that a program assertion that precedes a program segment can be replaced by a stronger one and an assertion that follows a program segment can be replaced by a weaker one without affecting the correctness of the segment. The assertion P is stronger than the assertion Q if P implies Q, $P => Q$. These rules can be formally stated as:

If Q1 => Q2 and Q2{S}Q3, then Q1{S}Q3.

If Q1{S}Q2 and Q2 => Q3, then Q1{S}Q3.

The two rules of consequence permit us to ignore information about the program variables if it is not important for the proof of correctness. For example, the value of a loop index may be important in the assertions within the loop, but when the execution continues past the loop, the value of this variable may not be significant. Indeed, in Ada the value of a loop index is not available outside the loop. The implications $Q1 => Q2$ and $Q2 => Q3$ relate two assertions. These implications must be proved independent of the program.

As an example, if the program segment

```
A1  :  TRUE
X  := 5;
Y  := X + Z;
A2  :  Y=Z+5
```

is shown to be correct, then since $Y = Z + 5 => Y > Z + 1$, we can conclude that

```
A1   :  TRUE
X   := 5;
Y   := X + Z;
A2'  :  Y>Z+1
```

is correct.

We next consider the rules of inference for several control statements in Ada and Modula-2. We examine the statements "if CONDITION then S;", "if CONDITION then S1 else S2;", and "while CONDITION loop S;". To prove that a nontrivial program is correct, we would also need to examine the rules of inference for other loop structures, for the null statement, for the case statement, for procedure invocation, and so on. In the statements that we consider, CONDITION is an assertion about the program variables. Whenever CONDITION is evaluated, the portion of the program to be executed next is determined by whether CONDITION is true or false. The effect of executing each of these statements is characterized by a rule of inference.

The If-Then Rule

When the program executes the statement "if CONDITION then S;", the program segment S is executed if and only if CONDITION is true. A rule of inference for this type of statement must involve preceding and following assertions that will be true regardless of whether the program segment S is executed. The rule can be formalized as follows.

If (Q1 and CONDITION){S}Q2 and
(Q1 and not CONDITION) => Q2, then
Q1{if CONDITION then S}Q2.

Note that this rule contains the proposition (Q1 and not CONDITION) => Q2, which must be proved independent of the program.

In terms of program segments, the if-then rule is:

If the implication
    (Q1 and not CONDITION) => Q2
is true and
    A1 : Q1 and CONDITION
    S
    A2 : Q2
is correct, then
    A1 : Q1
    if CONDITION then S
    A2 : Q2
is correct.

As an example, to show that the program segment

    A1 : TRUE
    if $X < 0$ then $Y := 5$;
    A2 : $X >= 0$ or $Y = 5$

is correct, we must show that the implication

$$(\text{TRUE and not}(X < 0)) => (X >= 0 \text{ or } Y = 5)$$

is true and that

    A1' : TRUE and $X < 0$
    $Y := 5$;
    A2 : $X >= 0$ or $Y = 5$

is correct. It follows from the if-then rule that the program segment is correct. The proof of implications uses identities established in the propositional calculus. The proof of the implication above is:

$$
\begin{array}{lll}
(\text{TRUE and not}(X < 0)) & => \text{not}(X < 0) & \text{Simplification} \\
\text{not}(X < 0) <==> X >= 0 & & \text{Definition of} >= \\
X >= 0 & => X >= 0 \text{ or } Y = 5 & \text{Addition}
\end{array}
$$

To prove that

$$
\begin{array}{l}
\text{A1}' : \text{TRUE and } X < \emptyset \\
Y := 5; \\
\text{A2} : X >= 0 \text{ or } Y = 5
\end{array}
$$

is correct, we note that since Y is assigned the value 5 and the value of X is not changed,

$$
\begin{array}{l}
\text{A1}' : \text{TRUE and } X < 0 \\
Y := 5; \\
\text{A2}' : \text{TRUE and } X < 0 \text{ and } Y = 5
\end{array}
$$

is correct. Since A2′ => A2, if follows from one of the rules of consequence that

$$
\begin{array}{l}
\text{A1}' : \text{TRUE and } X < \emptyset \\
Y := 5; \\
\text{A2} : X >= 0 \text{ or } Y = 5
\end{array}
$$

is correct.

The If-Then-Else Rule

When the statement "if CONDITION then S1 else S2;" is executed, if CONDITION is true then S1 is executed, otherwise S2 is executed. The if-then-else rule of inference is:

> If (Q1 and CONDITION){S1}Q2 and
>   (Q1 and not CONDITION){S2}Q2, then
>   Q1{if CONDITION then S1 else S2}Q2.

For example, suppose that we wish to establish that

    A1 : TRUE
    if X < 0 then Y := 10 else Y := −5;
    A2 : (X < 0 and Y = 10)   or   (X >= 0 and Y = −5)

is correct. Then by the if-then-else rule, it suffices to show that both

    A1′ : TRUE
    Y := 10;
    A2 : (X < 0 and Y = 10)   or   (X >= 0 and Y = −5)

and

    A1″ : TRUE
    Y := −5;
    A2 : (X < 0 and Y = 10)   or   (X >= 0 and Y = −5)

are correct.

The Iteration Rule

When the statement "while CONDITION loop S;" is executed, if CONDITION is false then execution proceeds to the next statement of the program. Otherwise, the program segment S is executed repeatedly until CONDITION becomes false. CONDITION is evaluated after each execution of S. If CONDITION fails to become false, execution of this statement will not terminate.

    The rule of inference for this statement is called the iteration rule. It requires an assertion that is true before S is executed and remains true after each execution of S. This assertion is called the "loop invariant relation" or "loop invariant condition." It describes a relationship that holds among the program variables each time CONDITION is evaluated, hence after every execution of S. Determining the proper loop invariant condition is often a difficult step in proving a program correct. If Q is the loop invariant condition, the iteration rule can be formally stated as:

If (Q and CONDITION){S}Q, then
    Q{while CONDITION loop S}(not CONDITION and Q).

In terms of programs, the iteration rule is:

```
If
    A1 : Q and CONDITION
    S
    A2 : Q
is correct, then
    A1 : Q
    while CONDITION loop S
    A2 : Q and not CONDITION
is correct.
```

Before presenting an example to illustrate the iteration rule, we describe the steps required to prove a program correct.

The Program Proof Method

1. Formulate initial and final assertions that characterize what task the program is supposed to do.
2. Subdivide the program into segments that accomplish subtasks and formulate initial and final assertions for each subtask. When a program segment S1 is immediately executed before a program segment S2, the final assertion of S1 should imply the initial assertion of S2.
3. Prove that each program segment is correct with respect to its initial and final assertions.
4. Conclude that the program is correct with respect to the initial and final assertions.

If the intermediate assertions have been chosen correctly and if the initial assertion was true before program execution, each assertion is true at the appropriate point of the computation. Hence, if execution reaches the end of the program (i.e., the program terminates), the final assertion will be true when execution is complete.

An Example of a Program Proof

We assume that the variables I, Y, A, and B are all integer variables that are visible to the following Ada program.

```
procedure PRODUCT is

--This procedure sets Y equal to the product of A times
--B where A in a nonnegative integer. The product is
```

--calculated by repeated addition. Y is initialized to
--0 and then B is added to Y A times.

```
begin
    I := 0;
    Y := 0;
    while I < A loop
        Y := Y + B;
        I := I + 1;
    end loop;
end PRODUCT;
```

The initial assertion is "A >= 0" and the final assertion is "Y = A * B", which is step 1 above. If we now perform step 2, we obtain the following version of the program, with appropriate assertions inserted into the program as comments.

```
procedure PRODUCT is

    --This procedure sets Y equal to the product of A times
    --B where A in a nonnegative integer. The product is
    --calculated by repeated addition. Y is initialized to
    --0 and then B is added to Y A times.

begin
        --A1 : A >= 0
        I := 0;
        --A2 : A >= 0 and I = 0
        Y := 0;
        --A3 : A >= 0 and I = 0 and Y = 0
        --A4 : Y = I*B and I <= A
        while I < A loop
            --A5 : Y = I*B and I < A
            Y := Y + B;
            --A6 : Y = (I+1)*B and I < A
            I := I + 1;
            --A4 : Y = I*B and I <=A
        end loop;
        --A7 : Y = A*B
end PRODUCT;
```

We now describe how to prove that PRODUCT is correct with respect to A1 and A7. The proof can be divided into two parts by proving that

1. A1 {I := 0; Y := 0} A4.
2. A4 {while I < A loop Y := Y + B; I := I + 1; end loop} A7.

It would then follow by the rule of composition that PRODUCT is correct with respect to A1 and A7.

To prove part 1, we use the intermediate assertion A2 and observe that:

A1 {I := 0} A2

That is,

A >= 0 {I := 0} A >= 0 and I = 0

since the assignment statement does not affect the value of A and it sets the value of I to 0. Similarly,

A2 {Y := 0} A3

That is,

A >= 0 and I = 0 {Y := 0} A >= 0 and I = 0 and Y = 0

By the rule of composition, we conclude that

A1 {I := 0; Y := 0} A3

From the rules of arithmetic and the properties of <=, it is obvious that A3 => A4. Therefore, by the rule of consequence we can conclude that:

A1 {I := 0; Y := 0} A4

which completes the proof of part 1.

To prove that the while loop in part 2 is correct with respect to the initial assertion A4 and the final assertion A7, we must first establish that the hypothesis of the iteration rule holds. That is, we must prove that

A4 and I < A {Y := Y + B; I := I + 1} A4

We observe that (A4 and I < A) <==> A5, so it suffices to show that

A5 {Y := Y + B; I := I + 1} A4

We use the intermediate assertion A6 and first show that

A5 {Y := Y + B} A6

Since the value of Y is changed by the assignment statement, we let Y' denote the value of Y before the assignment statement is executed. Then A5 is the assertion

Y' = I * B and I < A

The assignment statement sets Y equal to Y' + B. The conjunction of (Y' = I * B and I < A) and (Y = Y' + B) implies A6, so we can conclude

A5 { Y := Y + B } A6

Similarly, letting I' denote the value of I before the statement I := I + 1 is executed,

(Y= (I'+1)*B and I' < A and I= I'+1) => (Y= I*B and I <= A)

so we conclude that

A6 {I := I + 1} A4

By the rule of composition, we can infer that

A5 { Y := Y + B; I := I + 1} A4

and therefore the hypothesis of the iteration rule holds.
    Applying the iteration rule, we conclude that

A4 {while I < A loop Y := Y + B; I := I + 1; end loop} A4 and I >=A

We can then show that

(A4 and I >= A) => A7

and apply a rule of consequence to complete the proof of part 2.

We now know that this program is correct if assertion A1 is true when PRODUCT begins execution.

Sometimes it is useful to have assertions checked as part of the actual program execution. The program is "instrumented" with the assertions that must be true at selected steps in the program. If the assertion is false, the program will raise an error flag. For example, the preceding program may be instrumented as follows.

```
ASSERTION_ERROR : exception;

procedure ASSERT ( CONDITION : BOOLEAN ) is
begin
    if not CONDITION then
        raise ASSERTION_ERROR;
    end if;
end ASSERT;

procedure PRODUCT is
--This procedure sets Y equal to the product of A times
--B where A in a nonnegative integer. The product is
--calculated by repeated addition. Y is initialized to
--0 and then B is added to Y A times.

begin
    ASSERT ( A >= 0 );
    I := 0;
    ASSERT ( A >= 0 and I = 0 );
    Y := 0;
    ASSERT ( A >= 0 and I = 0 and Y = 0 );
    ASSERT ( Y = I*B and I <= A );
    while I < A loop
        ASSERT ( Y = I*B and I < A );
        Y := Y + B;
        ASSERT ( Y = (I+1)*B and I < A );
        I := I + 1;
        ASSERT ( Y = I*B and I <= A );
    end loop;
```

```
        ASSERT ( Y = A*B );
    end PRODUCT;
```

Clearly, instrumenting a program with assertions as above drastically affects the execution speed of the program.

The preceding discussion of program verification has treated the rules of inference for only a few selected statements in the programming language. Unless we have a set of axioms, we cannot apply the rules of inference. Typically the axioms for program proofs relate to the assignment statement. We do not pursue this matter further in this chapter.

Additional considerations often have to be taken into account to prove programs correct. For example, the assignment statement, $X := X + 1$, with X an integer looks innocent enough. What type of initial assertion should it have, if any? If the data manipulated by programs behaved like mathematical objects, this statement might not need an initial assertion. However, they do not. In this particular case, we must account for the fact that integers in a computer have some fixed maximum size, usually something like $2**m - 1$ where m is the word size in bits. We can execute the statement $X := X + 1$ only if the resulting value is in the range of the integers on the computer. Thus, we might write

$$X' = X \text{ and } (X + 1) <= 2**m - 1 \{ X := X + 1 \} X := X' + 1$$

In practice, we usually ignore such details, but sometimes they must be considered.

From the preceding examples and discussion, the reader may conclude that program verification is a difficult task. Only relatively simple programs can be verified by the techniques we have described. Programs will not be verified to this level of detail unless tools become available that automate this process. Some success has been achieved, but much work remains to be done. It seems likely that many programs will never yield to formal verification. If a programmer understands the techniques for proving programs correct, he or she may write programs that can be verified if the need arises. The resulting program is likely to be easy to read, understand, and modify.

8.7 SUMMARY

- Software testing can demonstrate only the presence of errors in a software system, never the absence of errors.
- The process of software testing begins during the implementation phase of the software life cycle and continues after implementation as a separate phase of the software life cycle.

- The objective of debugging is to locate and correct the errors found during testing.

- It is often desirable that an individual or group of people separate from the group that performed the implementation be responsible for software testing.

- The major stages of testing are code inspection, function testing, module testing, subsystem testing (integration testing), acceptance testing, and installation testing.

- The advantage of code inspection is that many errors may be detected during a single pass of the software system.

- Top-down testing starts at a high level (module level) with subprograms (procedures and functions) represented by stubs. The goal of testing at this level is to confirm that the major architectural blocks of the software system mesh together and that the appropriate interfaces exist between cooperating subprograms.

- Bottom-up testing starts by developing and testing small blocks of code (e.g., the implementation of an algorithm). The individual functions and procedures that make up a module are tested thoroughly before an actual module is assembled and tested with other modules.

- The main advantage of top-down testing is that serious design errors often are revealed at the highest levels of a software system.

- A shortcoming of top-down testing and software development is that subtleties of algorithm design may be covered up and not revealed until a lower level of program development is reached.

- The testing of a software system involves the construction of a set of test cases. Each test case requires an input specification, a description of the system functions tested by the input, and a statement of the expected output.

- Test data consist of the input information that is used in a particular test case.

- The goal in designing test cases is to exercise many possible program paths at every level of the software system.

- Test data generators are programs or modules that automatically generate a large number of test inputs for a given system.

- A program analyzer determines how many times each statement in a given program is executed during the run time of the program.

- A trace program provides information about the dynamic properties of a program, that is, the performance of the program as it runs.

- Static analyzers examine a program before it is executed.

- The most powerful debugging tools are those that allow a programmer to interact with a program while it is running.

- Formal proofs of program correctness are seldom used on large programs because of the extensive work required.

- A formal proof of correctness is dependent on initial final assertions that correctly characterize the purpose of the program.

REFERENCES

1. Fagen, M. E., "Design and Code Inspections to Reduce Errors in Program Development," *IBM Syst. J.,* Vol. 15, No. 3, pp. 182–211, 1976.
2. Osterweil, L. J., and L. D. Fosdick, "DAVE—A Validation, Error Detection and Documentation System for FORTRAN Programs," *Software Pract. Exp.,* Vol. 6, pp. 473–486, 1976.
3. Balzer, R. W., "EXDAMS—Extendable Debugging and Monitoring System," *AFIPS,* Vol. 34, 1969.
4. Manna, Zohar, *Mathematical Theory of Computation,* New York: McGraw-Hill, 1974.

EXERCISES

1. Show the test plan that you used to test the text formatter program given in Exercise 1 of Chapter 2.
2. Show the test plan that you used to test the screen editor program given in Exercise 2 of Chapter 2.
3. Show the test plan that you used to test the registration program given in Exercise 3 of Chapter 2.
4. Show the test plan that you used to test the business inventory system given in Exercise 4 of Chapter 2.
5. Show the test plan that you used to test the grammar checker system given in Exercise 5 of Chapter 2.
6. Show the test plan that you used to test the airline reservation system given in Exercise 6 of Chapter 2.
7. Show the test plan that you used to test the rollbook program given in Exercise 7 of Chapter 2.
8. Develop the implementation for the final revision of FunctionEvaluator using the new Stacks1 module, as described in Section 8.2.
9. Prove that the following program segments are correct.
   (a) A1 : A > 0

           C := A + B;

       A2 : C > B

   (b) Let X' be an auxiliary variable.
       A1 : X = X'

$$\text{IF } X < 0 \text{ THEN } X := -X;$$

A2 : $(X' < 0 => X = - X')$ AND $(X' >= 0 => X = X')$

10. Write a procedure SUM, to sum the elements of a vector X with subscript range 1 to N. Let the initial assertion be $N > 0$ and the final assertion be

$$\text{SUM} := X(1) + X(2) + \cdots + X(N)$$

Construct intermediate assertions, identify the loop invariant relation, and prove that the procedure is correct with respect to the initial and final assertions.

11. Suppose we have the following program segment S and we wish to prove that is sorts a vector X into ascending order:

A1 : $N > 0$

S

A2 : The elements X(1) to X(N) are in ascending order.

If we assume that this segment is proved correct, can we conclude that A sorts the first N elements of the vector X? If not, restate assertions A1 and A2 so that the formal specification corresponds to what the program segment is intended to do.

Chapter 9 _____

A CASE STUDY IN MODULAR
SOFTWARE CONSTRUCTION

In this chapter we present a case study that illustrates modern software engineering methodology—from requirements analysis to object-oriented design and modular software implementation. The software system that we specify, design, and implement is a spelling checker. Chapter 2 gave the requirements for a spelling checker, to illustrate the process of software specifications. Now we modify those requirements somewhat for the sake of presenting a tractable solution to the spelling checker in the space available.

We illustrate the development of a spelling checker because it is complex enough to warrant the high-powered methodology of object-oriented design, yet simple enough to be presented within the space constraints of a chapter. Furthermore, we believe that most readers have a natural interest in such a system because of its tremendous practical value.

We begin by stating the formal requirements, a modified version of the requirements presented in Chapter 2.

The design is presented as a series of refinements, using both pseudo-code and modular design charts. The framework for the entire software system is created first in Modula-2, then in Ada, to illustrate how each language may be used at the design level. Modula-2 and Ada compilers are used to verify that all the high level interfaces between modules and between the main program and the modules are correct.

The design of the system employs a high degree of data and functional abstraction. Data hiding is used extensively. This case study, moreover, reveals the full power of modular design charts in representing software system architecture.

The full implementation details of the system (a working spelling checker) are displayed in Modula-2, to show the reader a fairly large finished software product designed using an object-oriented methodology and modular construction.

An important section of this chapter is the section containing exercises. Here the reader is urged to probe deeper into the system design and to develop alternative strategies for optimizing the performance of the system. Some of the exercises provide an opportunity for the reader to perform perfective maintenance on a software system with modular architecture. Some of the exercises form the basis for instructive software engineering projects.

9.1 SPELLING CHECKER REQUIREMENTS

General Goals

Spell is a general-purpose spelling checker that operates on an existing editor-created text file to produce an output text file that has been checked for spelling errors. Spell parses out the words from an input file and compares them with the entries in its dictionaries. Whenever a word is not found in its dictionaries, the checker will indicate the word and the line of text that contains the word and seek the user's directions regarding the word.

Spell features a large main permanent dictionary accessed from disk, as well as a small "fast" permanent dictionary that is loaded into fast memory and contains the most commonly used words in the English language. In addition, an auxiliary dictionary that contains words inserted by the user is on line. This auxiliary dictionary is the only one that may be modified and maintained. Unknown words that are correctly spelled may be automatically added to the auxiliary dictionary.

Spell is required to run on a microcomputer in an interactive manner. The microcomputer must have at least a video terminal, two disk drives (floppy or hard) and at least 128,000 bytes of random access memory. Spell should be able to process at least 200 words per minute.

Functional Requirements

1. When an unidentified word is encountered, the user should have the option of replacing the word with a substitute word, inserting the word in the auxiliary dictionary, or temporarily accepting this word and all future occurrences of it as correct.

2. The full line of text containing the unidentified word is to be displayed on the video terminal.

3. Unusual or seldom used words (such as proper nouns) that are not in the main dictionary and are not wanted by the user in the auxiliary dictionary should be "remembered" so that they can be identified as correctly spelled if they should appear later in the text.

4. The program should not fail if the temporary or auxiliary dictionary is full and there is no more space to add additional words. If this happens, the "remembered" words should function like a queue (new words entered should displace words previously entered).

5. Statistics should be available to occasionally indicate the line and word being processed, and the number of words that can be added to the auxiliary dictionary.

6. When Spell is excited, the number of words and lines that were processed should be displayed.

7. Hyphens and all other punctuation marks except apostrophes should be treated as delimiters of words. Apostrophes should be considered to be legal word characters, except if they occur at the beginning or end of a word.

8. Line overflow should not be allowed.

Nonfunctional Requirements

1. The software must be able to correctly identify the spelling of at least 40,000 words. Dictionary compression techniques are acceptable.

2. At least 200 correctly spelled words per minute should be identified by the system.

3. A word is defined as a string of one or more legal characters delimited by nonword characters. Legal characters are upper- and lowercase letters (with no distinction between them) and apostrophes.

4. The internal sorting and searching methods are not critical in defining the overall system. The methods should be computationally efficient and should use a minimum amount of memory.

5. Common abbreviations should be considered to be legal words.

6. The dictionary should fit on a 5 1/4-in. double-sided floppy disk that holds 400,000 bytes.

7. Because of memory space constraints, the dictionary may be limited to words up to 13 characters long. Longer words may be ignored by the system.

8. The dictionaries should consist of words in uppercase letters and apostrophes.

9. The plurals of most root words should be identifiable by the software.

10. All ASCII characters may appear in the text file.

11. Spell should be "user-friendly" software; that is, the user should not need to keep referring to the user's guide for instructions on the operation of the software.

12. Spell should be menu driven, with clear, concise menus prompting the user for a response.

13. Wherever possible, all user inputs should be checked for validity and an appropriate message generated if invalid input is detected.

Maintenance Information

1. The software may eventually be incorporated into a word-processing system.
2. The user may purchase one large central computer, and it should be possible to move the software to the new multiuser system with little difficulty.
3. The dictionary may be expanded with the use of additional dictionary compression techniques.
4. The dictionary may need to be modified to correct misspelled words, to add new words, or to delete existing words.

User's Guide

A user's guide is left as an exercise for the reader.

9.2 SPELLING CHECKER DESIGN

We plan to employ an object-oriented design and modular construction for our system design. You may be wondering about the "objects" that form the basis for the so called object-oriented design and problem abstraction. We must begin by developing an informal strategy—a general sequence of steps that satisfy the system requirements.

INFORMAL STRATEGY FOR CHECKING A TEXT FILE FOR SPELLING

Algorithm General Strategy for Spelling Checker
    Initialize line counter and word counters to zero
    Get input text file to be processed
    Create an output text file
    Load dictionaries
    while (*more lines of text*) *loop*
        get line of text
        increment line counter
        while (*more words on line*) *loop*
            get word from line
            increment word counter
            if the word length qualifies
            then

test word against dictionaries
    if word is not found then handle word end if
    end if
end loop
send line to output text file
end loop
Print out number of lines and words processed
Print out the number of words found in each dictionary
Update dictionaries
end Algorithm

The informal strategy omits detail but establishes the major tasks that must be performed by the software system. It is not important at this initial stage of problem abstraction to indicate what is meant by "handle word" or "test word against dictionaries." These are implementation details (albeit quite important details) that are determined later.

From the informal strategy, we may identify a set of abstract objects. Table 9.1 lists the objects, in the order in which they occur. Table 9.2 lists the operations mentioned in connection with the abstract objects, in the order in which they occur.

Tables 9.1 and 9.2 form the basis for our initial data and functional abstraction in our object-oriented design. A modular design chart may be used to represent this initial state of design. This modular design chart represents our initial concept of the software system architecture. Figure 9.1 presents such a modular design chart.

The initial stage of design, depicted in Figure 9.1, may be represented by a set of modules or packages. That is, we may immediately proceed to establish the framing for the software implementation in either Modula-2 or Ada by representing both the abstract data types and the associated operations on these types in modules or packages. In either case, the initial modular structure of the software system may be established. Modular Design Listing 9.1 presents the Modula-2 version of our initial design. Modular Design Listing 9.2 gives the equivalent Ada version of our initial design.

The initial version of the main driver programs are displayed in both the Modula-2 and Ada versions. These main programs mimic, almost line by line, the informal strategy given above. In studying Modular Design Listings 9.1 and

Table 9.1 Abstract Objects Used in Informal Strategy

Line count
Word count
Input text file
Output text file
Dictionaries
Word Line

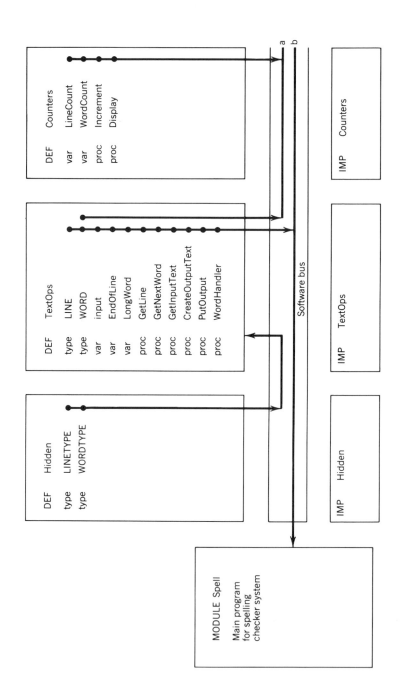

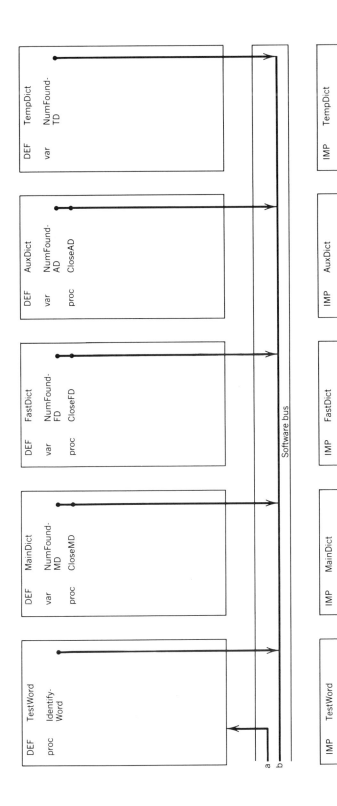

Figure 9.1 First modular design chart for spelling checker.

Table 9.2 Operations on the Abstract Objects

Initialize line count.
Initialize word count.
Get input text file.
Create output text file.
Load dictionaries.
Get line of text.
Increment line counter.
Get word from line.
Obtain length of word.
Test word against dictionaries.
Handle word.
Put line into output file.
Display line count.
Display word count.
Display words found in each dictionary.
Update dictionaries.

9.2, can you identify the abstract data types and procedures that correspond to the entities given in Tables 9.1 and 9.2? Note that we have identified the existence of the three dictionary files: main dictionary (the permanent large dictionary file), fast dictionary (the small file of the most commonly used words), and auxiliary dictionary (the user's own custom dictionary), without revealing the structural details of these objects. This is a central feature of object-oriented design. We may develop the architecture of the software system without concerning ourselves with the representational details of the various objects and the manipulations on these objects. Although these representational details are ultimately important, the design architecture of the system is not and should not be dependent on these details. This is precisely why object-oriented and modular design promotes smoother maintenance.

The modules given in Modular Design Listing 9.1 and the packages and procedures given in Modular Design Listing 9.2 may be compiled to ensure high level system integration. Study these listings carefully.

The module Hidden contains the representational details for the abstract data types defined in the system. This is done to hide these representational details from other modules while avoiding the necessity to declare these hidden data types as pointer types. You may recall that in Modula-2 opaque types often are implemented as pointer types.

MODULAR DESIGN LISTING 9.1   Initial Modula-2 Framework

```
DEFINITION MODULE Hidden;
(* $SEG:=18; *)
```

```
        FROM Files IMPORT FilePos;

        EXPORT QUALIFIED
                (* type *) LINETYPE,
                (* type *) WORDTYPE;

        CONST
            LineLength    = 80;
            WordLength    = 13;

        TYPE LINETYPE     = ARRAY[1..LineLength] OF CHAR;
        (* Used as the hidden data structure for a line.                *)

        TYPE WORDTYPE     = ARRAY[0..WordLength] OF CHAR;
        (* Used as the hidden data structure for a word.                *)

END Hidden.
```

```
DEFINITION MODULE Counters;
(* $SEG:=15; *)

        EXPORT QUALIFIED
                (* var  *) LineCount,
                (* var  *) WordCount,
                (* proc *) Increment,
                (* proc *) Display;

        TYPE Counter;

        VAR
            LineCount: Counter; (* Initialized to zero. *)
            WordCount: Counter; (* Initialized to zero. *)

        PROCEDURE Increment(VAR g: Counter);
        (* Used to increment either LineCount or WordCount.             *)

        PROCEDURE Display(g: Counter);
        (* Used to display the value of either LineCount
           or WordCount.                                                *)

END Counters.
```

```
DEFINITION MODULE TextOps;
(* $SEG:=16; *)

        FROM Hidden IMPORT LINETYPE, WORDTYPE;
```

```
FROM Texts IMPORT TEXT;

EXPORT QUALIFIED
            (* type *) LINE,
            (* type *) WORD,
            (* var   *) input,
            (* var   *) EndOfLine,
            (* var   *) LongWord,
            (* proc *) GetLine,
            (* proc *) GetNextWord,
            (* proc *) GetInputText,
            (* proc *) CreateOutputText,
            (* proc *) PutOutput,
            (* proc *) WordHandler;


TYPE LINE = LINETYPE;

TYPE WORD = WORDTYPE;

VAR input     : TEXT;

VAR EndOfLine : BOOLEAN;
(* Set of GetLine to true at the end of a line.                          *)

VAR LongWord : BOOLEAN;
(* Set by GetNextWord to true if word is over 13 characters.             *)

PROCEDURE GetLine(): LINE;
(* Obtains next line of text file for processing.                        *)

PROCEDURE GetNextWord(line: LINE): WORD;
(* Obtains next word in line for processing.                             *)

PROCEDURE GetInputText(name: ARRAY OF CHAR);
(* Fetches an existing text file with name.                              *)

PROCEDURE CreateOutputText(name: ARRAY OF CHAR);
(* Opens a new text file name.                                           *)

PROCEDURE PutOutput(line: LINE);
(* Sends line to the output text file.                                   *)

PROCEDURE WordHandler(word: WORD; VAR line: LINE);
(* Handles an unidentified word.                                         *)

END TextOps.
```

```
DEFINITION MODULE TestWord;
(* $SEG:=17; *)

    FROM TextOps IMPORT WORD;

    EXPORT QUALIFIED
            (* proc *) IdentifyWord;


    PROCEDURE IdentifyWord(VAR word: WORD): BOOLEAN;
    (* Returns true whenever word is found in one of
       the available dictionaries.                                      *)

END TestWord.
```

```
DEFINITION MODULE MainDict;
(* $SEG:=30; *)

    EXPORT QUALIFIED
            (* var   *) NumFoundMD,
            (* proc *) CloseMD;

    VAR NumFoundMD: INTEGER;
    (* NumFoundMD is incremented by one every time a word is found
       in the main dictionary.                                          *)

    PROCEDURE CloseMD();
    (* This procedure closes the main dictionary file.                  *)

END MainDict.
```

```
DEFINITION MODULE FastDict;
(* $SEG:=31; *)

    EXPORT QUALIFIED
            (* var   *) NumFoundFD,
            (* proc *) CloseFD;

    VAR NumFoundFD : INTEGER;
    (* NumFoundFD is incremented by one whenever a word is
       found in the fast dictionary.                                    *)

    PROCEDURE CloseFD();
    (* This procedure closes the fast dictionary file.                  *)

END FastDict.
```

```
DEFINITION MODULE AuxDict;
(* $SEG:=33; *)

        EXPORT QUALIFIED
                (* var  *) NumFoundAD,
                (* proc *) CloseAD;

        VAR NumFoundAD : INTEGER;
        (* NumFoundAD is incremented whenever a word is
           found in the auxiliary dictionary.                              *)

        PROCEDURE CloseAD();
        (* This procedure closes the auxiliary dictionary file.            *)

END AuxDict.
```

```
DEFINITION MODULE TempDict;
(* $SEG:=32; *)

        EXPORT QUALIFIED
                (* var *) NumFoundTD;

        VAR NumFoundTD : INTEGER;
        (* NumFoundTD is incremented whenever a word is
           found in the temporary dictionary.                              *)

END TempDict.
```

```
MODULE Spell;

        FROM Counters IMPORT LineCount, WordCount, Increment, Display;

        FROM TextOps IMPORT LINE, WORD, GetLine, GetNextWord, EndOfLine,
                            LongWord, input, GetInputText,
                            CreateOutputText, PutOutput, WordHandler;

        FROM TestWord IMPORT IdentifyWord;

        FROM MainDict IMPORT NumFoundMD, CloseMD;

        FROM FastDict IMPORT NumFoundFD, CloseFD;

        FROM AuxDict IMPORT NumFoundAD, CloseAD;

        FROM TempDict IMPORT NumFoundTD;
```

```
FROM Texts IMPORT EOT;

FROM InOut IMPORT WriteLn, WriteString, ReadString, WriteInt,
                  Write;

CONST bell = 7;

VAR
    inputline : LINE;
    word      : WORD;
    name      : ARRAY[0. .19] OF CHAR;

    PROCEDURE Information;
    BEGIN
        WriteString("What is the name of text to be checked?");
        WriteLn;
        WriteString("You must use the '.TEXT' suffix --> ");
        ReadString(name);
        GetInputText(name);
        WriteLn; WriteLn;WriteLn;
        WriteString("What is the name of the new text: ");
        WriteLn;
        WriteString("You must use the '.TEXT' suffix --> ");
        ReadString(name);
        CreateOutputText(name);
    END Information;

BEGIN (* Spell *)
    (* The line and word counters are initialized in module Counters.    *)
    (* Procedure Information gets input and output text files.           *)
    Information;
    LOOP
        inputline:=GetLine();
        IF EOT(input)
        THEN
            EXIT
        END(* if then *);
        Increment(LineCount);
        LOOP
            word:=GetNextWord(inputline);
            IF EndOfLine THEN EXIT; END(* if then *);
            IF NOT LongWord
            THEN
                Increment(WordCount);
                IF NOT IdentifyWord(word)
```

```
                THEN
                    Write( CHR(bell) );
                    WordHandler(word,inputline);
                END(* if then *);
            END(* if then *);
        END(* loop *);
        PutOutput(inputline);
    END(* loop *);
    WriteLn; WriteLn; WriteLn;
    WriteString("The number of lines processed is ");
    Display(LineCount);
    WriteLn;
    WriteString("The number of words processed is ");
    Display(WordCount);
    WriteLn;
    WriteString("The number of words found in main dictionary: ");
    WriteInt(NumFoundMD,1);
    WriteLn;
    WriteString("The number of words found in fast dictionary: ");
    WriteInt(NumFoundFD,1);
    WriteLn;
    WriteString("The number of words found in auxiliary dictionary: ");
    WriteInt(NumFoundAD,1);
    WriteLn;
    WriteString("The number of words found in temporary dictionary: ");
    WriteInt(NumFoundTD,1);
    WriteLn;
    CloseMD();
    CloseFD();
    CloseAD();
END Spell.
```

MODULAR DESIGN LISTING 9.2   Initial Ada Framework

```
package COUNTERS is

    type COUNTER is limited private;

    procedure INITIALIZE ( C : out COUNTER );
        --Used to initialize an object C of type COUNTER to zero.

    procedure INCREMENT ( C : in out COUNTER );
        --Used to increment an object C of type COUNTER by one.
```

```
    procedure DISPLAY ( C : in COUNTER );
        --Used to display the value of an object of type COUNTER.

private

    type COUNTER is new INTEGER;

end COUNTERS;
```

```
with DIRECT_IO, COUNTERS;
use COUNTERS;

package TEXT_OPS is

    --From DIRECT_IO import type FILE_TYPE.

    --From COUNTERS import type COUNTER.

    type LINE is limited private;

    type WORD is limited private;

    INPUT : DIRECT_IO.FILE_TYPE;

    END_OF_LINE, LONG_WORD : BOOLEAN;
        --END_OF_LINE is set by GET_LINE to true at the end of a line.
        --LONG_WORD is set by GET_NEXT_WORD to true if word is over 13
        --characters.

    function GET_LINE return LINE;
        --Obtains the next line of text for processing.

    function GET_NEXT_WORD ( L : LINE ) return WORD;
        --Obtains the next word in line for processing.

    procedure GET_INPUT_TEXT ( NAME : in STRING );
        --Fetches an existing text file with NAME.

    procedure CREATE_OUTPUT_TEXT ( NAME : in out STRING );
        --Opens a new text file NAME.

    procedure PUT_OUTPUT ( L : in LINE );
        --Sends line to the output text file.

    procedure WORD_HANDLER ( W : in WORD; L : in out LINE;
                             W_COUNT, L_COUNT : in COUNTER);
        --Handles an unidentified word.
```

```
private
        LINE_LENGTH   : constant := 80;
        WORD_LENGTH : constant := 13;

    type LINE is array (1..LINE_LENGTH) of CHARACTER;
    type WORD is array (1..WORD_LENGTH) of CHARACTER;

end TEXT_OPS;
```

```
with TEXT_OPS; use TEXT_OPS;

package TEST_WORD is

    --From TEXT_OPS import WORD.

    function IDENTIFY_WORD ( W : in out WORD ) return BOOLEAN;
        --Returns true whenever word is found in one of the
        --available dictionaries.

end TEST_WORD;
```

```
package MAIN_DICT is

    NUM_FOUND_MD : INTEGER;
        --NUM_FOUND_MD is incremented by one every time a word is found
        --in the main dictionary.

    procedure CLOSE_MD;
        --This procedure closes the main dictionary file.

end MAIN_DICT;
```

```
package FAST_DICT is

    NUM_FOUND_FD : INTEGER;
        --NUM_FOUND_FD is incremented by one whenever a word is
        --found in the fast dictionary.

    procedure CLOSE_FD;
        --This procedure closes the fast dictionary.

end FAST_DICT;
```

```
package AUX_DICT is
    NUM_FOUND_AD : INTEGER;
```

--NUM_FOUND_AD is incremented whenever a word is found in
--the auxiliary dictionary.

    procedure CLOSE_AD;
        --This procedure closes the auxiliary dictionary file.

end AUX_DICT;

----

package TEMP_DICT is

    NUM_FOUND_TD : INTEGER;
        --NUM_FOUND_TD is incremented whenever a word is found in
        --the temporary dictionary.

end TEMP_DICT;

----

with TEXT_OPS, COUNTERS, TEST_WORD, MAIN_DICT, FAST_DICT,
    AUX_DICT, TEMP_DICT, TEXT_IO, DISK_IO;

 use TEXT_OPS, COUNTERS, TEST_WORD, MAIN_DICT, FAST_DICT,
    AUX_DICT, TEMP_DICT, TEXT_IO, DISK_IO;

procedure SPELL is

--From COUNTERS import INCREMENT and DISPLAY.

--From TEXT_OPS import LINE, WORD, GET_LINE, GET_NEXT_WORD,
--   END_OF_LINE, LONG_WORD, INPUT,
--   GET_INPUT_TEXT, CREATE_OUTPUT_TEXT,
--   PUT_OUTPUT, AND WORD_HANDLER.

--From TEST_WORD import IDENTIFY_WORD.

--From MAIN_DICT import NUM_FOUND_MD and CLOSE_MD.

--From FAST_DICT import NUM_FOUND_FD and CLOSE_FD.

--From AUX_DICT and import NUM_FOUND_AD and CLOSE_AD.

--From TEMP_DICT import NUM_FOUND_TD.

--From TEXT_IO import put, get, new_line, and put_line.

--From DISK_IO import END_OF_FILE.

```
INPUT_LINE                   : LINE;
WRD                          : WORD;
NAME                         : STRING(1..20);
LINE_COUNT  WORD_COUNT  : COUNTER;

procedure INFORMATION;
begin
    put ("What is the name of the text to be checked?");
    new_line;
    put ("You must use the '.TEXT' suffix > ");
    get (NAME);
    new_line(3);
    put ("What is the name of the new text: ");
    new_line;
    put ("You must use the '.TEXT' suffix > ");
    get (NAME);
    CREATE_OUTPUT_TEXT (NAME);
end INFORMATION;

begin    --SPELL
    INITIALIZE (LINE_COUNT);
    INITIALIZE (WORD_COUNT);
    INFORMATION;
    loop
        INPUT_LINE := GET_LINE;
        exit when END_OF_FILE (INPUT);
        INCREMENT (LINE_COUNT);
        loop
            WRD := GET_NEXT_WORD (INPUT_LINE);
            exit when END_OF_LINE;
            if not LONG_WORD then
                INCREMENT (WORD_COUNT);
                if not IDENTIFY_WORD (WRD) then
                    put (ASCII.BEL);
                    WORD_HANDLER (WRD, INPUT_LINE, WORD_COUNT,
                                        LINE_COUNT);
                end if;
            end if;
        end loop;
        PUT_OUTPUT (INPUT_LINE);
    end loop;
    new_line(3);
    put ("The number of lines processed is ");
    DISPLAY (LINE_COUNT);
    new_line;
```

```
    put ("The number of words processed is ");
    DISPLAY (WORD_COUNT);
    new_line;
    put ("The number of words found in main dictionary: ");
    put_line (NUM_FOUND_MD);
    new_line;
    put ("The number of words found in fast dictionary: ");
    put_line (NUM_FOUND_FD);
    new_line;
    put ("The number of words found in auxiliary dictionary: ");
    put_line (NUM_FOUND_AD);
    new_line;
    put ("The number of words found in temporary dictionary: ");
    put_line (NUM_FOUND_TD);
    new_line;
end SPELL;
```

At the next stage of refinement in our design, we examine the most important tasks given in the initial informal strategy. The two major tasks are:

1. Testing words against the dictionaries.

2. Handling words.

We present informal strategies for each task below.

INFORMAL STRATEGY FOR TESTING WORDS AGAINST DICTIONARIES

Algorithm Test_Word(input ORIGWORD)
    (Returns true if the word is found in the dictionaries
            and false otherwise.)
    change ORIGWORD to uppercase
    remove first or last apostrophes if length of word > 1
    WORD = ORIGWORD
    if WORD ending is in the set { "S", "D", "ED", "LY", "ER",
                                    "EDS", "ERS", "ING" }
    then
        strip off the ending of WORD
        test to see whether WORD is in one of the dictionaries
            using Algorithm TestDictionaries
        if it is
        then
            return TRUE
        end if

> *if ORIGWORD ends in "ING"*
> *then*
> > *add "E" to WORD*
> > *test to see whether WORD is in one of the dictionaries*
> > > *using Algorithm TestDictionaries*
> >
> > *if it is*
> > *then*
> > > *return TRUE*
> >
> > *end if*
>
> *end if*
> *WORD = ORIGWORD*
> *test to see whether WORD is in one of the dictionaries*
> > *using Algorithm TestDictionaries*
>
> *if it is*
> *then*
> > *return TRUE*
>
> *else*
> > *return FALSE*
>
> *end if*

end Algorithm

The reason for removing various word endings is to compress the size of the main dictionary. One hazard associated with this design concept is that some incorrectly spelled words may be identified as correctly spelled. For example, if the root word "beast" is in the main dictionary, then the incorrectly spelled words "beasted" or "beasting" or "beaster" will be identified as correctly spelled. This initial design decision may be changed later with little fall-out effect. For now, it produces the beneficial effect of lowering the required size of the main dictionary thus allowing the main dictionary to be stored on disk within the given space constraint.

The informal strategy for testing words suggests additional operations on the objects listed in Table 9.1. These are listed in Table 9.3.

The algorithm TestDictionaries, mentioned in the informal strategy for testing words against dictionaries, is given below.

Table 9.3 Additional Operations for Spelling Checker

Change word to uppercase.
Test ending of word for 'S' or 'D'.
Test ending of word for 'ED', 'LY', or 'ER'.
Strip off ending of word for 'S' or 'D'.
Strip off ending of word for 'ED', 'LY', or 'ER'.
Strip off ending of word for 'EDS', 'ERS', or 'ING'.

INFORMAL STRATEGY FOR TEST DICTIONARIES

Algorithm TestDictionaries
   If WORD qualifies for fast dictionary
   then
         if WORD in fast dictionary then return TRUE end if
   end if
   if WORD in auxiliary dictionary then return TRUE end if
   if WORD in temporary dictionary then return TRUE end if
   if WORD in main dictionary
   then
         insert word in unused portion of auxiliary dictionary
         return TRUE
   else
         return FALSE
   end if
end Algorithm

Let us discuss the concept for "dictionary lookup" that is contained in the informal algorithm TestDictionaries, given above.

A word is potentially checked in four dictionaries. If the word is small enough (the fast dictionary only contains small words), it is checked against this dictionary. If it is not found there, it is checked against the user's own auxiliary dictionary. If it is not found there, it is checked against the dictionary of words temporarily stored in memory. If it is not found there, it is checked against the main permanent dictionary stored on disk. Since main dictionary accesses are relatively slow, the concept in our initial design is to store all words found in the main dictionary in random access memory. The location for this storage of main dictionary words is the unused portion of the auxiliary dictionary.

The predefined storage space for the auxiliary dictionary may not be fully utilized. In fact, in practice, only a small portion of the available space may be actually used. For example, if space for 1200 auxiliary dictionary words is provided, the user may have only 150 words stored in this dictionary. The memory space for the additional 1050 words can be used to store words that have been found in the main dictionary.

Using this scheme of sharing the memory space of the auxiliary dictionary, priority must be given to words that the user wishes to store in the auxiliary dictionary. Thus, when the auxiliary dictionary becomes full, a new entry earmarked as an auxiliary dictionary word must bump a main dictionary word out.

We are getting ahead of ourselves at this point, since we are becoming concerned too early with structural details in the design.

We now examine the informal strategy for handling words.

INFORMAL STRATEGY FOR HANDLING WORDS NOT FOUND IN DICTIONARIES

Algorithm WordHandler
display line number that contains unidentified word
display the unidentified word
display the line that contains the unidentified word
display the following menu:

R --> Replace unidentified word with a correctly spelled word
T --> Add unidentified word to the temporary dictionary
A --> Add unidentified word to the auxiliary dictionary

prompt user to choose one of the menu items above
if user response = R then
    replace unidentified word with new word
end if
if user response = T then
    add word to the temporary dictionary
end if
if user response = A then
    add word to the auxiliary dictionary
end if
end Algorithm

As before, additional operations are introduced by the refinements in problem solution represented by the informal strategies. The additional operations on the abstract data objects are listed in Table 9.4.

The refinements to the initial design that lead to the additional abstract operations given in Tables 9.3 and 9.4 may be represented by a second modular design chart, Figure 9.2, which is a refinement of the modular design chart of Figure 9.1. The architecture of the system is beginning to take final shape.

Table 9.4   Additional Operations on Abstract Objects

Look up word in fast dictionary.
Look up word in auxiliary dictionary.
Look up word in temporary dictionary.
Look up word in main dictionary.
Display word.
Display line.
Replace unidentified word.
Add word to temporary dictionary.
Add word to auxiliary dictionary.
Insert word in unused portion of the auxiliary dictionary.

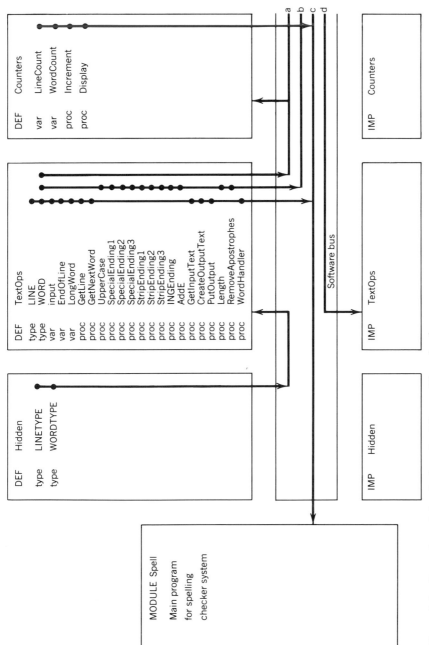

Figure 9.2 Second modular design chart for spelling checker.

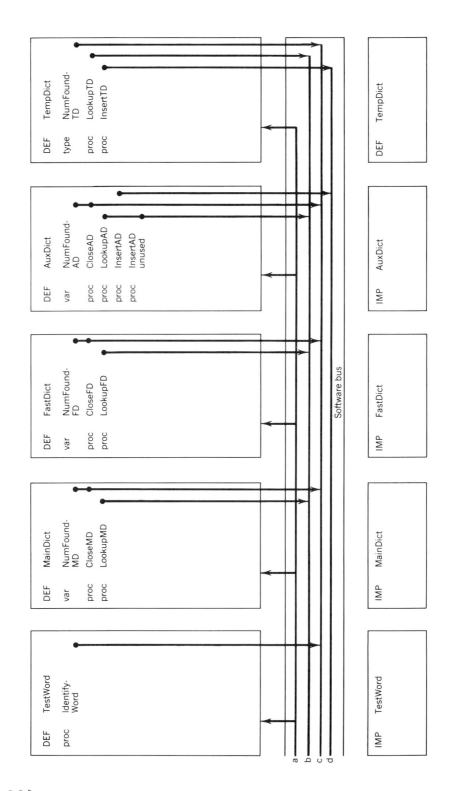

The Modula-2 or Ada framework for the software implementation may now be expanded to include the new features indicated in Figure 9.2. We present the expanded Modula-2 system design in Modular Design Listing 9.3, and the expanded Ada system design in Modular Design Listing 9.4.

MODULAR DESIGN LISTING 9.3   Expanded Modula-2 Framework

```
DEFINITION MODULE Hidden;
(* $SEG:=18; *)

    EXPORT QUALIFIED
            (* type *) LINETYPE,
            (* type *) WORDTYPE;
    CONST
            LineLength  = 80;
            WordLength = 13;

    TYPE LINETYPE     = ARRAY[1..LineLength] OF CHAR;
    (* Used as the hidden data structure for a line.                    *)

    TYPE WORDTYPE     = ARRAY[0..WordLength] OF CHAR;
    (* Used as the hidden data structure for a word.                    *)

END Hidden.
-----------------------------------------------------------------------------
DEFINITION MODULE TextOps;
(* $SEG:=16; *)

    FROM Hidden IMPORT LINETYPE, WORDTYPE;

    FROM Texts IMPORT TEXT;

    EXPORT QUALIFIED
            (* type *) LINE,
            (* type *) WORD,
            (* var  *) input,
            (* var  *) EndOfLine,
            (* var  *) LongWord,
            (* proc *) GetLine,
            (* proc *) GetNextWord,
            (* proc *) Uppercase,
            (* proc *) SpecialEnding1,
            (* proc *) SpecialEnding2,
            (* proc *) SpecialEnding3,
```

```
                    (* proc *) StripEnding1,
                    (* proc *) StripEnding2,
                    (* proc *) StripEnding3,
                    (* proc *) INGEnding,
                    (* proc *) AddE,
                    (* proc *) GetInputText,
                    (* proc *) CreateOutputText,
                    (* proc *) PutOutput,
                    (* proc *) Length,
                    (* proc *) RemoveApostrophes,
                    (* proc *) WordHandler;

TYPE LINE = LINETYPE;

TYPE WORD = WORDTYPE;

VAR input      : TEXT;

VAR EndOfLine : BOOLEAN;

VAR LongWord  : BOOLEAN;

PROCEDURE GetLine(): LINE;
(* Obtains next line of text file for processing.                        *)

PROCEDURE GetNextWord(line: LINE): WORD;
(* Obtains next word in line for processing.                             *)

PROCEDURE Uppercase(word: WORD): WORD;
(* Converts word to uppercase.                                           *)

PROCEDURE SpecialEnding1(word: WORD): BOOLEAN;
(* Returns true if word ends in 'S' or 'D'.                              *)

PROCEDURE SpecialEnding2(word: WORD): BOOLEAN;
(* Returns true if word ends in 'ED' or 'LY' or 'ER'.                    *)

PROCEDURE SpecialEnding3(word: WORD): BOOLEAN;
(* Returns true if word ends in 'EDS', 'ERS', or 'ING'.                  *)

PROCEDURE StripEnding1(word: WORD): WORD;
(* Removes 'S' or 'D' ending from word.                                  *)

PROCEDURE StripEnding2(word: WORD): WORD;
(* Removes 'ED', 'LY', or 'ER' ending from word.                         *)
```

```
PROCEDURE StripEnding3(word: WORD): WORD;
(* Removes 'EDS', 'ERS', or 'ING' ending from word.                    *)


PROCEDURE INGEnding(word: WORD): BOOLEAN;
(* Returns true if word ends in 'ING'.                                  *)


PROCEDURE AddE(word: WORD): WORD;
(* Adds 'E' to word.                                                    *)


PROCEDURE GetInputText(name: ARRAY OF CHAR);
(* Fetches an existing text file with name.                             *)


PROCEDURE CreateOutputText(name: ARRAY OF CHAR);
(* Opens a new text file name.                                          *)


PROCEDURE PutOutput(line: LINE);
(* Sends line to the output text file.                                  *)


PROCEDURE WordHandler(word: WORD; VAR line: LINE);
(* Handles an unidentified word.                                        *)


PROCEDURE RemoveApostrophes(VAR word: WORD);
(* Removes first and last apostrophes, if present
   in either first or last character of word.                           *)


PROCEDURE Length(word: WORD): INTEGER;
(* Returns the number of nonblank characters in word.                   *)

END TextOps.
```

```
DEFINITION MODULE Counters;
(* $SEG:=15; *)

    EXPORT QUALIFIED
            (* var  *) LineCount,
            (* var  *) WordCount,
            (* proc *) Increment,
            (* proc *) Display;

    TYPE Counter;

    VAR
        LineCount : Counter; (* Initialized to zero. *)
        WordCount: Counter; (* Initialized to zero. *)
```

```
    PROCEDURE Increment(VAR g: Counter);
    (* Used to increment either LineCount or WordCount.                 *)

    PROCEDURE Display(g: Counter);
    (* Used to display the value of either LineCount
       or WordCount.                                                    *)

END Counters.
```

```
DEFINITION MODULE MainDict;
(* $SEG:=30; *)

    FROM TextOps IMPORT WORD;

    EXPORT QUALIFIED

            (* var   *) NumFoundMD,
            (* proc *) CloseMD,
            (* proc *) LookupMD;

    VAR NumFoundMD: INTEGER;
    (* NumFoundMD is incremented by one every time a word is found
       in the main dictionary.                                         *)

    PROCEDURE CloseMD();
    (* Closes the main dictionary file.                                *)

    PROCEDURE LookupMD(word: WORD): BOOLEAN;
    (* Returns true if word is found in the main dictionary.           *)

END MainDict.
```

```
DEFINITION MODULE FastDict;
(* $SEG:=31; *)

    FROM TextOps IMPORT WORD;

    EXPORT QUALIFIED
            (* var   *) NumFoundFD,
            (* proc *) CloseFD,
            (* proc *) LookupFD;

    VAR NumFoundFD : INTEGER;
    (* NumFoundFD is incremented by one whenever a word is
       found in the fast dictionary.                                   *)
```

PROCEDURE CloseFD();
(* This procedure closes the fast dictionary file.   *)

PROCEDURE LookupFD(word: WORD): BOOLEAN;
(* Returns true whenever word is found in fast dictionary. *)

END FastDict.

DEFINITION MODULE TempDict;
(* $SEG:=32; *)

FROM TextOps IMPORT WORD;

EXPORT QUALIFIED
        (* var   *) NumFoundTD,
        (* proc *) LookupTD,
        (* proc *) InsertTD;

VAR NumFoundTD : INTEGER;
(* NumFoundTD is incremented whenever a word is
   found in the temporary dictionary.   *)

PROCEDURE InsertTD(word: WORD);
(* Inserts word in the temporary dictionary.   *)

PROCEDURE LookupTD(word: WORD): BOOLEAN;
(* Returns true whenever word is found in
   temporary dictionary.   *)

END TempDict.

DEFINITION MODULE AuxDict;
(* $SEG:=33; *)

FROM TextOps IMPORT WORD;

EXPORT QUALIFIED
        (* var   *) NumFoundAD,
        (* proc *) CloseAD,
        (* proc *) LookupAD,
        (* proc *) InsertAD,
        (* proc *) InsertADunused;

VAR NumFoundAD : INTEGER;
(* NumFoundAD is incremented whenever a word is
   found in the auxiliary dictionary.   *)

```
    PROCEDURE CloseAD();
    (* Used to close the auxiliary dictionary file.                    *)

    PROCEDURE LookupAD(word: WORD): BOOLEAN;

    PROCEDURE InsertAD(word: WORD);
    (* Used to insert word into auxiliary dictionary.                  *)

    PROCEDURE InsertADunused(word: WORD);
    (* Used to insert word into unused portion of
       auxiliary dictionary.                                           *)

END AuxDict.
```

```
DEFINITION MODULE TestWord;
(* $SEG:=17; *)

    FROM TextOps IMPORT WORD;

    EXPORT QUALIFIED
            (* proc *) IdentifyWord;

    PROCEDURE IdentifyWord(VAR word: WORD): BOOLEAN;
    (* Returns true whenever word is found in one of
       the available dictionaries.                                     *)

END TestWord.
```

```
IMPLEMENTATION MODULE TestWord;

    FROM TextOps IMPORT WORD, Uppercase, Length, SpecialEnding1,
                        SpecialEnding2, SpecialEnding3,
                        StripEnding1, StripEnding2, StripEnding3,
                        INGEnding, AddE, RemoveApostrophes;

    FROM MainDict IMPORT LookupMD;

    FROM FastDict IMPORT LookupFD;

    FROM TempDict IMPORT LookupTD;

    FROM AuxDict IMPORT InsertADunused, LookupAD;

    PROCEDURE IdentifyWord(VAR word: WORD): BOOLEAN;
```

```
VAR
    tempword : WORD;
    i          : INTEGER;

    PROCEDURE IsInDictionaries(word: WORD): BOOLEAN;
    BEGIN
        IF (Length(word) <= 6)
        THEN
            IF LookupFD(word)
            THEN
                RETURN TRUE
            END(* if then *);
        END(* if then *);
        IF LookupAD(word)
        THEN
            RETURN TRUE
        END(* if then *);
        IF LookupTD(word)
        THEN
            RETURN TRUE
        END(* if then *);
        IF LookupMD(word)
        THEN
            InsertADunused(word);
            RETURN TRUE
        ELSE
            RETURN FALSE
        END(* if then else *);
    END IsInDictionaries;

BEGIN (* IdentifyWord *)
    word:=Uppercase(word);
    (* We remove apostrophe if it is the first symbol
       or last symbol.                                                    *)
    RemoveApostrophes(word);
    IF SpecialEnding1(word)      (* S or D *)
    THEN
        tempword:=StripEnding1(word);
        IF IsInDictionaries(tempword)
        THEN
            RETURN TRUE
        END(* if then *);
    END(* if then *);
    IF SpecialEnding2(word)      (* ED or LY or ER *)
    THEN
        tempword:=StripEnding2(word);
```

```
            IF IsInDictionaries(tempword)
            THEN
                RETURN TRUE
            END(* if then *);
        END(* if then *);
        IF SpecialEnding3(word)      (* EDS or ERS or ING *)
        THEN
            tempword:=StripEnding3(word);
            IF IsInDictionaries(tempword)
            THEN
                RETURN TRUE
            END(* if then *);
            IF INGEnding(word)
            THEN
                tempword:=AddE(tempword);
                IF IsInDictionaries(tempword)
                THEN
                    RETURN TRUE
                END(* if then *);
            END(* if then *);
        END(* if then *);
        IF IsInDictionaries(word)
        THEN
            RETURN TRUE
        ELSE
            RETURN FALSE
        END(* if then else *);
    END IdentifyWord;

END TestWord.
```

(* We show only procedure WordHandler from the implementation module for
 TextOps. Procedure WordHandler uses several procedures that are defined
 local to this implementation module but are not exported from the definition
 module. The implementation module TextOps also imports several procedures from other modules. For example, procedure InsertTD is imported from
 module TempDict.   *)

```
PROCEDURE WordHandler(word: WORD; VAR line: LINE);

VAR
    i        : INTEGER;
    k        : INTEGER;
    newword : WORD;
    oldlen   : INTEGER;
```

```
    newlen   : INTEGER;
    linelen  : INTEGER;
    ch       : CHAR;
    choice   : CHAR;

    PROCEDURE Replace(word: WORD; VAR line: LINE);
    BEGIN
        (* Code for replacing word in line *)
    END Replace;

BEGIN (* WordHandler *)
    Utilities.Clear;
    WriteLn; WriteLn;
    WriteString("There is an unidentified word on line ");
    Counters.Display(Counters.LineCount);
    WriteString(", word number ");
    Counters.Display(Counters.WordCount);
    WriteString(". ");
    WriteLn;
    WriteString("The unidentified word is --> ");
    DisplayWord(word);
    WriteLn; WriteLn;
    Utilities.CenterMessage("The line containing the unidentified
                            word -->");
    WriteLn; WriteLn;
    DisplayLine(line);
    WriteLn; WriteLn; WriteLn;
    oldlen:=Length(word);
    WriteLn;
    WriteLn;
    WriteString("    R --> Replace word with a correctly spelled word");
    WriteLn; WriteLn;
    WriteString("    A --> Add word to auxiliary dictionary");
    WriteLn; WriteLn;
    WriteString("    T --> Temporarily accept word");
    WriteLn; WriteLn;
    WriteString("    Please enter your choice: ");
    choice:=Utilities.ReadKey(Utilities.setofchar
            {'R','A','T','r','a','t'});
    WriteLn; WriteLn;
    CASE choice OF
        'R','r': Replace (word,line); |
        'A','a': InsertAD(word);      |
        'T','a': InsertTD(word);
    END(* case *);
END WordHandler;
```

You will again note how the main body of code in both the TestWord module and the WordHandler procedure follow the informal strategy closely. This is possible because of the high degree of data and functional abstraction used in the design.

MODULAR DESIGN LISTING 9.4   Expanded Ada Framework

```
package COUNTERS is

    type COUNTER is limited private;

    procedure INITIALIZE ( C : out COUNTER );
        --Used to initialize an object C of type COUNTER to zero.

    procedure INCREMENT ( C : in out COUNTER );
        --Used to increment an object of type COUNTER by one.

    procedure DISPLAY ( C : in COUNTER );
        --Used to display the value of an object of type COUNTER.

private

    type COUNTER is new INTEGER;

end COUNTERS;
```

```
with DIRECT_IO, COUNTERS;
use  COUNTERS;

package TEXT_OPS is

    --From DIRECT_IO import type FILE_TYPE;

    --From COUNTERS import type COUNTER;

    type LINE is limited private;

    type WORD is limited private;

    INPUT : DIRECT_IO.FILE_TYPE;

    END_OF_LINE, LONG_WORD : BOOLEAN;
        --END_OF_LINE is set by GET_LINE to true at the end of a line.
```

--LONG_WORD is set by GET_NEXT_WORD to true if word is over 13
--characters.

function GET_LINE return LINE;
    --Obtains the next line of text for processing.

function GET_NEXT_WORD (L : LINE) return WORD;
    --Obtains the next word in line for processing.

procedure GET_INPUT_TEXT (NAME : in STRING);
    --Fetches an existing text file with NAME.

procedure CREATE_OUTPUT_TEXT (NAME : in out STRING);
    --Opens a new text file NAME.

procedure PUT_OUTPUT (L : in LINE);
    --Sends line to the output text file.

procedure WORD_HANDLER (W : in WORD; L : in out LINE;
                         W_COUNT, L_COUNT : in COUNTER);
    --Handles an unidentified word.

function UPPERCASE (W : WORD) return WORD;
    --Converts a word to uppercase.

function SPECIAL_ENDING_1 (W : WORD) return BOOLEAN;
    --Returns true if word ends in 'S' or 'D'.

function SPECIAL_ENDING_2 (W : WORD) return BOOLEAN;
    --Returns true if word ends in 'ED', 'LY', or 'ER'.

function SPECIAL_ENDING_3 (W : WORD) return BOOLEAN;
    --Returns true if word ends in 'EDS', 'ERS', or 'ING'.

function STRIP_ENDING _1 (W : WORD) return WORD;
    --Removes 'S' or 'D' ending from word.

function STRIP_ENDING _2 (W : WORD) return WORD;
    --Removes 'ED', 'LY', or 'ER' ending from word.

function STRIP_ENDING _3 (W : WORD) return WORD;
    --Removes 'EDS', 'ERS', or 'ING' ending from word.

function ING_ENDING (W : WORD) return BOOLEAN;
    --Returns true if word ends in 'ING'.

```
function ADD_E ( W : WORD ) return WORD;
    --Adds 'E' to word.

procedure DISPLAY_LINE ( L : in LINE );
    --Displays a line on a video terminal.

procedure DISPLAY_WORD ( W : in WORD );
    --Displays a word on a video terminal.

procedure REMOVE_APOSTROPHES ( W : in out WORD );
    --Removes first and last apostrophes, if present in
    --either the first or last character of the word.

function LENGTH ( W : WORD ) return INTEGER;
    --Returns the number of nonblank characters in the
    --word.

private

    LINE_LENGTH   : constant := 80;
    WORD_LENGTH : constant := 13;

    type LINE is array (1..LINE_LENGTH) of CHARACTER;
    type WORD is array (1..WORD_LENGTH) of CHARACTER;

end TEXT_OPS;
```

```
with TEXT_OPS;    use TEXT_OPS;

package TEST_WORD is

    --From TEXT_OPS import WORD.

    function IDENTIFY_WORD ( W : in out WORD ) return BOOLEAN;
        --Returns true whenever word is found in one of the
        --available dictionaries.

end TEST_WORD;
```

```
with TEXT_OPS;    use TEXT_OPS;

package MAIN_DICT is

    --From TEXT_OPS import WORD.
```

NUM_FOUND_MD : INTEGER;
   --NUM_FOUND_MD is incremented by one every time a word
   --is found in the main dictionary.

procedure CLOSE_MD;
   --This procedure closes the main dictionary file.

function LOOKUP_MD (W : WORD) return BOOLEAN;
   --Returns true if word is found in the main dictionary.

end MAIN_DICT;
----
with TEXT_OPS;   use TEXT_OPS;

package FAST_DICT is

   --From TEXT_OPS import WORD.

   NUM_FOUND_FD : INTEGER;
      --NUM_FOUND_FD is incremented by one whenever a word is
      --found in the fast dictionary.

   procedure CLOSE_FD;
      --This procedure closes the fast dictionary.

   function LOOKUP_FD (W : WORD) return BOOLEAN;
      --Returns true whenever word is found in the fast dictionary.

end FAST_DICT;
----
with TEXT_OPS; use TEXT_OPS;

package AUX_DICT is
   --From TEXT_OPS import WORD.

   NUM_FOUND_AN : INTEGER;
      --NUM_FOUND_AD is incremented whenever a word is found in
      --the auxiliary dictionary.

   procedure CLOSE_AD;
      --This procedure closes the auxiliary dictionary file.

   function LOOKUP_AD (W : WORD) return BOOLEAN;
      --Returns true whenever word is found in the auxiliary
      --dictionary.

```
procedure INSERT_AD ( W : in WORD );
    --Used to insert a word into the auxiliary dictionary.

procedure INSET_AD_UNUSED ( W : in WORD );
    --Used to insert a word into the unused portion of the
    --auxiliary dictionary.

end AUX_DICT;
```

```
with TEXT_OPS; use TEXT_OPS;

package TEMP_DICT is
    --From TEXT_OPS import WORD.

    NUM_FOUND_TD : INTEGER;
        --NUM_FOUND_TD is incremented whenever a word is found in
        --the temporary dictionary.

    procedure INSERT_TD ( W : in WORD );
        --Used to insert a word into the temporary dictionary.

    function LOOKUP_TD ( W : WORD ) return BOOLEAN;
        --Returns true whenever word is found in the temporary
        --dictionary.

end TEMP_DICT;
```

```
with TEXT_OPS, MAIN_DICT, FAST_DICT, AUX_DICT, TEMP_DICT;

use  TEXT_OPS, MAIN_DICT, FAST_DICT, AUX_DICT, TEMP_DICT;

    package body TEST_WORD is

    --From TEXT_OPS import WORD, UPPERCASE, LENGTH,
    --                    SPECIAL_ENDING_1, SPECIAL_ENDING_2,
    --                    SPECIAL_ENDING_3, STRIP_ENDING_1,
    --                    STRIP_ENDING_2, STRIP_ENDING_3,
    --                    ING_ENDING, ADD_E, REMOVE_APOSTROPHES.

    --From MAIN_DICT  import LOOKUP_MD.

    --From FAST_DICT  import LOOKUP_FD.
```

--From TEMP_DICT import LOOKUP_TD.

--From AUX_DICT   import LOOKUP_AD, INSERT_AD_UNUSED.

```
function IDENTIFY_ WORD ( W : in out WORD ) return BOOLEAN is

    TEMP_WORD : WORD;
    I              : INTEGER;

    function IS_IN_DICTIONARIES ( W : WORD ) return BOOLEAN is
    begin
        if ( LENGTH (W) <= 6 ) and then LOOKUP_FD (W) then
            return TRUE;
        elsif LOOKUP_AD (W) then
            return TRUE;
        elsif LOOKUP_TD (W) then
            return TRUE;
        elsif LOOKUP_MD (W) then
            INSERT_AD_UNUSED (W);
            return TRUE;
        else
            return FALSE;
        end if;
    end IS_IN_DICTIONARIES;                         .

begin   --IDENTIFY_WORD
    W := UPPERCASE (W);
        --We remove apostrophe if it is the first or last symbol.
    REMOVE_APOSTROPHES (W);
    if SPECIAL_ENDING_1 (W) then      -- S or D ending.
        TEMP_WORD := STRIP_ENDING_1 (W);
        if IS_IN_DICTIONARIES (TEMP_WORD) then
            return TRUE;
        end if;
    elsif SPECIAL_ENDING_2 (W) then   -- ED or LY or ER ending.
        TEMP_WORD := STRIP_ENDING_2 (W);
        if IS_IN_DICTIONARIES (TEMP_WORD) then
            return TRUE;
        end if;
    elsif SPECIAL_ENDING_3 (W) then   -- EDS or ERS or ING ending.
        TEMP_WORD := STRIP_ENDING_3 (W);
        if IS_IN_DICTIONARIES (TEMP_WORD)  then
```

```
                        return TRUE;
                end if;
                if ING_ENDING (W) then
                        TEMP_WORD := ADD_E (TEMP_WORD);
                        if IS_IN_DICTIONARIES (TEMP_WORD) then
                            return TRUE;
                        end if;
                end if;
            end if;
            if IS_IN_DICTIONARIES (W) then
            return TRUE;
        else
            return FALSE;
        end if;
    end IDENTIFY_WORD;


end TEST_WORD;
-------------------------------------------------------------------------
--The following procedure is in package body TEXT_OPS.

--We assume that we have available to us, in Ada, a
--package that has the features specified in Program 7.3.
--In particular, we assume that we have the following
--routines:
--      CLEAR, which clears the screen.
--      CENTER_MESSAGE, which centers a message on the screen.
--      READ_KEY, which is used to input a character from the
--          terminal.

procedure WORD_HANDLER ( W : WORD; L : in out LINE;
                            W_COUNT, L_COUNT : in COUNTER ) is

    I, K          : INTEGER;
    NEW_WORD : WORD;
    OLD_LEN    : INTEGER;
    NEW_LEN    : INTEGER;
    LINE_LEN   : INTEGER;
    CH            : CHARACTER;
    CHOICE      : CHARACTER;

    procedure REPLACE (W : WORD; L : in out LINE) is
    begin
        --Code for replacing a word in a line.
    end REPLACE;
```

```
begin    --WORD_HANDLER
    CLEAR;
    new_line(2);
    put ("There is an unidentified word on line ");
    COUNTERS.DISPLAY (L_COUNT);
    put_line (", word number ");
    COUNTERS.DISPLAY (W_COUNT);
    put_line (".");
    new_line;
    put ("The unidentified word is --> ");
    DISPLAY_WORD (W);
    new_line(2);
    CENTER_MESSAGE ("The line containing the unidentified word -->");
    new_line(2);
    DISPLAY_LINE (L);
    new_line(3);
    OLD_LEN := LENGTH (W);
    new_line(2);
    put ("     R --> Replace word with a correctly spelled word");
    new_line(2);
    put ("     A --> Add word to auxiliary dictionary");
    new_line(2);
    put ("     T --> Temporarily accept word");
    new_line(2);
    put ("     Please enter your choice: ");
    CHOICE := READ_KEY ('R', 'A', 'T', 'r', 'a', 't');
    new_line(2);
    case CHOICE is
        when 'R' : 'r' => REPLACE (W, L);
        when 'A' : 'a' => INSERT_AD (W);
        when 'T' : 't' => INSERT_TD (W);
    end case;
end WORD_HANDLER;
```

In Modular Design Listings 9.3 and 9.4, we have shown some of the implementation details for TestWord and WordHandler. You will note how all the word manipulations that are performed in these implementations are done in terms of the functional abstractions defined in TextOps. For example, we perform the operations of LookupMD, or InsertAD. This high level of abstraction separates the system designer from representational details. The high level of modularity will support later system maintenance.

The Modula-2 and Ada design framework, given in Listings 9.3 and 9.4, may be compiled to verify that high level system integration is correctly in place. With the establishment of 10 modules, we have the major features of the software system architecture.

We move on, in the next section, to the final implementation of the spelling checker.

9.3 IMPLEMENTATION OF SPELLING CHECKER

With the framework of the software system in place and represented by the Modula Design Chart of Figure 9.2 and the Modular Design Listings 9.3 and 9.4, the next steps involve the implementation of each of the modules and packages in the system. There are many ways to implement the various modules and packages. Indeed, changes may and probably will be made in some or all of the implementation details. The extent to which these maintenance changes are isolated from the rest of the software system is a measure of the effectiveness of our modular design.

As each module or package is implemented, it is tested thoroughly. Thus, the testing phase of software development is integrated with the implementation stage. Rather than showing the detailed test cases that were used at each stage of the implementation process, we ask the reader to develop some test cases in the exercises at the end of the chapter.

Space does not allow us to show the additional stages of refinement from the original two modular design charts that lead to the final implementation. As the bodies for each module or package specification are implemented, additional data and functional abstraction become necessary. This follows because the representational details of the abstract data objects such as "word" or "line" are not visible to the implementation modules. Any new operations that must be performed on these objects must be made available in the TextOps module or package. Thus, the module TextOps acquires several additional data types and procedures. From this point on, we display only the Modula-2 version of the implementation. It is left as an exercise for the reader to develop the equivalent Ada version.

Object-oriented design imposes a new and curious discipline on those involved in a team programming environment. Suppose that programmer A has the job of writing the module TextOps and that programmer B is writing the code for module AuxDict. Programmer B suddenly discovers that she needs to compare two words with respect to alphabetical order (e.g., in sorting the auxiliary dictionary using the heapsort algorithm) but does not have access to the representational details of the data type WORD. Programmer B must communicate with programmer A and request that A write a procedure

```
PROCEDURE LessThan(w1,w2: WORD): BOOLEAN;
```

that returns true if word w1 is less than word w2 and false otherwise. Programmer A delivers a new compiled version of definition module TextOps that contains the desired functional abstraction LessThan. Now Programmer B may continue to develop her code. It is important to note that programmer B may still have no idea about the structure of the data type WORD, but nevertheless her implementation work may proceed without hitch.

We ask you, the reader, to allocate some time to carefully study the listing of the full program for the spelling checker given in Program 9.1. In this listing, you will see the old design framework surrounded by a great deal of implementation code. All the software specifications are met by this implementation. Since the "program" is partitioned into 17 modules (including the main driver program), each module may be studied carefully in relative isolation from the adjoining modules. This should significantly add to the readability of the "program."

You may wonder as you read this long listing, whether all the overhead imposed by object-oriented design and modular software construction is worth it? The real answer to this question occurs when maintenance is attempted. We illustrate perfective maintenance in the next section.

It has been our experience with both Ada and Modula-2 that the discipline of object-oriented design virtually forces the software developer to carefully think through the problem and map real-world objects into the entities used in the software system. This exercise alone usually assures sound design. Although it is too early to document this opinion, we believe that in addition to greatly improving software maintenance, software reliability will also be significantly improved by using object-oriented design and modular construction.

PROGRAM 9.1   The Completed Spelling Checker in Modula-2

```
DEFINITION MODULE Hidden;
(* $SEG:=18; *)


    FROM Files IMPORT FilePos;


    EXPORT QUALIFIED
            (* type  *) LINETYPE,
            (* type  *) WORDTYPE,
            (* type  *) AUXDICTTYPE,
            (* type  *) MAINDICTTYPE,
            (* type  *) FASTDICTTYPE,
            (* type  *) TEMPDICTTYPE,
            (* type  *) INDEXTYPE,
```

```
            (* type  *) FPTYPE,
            (* const *) AuxDictLength;

       CONST
            LineLength      = 80;
            WordLength      = 13;
            BlockLength     = 128;
            TempDictLength  = 100;
            FastDictLength  = 1024;
            AuxDictLength   = 1200;
            IndexLength     = 186;
```

```
    TYPE LINETYPE       = ARRAY[1..LineLength] OF CHAR;
    (* Used as the hidden data structure for a line.                      *)

    TYPE WORDTYPE       = ARRAY[0..WordLength] OF CHAR;
    (* Used as the hidden data structure for a word.                      *)

    TYPE AUXDICTTYPE    = ARRAY[1..1200] OF WORDTYPE;
    (* Used as the hidden data structure for the auxiliary dictionary.    *)

    TYPE MAINDICTTYPE   = ARRAY[1..128] OF WORDTYPE;
    (* Used as the hidden data structure for the main dictionary.         *)

    TYPE FASTDICTTYPE   = ARRAY[1..1024] OF WORDTYPE;
    (* Used as the hidden data structure for the fast dictionary.         *)

    TYPE INDEXTYPE      = ARRAY[0..IndexLength] OF WORDTYPE;
    (* Used as the hidden data structure for the dictionary index.        *)

    TYPE TEMPDICTTYPE   = ARRAY[1..TempDictLength] OF WORDTYPE;
    (* Used as the hidden data structure for the temporary dictionary.    *)

    TYPE FPTYPE         = ARRAY[0..IndexLength] OF FilePos;
    (* Used as the hidden data structure for the file position index.     *)

END Hidden.
```

```
IMPLEMENTATION MODULE Hidden;

    FROM Utilities IMPORT Clear, CenterMessage;

    FROM InOut IMPORT WriteLn;
```

```
BEGIN (* Initialization Code *)
    Clear;
    WriteLn; WriteLn; WriteLn; WriteLn; WriteLn; WriteLn;
    CenterMessage("Spelling Checker Program Developed");
    WriteLn;WriteLn;
    CenterMessage("by");
    WriteLn;WriteLn;
    CenterMessage("Richard Wiener and Richard Sincovec");
    WriteLn; WriteLn;WriteLn; WriteLn;
END Hidden.
```

```
DEFINITION MODULE Counters;
(* $SEG:=15; *)

    EXPORT QUALIFIED
                (* var  *) LineCount,
                (* var  *) WordCount,
                (* proc *) Increment,
                (* proc *) Display,
                (* proc *) DivideByTen;


    TYPE Counter;


    VAR
        LineCount  : Counter; (* Initialized to zero. *)
        WordCount: Counter; (* Initialized to zero. *)


    PROCEDURE Increment(VAR g: Counter);
    (* Used to increment either LineCount or WordCount.                    *)


    PROCEDURE Display(g: Counter);
    (* Used to display the value of either LineCount
        or WordCount.                                                       *)


    PROCEDURE DivideByTen(c: Counter): BOOLEAN;
    (* Returns true whenever LineCount or WordCount
        is evenly divisible by 10.                                         *)


END Counters.
```

```
IMPLEMENTATION MODULE Counters;

    FROM InOut IMPORT WriteInt;

    FROM Storage IMPORT ALLOCATE;

    TYPE Counter = POINTER TO INTEGER;

    PROCEDURE Increment(VAR g: Counter);
    BEGIN
        INC(g↑);
    END Increment;

    PROCEDURE Display(g; Counter);
    BEGIN
        WriteInt(g↑,1)
    END Display;

    PROCEDURE DivideByTen(c: Counter): BOOLEAN;
    BEGIN
        IF c↑ MOD 10 = 0
        THEN
            RETURN TRUE
        ELSE
            RETURN FALSE
        END(* if then else *);
    END DivideByTen;

BEGIN (* Counters *)
    NEW(LineCount);
    NEW(WordCount);
    LineCount↑:=0;
    WordCount↑:=0;
END Counters.
```

```
DEFINITION MODULE TextOps;
(* $SEG:=16; *)

    FROM Hidden IMPORT LINETYPE, WORDTYPE;

    FROM Texts IMPORT TEXT;

    EXPORT QUALIFIED
            (* const *) WordLength,
            (* type  *) LINE,
```

```
(* type  *) WORD,
(* var   *) input,
(* var   *) EndOfLine,
(* var   *) LongWord,
(* proc  *) GetLine,
(* proc  *) GetNextWord,
(* proc  *) Length,
(* proc  *) Uppercase,
(* proc  *) SpecialEnding1,
(* proc  *) SpecialEnding2,
(* proc  *) SpecialEnding3,
(* proc  *) StripEnding1,
(* proc  *) StripEnding2,
(* proc  *) StripEnding3,
(* proc  *) INGEnding,
(* proc  *) AddE,
(* proc  *) GetInputText,
(* proc  *) CreateOutputText,
(* proc  *) PutOutput,
(* proc  *) DisplayWord,
(* proc  *) WordHandler,
(* proc  *) Equal,
(* proc  *) LessThan,
(* proc  *) RemoveApostrophes,
(* proc  *) Assign;
```

TYPE LINE = LINETYPE;

TYPE WORD = WORDTYPE;

CONST WordLength = 13;

VAR input   : TEXT;

VAR EndOfLine : BOOLEAN;

VAR LongWord : BOOLEAN;

PROCEDURE GetLine(): LINE;
(* Obtains next line of text file for processing.   *)

PROCEDURE GetNextWord(line: LINE): WORD;
(* Obtains next word in line for processing.   *)

PROCEDURE Length(word: WORD): INTEGER;
(* Returns the number of nonblank characters in word.   *)

```
PROCEDURE Uppercase(word: WORD): WORD;
(* Converts word to uppercase.                                    *)

PROCEDURE SpecialEnding1(word: WORD): BOOLEAN;
(* Returns true if word ends in 'S' or 'D'.                       *)

PROCEDURE SpecialEnding2(word: WORD): BOOLEAN;
(* Returns true if word ends in 'ED', 'LY', or 'ER'.             *)

PROCEDURE SpecialEnding3(word: WORD): BOOLEAN;
(* Returns true if word ends in 'EDS', 'ERS', or 'ING'.         *)

PROCEDURE StripEnding1(word: WORD): WORD;
(* Removes 'S' or 'D' ending from word.                          *)

PROCEDURE StripEnding2(word: WORD): WORD;
(* Removes 'ED', 'LY', or 'ER' ending from word.                *)

PROCEDURE StripEnding3(word: WORD): WORD;
(* Removes 'EDS', 'ERS', or 'ING' ending from word.             *)

PROCEDURE INGEnding(word: WORD): BOOLEAN;
(* Returns true if word ends in 'ING'.                           *)

PROCEDURE AddE(word: WORD): WORD;
(* Adds 'E' to word.                                             *)

PROCEDURE GetInputText(name: ARRAY OF CHAR);
(* Fetches an existing text file with name.                      *)

PROCEDURE CreateOutputText(name: ARRAY OF CHAR);
(* Opens a new text file name.                                   *)

PROCEDUE PutOutput(line: LINE);
(* Sends line to the output text file.                           *)

PROCEDURE DisplayWord(word: WORD);
(* Displays word on a video terminal.                            *)

PROCEDURE WordHandler(word: WORD; VAR line: LINE);
(* Handles an unidentified word.                                 *)

PROCEDURE Equal(w1,w2: WORD): BOOLEAN;
(* Returns true if word w1 = w2.                                 *)
```

```
    PROCEDURE LessThan(w1,w2: WORD): BOOLEAN;
    (* Returns true if w1 < w2.                                    *)

    PROCEDURE Assign(w1: WORD; VAR w2: WORD);
    (* Assigns value of w1 to w2.                                  *)

    PROCEDURE RemoveApostrophes(VAR word: WORD);
    (* Removes apostrophes from word if they are either
        the first or last character of word.                       *)

END TextOps.
-----------------------------------------------------------------------------
DEFINITION MODULE MainDict;
(* $SEG:=30; *)

    FROM TextOps IMPORT WORD;

    EXPORT QUALIFIED
            (* var   *) NumFoundMD,
            (* proc *) CloseMD,
            (* proc *) LookupMD;

    VAR NumFoundMD: INTEGER;
    (* NumFoundMD is incremented by one every time a word is found
        in the main dictionary.                                    *)

    PROCEDURE CloseMD();
    (* Closes the main dictionary file.                            *)

    PROCEDURE LookupMD(word: WORD): BOOLEAN;
    (* Returns true if word is found in the main dictionary.       *)

END MainDict.
-----------------------------------------------------------------------------
IMPLEMENTATION MODULE MainDict;

    FROM TextOps IMPORT WORD, Equal, LessThan;

    FROM Files IMPORT Open, Close, FILE, FileState, ReadRec, FilePos,
                      SetPos;

    FROM Hidden IMPORT MAINDICTTYPE, INDEXTYPE, FPTYPE;

    FROM Utilities IMPORT CenterMessage;
```

```
FROM InOut IMPORT WriteLn;

VAR
    MAINDICT : FILE;
    INDEX    : FILE;
    FILEP    : FILE;
    maindict : MAINDICTTYPE;
    index    : INDEXTYPE;
    fp       : FPTYPE;
    fs       : FileState;

PROCEDURE Stop;
BEGIN
    WriteLn;
    CenterMessage("Trouble loading one of the main dictionaries.");
    WriteLn;
    HALT
END Stop;

PROCEDURE CloseMD();
BEGIN
    fs:=Close(MAINDICT);
    fs:=Close(INDEX);
    fs:=Close(FILEP);
END CloseMD;

PROCEDURE BlockNumber(word: WORD): FilePos;
(* This procedure returns the appropriate block number
   in the main dictionary file.                                    *)

VAR pos : INTEGER;

    PROCEDURE BinarySindex(x: WORD; low,high: INTEGER;
                                VAR pos: INTEGER);

    VAR mid: INTEGER;

    BEGIN
        pos:=high;
        WHILE (low <= high) DO
            mid:=(low + high) DIV 2;
            IF Equal(x,index[mid])
            THEN
                pos:=mis-1;
                RETURN
            END(* if then *);
```

```
        IF LessThan(x,index[mid])
        THEN
            high:=mid−1;
            pos:=high
        ELSE
            low:=mid+1
        END(* if then else *);
    END(* while loop *);
  END BinarySindex;

BEGIN (* BlockNumber *)
    BinarySindex(word,1,186,pos);
    RETURN fp[pos]
END BlockNumber;

PROCEDURE LookupMD(word: WORD): BOOLEAN;

VAR f : FilePos;

    PROCEDURE BinarySmaindict(word: WORD): BOOLEAN;

    VAR
        mid  : INTEGER;
        low  : INTEGER;
        high : INTEGER;
        t    : BOOLEAN;

    BEGIN
        t:=FALSE;
        low:=1;
        high:=128;
        WHILE (low <= high) DO
            mid:=(low + high) DIV 2;
            IF Equal(word,maindict[mid])
            THEN
                t:=TRUE;
                RETURN t
            END(* if then *);
            IF LessThan(word,maindict[mid])
            THEN
                high:=mid−1
            ELSE
                low:=mid+1
            END(* if then else *);
        END(* while loop *);
        RETURN t
    END BinarySmaindict;
```

```
BEGIN (* LookupMD *)
    f:=BlockNumber(word);
    SetPos(MAINDICT,f);
    ReadRec(MAINDICT,maindict);
    IF BinarySmaindict(word)
    THEN
        INC(NumFoundMD);
        RETURN TRUE
    ELSE
        RETURN FALSE;
    END(* if then else *);
END LookupMD;

BEGIN (* Initialization Code *)
    fs:=Open(MAINDICT,"MAINDICT");
    IF fs # FileOK
    THEN
        Stop;
    END(* if then *);
    fs:=Open(INDEX,"INDEXFILE");
    IF fs # FileOK
    THEN
        Stop;
    END(* if then *);
    fs:=Open(FILEP,'FP');
    IF fs # FileOK
    THEN
        Stop;
    END(* if then *);
    ReadRec(INDEX, index);
    ReadRec(FILEP, fp);
    NumFoundMD:=0;
END MainDict.
```

```
DEFINITION MODULE FastDict;
(* $SEG:=31; *)

    FROM TextOps IMPORT WORD;

    EXPORT QUALIFIED
            (* var  *) NumFoundFD,
            (* proc *) CloseFD,
            (* proc *) LookupFD;
```

```
    VAR NumFoundFD : INTEGER;
    (* NumFoundFD is incremented by one whenever a word is
       found in the fast dictionary.                             *)

    PROCEDURE CloseFD();
    (* This procedure closes the fast dictionary file.           *)

    PROCEDURE LookupFD(word: WORD): BOOLEAN;
    (* Returns true whenever word is found in fast dictionary.   *)

END FastDict.
```

```
IMPLEMENTATION MODULE FastDict;

    FROM TextOps IMPORT WORD, Equal, LessThan;

    FROM Files IMPORT Open, FileState, Close, FILE, ReadRec;

    FROM Hidden IMPORT FASTDICTTYPE;

    FROM InOut IMPORT WriteLn;

    FROM Utilities IMPORT CenterMessage;

    VAR
        fs              : FileState;
        FAST            : FILE;
        fast            : FASTDICTTYPE;

    PROCEDURE Stop;
    BEGIN
        WriteLn;
        CenterMessage("Trouble loading fast dictionary.");
        WriteLn;
        HALT
    END Stop;

    PROCEDURE CloseFD();
    BEGIN
        fs:=Close(FAST);
    END CloseFD;

    PROCEDURE LookupFD(word: WORD): BOOLEAN;
    VAR pos : INTEGER;
```

```
PROCEDURE BinarySfastdict (word: WORD; low,high: INTEGER;
                                    VAR pos: INTEGER);

VAR mid: INTEGER;

BEGIN
    WHILE low <= high DO
        mid:=(low + high) DIV 2;
        IF Equal(word,fast[mid])
        THEN
            pos:=mid;
            RETURN
        END(* if then *);
        IF LessThan(word,fast[mid])
        THEN
            high:=mid-1
        ELSE
            low:=mid+1
        END(* if then else *);
    END(* while loop *);
END BinarySfastdict;

BEGIN (* LookupFD *)
    pos:=0;
    BinarySfastdict(word,1,1024,pos);
    IF pos = 0
    THEN
        RETURN FALSE
    ELSE
        INC(NumFoundFD);
        RETURN TRUE
    END(* if then else *);
END LookupFD;

BEGIN (* Initialization Code *);
    fs:=Open(FAST, "FASTFILE");
    IF fs # FileOK
    THEN
        Stop;
    END(* if then *);
    ReadRec(FAST,fast);
    NumFoundFD:=0;
END FastDict.
```

```
DEFINITION MODULE TempDict;
(* $SEG:=32; *)

    FROM TextOps IMPORT WORD;

    EXPORT QUALIFIED
            (* var   *) NumFoundTD,
            (* proc *) LookupTD,
            (* proc *) InsertTD;

    VAR NumFoundTD : INTEGER;
    (* NumFoundTD is incremented whenever a word is
       found in the temporary dictionary.                          *)

    PROCEDURE InsertTD(word: WORD);
    (* Inserts word in the temporary dictionary.                   *)

    PROCEDURE LookupTD(word: WORD): BOOLEAN;
    (* Returns true whenever word is found in
       temporary dictionary.                                       *)

END TempDict.
```

```
IMPLEMENTATION MODULE TempDict;

    FROM TextOps IMPORT WORD, Equal, Uppercase, Assign;

    FROM Hidden IMPORT TEMPDICTTYPE;

    FROM InOut IMPORT WriteLn, WriteString;

    FROM Utilities IMPORT Spacebar;

    VAR
        temp     : TEMPDICTTYPE;
        next     : INTEGER;

    PROCEDURE InsertTD(word: WORD);

    VAR i : INTEGER;

    BEGIN
        word:=Uppercase(word);
        IF next = 100
```

```
    THEN
        WriteLn;
        WriteString("The temporary dictionary is filled up.");
        WriteLn;
        WriteString("Any additional temporary words will displace");
        WriteLn;
        WriteString("Words inserted earlier in the temporary
                    dictionary.");
        WriteLn;
        Spacebar;
        next:=1
    END(* if then *);
    Assign(word,temp[next]);
    INC(next);
END InsertTD;

PROCEDURE LookupTD(word: WORD): BOOLEAN;

VAR i : INTEGER;

BEGIN
    i:=1;
    WHILE (i <= 100) AND (temp[i,1] # ' ') AND
          ( NOT Equal(temp[i],word) ) DO
        INC(i);
    END(* while loop *);
    IF Equal(temp[i],word)
    THEN
        INC(NumFoundTD);
        RETURN TRUE
    ELSE
        RETURN FALSE;
    END(* if then else *);
END LookupTD;

VAR
    i : INTEGER;
    j : INTEGER;

BEGIN (* Initialization Code *)
    FOR i:=1 TO 100 DO
        FOR j:=1 TO 13 DO
            temp[i,j]:=' ';
        END(* for loop *);
    END(* for loop *);
```

```
      next :=1;
      NumFoundTD:=0;
END TempDict.
```

```
DEFINITION MODULE AuxDict;
(* $SEG:=33; *)

      FROM TextOps IMPORT WORD;

      EXPORT QUALIFIED
            (* var   *) NumFoundAD,
            (* var   *) currentauxmarker,
            (* proc *) CloseAD,
            (* proc *) LookupAD,
            (* proc *) InsertAD,
            (* proc *) InsertADunused;

      VAR currentauxmarker : INTEGER;
      (* Marks the current position of the next available
         space for insertion into the auxiliary dictionary.          *)

      VAR NumFoundAD : INTEGER;
      (* NumFoundAD is incremented whenever a word is
         found in the auxiliary dictionary.                           *)

      PROCEDURE CloseAD();
      (* Used to close the auxiliary dictionary file.                 *)

      PROCEDURE LookupAD(word: WORD): BOOLEAN;

      PROCEDURE InsertAD(word: WORD);
      (* Used to insert word into auxiliary dictionary.               *)

      PROCEDURE InsertADunused(word: WORD);
      (* Used to insert word into unused portion of
         auxiliary dictionary.                                        *)

END AuxDict.
```

```
IMPLEMENTATION MODULE AuxDict;

      FROM TextOps IMPORT WORD, Equal, LessThan, DisplayWord,
                          Uppercase, Assign;

      FROM Files IMPORT Open, FileState, Close, FILE, ReadRec,
                        WriteRec, FilePos, SetPos, GetPos;
```

```
FROM Hidden IMPORT AUXDICTTYPE, AuxDictLength;

FROM TempDict IMPORT InsertTD;

FROM InOut IMPORT WriteLn, WriteString;

FROM Utilities IMPORT CenterMessage, Spacebar;

VAR
    fs                  : FileState;
    fp                  : FilePos;
    AUX                 : FILE;
    aux                 : AUXDICTTYPE;
    oldauxmarker        : INTEGER;
    maindictmarker      : INTEGER;

PROCEDURE Stop;
BEGIN
    WriteLn;
    CenterMessage("Trouble loading auxiliary dictionary.");
    WriteLn;
    HALT
END Stop;

PROCEDURE CloseAD();
```

(∗ Before closing the file AUX, the new components must be added to the old AUX file, the file realphabetized, and the unused space set to blanks once again.   ∗)

```
PROCEDURE HeapSort(VAR a: AUXDICTTYPE; n: INTEGER);

    PROCEDURE CreateHeap(VAR a: AUXDICTTYPE; n: INTEGER);

    VAR
        node : INTEGER;
        i     : INTEGER;
        j     : INTEGER;
        t     : WORD;

    BEGIN (∗ CreateHeap ∗)
        FOR node:=2 TO n DO
            i:=node;
            j:=i DIV 2;
```

```
        WHILE (j # 0 ) AND (   (LessThan(a[j],a[i])) OR
                            (Equal(a[j],a[i]))   )
        DO
            (* Interchange a[j],a[i] *)
            Assign(a[i],t);
            Assign(a[j],a[i]);
            Assign(t,a[j]);
            i:=j;
            j:=i DIV 2;
        END(* while loop *);
    END(* for loop *);
END CreateHeap;


PROCEDURE Adjust(VAR a: AUXDICTTYPE; k: INTEGER);

VAR
    i : INTEGER;
    j : INTEGER;
    t : WORD;

BEGIN (* Adjust *)
    i:=1;
    j:=2;
    IF (k >=3)
    THEN
        IF LessThan(a[2],a[3])
        THEN
            j:=3;
        END(* if then *);
    END(* if then *);
    WHILE (j <= k) AND (LessThan(a[i],a[j])) DO
        (* Interchange a[i] and a[j] *)
        Assign(a[j],t);
        Assign(a[i],a[j]);
        Assign(t,a[i]);
        i:=j;
        IF i > currentauxmarker
        THEN
            RETURN
        END(* if then *);
        j:=2*i;
        IF j > currentauxmarker
        THEN
            . RETURN
        END(* if then *);
```

```
                IF j+1 <=k
                THEN
                    IF LessThan(a[j],a[j+1])
                    THEN
                        INC(j);
                    END(* if then *);
                END(* if then *);
            END(* while loop *);
        END Adjust;

VAR
    i : INTEGER;
    t : WORD;

BEGIN (* HeapSort *)
    CreateHeap(a,n);
    FOR i:=n TO 2 BY −1 DO
        (* Interchange a[1] and a[i]. *)
        Assign(a[i],t);
        Assign(a[1],a[i]);
        Assign(t,a[1]);
        Adjust(a,i−1);
    END(* for loop *);
END HeapSort;

VAR
    i : INTEGER;
    j : INTEGER;

BEGIN
    WriteLn; WriteLn;
    CenterMessage("Closing Files.");
    WriteLn;
    FOR i:=currentauxmarker TO AuxDictLength DO
        FOR j:=1 TO 13 DO
            aux[i,j]:=' ';
        END(* for loop *);
    END(* for loop *);
    IF currentauxmarker > oldauxmarker
    THEN
        HeapSort(aux,currentauxmarker−1);
    END(* if then *);
    SetPos(AUX,fp);
```

```
        WriteRec(AUX,aux);
        fs:=Close(AUX);
END CloseAD;

PROCEDURE LookupAD(word: WORD): BOOLEAN;
(* First do a binary search from 1 to oldauxmarker, then
    do a linear search from oldauxmarker to currentauxmarker,
    then do a linear search from 1200 down to maindictmarker.          *)

VAR
    i    : INTEGER;
    pos : INTEGER;

    PROCEDURE BinarySauxdict(word: Word; low,high: INTEGER;
                                VAR pos: INTEGER);

    VAR mid : INTEGER;

    BEGIN
        WHILE (low <= high) DO
            mid:=(low + high) DIV 2;
            IF Equal(word,aux[mid])
            THEN
                pos:=mid;
                RETURN;
            END(* if then *);
            IF LessThan(word,aux[mid])
            THEN
                high:=mid-1
            ELSE
                low:=mid+1
            END(* if then else *);
        END(* while loop *);
    END BinarySauxdict;

BEGIN (* LookupAd *)
    pos:=0;
    BinarySauxdict(word,1,oldauxmarker,pos);
    IF pos # 0
    THEN
        INC(NumFoundAD);
        RETURN TRUE
    END(* if then *);
    IF currentauxmarker > oldauxmarker
```

```
THEN
    FOR i:=oldauxmarker+1 TO currentauxmarker DO
        IF Equal(aux[i],word)
        THEN
            INC(NumFoundAD);
            RETURN TRUE;
        END(* if then *);
    END(* for loop *);
END(* if then *);
IF currentauxmarker # AuxDictLength
THEN
    FOR i:=AuxDictLength TO maindictmarker BY −1 DO
        IF Equal(aux[i],word)
        THEN
            INC(NumFoundAD);
            RETURN TRUE;
        END(* if then *);
    END(* for loop *);
END(* if then *);
RETURN FALSE;
END LookupAD;

PROCEDURE InsertAD(word: WORD);

VAR i : INTEGER;

BEGIN
    word:=Uppercase(word);
    IF currentauxmarker = AuxDictLength
    THEN
        WriteLn;
        WriteString("Cannot add more words to auxiliary dictionary.");
        WriteLn; WriteLn;
        DisplayWord(word);
        WriteString(" will be added to temporary dictionary.");
        WriteLn; WriteLn;
        InsertTD(word);
        Spacebar
    ELSE
        Assign(word,aux[currentauxmarker]);
        INC(currentauxmarker);
    END(* if then else *);
END InsertAD;

PROCEDURE InsertADunused(word: WORD);
```

```
    VAR i : INTEGER;

    BEGIN
        word:=Uppercase(word);
        IF maindictmarker > currentauxmarker+1
        THEN
            DEC(maindictmarker);
            Assign(word,aux[maindictmarker]);
        ELSE
            maindictmarker:=AuxDictLength;
            IF currentauxmarker < AuxDictLength
            THEN
                Assign(word,aux[maindictmarker]);
            END(* if then *);
        END(* if then else *);
    END InsertADunused;

VAR
    i : INTEGER;
    j : INTEGER;

BEGIN (* Initialization Code *)
    fs:=Open(AUX, "AUXDICT");
    IF fs # FileOK
    THEN
        Stop;
    END(* if then *);
    GetPos(AUX,fp);
    ReadRec(AUX, aux);
    i:=1;
    WHILE (i <= AuxDictLength) AND (aux[i,1] # ' ') DO
        INC(i);
    END(* while loop *);
    maindictmarker:=1201;
    oldauxmarker:=i;
    currentauxmarker:=i;
    NumFoundAD:=0;
END AuxDict.
```

--------------------- --

```
IMPLEMENTATION MODULE TextOps;

    IMPORT Texts;

    IMPORT Counters;

    IMPORT Utilities;
```

```
    FROM Files IMPORT FILE, FileState, Open, Create;

    FROM InOut IMPORT WriteLn, WriteString, Write, Read, EOL;

    FROM TempDict IMPORT InsertTD;

    FROM AuxDict IMPORT InsertAD, InsertADunused;

CONST ap = " ' ";
        n1 = 97;              (* ORD('a') *)
        n2 = 65;              (* ORD('A') *)

    VAR word      : WORD;
        line      : LINE;
        lineindex : INTEGER;
        oldindex  : INTEGER;
        legalchar : Utilities.setofchar;
        output    : FILE;

    PROCEDURE Equal(w1,w2: WORD): BOOLEAN;

    VAR
        t         : BOOLEAN;
        len1      : INTEGER;
        len2      : INTEGER;
        i         : INTEGER;

    BEGIN
        len1:=Length(w1);
        len2:=Length(w2);
        IF len1 # len2
        THEN
            RETURN FALSE
        ELSE
            t:=TRUE;
            i:=0;
            REPEAT
                INC(i);
                IF w1[i] # w2[i]
                THEN
                    t:=FALSE;
                END(* if then *);
            UNTIL (i = len1) OR (NOT t);
            RETURN t
        END(* if then else *);
    END Equal;
```

```
PROCEDURE LessThan(w1,w2: WORD): BOOLEAN;

VAR
    t        : BOOLEAN;
    i        : INTEGER;

BEGIN
    i:=0;
    t:=TRUE;
    REPEAT
        INC(i);
        IF w1[i] > w2[i]
        THEN
            RETURN FALSE
        END(* if then *);
    UNTIL (i = WordLength) OR (w1[i] # w2[i]);
    RETURN t
END LessThan;


PROCEDURE Assign(w1: WORD; VAR w2: WORD);

VAR i : INTEGER;

BEGIN
    FOR i:=1 TO WordLength DO
        w2[i]:=w1[i];
    END(* for loop *);
END Assign;


PROCEDURE GetLine(): LINE;

VAR
        ln : LINE;
        i  : INTEGER;

BEGIN
    FOR i:=1 TO 80 DO
        ln[i]:=' ';
    END(* for loop *);
    Texts.ReadLn(input,ln);
    lineindex:=1;
    EndOfLine:=FALSE;
    RETURN ln
END GetLine;
```

```
PROCEDURE GetNextWord(line: LINE): WORD;

VAR
        i           : INTEGER;
        j           : INTEGER;
        t           : WORD;

BEGIN
    (* Initialize word to blank. *)
    FOR j:=1 TO WordLength DO
        word[j]:= ' ';
    END(* for loop *);
    i:=lineindex;
    (* Advance lineindex to the next legal character. *)
    WHILE ( i <= 80 ) AND ( NOT (line[i] IN legalchar) ) DO
        INC(i)
    END(* while loop *);
    IF i > 80
    THEN
        EndOfLine:=TRUE;
        RETURN word; (* a blank array of characters *)
    END(* if then *);
    oldindex:=i;
    (* Advance lineindex to the first illegal character. *)
    WHILE ( i <= 80 ) AND ( line[i] IN legalchar ) DO
        INC(i);
    END(* while loop *);
    IF i-oldindex > WordLength
    THEN
        LongWord:=TRUE
    ELSE
        LongWord:=FALSE;
    END(* if then *);
    (* Copy from line to word over appropriate range. *)
    FOR j:=oldindex TO i-1 DO
        word[j-oldindex+1]:=line[j];
    END(* for loop *);
    lineindex:=i;
    RETURN word
END GetNextWord;

PROCEDURE Length(word: WORD): INTEGER;

VAR i : INTEGER;
```

```
BEGIN
    i:=1;
    WHILE ( i <= WordLength ) AND ( word[i] # ' ' ) DO
        INC(i);
    END(* while loop *);
    RETURN i-1
END Length;

PROCEDURE LineLength(line: LINE): INTEGER;

VAR i : INTEGER;

BEGIN
    i:=80;
    WHILE ( i >= 1 ) AND ( line[i] = ' ' ) DO
        DEC(i);
    END(* while loop *);
    RETURN i-1
END LineLength;

PROCEDURE Uppercase(word: WORD): WORD;

Var j : INTEGER;

BEGIN
    FOR j:=1 TO Length(word) DO
        IF word[j] IN Utilities.setofchar{'a'..'z'}
        THEN
            word[j]:=CHR(ORD(word[j])-n1+n2);
        END(* if then *);
    END(* for loop *);
    RETURN word
END Uppercase;

PROCEDURE SpecialEnding1(word: WORD): BOOLEAN;

VAR L: INTEGER;

BEGIN
    L:=Length(word);
    IF (L < 1)
    THEN
        RETURN FALSE
    END(* if then *);
    IF (word[L] = 'S') OR (word[L]='D')
    THEN
        RETURN TRUE
```

```
        ELSE
            RETURN FALSE;
        END(* if then else *);
    END SpecialEnding1;


    PROCEDURE SpecialEnding2(word: WORD): BOOLEAN;

    VAR L: INTEGER;

    BEGIN
        L:=Length(word);
        IF (L < 2)
        THEN
            RETURN FALSE
        END(* if then *);
        IF (  (word[L−1]='E') AND (word[L]='D')  ) OR
           (  (word[L−1]='L') AND (word[L]='Y')  ) OR
           (  (word[L−1]='E') AND (word[L]='R')  )
        THEN
            RETURN TRUE
        ELSE
            RETURN FALSE;
        END(* if then else *);
    END Special Ending2;


    PROCEDURE SpecialEnding3(word: WORD): BOOLEAN;

    VAR L: INTEGER;

    BEGIN
        L:=Length(word);
        IF (L < 3)
        THEN
            RETURN FALSE
        END(* if then *);
        IF (  (word[L−2]='E') AND (word[L−1]='D') AND (word[L]='S')  ) OR
           (  (word[L−2]='E') AND (word[L−1]='R') AND (word[L]='S')  ) OR
           (  (word[L−2]='I') AND (word[L−1]='N') AND (word[L]='G')  )
        THEN
            RETURN TRUE
        ELSE
            RETURN FALSE;
        END(* if then else *);
    END SpecialEnding3;
```

```
PROCEDURE StripEnding1(word: WORD): WORD;

VAR
        w   : WORD;
        i    : INTEGER;
        L   : INTEGER;

BEGIN
    L:=Length(word);
    FOR i:=1 TO WordLength DO
        w[i]:=' ';
    END(* for loop *);
    IF NOT SpecialEnding1(word)
    THEN
        RETURN word
    END(* if then *);
    FOR i:=1 TO L-1 DO
        w[i]:=word[i];
    END(* for loop *);
    RETURN w;
END StripEnding1;


PROCEDURE StripEnding2(word: WORD): WORD;

VAR
        w   : WORD;
        i    : INTEGER;
        L   : INTEGER;

BEGIN
    L:=Length(word);
    FOR i:=1 TO WordLength DO
        w[i]:=' ';
    END(* for loop *);
    IF NOT SpecialEnding2(word)
    THEN
        RETURN word
    END(* if then *);
    FOR i:=1 TO L-2 DO
        w[i]:=word[i];
    END(* for loop *);
    RETURN w;
END StripEnding2;


PROCEDURE StripEnding3(word: WORD): WORD;
```

```
VAR
      w   : WORD;
      i    : INTEGER;
      L    : INTEGER;

BEGIN
    L:=Length(word);
    FOR i:=1 TO WordLength DO
        w[i]:=' ';
    END(* for loop *);
    IF NOT SpecialEnding3(word)
    THEN
        RETURN word
    END(* if then *);
    FOR i:=1 TO L-3 DO
        w[i]:=word[i];
    END(* for loop *);
    RETURN w;
END StripEnding3;

PROCEDURE INGEnding(word: WORD): BOOLEAN;

VAR L : INTEGER;

BEGIN
    L:=Length(word);
    IF L < 3
    THEN
        RETURN FALSE
    END(* if then *);
    IF (word[L-2]='I') AND (word[L-1]='N') AND (word[L]='G')
    THEN
        RETURN TRUE
    ELSE
        RETURN FALSE;
    END(* if then else *);
END INGEnding;

PROCEDURE AddE(word: WORD): WORD;

VAR L : INTEGER;
    w : WORD;
    i  : INTEGER;

BEGIN
    L:=Length(word);
```

```
    FOR i:=1 TO WordLength DO
        w[i]:=' ';
    END(* for loop *);
    FOR i:=1 TO L DO
        w[i]:=word[i];
    END(* for loop *);
    w[L+1]:='E';
    RETURN w;
END AddE;


VAR ts   : Texts.TextState;
    fs   : FileState;
    in   : FILE;
    out  : FILE;


PROCEDURE GetInputText(name: ARRAY OF CHAR);
BEGIN
    fs:=Open(in,name);
    IF NOT (fs = FileOK)
    THEN
        WriteLn;
        WriteString("No such text file on disk.");
        WriteLn;
        WriteString("Program execution will halt.");
        WriteLn;
        HALT
    END(* if then *);
    ts:=Texts.Connect(input,in);
    IF NOT (ts = Texts.TextOK)
    THEN
        WriteLn;
        WriteString("Text File IO Problem.");
        WriteLn;
        WriteString("Program execution will halt.");
        WriteLn;
        HALT
    END(* if then *);
END GetInputText;


PROCEDURE CreateOutputText(name: ARRAY OF CHAR);
BEGIN
    fs:=Create(out,name);
    IF NOT (fs = FileOK)
    THEN
        WriteLn;
```

```
                WriteString("Trouble creating output text file on disk.");
                WriteLn;
                WriteString("Program execution will halt.");
                WriteLn;
                HALT
            END(* if then *);
        ts:=Texts.Connect(output,out);
        IF NOT (ts = Texts.TextOK)
        THEN
            WriteLn;
            WriteString("Text File IO Problem.");
            WriteLn;
            WriteString("Program execution will halt.");
            WriteLn;
            HALT
        END(* if then *);
    END CreateOutputText;


    PROCEDURE PutOutput(line: LINE);
    BEGIN
        Texts.WriteString(output,line);
        Texts.WriteLn(output);
    END PutOutput;


    PROCEDURE DisplayLine(line: LINE);

    VAR i : INTEGER;

    BEGIN
        FOR i:=1 TO 80 DO
            Write(line[i]);
        END(* for loop *);
    END DisplayLine;


    PROCEDURE DisplayWord(word: WORD);

    VAR i : INTEGER;

    BEGIN
        FOR i:=1 TO Length(word) DO
            Write(word[i]);
        END(* for loop *);
    END DisplayWord;


    PROCEDURE WordHandler(word: WORD; VAR line: LINE);
```

```
VAR
      i         : INTEGER;
      k         : INTEGER;
      newword : WORD;
      oldlen    : INTEGER;
      newlen    : INTEGER;
      linelen   : INTEGER;
      ch        : CHAR;
      choice    : CHAR;

   PROCEDURE Replace(word: WORD; VAR line: LINE);
   BEGIN
      WriteString("Replace --> ");
      DisplayWord(word);
      WriteString(" <-- with what correctly spelled word: ");
      i:=0;
      REPEAT
         INC(i);
         Read(ch);
         IF (ch = EOL) AND (i=1)
         THEN (* The first character is EOL. *)
             ch:=' ';
             DEC(i);
         END(* if then *);
         IF NOT (ch = EOL)
         THEN
             newword[I]:=ch;
         END(* if then *);
      UNTIL (i = WordLength) OR (ch = EOL);
      IF i < WordLength
      THEN
         FOR k:=i TO WordLength DO
             newword[k]:=' ';
         END(* for loop *);
      END(* if then *);
      newlen:=i-1;
      linelen:=LineLength(line);
      IF linelen + newlen - oldlen > 80
      THEN
         WriteLn;
         WriteString("Cannot replace word because of line overflow.");
         WriteLn;
         WriteString("Mark the word down and make change later.");
         WriteLn;
         Utilities.Spacebar;
```

```
            RETURN;
        END(* if then *);
        IF newlen < oldlen
        THEN
            (* Substitute new word for old word. *);
            FOR i:=oldindex TO oldindex + newlen −1 DO
                line[i]:=newword[i−oldindex+1];
            END(* for loop *);
            (* Compress the remainder of the line. *)
            FOR i:=oldindex + newlen TO 80−(oldlen−newlen) DO
                line[i]:=line[i+oldlen−newlen];
            END(* for loop *);
            lineindex:=oldindex+newlen;
        ELSIF newlen > oldlen
        THEN
        (* Expand the remainder of the line to make room for new word. *)
            linelen:=linelen+(newlen−oldlen);
            FOR i:=(linelen + newlen − oldlen) TO
                    (oldindex + newlen) BY −1 DO
                line[i]:=line[i−(newlen−oldlen)];
            END(* for loop *);
            (* Substitute new word for old word. *)
            FOR i:=oldindex TO oldindex + newlen−1 DO
                line[i]:=newword[i−oldindex+1];
            END(* for loop *);
            lineindex:=oldindex+newlen;
        ELSE
            (* Substitute new word for old word. *)
            FOR i:=oldindex TO oldindex + newlen−1 DO
                line[i]:=newword[i−oldindex+1];
            END(* for loop *);
        END(* if then elsif else *);
        InsertADunused(newword);
    END Replace;

BEGIN (* WordHandler *)
    Utilities.Clear;
    WriteLn; WriteLn;
    WriteString("There is an unidentified word on line.");
    Counters.Display(Counters.LineCount);
    WriteString(", word number ");
    Counters.Display(Counters.WordCount);
    WriteString(". ");
    WriteLn;
```

```
WriteString("The unidentified word is --> ");
DisplayWord(word);
WriteLn; WriteLn;
Utilities.CenterMessage("The line containing the unidentified word -->");

WriteLn; WriteLn;
DisplayLine(line);
WriteLn; WriteLn; WriteLn;
oldlen:=Length(word);
WriteLn;
WriteLn;
WriteString("R --> Replace word with a correctly spelled word");
WriteLn; WriteLn;
WriteString("A --> Add word to auxiliary dictionary");
WriteLn; WriteLn;
WriteString("T --> Temporarily accept word");
WriteLn; WriteLn;
WriteString("          Please enter your choice: ");
choice:=Utilities.ReadKey(Utilities.setofchar)
           {'R', 'A', 'T', 'r', 'a', 't'});
WriteLn; WriteLn;
CASE choice OF
    'R', 'r': Replace(word,line); |
    'A', 'a': InsertAD(word); |
    'T', 't': InsertTD(word);
END(* case *);
END WordHandler;


PROCEDURE RemoveApostrophes(VAR word: WORD);


VAR i : INTEGER;


BEGIN
    IF (word[1] = " ' ") AND (Length(word) > 1)
        THEN
            FOR i:=1 TO 12 DO
                word[i]:=word[i+1];
            END(* for loop *);
        END(* if then *);
    IF (word[Length(word)] = " ' ") AND (Length(word) >1)
    THEN
        word[Length(word)]:=' ';
    END(* if then *);
END RemoveApostrophes;
```

```
BEGIN (* Initialization Code *)
    legalchar:=Utilities.setofchar{'A'..'Z'} +
                Utilities.setofchar{'a'..'z'} +
                Utilities.setofchar{ap};
END TextOps.
```

```
DEFINITION MODULE TestWord;
(* $SEG:=17; *)

    FROM TextOps IMPORT WORD;

    EXPORT QUALIFIED
            (* proc *) IdentifyWord;

    PROCEDURE IdentifyWord(VAR word: WORD): BOOLEAN;
    (* Returns true whenever word is found in one of
        the available dictionaries.                                    *)

END TestWord.
```

```
IMPLEMENTATION MODULE TestWord;

    FROM TextOps IMPORT WORD, Uppercase, Length, SpecialEnding1,
                        SpecialEnding2, SpecialEnding3,
                        StripEnding1, StripEnding2, StripEnding3,
                        INGEnding, AddE, RemoveApostrophes;

    FROM MainDict IMPORT LookupMD;

    FROM FastDict IMPORT LookupFD;

    FROM TempDict IMPORT LookupTD;

    FROM AuxDict IMPORT InsertADunused, LookupAD;

    PROCEDURE IdentifyWord(VAR word: WORD): BOOLEAN;

    VAR
            tempword : WORD;
            i              : INTEGER;

        PROCEDURE IsInDictionaries(word: WORD): BOOLEAN;
        BEGIN
            IF (Length(word) <= 6)
```

```
        THEN
            IF LookupFD(word)
            THEN
                RETURN TRUE
            END(* if then *);
        END(* if then *);
        IF LookupAD(word)
        THEN
            RETURN TRUE
        END(* if then *);
        IF LookupTD(word)
        THEN
            RETURN TRUE
        END(* if then *);
        IF LookupMD(word)
        THEN
            InsertADunused(word);
            RETURN TRUE
        ELSE
            RETURN FALSE
        END(* if then else *);
    END IsInDictionaries;

BEGIN
    word:=Uppercase(word);
    RemoveApostrophes(word);
    IF SpecialEnding1(word)      (* S or D *)
    THEN
        tempword:=StripEnding1(word);
        IF IsInDictionaries(tempword)
        THEN
            RETURN TRUE
        END(* if then *);
    END(* if then *);
    IF SpecialEnding2(word)      (* ED or LY or ER *)
    THEN
        tempword:=StripEnding2(word);
        IF IsInDictionaries(tempword)
        THEN
            RETURN TRUE
        END(* if then *);
    END(* if then *);
    IF SpecialEnding3(word)      (* EDS or ERS or ING *)
    THEN
        tempword:=StripEnding3(word);
```

```
            IF IsInDictionaries(tempword)
            THEN
                RETURN TRUE
            END(* if then *);
            IF INGEnding(word)
            THEN
                tempword:=AddE(tempword);
                IF IsInDictionaries(tempword)
                THEN
                    RETURN TRUE
                END(* if then *);
            END(* if then *);
        END(* if then *);
        IF IsInDictionaries(word)
        THEN
            RETURN TRUE
        ELSE
            RETURN FALSE
        END(* if then else *);
    END IdentifyWord;

END TestWord.
```

```
MODULE Spell;

    FROM Hidden IMPORT AuxDictLength;

    FROM Counters IMPORT LineCount, WordCount, Increment, Display,
                    DivideByTen;

    FROM TextOps IMPORT LINE, WORD, GetLine, GetNextWord, Length,
                    EndOfLine, LongWord, WordLength, input,
                    GetInputText, CreateOutputText, PutOutput,
                    WordHandler;

    FROM TestWord IMPORT IdentifyWord;

    FROM Texts IMPORT EOT;

    FROM MainDict IMPORT CloseMD, NumFoundMD;

    FROM FastDict IMPORT CloseFD, NumFoundFD;

    FROM AuxDict IMPORT CloseAD, currentauxmarker, NumFoundAD;
```

```
FROM TempDict IMPORT NumFoundTD;

FROM InOut IMPORT WriteLn, WriteString, ReadString, WriteInt,
                    Write;

FROM Utilities IMPORT Clear, CenterMessage, Spacebar;

FROM Files IMPORT Open, FileState, FILE;

CONST bell = 7;

VAR
        fs         : FileState;
        auxdict    : FILE;
        inputline  : LINE;
        word       : WORD;
        name       : ARRAY[0. .19] OF CHAR;

PROCEDURE DisplayStatus;
BEGIN
    Clear;
    WriteLn; WriteLn; WriteLn; WriteLn;
    WriteString("         Number of lines processed: ");
    Display(LineCount);
    WriteLn; WriteLn;
    WriteString("         Number of words processed: ");
    Display(WordCount);
    WriteLn; WriteLn;
    WriteString("         Remaining size of auxiliary dictionary: ");
    WriteInt(1+AuxDictLength−currentauxmarker,1);
    WriteLn;
END DisplayStatus;

PROCEDURE Information;
BEGIN
    WriteString("What is the name of text to be checked?");
    WriteLn;
    WriteString("You must use the '.TEXT' suffix --> ");
    ReadString(name);
    GetInputText(name);
    WriteLn; WriteLn;WriteLn;
    WriteString("What is the name of the new text: ");
    WriteLn;
    WriteString("You must use the '.TEXT' suffix --> ");
```

```
        ReadString(name);
        CreateOutputText(name);
        Clear;
        WriteLn; WriteLn; WriteLn; WriteLn; WriteLn;
        WriteString("        You must have the dictionaries:");
        WriteLn; WriteLn;
        WriteString("                MAINDICT");
        WriteLn; WriteLn;
        WriteString("                INDEXFILE");
        WriteLn; WriteLn;
        WriteString("                FP");
        WriteLn; WriteLn;
        WriteString("                FASTFILE");
        WriteLn; WriteLn;
        WriteString("                AUXDICT");
        WriteLn; WriteLn;
        WriteString("        on disk in order for this program to run.");
        Spacebar;
        WriteLn; WriteLn;WriteLn;
    END Information;


BEGIN (* Spell *)
    Information;
    (* The dictionaries MAINDICT, FP, INDEX, FASTFILE, and AUXDICT
      are loaded during the initialization process from modules
      MainDict, FastDict, and AuxDict respectively.                      *)
    LOOP
        inputline:=GetLine( );
        IF EOT(input)
        THEN
            EXIT
        END(* if then *);
        Increment(LineCount);
        IF DivideByTen(LineCount)
        THEN
            DisplayStatus;
        END(* if then *);
        LOOP
            word:=GetNextWord(inputline);
            IF EndOfLine THEN EXIT; END(* if then *);
            IF NOT LongWord
            THEN
                Increment(WordCount);
                IF NOT IdentifyWord(word)
                THEN
                    Write( CHR(bell) );
```

```
                    WordHandler(word,inputline);
                 END(* if then *);
              END(* if then *);
           END(* loop *);
           PutOutput(inputline);
        END(* loop *);
        WriteLn; WriteLn; WriteLn;
        WriteString("The number of lines processed is ");
        Display(LineCount);
        WriteLn;
        WriteString("The number of words processed is ");
        Display(WordCount);
        WriteLn;
        WriteString("The number of words found in main dictionary: ");
        WriteInt(NumFoundMD,1);
        WriteLn;
        WriteString("The number of words found in fast dictionary: ");
        WriteInt(NumFoundFD,1);
        WriteLn;
        WriteString("The number of words found in auxiliary dictionary: ");
        WriteInt(NumFoundAD,1);
        WriteLn;
        WriteString("The number of words found in temporary dictionary: ");
        WriteInt(NumFoundTD,1);
        WriteLn;
        CloseMD( );
        CloseFD( );
        CloseAD( );
END Spell.
```

9.4 MAINTENANCE OF THE SPELLING CHECKER

Have you carefully studied the long listing for Program 9.1? Each of the abstract data types and functional components given in the system design (see Figures 9.1 and 9.2) is implemented. We probe deeper into many of the lower level design decisions in the exercises.

The performance of the spelling checker degrades considerably after several hundred words have been processed. Why might this be so?

The degradation in performance occurs because the unused portion of the auxiliary dictionary fills up with words found in the main dictionary as text processing progresses. Each new word not found in the fast dictionary or in the first portion of the auxiliary dictionary is tested, using a relatively inefficient linear search, against the words in the unused portion of the auxiliary dictionary. It is noted that a binary search is used to test new words against the original portion of the auxiliary dictionary.

In the tests that were performed, the auxiliary dictionary originally had no words in it. Therefore, before long, the full 1200-word array space is filled with main dictionary words. The linear search of this 1200-word array, even though it is performed in fast memory, loads the system down and causes its performance to degrade.

This observation causes us to consider perfective maintenance. Why not remove the unused portion of the auxiliary dictionary and dedicate the entire 1200-word array space for user-inserted auxiliary words?

Where must changes be made in the software system to modify the dictionary structure? The basic system design is hardly affected by our proposed maintenance. Only the definition module AuxDict (i.e., the removal of Insert ADunused) and the implementation modules AuxDict, TestWord, and TextOps (in procedure Replace) must be changed. All in all, only a few lines of code must be changed. Can you identify the changes that are required?

We display the modified implementation modules in Program 9.2. Since only one line of code must be omitted from procedure Replace in implementation module TextOps, we do not repeat this lengthy module.

PROGRAM 9.2   Modifications to Original Spelling Checker

```
DEFINITION MODULE AuxDict;
(* $SEG:=33; *)

    FROM TextOps IMPORT WORD;

    EXPORT QUALIFIED
            (* var  *) NumFoundAD,
            (* var  *) currentauxmarker,
            (* proc *) CloseAD,
            (* proc *) LookupAD,
            (* proc *) InsertAD;

    VAR currentauxmarker : INTEGER;
    (* Marks the current position of the next available
        space for insertion into the auxiliary dictionary.        *)

    VAR NumFoundAD : INTEGER;
    (* NumFoundAD is incremented whenever a word is
        found in the auxiliary dictionary.                        *)

    PROCEDURE CloseAD( );
    (* Used to close the auxiliary dictionary file.               *)
```

```
PROCEDURE LookupAD(word: WORD): BOOLEAN;

PROCEDURE InsertAD(word: WORD);
(* Used to insert word into auxiliary dictionary.                    *)

END AuxDict.
```

```
IMPLEMENTATION MODULE AuxDict;
    FROM TextOps IMPORT WORD, Equal, LessThan, DisplayWord, Uppercase,
                        Assign;

    FROM Files IMPORT Open, FileState, Close, FILE, ReadRec,
                      WriteRec, FilePos, SetPos, GetPos;

    FROM Hidden IMPORT AUXDICTTYPE, AuxDictLength;

    FROM TempDict IMPORT InsertTD;

    FROM InOut IMPORT WriteLn, WriteString;

    FROM Utilities IMPORT CenterMessage, Spacebar;

    VAR
            fs              : FileState;
            fp              : FilePos;
            AUX             : FILE;
            aux             : AUXDICTTYPE;
            oldauxmarker    : INTEGER;

PROCEDURE Stop;
BEGIN
    WriteLn;
    CenterMessage("Trouble loading auxiliary dictionary.");
    WriteLn;
    HALT
END Stop;

PROCEDURE CloseAD( );
(* Before closing the file AUX, the new components must be
   added to the old AUX file, the file realphabetized, and the
   unused space set to blanks once again.                           *)

PROCEDURE HeapSort(VAR a: AUXDICTTYPE; n: INTEGER);

    PROCEDURE CreateHeap(VAR a: AUXDICTTYPE; n: INTEGER);
```

```
VAR
        node : INTEGER;
        i     : INTEGER;
        j     : INTEGER;
        t     : WORD;

BEGIN (* CreateHeap *)
    FOR node:=2 TO n DO
        i:=node;
        j:=i DIV 2;
        WHILE (j # 0 ) AND ( (LessThan(a[j],a[i])) OR
                            (Equal(a[j],a[i])) )
        DO
            (* Interchange a[j],a[i] *)
            Assign(a[i],t);
            Assign(a[j],a[i]);
            Assign(t,a[j]);
            i:=j;
            j:=i DIV 2;
        END(* while loop *);
    END(* for loop *);
END CreateHeap;

PROCEDURE Adjust(VAR a: AUXDICTTYPE; k: INTEGER);

VAR
        i : INTEGER;
        j : INTEGER;
        t : WORD;

BEGIN (* Adjust *)
    i:=1;
    j:=2;
    IF (k >=3)
    THEN
        IF LessThan(a[2],a[3])
        THEN
            j:=3;
        END(* if then *);
    END(* if then *);
    WHILE (j <= k) AND (LessThan(a[i],a[j])) DO
        (* Interchange a[i] and a[j] *)
        Assign(a[j],t);
        Assign(a[i],a[j]);
        Assign(t,a[i]);
        i:=j;
```

```
                IF i > currentauxmarker
                THEN
                    RETURN
                END(* if then *);
                j:=2*i;
                IF j > currentauxmarker
                THEN
                    RETURN
                END(* if then *);
                IF j+1 <=k
                THEN
                    IF LessThan(a[j],a[j+1])
                    THEN
                        INC(j);
                    END(* if then *);
                END(* if then *);
            END(* while loop *);
    END Adjust;

    VAR
            i : INTEGER;
            t : WORD;

    BEGIN (* HeapSort *)
        CreateHeap(a,n);
        FOR i:=n TO 2 BY -1 DO
            (* Interchange a[i] and a[i] *)
            Assign(a[i],t);
            Assign(a[1],a[i]);
            Assign(t,a[1]);
            Adjust(a,i-1);
        END(* for loop *);
    END HeapSort;

VAR
            i : INTEGER;
            j : INTEGER;

BEGIN
    WriteLn; WriteLn;
    CenterMessage("Closing Files.");
    WriteLn;
    IF currentauxmarker > oldauxmarker
    THEN
        HeapSort(aux,currentauxmarker-1);
    END(* if then *);
```

```
            SetPos(AUX,fp);
            WriteRec(AUX,aux);
            fs:=Close(AUX);
        END CloseAD;

PROCEDURE LookupAD(word: WORD): BOOLEAN;
(* First do a binary search from 1 to oldauxmarker, then
   do a linear search from oldauxmarker to currentauxmarker,
   then do a linear search from 1200 down to maindictmarker.        *)

VAR
        i    : INTEGER;
        pos : INTEGER;

    PROCEDURE BinarySauxdict(word: WORD; low,high: INTEGER;
                                VAR pos: INTEGER);

    VAR mid : INTEGER;

    BEGIN
        WHILE (low <= high) DO
            mid:=(low + high) DIV 2;
            IF Equal(word,aux[mid])
            THEN
                pos:=mid;
                RETURN;
            END(* if then *);
            IF LessThan(word,aux[mid])
            THEN
                high:=mid-1
            ELSE
                low:=mid+1
            END(* if then else *);
        END(* while loop *);
    END BinarySauxdict;

BEGIN (* LookupAd *)
    pos:=0;
    BinarySauxdict(word,1,oldauxmarker,pos);
    IF pos # 0
    THEN
        INC(NumFoundAD);
        RETURN TRUE
    END(* if then *);
    IF currentauxmarker > oldauxmarker
```

```
      THEN
          FOR i:=oldauxmarker+1 TO currentauxmarker DO
              IF Equal(aux[i],word)
              THEN
                  INC(NumFoundAD);
                  RETURN TRUE;
              END(* if then *);
          END(* for loop *);
      END(* if then *);
      RETURN FALSE;
  END LookupAD;


PROCEDURE InsertAD(word: WORD);


VAR i : INTEGER;


BEGIN
    word:=Uppercase(word);
    IF currentauxmarker = AuxDictLength
    THEN
        WriteLn;
        WriteString("Cannot add more words to auxiliary dictionary.");
        WriteLn; WriteLn;
        DisplayWord(word);
        WriteString(" will be added to temporary dictionary.");
        WriteLn; WriteLn;
        InsertTD(word);
        Spacebar
    ELSE
        Assign(word,aux[currentauxmarker]);
        INC(currentauxmarker);
    END(* if then else *);
  END InsertAD;

VAR
      i : INTEGER;
      j : INTEGER;


BEGIN (* Initialize Code *)
      fs:=Open(AUX, "AUXDICT");
      IF fs # FileOK
      THEN
          Stop;
      END(* if then *);
      GetPos(AUX,fp);
```

```
        ReadRec(AUX, aux);
        i:=1;
        WHILE (i <= AuxDictLength) AND (aux[i,1] # ' ') DO
            INC(i);
        END(* while loop *);
        oldauxmarker:=i;
        currentauxmarker:=i;
        NumFoundAD:=0;
END AuxDict.
```

We now compare the performance of the two versions by measuring the time required to process the first 200 lines, of text in Chapter 1 of this book. The results are:

Version 1 --> 475 seconds

Version 2 --> 181 seconds

These results were obtained using a Sage IV 16-bit computer and a Volition Systems Modula-2 compiler. The difference in performance would be even more dramatic if the processing time for the first 1000 lines of text were compared. Since version 1 slows down considerably once the unused portion of the auxiliary dictionary has filled up, its speed falls to below the required 200 words per minute. Version 2's speed remains about the same and averages about 425 words per minute.

After processing Chapter 1 with version 2 of the spelling checker, we can report the following mix of words found in the various dictionaries.

Words found in main dictionary --> 2497
Words found in fast dictionary   --> 3336

Perhaps the conclusion to be drawn from this experiment is that Wiener and Sincovec need to expand their active vocabularies!

9.5 EXERCISES AND FURTHER PROBING INTO THE SPELLING CHECKER

In this final section of the chapter we ask the reader to examine some of the design decisions made in two versions of the spelling checker. We believe that the best way to appreciate the benefits of modular software construction is to attempt perfective maintenance.

Some of the perfective maintenance exercises may be suitable as semester projects in a software engineering course. They may also be suitable as team projects in an intensive seminar on software engineering.

1. Write a Modula-2 program that generates the dictionary files for versions 1 and 2 of the spelling checker program. The data structures for these files may be found in the definition module Hidden. The input data for your dictionary generator is assumed to be a text file of main dictionary words.

2. Implement the spelling checker, version 2, in Ada. Use Modular Design Listing 9.4 as a starting point.

3. Write an Ada program that generates the same dictionary files as Exercise 1.

4. Test every module of the Modula-2 version 1, given in this chapter. Show your test cases and the additional code that you must write to perform these tests. Each module should be tested individually.

5. Write a complete user's guide that supports either version 1 or version 2 of the spelling checker.

The following perfective maintenance exercises may be performed in either Ada or Modula-2. Depending on your available compilers and time, you may wish to attempt maintenance in both the Ada and the Modula-2 version.

6. Modify version 2 so that root words that end in an apostrophe followed by an s ('s) may be identified as spelled correctly. Test your modification.

7. Modify version 1 by creating an AVL tree (dynamically) to store words found in the main dictionary rather than using the linear array, used in version 1. You must make provision for some signal that stops the process of building the AVL tree after a certain number of words have been added (this number is a function of the memory of your machine and the value of variable currentauxdict). Since the search time in an AVL tree is approximately of order log $2n$ as compared to order n for the array, significant improvements in processing time might be expected. Compare the timing of the old version 1 implementation with your new version. What strategy do you propose to follow after the AVL tree reaches its capacity? To preserve the object-oriented character of your software system, the structural details of the AVL tree must be hidden.

8. Modify version 2 by adding a menu item that allows the user to print out selected parts of the main dictionary. The user may input a subset of the first several letters of a word. The program must then print out all the main dictionary words that contain the subset that the user inputs. Since there may be hundreds of words that must be displayed on the screen, take care

to print only one screen-full at a time, giving an exit option to the user after each screen display. This new menu option should be presented in both procedure WordHandler and a main program menu.

9. Modify version 2 so that the user may print out the contents of the auxiliary dictionary. In addition, the user should be provided with a main menu option of being able to delete words from the auxiliary dictionary.

10. Modify the hidden data structure for the main dictionary by using a B-tree. Write a new dictionary generation program that converts a text file of words to the new data structure. Modify module MainDict, and in particular, procedure LookupMD, to reflect the new structure for the main dictionary. Compare the processing time of your new version with version 2.

11. Develop a hash table approach for testing words in the main dictionary. You must write a program for generating the appropriate hash table from the input text file of dictionary words. What hazards are associated with using a hash table for main dictionary word lookup? Make the appropriate modifications in the spelling checker program, again focusing on module MainDict and procedure LookupMD, to reflect the use of the hash table. Compare the processing time and accuracy of your modified version with version 2.

12. Modify version 2 so that the user has the option of directing all words of length greater than 13 to a user-named file. This file may be a line printer.

13. Modify versions 1 and 2 by experimenting with the size of the block that is used for the main dictionary. As you modify the block size, you must make appropriate changes in both the dictionary generation program and the spelling checker. As the block size is made smaller, the size of the index file will grow but the disk access time will decrease. The converse will occur when the block size is increased. Experimentally determine the best choice for the main dictionary block size by comparing the processing times associated with different block sizes.

14. All the versions, except perhaps the hash table version, involve storing a complete word in the main dictionary disk file. Using data compression, more words can be packed into a smaller disk space. The usual consequence of such data compression is lowered processing speed. Modify version 2 by using data compression to decrease the size of the main dictionary file. You may wish to encode each letter into a bit stream of five bits. For example, the letter 'A' maps into 00001, 'B' into 00010, 'C' into 00011, and so forth. The bit streams can be stored instead of the complete word. Using such a scheme it may be possible to achieve significant savings in main dictionary storage space. Explore other data compression techniques. For each scheme used, modify version 2, test your modified program, and compare its processing speed with that of version 2.

15. Draw a modular design chart that represents the system architecture for the version 2 of the spelling checker.

Appendix

LIBRARY MODULES
THAT SUPPORT MODULA-2

The following library modules are supplied with the Volition Systems Modula-2 compiler. Most of the modules are standard. A few of the modules are machine dependent.

MODULE InOut

```
EXPORT QUALIFIED
     EOL, Done, termCH,
     OpenInput, OpenOutput, CloseInput, CloseOutput,
     Read, ReadString, ReadInt, ReadCard,
     Write, WriteLn, WriteString, WriteInt, WriteCard, WriteOct, WriteHex;

CONST EOL = 15C; (* SYSTEM DEPENDENT *)

VAR Done: BOOLEAN;
VAR termCH: CHAR;

PROCEDURE OpenInput     (defext: ARRAY OF CHAR);
PROCEDURE OpenOutput   (defext: ARRAY OF CHAR);
PROCEDURE CloseInput;
PROCEDURE CloseOutput;

PROCEDURE Read          (VAR ch: CHAR);
PROCEDURE ReadString    (VAR  s: ARRAY OF CHAR);
```

```
PROCEDURE ReadInt      (VAR  x: INTEGER);
PROCEDURE ReadCard     (VAR  x: CARDINAL);

PROCEDURE Write        (ch : CHAR);
PROCEDURE WriteLn;
PROCEDURE WriteString  (s  : ARRAY OF CHAR);
PROCEDURE WriteInt     (x  : INTEGER; n: CARDINAL);
PROCEDURE Writecard    (x,n: CARDINAL);
PROCEDURE WriteOct     (x,n: CARDINAL);
PROCEDURE WriteHex     (x,n: CARDINAL);
```

MODULE Files

```
FROM SYSTEM IMPORT WORD, ADDRESS;

EXPORT QUALIFIED
    FILE, EOF, FileStatus, FileState, SetFileHandler,
    Open, Create, Close, Release, Rename, Delete,
    FilePos, SetPos, GetPos, SetEOF, GetEOF, CalcPos
    Read, Write, ReadRec, WriteRec, ReadBytes, WriteBytes;

TYPE FILE;

PROCEDURE EOF(f: FILE): BOOLEAN;   (*End of file encountered. *)

TYPE FileState = (FileOK, NameError, UseError, StatusError, DeviceError,
                EndError);

PROCEDURE FileStatus(f: FILE): FileState;   (* File I/O status. *)

TYPE FileHandler = PROCEDURE (FileState);

PROCEDURE SetFileHandler (f: FILE; handler: Filehandler);

PROCEDURE Open     (VAR f: FILE; name: ARRAY OF CHAR): FileState;
PROCEDURE Create   (VAR f: FILE; name: ARRAY OF CHAR): FileState;

PROCEDURE Close     (VAR f: FILE): FileState;
PROCEDURE Release   (VAR f: FILE): FileState;

PROCEDURE Delete    (name: ARRAY OF CHAR): FileState;
PROCEDURE Rename    (old,new: ARRAY OF CHAR): FileState;

TYPE FilePos;
```

```
PROCEDURE GetPos    (f: FILE; VAR pos: FilePos);
PROCEDURE GetEOF    (f: FILE; VAR pos: FilePos);

PROCEDURE SetPos    (f: FILE; pos: FilePos);
PROCEDURE SetEOF    (f: FILE; pos: FilePos);

PROCEDURE CalcPos (recnum,recsize: CARDINAL; VAR pos: FilePos);

PROCEDURE Read         (f: FILE; VAR ch: CHAR);
PROCEDURE ReadRec      (f: FILE; VAR rec: ARRAY OF WORD);
PROCEDURE ReadBytes    (f: FILE; buf: ADDRESS; nbytes: CARDINAL):
                       CARDINAL;

PROCEDURE Write        (f: FILE; ch: CHAR);
PROCEDURE WriteRec     (f: FILE; VAR rec: ARRAY OF WORD);
PROCEDURE WriteBytes   (f: FILE; buf: ADDRESS; nbytes: CARDINAL):
                       CARDINAL;
```

MODULE MathLib

```
EXPORT QUALIFIED
    sqrt, exp, ln, sin, cos, arctan, real, entier;

PROCEDURE sqrt     (x: REAL): REAL;

PROCEDURE exp      (x: REAL): REAL;

PROCEDURE ln       (x: REAL): REAL;

PROCEDURE sin      (x: REAL): REAL;

PROCEDURE cos      (x: REAL): REAL;

PROCEDURE arctan   (x: REAL): REAL;

PROCEDURE real     (x: INTEGER): REAL;

PROCEDURE entier   (x: REAL): INTEGER;
```

MODULE Processes

```
EXPORT QUALIFIED SIGNAL, StartProcess, SEND, WAIT, Awaited, Init;

TYPE SIGNAL;
```

PROCEDURE StartProcess (P: PROC; n: CARDINAL);
(* Start a sequential process with program P and workspace of size n.   *)

PROCEDURE SEND (VAR s: SIGNAL);
(* One process waiting for s is resumed.   *)

PROCEDURE WAIT (VAR s: SIGNAL);
(* Wait for some other process to send s.   *)

PROCEDURE Awaited (s: SIGNAL): BOOLEAN;
(* Awaited(s) = 'at least one process waiting for s'.   *)

PROCEDURE Init (VAR s: SIGNAL);
(* Compulsory initialization.   *)

MODULE Program

EXPORT QUALIFIED
    Call, CallMode, ErrorMode, CallResult,
    Terminate, SetEnvelope, EnvMode;

TYPE CallResult = (NormalReturn, ProgramHalt, RangeError,SystemError,
                   FunctionError, StackOverflow, IntegerError,
                   DivideByZero, AddressError, UserHalt,CodeIOError,
                   UserIOError, InstructionError, FloatingError,
                   StringError, StorageError, VersionError,
                   MissingProgram, MissingModule, LibraryError,
                   NotMainProcess, DuplicateName);

TYPE CallMode = (Shared,Unshared);
TYPE ErrorMode = (SystemTrap, CallerTrap);

PROCEDURE Terminate (exception: CallResult);
PROCEDURE Call (programNAME: ARRAY OF CHAR;
                calltype   : CallMode;
                errors   : ErrorMode): CallResult;

TYPE EnvMode   = (AllCalls, UnsharedCalls, FirstCall);

PROCEDURE SetEnvelope (init, term: PROC; mode: EnvMode);

MODULE RealInOut

EXPORT QUALIFIED
ReadReal, WriteReal, WriteRealOct, Done;

VAR Done: BOOLEAN;

PROCEDURE ReadReal   (VAR x: REAL);
PROCEDURE WriteReal   (x: REAL; n: CARDINAL);
PROCEDURE WriteRealOct   (x: REAL);

MODULE Reals

FROM Texts IMPORT TEXT;

EXPORT QUALIFIED RealToStr, StrToReal, ReadReal, WriteReal;

PROCEDURE ReadReal   (t: TEXT; VAR r: REAL);

PROCEDURE WriteReal   (t: TEXT; r: REAL);
                       n: CARDINAL; digits: INTEGER);

PROCEDURE RealToStr   (r: REAL; digits: INTEGER;
                       VAR s: ARRAY OF CHAR):BOOLEAN;

PROCEDURE StrToReal   (s: ARRAY OF CHAR;
                       VAR r: REAL): BOOLEAN;

MODULE Screen

EXPORT QUALIFIED HomeCursor, ClearScreen, EraseLine, GotoXY;
PROCEDURE HomeCursor;   (* Move the cursor to upper left.   *)
PROCEDURE ClearScreen; (* Erase from cursor to end of screen.   *)
PROCEDURE EraseLine;   (* Erase from cursor to end of line.   *)
PROCEDURE GotoXY(x, y: CARDINAL); (* Move to column x, row y.   *)

MODULE Strings

EXPORT QUALIFIED STRING, Assign, Insert, Delete,
                 Pos, Copy, Concat, Length, CompareStr;

```
TYPE STRING = ARRAY[0. .80] OF CHAR;

PROCEDURE Assign (VAR source, dest: ARRAY OF CHAR);

PROCEDURE Insert (VAR str:  ARRAY OF CHAR;
                       inx: CARDINAL;
                       len: CARDINAL);

PROCEDURE Delete (VAR str:  ARRAY OF CHAR;
                       inx: CARDINAL;
                       len: CARDINAL);

PROCEDURE Pos (substr, str: ARRAY OF CHAR): CARDINAL;

PROCEDURE Copy (str:  ARRAY OF CHAR;
                    inx: CARDINAL;
                    len: CARDINAL;
                    VAR result: ARRAY OF CHAR);

PROCEDURE Concat (s1, s2: ARRAY OF CHAR;
                     VAR result: ARRAY OF CHAR);

PROCEDURE Length (VAR str: ARRAY OF CHAR): CARDINAL;

PROCEDURE CompareStr (s1, s2: ARRAY OF CHAR): INTEGER;
```

MODULE Terminal

```
EXPORT QUALIFIED Read, BusyRead, ReadAgain, ReadLn,
                    Write, WriteString, WriteLn;

PROCEDURE Read       (VAR ch: CHAR);
PROCEDURE ReadLn     (VAR  s: ARRAY OF CHAR);
PROCEDURE BusyRead   (VAR ch: CHAR);
PROCEDURE ReadAgain;

PROCEDURE Write       (ch: CHAR);
PROCEDURE WriteString  (  s: ARRAY OF CHAR);
PROCEDURE WriteLn;
```

MODULE SystemTypes

EXPORT QUALIFIED
    MinInt, MaxInt, MaxCard, AdrsPerWord, CharsPerWord;

```
CONST   MinInt      = −32768;
        MaxInt      =   32767;
        MaxCard     =   65535;

        AdrsPerWord  =     2;
        CharsPerWord =     2;
```

MODULE Storage

FROM SYSTEM IMPORT ADDRESS;

EXPORT QUALIFIED ALLOCATE, DEALLOCATE, Available;

```
PROCEDURE ALLOCATE      (VAR p: ADDRESS; size: CARDINAL);
PROCEDURE DEALLOCATE   (VAR p: ADDRESS; size: CARDINAL);

PROCEDURE Available (size: CARDINAL): BOOLEAN;
```

MODULE Texts

EXPORT QUALIFIED
    TEXT, input, output, console, Connect, Disconnect,
    EOT, EOL, TextStatus, TextState, SetTextHandler,
    Read, ReadInt, ReadCard, ReadLn, ReadAgain,
    Write, WriteString, WriteInt, WriteCard, WriteLn;

TYPE TEXT;

VAR input, output, console: TEXT;   (* Predeclared text files *)

PROCEDURE EOT(t: TEXT): BOOLEAN; (* End of text read. *)
PROCEDURE EOL(t: TEXT): BOOLEAN; (* End of line read. *)

TYPE TextState = (TextOk, FormatError, FileError, ConnectError);

PROCEDURE TextStatus   (t: TEXT): TextState;

TYPE TextHandler = PROCEDURE (TextState);

PROCEDURE SetTextHandler (t: TEXT; handler: TextHandler);

PROCEDURE Connect   (VAR t: TEXT; f: FILE): TextState;
PROCEDURE Disconnect   (VAR t: TEXT): TextState;

PROCEDURE Read   (t: TEXT; VAR ch: CHAR);
PROCEDURE Readint   (t: TEXT; VAR i: INTEGER);
PROCEDURE ReadCard   (t: TEXT; VAR c: CARDINAL);
PROCEDURE ReadLn   (t: TEXT; VAR s: ARRAY OF CHAR);
PROCEDURE ReadAgain   (t: TEXT);

PROCEDURE Write   (t: TEXT; ch: CHAR);
PROCEDURE WriteString (t: TEXT;   s: ARRAY OF CHAR);
PROCEDURE WriteInt   (t: TEXT;   i: INTEGER; n: CARDINAL);
PROCEDURE WriteCard   (t: TEXT; c,n: CARDINAL);
PROCEDURE WriteLn   (t: TEXT);

MODULE UnitIO

FROM SYSTEM IMPORT WORD, ADDRESS;

EXPORT QUALIFIED UnitRead, UnitWrite, UnitStatus, UnitClear,
                 UnitBusy, IOResult, IOResultType;

TYPE IOResultType = (INoError,   (* 0 *)
                     IHardErr,
                     IBadUnit,
                     IBadMode,
                     ITimeout,
                     ILostUnit,   (* 5 *)
                     ILostFile,
                     IBadTitle,
                     INoSpace,
                     INoUnit,
                     INoFile,   (* 10 *)
                     IDupFile,
                     IFileOpen,
                     INotOpen,
                     IBadFormat,
                     IBufOflow);   (* 15 *)

```
PROCEDURE IOResult(): IOResultType;
(* Return value indicating the result of the previous I/O operation.          *)

PROCEDURE UnitStatus (UnitNo: CARDINAL;
                       Result : ADDRESS;
                       Option: CARDINAL);
(* Return status of the specified unit
   --see UCSD Pascal manual for details.                                      *)

PROCEDURE UnitBusy (UnitNo: CARDINAL): BOOLEAN;
(* Return TRUE if the specified unit is waiting
   for an I/O operation to complete.                                          *)

PROCEDURE  UnitClear (UnitNo: CARDINAL);
(* Set the specified unit back to its initial operating state.                *)

PROCEDURE UnitRead (UnitNo  : CARDINAL;
                    Buffer  : ADDRESS;
                    Index   : CARDINAL;
                    NBytes  : CARDINAL;
                    BlkNum: CARDINAL;
                    FlagWd : BITSET);

(* Read Bytes from I/O unit into buffer.                                      *)

PROCEDURE UnitWrite(UnitNo  : CARDINAL;
                    Buffer  : ADDRESS;
                    Index   : CARDINAL;
                    NBytes  : CARDINAL;
                    BlkNum: CARDINAL;
                    FlagWd : BITSET);

(* Write Bytes in Buffer out to I/O unit.                                     *)
```

MODULE Standards

```
FROM SYSTEM IMPORT ADDRESS

EXPORT QUALIFIED MoveLeft, MoveRight, FillChar, Scan, Time, ScanType,
                 PowerOfTen, Alloc, Mark, Release, MemAvail;

TYPE ScanType = (ScanUntil, ScanWhile);
```

```
PROCEDURE MoveLeft (SrcAddr : ADDRESS;
                    SrcInx   : CARDINAL;
                    DestAddr: ADDRESS;
                    DestInx  : CARDINAL;
                    NBytes   : CARDINAL);
```

(* Move bytes from Source to Destination starting with
   the first byte in Source.   *)

```
PROCEDURE MoveRight(SrcAddr : ADDRESS;
                    SrcInx   : CARDINAL;
                    DestAddr: ADDRESS;
                    DestInx  : CARDINAL;
                    NBytes   : CARDINAL);
```

(* Move bytes from Source to Destination starting with
   the last byte in Source.   *)

```
PROCEDURE FillChar (DestAddr: ADDRESS;
                    DestInx  : CARDINAL;
                    NBytes   : CARDINAL;
                    FillVal  : CHAR);
```

(* Initialize bytes in Dest with the byte value FillVal.   *)

```
PROCEDURE Scan (NumChars: INTEGER;
                ForPast   : ScanType;
                Target    : CHAR;
                Source    : ADDRESS;
                SrcInx    : CARDINAL): INTEGER;
```

(* Starting at Source, scan for Numchars characters until
   Target character is found. Return offset from Source.   *)

```
PROCEDURE Time (VAR Hi, Lo: CARDINAL;
```
(* Return 32-bit system clock value in Hi and Lo.   *)

```
PROCEDURE Alloc (VAR p: ADDRESS; words: CARDINAL);
```
(* Allocate space on top of heap.   *)

```
PROCEDURE Mark (VAR p: ADDRESS);
```
(* Save current heap position in p.   *)

```
PROCEDURE Release (VAR p: ADDRESS);
```
(* Cut heap back to position specified by p.   *)

```
PROCEDURE MemAvail(): CARDINAL;
(* Return # words between stack and heap top.                     *)

PROCEDURE PowerOfTen (e: CARDINAL): REAL;
(* Return 10 raised to the eth power.                             *)
```

MODULE Conversions

```
FROM SYSTEM IMPORT WORD

EXPORT QUALIFIED
    IntToStr, StrToInt, CardToStr, StrToCard, HexToStr, StrToHex;

PROCEDURE IntToStr   (i: INTEGER;
                      VAR s: ARRAY OF CHAR): BOOLEAN;

PROCEDURE StrToInt   (s: ARRAY OF CHAR;
                      VAR i: INTEGER): BOOLEAN;

PROCEDURE CardToStr (c: CARDINAL;
                     VAR s: ARRAY OF CHAR): BOOLEAN;

PROCEDURE StrToCard (s: ARRAY OF CHAR;
                     VAR c: CARDINAL): BOOLEAN;

PROCEDURE HexToStr  (w: WORD;
                     VAR s: ARRAY OF CHAR): BOOLEAN;

PROCEDURE StrToHex  (s: ARRAY OF CHAR;
                     VAR w: WORD): BOOLEAN;
```

MODULE BlockIO

```
FROM SYSTEM IMPORT ADDRESS, WORD;

EXPORT QUALIFIED FILE, BlockRead, BlockWrite, Reset, Rewrite,
                 Close, InitFile, FileName, CloseType;

TYPE
    FileName  = ARRAY [0..39] OF CHAR; (*UCSD format string*)
    CloseType = (Normal, Lock, Purge, Crunch);
    FILE      = ARRAY [0..30] OF WORD;
```

(* Note that INTEGER parameters are to be
used as CARDINAL. They are declared as
INTEGER to match UCSD operating systems declarations exactly.   *)

PROCEDURE InitFile(VAR f: FILE);
(* Initialize FILE variable. . .must be done before any other routines
can be called.   *)

PROCEDURE Reset(VAR f: FILE; VAR fn: FileName);
(* Open existing file.   *)

PROCEDURE Rewrite(VAR f: FILE; VAR fn: FileName);
(* Open new file.   *)

PROCEDURE Close(VAR f: FILE; ftype: CloseType);
(* Close file and update directory. . .

        Normal   Leave if opened with Reset, remove if
                        opened with Rewrite.
        Lock   Save permanent entry in directory.
        Purge   Remove entry from directory.
        Crunch   Save permanent entry, but truncate
                        file at current file position.   *)

PROCEDURE BlockRead(VAR f: FILE; buf: ADDRESS; byteindex: INTEGER;
                              nblocks, startblock: INTEGER): INTEGER;
(* Read nblocks of the file into memory.   *)

PROCEDURE BlockWrite(VAR f: FILE; buf: ADDRESS; byteindex: INTEGER:
                              nblocks, startblock: INTEGER): INTEGER;
(* Write nblocks of the file from memory.   *)

MODULE Bits

FROM SYSTEM IMPORT WORD, ADDRESS;

EXPORT QUALIFIED LoadByte, StoreByte, LoadField, StoreField;

PROCEDURE LoadByte (base: ADDRESS; offset: CARDINAL):CARDINAL;
(* Load byte from byte address base[offset].   *)

PROCEDURE StoreByte(base: ADDRESS; offset, ValueToStore: CARDINAL);
(* Store byte at byte address base[offset].   *)

```
PROCEDURE LoadField (VAR        w: WORD;
                     NumberOfBits: CARDINAL;
                     RightMostBit : CARDINAL): CARDINAL;
(* Load specified bit field from word w.                          *)

PROCEDURE StoreField (VAR        w: WORD;
                      NumberOfBits: CARDINAL;
                      RightMostBit : CARDINAL;
                      ValueToStore : CARDINAL);
(* Store specified bit field into word w.                         *)
```

Modula Library Units: MODULE ASCII

```
EXPORT QUALIFIED
    nul, soh, stx, etx, eot, enq, ack, bel,
    bs,  ht,  lf,  vt,  ff,  cr,  so, si,
    dle, dc1, dc2, dc3, dc4, nak, syn, etb,
    can, em, sub, esc, fs,  gs,  rs,  us,  del;
CONST
        nul = 00C;  soh = 01C;  stx = 02C;  etx = 03C;
        eot = 04C;  enq = 05C;  ack = 06C;  bel = 07C;
        bs  = 10C;  ht  = 11C;  lf  = 12C;  vt  = 13C;
        ff  = 14C;  cr  = 15C;  so  = 16C;  si  = 17C;
        dle = 20C;  dc1 = 21C;  dc2 = 22C;  dc3 = 23C;
        dc4 = 24C;  nak = 25C;  syn = 26C;  etb = 27C;
        can = 30C;  em  = 31C;  sub = 32C;  esc = 33C;
        fs  = 34C;  gs  = 35C;  rs  = 36C;  us  = 37C;
        del =177C;
```

INDEX